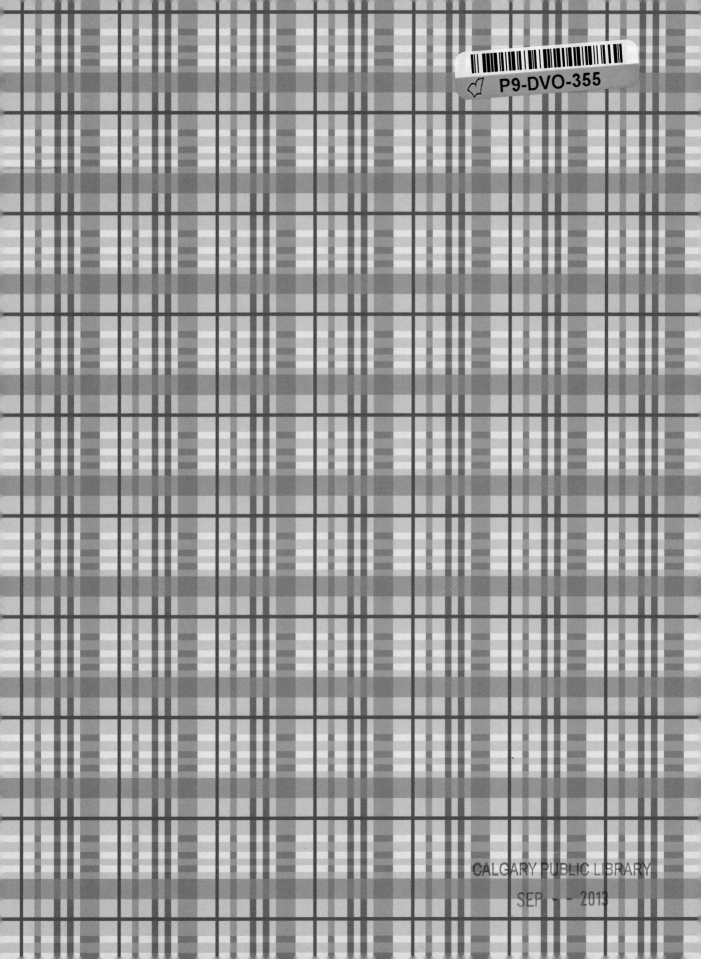

THE COMPLETE
Chocolate
BOOK

TRANSCONTINENTAL BOOKS
5800 Saint-Denis St.
Suite 900
Montreal, Que. H2S 3L5
Telephone: 514-273-1066
Toll-free: 1-800-565-5531
canadianliving.com

Bibliothèque et Archives nationales du
Québec and Library and Archives Canada
cataloguing in publication

Main entry under title :
The complete chocolate book : 100+
how-to photos and tips from Canada's
most-trusted kitchen
"Canadian living".
Includes index.
ISBN 978-0-9877474-6-4
1. Cooking (Chocolate). 2. Chocolate.
3. Cookbooks. I. Canadian Living Test
Kitchen. II. Title: Canadian living.

TX767.C5C65 2013   641.6'374
C2013-940284-5

Project editor: Tina Anson Mine
Copy editor: Lisa Fielding
Indexer: Beth Zabloski
Art director: Colin Elliott

Printed in Canada
© Transcontinental Books, 2013
Legal deposit – 4th quarter 2013
National Library of Quebec
National Library of Canada
ISBN 978-0-9877474-6-4

We acknowledge the financial support of
our publishing activity by the Government
of Canada through the Canada Book Fund.

For information on special rates for
corporate libraries and wholesale
purchases, please call 1-866-800-2500.

Canadian Living

THE COMPLETE
Chocolate
BOOK

100+ how-to photos and tips from Canada's most-trusted kitchen

BY THE CANADIAN LIVING TEST KITCHEN

Transcontinental Books

The Best Chocolate Brownies
(page 145)

There is no ingredient quite like chocolate. It is simultaneously sexy and comforting, finicky and forgiving, rustic and sophisticated.

Like the little black dress of the culinary world, chocolate can be dressed up or down for any occasion. It can be the luscious base for an elegant dessert at a fancy dinner party or the starting point for a simple, comforting hot chocolate to sip while chilling with your family in your pajamas on a Sunday afternoon.

No matter what you crave – something gooey, creamy, crunchy, chewy, melty, crumbly, chilly or cakey – chocolate can, and will, deliver.

Canadian Living has – literally – thousands of Tested-Till-Perfect chocolate recipes. We went through every luxurious one to create this ultimate collection. Then we added our helpful how-to photos and tips to create a go-to reference book for pro and beginner cooks alike.

It was such a delicious experience putting together this all-time favourite book. We wish you and your loved ones the ooiest, gooiest of culinary adventures as you find your favourites among our favourites.
We hope that, someday, your copy will be just as dog-eared and chocolate stained as ours.

Eat well and enjoy!

– Annabelle Waugh,
director, Food

8
gooey

42
creamy

90
crunchy

132
chewy

176
melty

218
crumbly

260
chilly

298
cakey

Contents

gooey

Chocolate Cheesecake With Caramel Pecan Sauce 11

Chocolate Toffee Pecan Tart 12

Maple Chocolate Butter Tarts 13

Chocolate, Caramel & Cashew Torte 14

Flourless Chocolate Lava Cakes 17

Chocolate Peanut Butter Pudding Cake 18

Molten Chocolate Cakes 19

Slow Cooker Hot Cocoa Cake 20

Chocolate Toffee Squares 22

Banana Chocolate Chunk Bread Pudding 23

Flourless Chocolate Truffle Cake 25

Chocolate Caramel Cookies 26

Chocolate-Covered Homemade Marshmallows 27

Chocolate Caramel Pecan Clusters 28

Caramel Chocolate Custard 30

Chocolate Hazelnut French Toast 31

Chocolate Cinnamon Buns 33

Boozy Chocolate Sauce 34

White Chocolate Coconut Sauce 34

Warm Cinnamon Chocolate Sauce 35

Peanut Butter Caramel Sauce 35

Rich Double-Chocolate Sauce 36

Silky Dark Chocolate Sauce 38

Mocha Fudge Sauce 38

S'mores Chocolate Fondue 41

This is what happens when all the flavours of Turtles, a favourite childhood candy, come together in a dessert that's perfect for entertaining. The contrast between the creamy chocolaty cheesecake base and the sticky caramel-pecan topping is just divine.

Chocolate Cheesecake With Caramel Pecan Sauce

ingredients

1 cup **graham cracker crumbs**
⅓ cup finely chopped **pecans**
¼ cup **butter,** melted

CHEESECAKE:
¾ cup packed **brown sugar**
3 pkg (each 250 g) **cream cheese,** softened
4 **eggs**
1 tsp **vanilla**

2 bars (each 100 g) **70% dark chocolate,** melted
¼ cup **whipping cream (35%)**

CARAMEL PECAN SAUCE:
¾ cup **granulated sugar**
½ cup **whipping cream (35%)**
2 tbsp **butter**
⅓ cup **pecan halves,** toasted and halved
Pinch **salt**

method

Grease then line side of 9-inch (2.5 L) springform pan with parchment paper. Centre pan on large square of heavy-duty foil; bring foil up and press to side of pan.

Stir together graham cracker crumbs, pecans and butter until moistened; press onto bottom of prepared pan. Bake in 350°F (180°C) oven until firm, about 10 minutes. Let cool in pan on rack.

CHEESECAKE: Press brown sugar through sieve to remove any lumps. In bowl, beat cream cheese with brown sugar on high for 5 minutes, scraping down side of bowl often. Beat in eggs, 1 at a time. Beat in vanilla.

Mix about 1 cup of the cream cheese mixture into chocolate until smooth; return to remaining cheese mixture and stir until combined. Beat in cream. Pour over crust.

Set pan in larger pan; pour in enough hot water to come 1 inch (2.5 cm) up side. Bake in 325°F (160°C) oven until set around edge and centre is still jiggly, about 1 hour.

Transfer springform pan to rack and remove foil; let cool completely. Cover and refrigerate until firm and chilled, about 4 hours. *(Make-ahead: Refrigerate for up to 24 hours.)*

CARAMEL PECAN SAUCE: In heavy saucepan, stir sugar with ¼ cup water over medium heat until dissolved. Bring to boil; boil vigorously, without stirring but brushing down side of pan often with pastry brush dipped in cold water, until dark amber, 6 to 10 minutes. Remove from heat.

Standing back and averting face, add cream; whisk until smooth. Whisk in butter until smooth. Stir in pecans and salt. Let cool. *(Make-ahead: Refrigerate in airtight container for up to 24 hours; gently rewarm to liquefy.)*

Serve sauce over cheesecake.

MAKES 16 SERVINGS.
PER SERVING: about 451 cal, 7 g pro, 34 g total fat (19 g sat. fat), 33 g carb, 2 g fibre, 124 mg chol, 224 mg sodium, 145 mg potassium. % RDI: 7% calcium, 22% iron, 27% vit A, 8% folate.

A press-in crust and easy filling make this showstopping dessert simple enough for novice bakers.
Cocoa powder gives the crust its beautiful dark colour and rich chocolate flavour.

Chocolate Toffee Pecan Tart

ingredients

1 cup chopped toasted **pecans**
¾ cup packed **dark brown sugar**
⅓ cup **sweetened condensed milk**
¼ cup **butter**
2 tbsp **corn syrup**
½ tsp **vanilla**

CHOCOLATE CRUST:
1¼ cups **all-purpose flour**
¼ cup **cocoa powder**
2 tbsp **icing sugar**
½ cup cold **butter**, cubed
1 **egg yolk**
1 tbsp cold **water**

GANACHE GLAZE:
5 oz (140 g) **bittersweet chocolate**, chopped
⅔ cup **whipping cream (35%)**

method

CHOCOLATE CRUST: In food processor, pulse together flour, cocoa powder and sugar until combined. Add butter; pulse just until in fine crumbs. Whisk egg yolk with cold water; drizzle over flour mixture and pulse just until dough starts to clump together.

Transfer dough to work surface; press into smooth ball. Press by small handfuls onto bottom and up side of 9-inch (23 cm) round tart pan with removable bottom. Refrigerate for 30 minutes. *(Make-ahead: Cover and refrigerate for up to 24 hours.)*

Prick bottom of pastry all over with fork. Bake on baking sheet in 350°F (180°C) oven until firm, about 20 minutes. Let cool in pan on rack. Spread pecans in tart shell.

In saucepan, stir brown sugar with ¼ cup water over medium-low heat until most of the sugar crystals are dissolved, about 5 minutes.

Stir in sweetened condensed milk, butter and corn syrup. Cook, stirring constantly, just until gently boiling; boil, stirring, for 3 minutes. Remove from heat; stir in vanilla. Let cool for 2 minutes. Pour into tart shell. Let cool to room temperature, about 1 hour.

GANACHE GLAZE: Place chocolate in heatproof bowl. In saucepan, bring cream just to boil; pour over chocolate, whisking until smooth. Let cool for 3 minutes. Spread over filling. Refrigerate until set, about 1 hour. *(Make-ahead: Cover with plastic wrap and refrigerate for up to 2 days.)*

Let stand at room temperature for 15 minutes before serving.

MAKES 12 SERVINGS.
PER SERVING: about 429 cal, 5 g pro, 29 g total fat (14 g sat. fat), 41 g carb, 3 g fibre, 73 mg chol, 144 mg sodium. % RDI: 6% calcium, 14% iron, 17% vit A, 10% folate.

Canadians are crazy about butter tarts. These chocolate-studded tarts are delightfully custardy and sweetened with very Canadian maple syrup instead of the more common corn syrup. Omit the walnuts if you want a nut-free version.

Maple Chocolate Butter Tarts

ingredients

¾ cup packed **brown sugar**
½ cup **maple syrup**
   (No. 1 medium grade)
⅓ cup **butter,** melted
2 **eggs**
1 tbsp **cider vinegar**
½ tsp **salt**
½ cup chopped **walnut halves**
½ cup chopped **bittersweet chocolate** or semisweet chocolate chips

SOUR CREAM PASTRY:
1¼ cups **all-purpose flour**
¼ tsp **salt**
¼ cup cold **butter,** cubed
¼ cup cold **lard,** cubed
2 tbsp ice **water** (approx)
4 tsp **sour cream**

method

SOUR CREAM PASTRY: In bowl, whisk flour with salt. Using pastry blender, cut in butter and lard until in fine crumbs with a few larger pieces. Whisk ice water with sour cream; drizzle over flour mixture, tossing briskly with fork and adding more water if necessary to form ragged dough. Press into disc; wrap and refrigerate until chilled, about 30 minutes. *(Make-ahead: Refrigerate for up to 3 days.)*

On lightly floured surface, roll out pastry to generous ⅛-inch (3 mm) thickness. Using 4-inch (10 cm) round cutter, cut out 12 circles, rerolling and cutting scraps. Fit circles into 12 muffin cups; refrigerate for 30 minutes.

Meanwhile, whisk together brown sugar, maple syrup, butter, eggs, vinegar and salt. Divide walnuts and chocolate among pastry shells. Spoon scant ¼ cup filling into each shell.

Bake in 350°F (180°C) oven until filling is set and pastry is golden, 20 to 25 minutes. Run thin knife around edges to release tarts. Let cool in pan on rack for 20 minutes. Transfer to rack; let cool completely. *(Make-ahead: Store in single layer in airtight container for up to 24 hours.)*

MAKES 12 TARTS.
PER TART: about 343 cal, 4 g pro, 21 g total fat (10 g sat. fat), 36 g carb, 1 g fibre, 59 mg chol, 225 mg sodium, 140 mg potassium. % RDI: 4% calcium, 11% iron, 10% vit A, 13% folate.

You won't need a candy thermometer to make the caramel for this sticky torte, but you will need to keep an eye on it, so make sure all of your ingredients are prepped before you start cooking. For a special touch, sprinkle a pinch of fleur de sel over each slice before serving.

Chocolate, Caramel & Cashew Torte

ingredients

½ cup **butter,** softened
⅓ cup **granulated sugar**
1 **egg yolk**
½ tsp **vanilla**
¾ cup **all-purpose flour**
⅓ cup **cocoa powder**
¼ cup ground **roasted cashews**
  (about ½ cup whole)
¼ tsp **baking powder**
Pinch **salt**

CARAMEL CASHEW FILLING:
⅔ cup **granulated sugar**
½ cup **whipping cream (35%)**
¾ cup chopped **roasted cashews**

GANACHE:
6 oz (170 g) **bittersweet chocolate,**
  finely chopped
¼ cup cold **butter,** cubed
¼ cup **whipping cream (35%)**

method

In bowl, beat butter with sugar until fluffy; beat in egg yolk and vanilla. Whisk together flour, cocoa powder, ground cashews, baking powder and salt; stir into butter mixture. Press onto bottom and up side of greased 9-inch (23 cm) round tart pan with removable bottom ❶; refrigerate until firm, 30 minutes.

Bake on baking sheet in 350°F (180°C) oven until surface looks dry, about 30 minutes. Let cool in pan on rack. *(Make-ahead: Cover and store in cool, dry place for up to 24 hours.)*

CARAMEL CASHEW FILLING: Meanwhile, in heavy saucepan, stir sugar with 2 tbsp water over medium heat until dissolved; brush down side of pan with pastry brush dipped in cold water. Bring to boil; boil vigorously, without stirring but brushing down side of pan often, until dark amber, about 10 minutes.

Standing back and averting face, add cream; whisk until smooth. Stir in cashews; boil for 1 minute. Pour into heatproof bowl; let cool for 30 minutes. Spread over tart shell ❷; refrigerate until set, about 2 hours.

GANACHE: Place chocolate and butter in heatproof bowl. In saucepan, bring cream just to boil over medium-high heat; pour over chocolate mixture, whisking until melted and smooth. Refrigerate until cool, about 30 minutes. Pour over tart; spread evenly ❸. Refrigerate until set, about 4 hours. *(Make-ahead: Cover and refrigerate for up to 3 days.)*

MAKES 10 TO 12 SERVINGS.

PER EACH OF 12 SERVINGS: about 414 cal, 5 g pro, 29 g total fat (15 g sat. fat), 36 g carb, 3 g fibre, 67 mg chol, 98 mg sodium, 251 mg potassium.
% RDI: 3% calcium, 18% iron, 15% vit A, 10% folate.

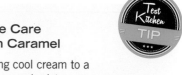

Take Care With Caramel

Adding cool cream to a hot caramel mixture causes some lively spattering, so you'll want to keep your face and hands out of the line of fire. Wear oven mitts and use a long-handled spoon to stir the mixture. And make sure your face is a safe distance away from the pan so it doesn't get splashed with hot caramel.

HOW-TO

1

2

3

You can easily make the batter for these decadent gluten-free desserts ahead, but the cakes are best immediately after baking; put them in the oven just before your guests are ready to dig in. If you're celebrating Passover or want a version that's dairy-free as well, try the variation below.

Flourless Chocolate Lava Cakes

ingredients

12 oz (340 g) **bittersweet chocolate** or semisweet chocolate, chopped
½ cup **butter,** cubed
Seeds of 1 **vanilla pod**
2 cups **granulated sugar**
6 **eggs**

6 **egg yolks**
¼ cup **cocoa powder,** sifted
Pinch **salt**
12 oz (340 g) **strawberries,** hulled and diced
Whipped cream (optional)

method

In heatproof bowl over hot (not boiling) water, melt chocolate with butter, stirring until smooth. Stir in vanilla seeds. Remove from heat.

Whisk in sugar. Whisk in eggs and egg yolks, 1 at a time. Whisk in cocoa powder and salt. Pour into twelve ¾-cup (175 mL) ramekins; place on rimmed baking sheet. *(Make-ahead: Cover and refrigerate for up to 24 hours. Bake as directed, adding 5 minutes to baking time.)*

Bake in 425°F (220°C) oven until edges are set and centres are slightly jiggly when lightly tapped, about 15 minutes. Let cool on pan on rack for 3 minutes.

Run knife around edges and turn out onto plates. Garnish with strawberries, and whipped cream (if using).

MAKES 12 SERVINGS.
PER SERVING: about 442 cal, 7 g pro, 24 g total fat (13 g sat. fat), 52 g carb, 3 g fibre, 210 mg chol, 93 mg sodium, 287 mg potassium. % RDI: 4% calcium, 21% iron, 17% vit A, 27% vit C, 16% folate.

CHANGE IT UP
Passover Dairy-Free Gluten-Free Flourless Chocolate Lava Cakes
Substitute kosher pareve margarine for the butter, kosher pareve cocoa powder (such as Ghirardelli) for the regular cocoa powder, kosher pareve bittersweet chocolate or semisweet chocolate (such as Lieber's) for the regular chocolate, and kosher nondairy whipped topping for the whipped cream.

17

CANADIAN LIVING • THE COMPLETE CHOCOLATE BOOK

Pudding cakes like this are so much fun. The ingredients, once baked, separate into a fluffy, light cake atop a layer of deliciously sticky pudding. They're perfect for making with kids, who will enjoy both the flavour and the apparent magic that happens in the oven.

Chocolate Peanut Butter Pudding Cake

ingredients

¾ cup **all-purpose flour**
⅓ cup **granulated sugar**
1 tsp **baking powder**
⅓ cup **milk**
1 **egg,** beaten

3 tbsp **natural peanut butter**
¾ cup packed **brown sugar**
¼ cup **cocoa powder**
1 cup boiling **water**

method

In large bowl, whisk together flour, granulated sugar and baking powder. Whisk together milk, egg and peanut butter; stir into flour mixture. Scrape into greased 8-inch (2 L) square baking dish.

In heatproof bowl, whisk brown sugar with cocoa powder; whisk in boiling water until smooth. Pour over cake; do not stir. Bake in 350°F (180°C) oven until cake is firm to the touch, about 30 minutes. Let cool in pan on rack for 10 minutes.

MAKE 4 TO 6 SERVINGS.
PER EACH OF 6 SERVINGS: about 281 cal, 6 g pro, 6 g total fat (1 g sat. fat), 54 g carb, 2 g fibre, 32 mg chol, 81 mg sodium. % RDI: 7% calcium, 16% iron, 2% vit A, 17% folate.

CHANGE IT UP
Slow Cooker Chocolate Peanut Butter Pudding Cake
Scrape batter into greased 5- to 6-quart (5 to 6 L) slow cooker. Pour cocoa mixture over top; do not stir. Cover and cook on high until cake is firm to the touch, about 2 hours.

No Stir, for Sure

The secret to the layers in pudding cakes like this lies in pouring the liquid over the batter and resisting the urge to stir. If you do, the sauce layer won't sink, and the cake layer won't rise.

Test Kitchen
TIP

These dramatic mini cakes with flowing chocolate centres are the classic version of everyone's favourite lava cakes (see page 17 for a gluten-free take on them). You can change up the liqueur in the truffles and crème anglaise to reinvent this dessert to suit your tastes.

Molten Chocolate Cakes

ingredients

¾ cup **butter**, softened
1 cup **granulated sugar** (approx)
12 oz (340 g) **bittersweet chocolate**, chopped
4 each **eggs** and **egg yolks**
1 tbsp **vanilla**
1 cup **all-purpose flour**

TRUFFLE:
4 oz (115 g) **bittersweet chocolate**, chopped
⅓ cup **whipping cream (35%)**
2 tbsp **Irish cream liqueur** (or 1 tsp vanilla)

CRÈME ANGLAISE:
1 cup **18% cream** or whipping cream (35%)
1 cup **milk**
¼ cup **granulated sugar**
6 **egg yolks**
1 tsp **cornstarch**
2 tbsp **Irish cream liqueur** (or 1 tsp vanilla)
1 tsp **vanilla**

method

CRÈME ANGLAISE: In heavy saucepan, heat cream, milk and half of the sugar over medium heat until bubbles form around edge. Meanwhile, in bowl, whisk together egg yolks, cornstarch and remaining sugar; whisk in hot cream mixture in thin stream. Return to pan; cook over medium-low heat, stirring constantly and without simmering, until thick enough to coat spoon, 3 to 5 minutes. Strain into clean bowl. Stir in liqueur and vanilla. Place plastic wrap directly on surface; let cool. Refrigerate until cold, about 1 hour. *(Make-ahead: Refrigerate for up to 3 days.)*

TRUFFLE: Place chocolate in heatproof bowl. In small saucepan, bring cream just to boil; pour over chocolate, whisking until melted and smooth. Whisk in liqueur; refrigerate until firm, about 1 hour. Spoon into 8 mounds onto plastic wrap–lined rimmed baking sheet. Roll into balls. Cover and freeze until firm, about 4 hours. *(Make-ahead: Freeze in airtight container for up to 1 week.)*

Using no more than 1 tbsp of the butter, grease eight ¾-cup (175 mL) custard cups or ramekins. Line bottoms with parchment paper; sprinkle scant 1 tsp of the sugar inside each. Set aside. In heatproof bowl over saucepan of hot (not boiling) water, melt chocolate with remaining butter, stirring until smooth. Let cool to room temperature.

In separate bowl, beat eggs, egg yolks and remaining ¾ cup sugar until thickened, about 5 minutes. Fold in chocolate mixture and vanilla. Stir in flour. Spoon half of the batter into prepared cups; place frozen truffle in centre of each. Spoon remaining batter over top. *(Make-ahead: Cover and refrigerate for up to 24 hours.)*

Bake on baking sheet in 350°F (180°C) oven until centres are sunken, soft and shiny, about 22 minutes. Let cool on rack for 2 minutes. Run thin knife around edges to gently loosen cakes. Unmould onto plates; peel off paper. Serve immediately with crème anglaise.

MAKES 8 SERVINGS.
PER SERVING: about 890 cal, 17 g pro, 69 g total fat (39 g sat. fat), 71 g carb, 9 g fibre, 436 mg chol, 262 mg sodium. % RDI: 15% calcium, 39% iron, 41% vit A, 32% folate.

{ gooey }

This rich, fudgy cake is not one you want to make ahead and store (you won't be able to resist its gooey charms anyway!). It's best served warm, scooped right out of the slow cooker into individual mugs. Dark chocolate lovers will enjoy their servings dusted with extra cocoa powder.

Slow Cooker Hot Cocoa Cake

ingredients

2 cups **all-purpose flour**
¾ cup **cocoa powder,** sifted
1½ tsp **baking powder**
1½ tsp **baking soda**
½ tsp **salt**
Pinch **cinnamon**
2 cups **granulated sugar**
2 **eggs**
½ cup **vegetable oil**
½ cup **milk**

½ cup cooled brewed **coffee**
  or water
2 tsp **vanilla**
½ cup **semisweet chocolate chips**

WHIPPED CREAM:
⅔ cup **whipping cream (35%)**
2 tbsp **granulated sugar**
½ tsp **vanilla**
Pinch **cinnamon**

method

Grease bottom of 5- to 6-quart (5 to 6 L) slow cooker; set aside.

In large bowl, whisk together flour, cocoa powder, baking powder, baking soda, salt and cinnamon. Whisk together sugar, eggs, oil, milk, coffee and vanilla until well combined. Add to flour mixture; stir just until moistened.

Pour into prepared slow cooker; sprinkle with chocolate chips. Cover and cook on high until cake tester inserted in centre comes out with a few moist crumbs clinging, about 2 hours.

Turn off slow cooker; uncover and let cool for 15 minutes.

WHIPPED CREAM: Meanwhile, whip together cream, sugar, vanilla and cinnamon until soft peaks form.

Spoon warm cake into mugs; top with whipped cream.

MAKES 12 TO 16 SERVINGS.
PER EACH OF 16 SERVINGS: about 300 cal, 4 g pro, 13 g total fat (4 g sat. fat), 45 g carb, 2 g fibre, 37 mg chol, 234 mg sodium, 170 mg potassium. % RDI: 4% calcium, 11% iron, 5% vit A, 17% folate.

Slow Cooker Size Matters

For soups and stews, the capacity of your slow cooker isn't too critical. For baking, however, it is a little more exacting. The right size of insert ensures your cake bakes through in the time suggested. Here, a 5- to 6-quart (5 to 6 L) slow cooker will give you a cake that's the right thickness. Anything smaller would make it too tall and the centre wouldn't cook through.

Test Kitchen TIP

{ gooey }

The ooey, gooey filling of these squares gets its decadent texture from a mixture of sweetened condensed milk and corn syrup. Watch your fillings with this treat!

Chocolate Toffee Squares

ingredients

1¾ cups **all-purpose flour**
¼ cup **granulated sugar**
2 tbsp **cornstarch**
¼ tsp **salt**
1 cup **unsalted butter,** softened

TOFFEE FILLING:
1 cup packed **dark brown sugar**
1 cup **unsalted butter**
1 can (300 mL) **sweetened condensed milk**
¼ cup **corn syrup**

GANACHE TOPPING:
6 oz (170 g) **bittersweet chocolate,** chopped
⅔ cup **whipping cream (35%)**

method

In food processor, pulse together flour, sugar, cornstarch and salt. Pulse in butter just until mixture holds together. Press evenly into parchment paper–lined 13- x 9-inch (3.5 L) cake pan. Prick all over with fork; refrigerate for 30 minutes.

Bake in 350°F (180°C) oven until light golden, 20 to 25 minutes. Let cool on rack.

TOFFEE FILLING: In saucepan over medium heat, melt together brown sugar, butter, condensed milk and corn syrup, stirring constantly. Reduce heat to medium-low; cook, stirring constantly, until candy thermometer reaches thread stage of 230 to 234°F (110 to 112°C), 25 to 30 minutes, or 1 tsp hot syrup dropped into cold water forms soft 2-inch (5 cm) thread. Pour over base. Refrigerate until cold, about 1 hour.

GANACHE TOPPING: Place chocolate in heatproof bowl. In saucepan, bring cream just to boil; pour over chocolate, whisking until smooth. Let cool to room temperature. Pour over toffee filling, spreading evenly. Refrigerate until set, about 1 hour.

Using parchment paper to lift, transfer to cutting board. Peel paper off sides. Wiping knife with damp cloth between cuts, trim edges even; cut into 1-inch (2.5 cm) squares.

MAKES ABOUT 96 SQUARES.
PER SQUARE: about 84 cal, 1 g pro, 6 g total fat (3 g sat. fat), 9 g carb, trace fibre, 14 mg chol, 14 mg sodium, 28 mg potassium. % RDI: 2% calcium, 1% iron, 4% vit A, 2% folate.

Chocolate and bananas are great friends in desserts, and here they liven up a classic bread pudding. Day-old bread is best for making puddings like this, because it gives them a soft but not-too-spongy texture.

Banana Chocolate Chunk Bread Pudding

ingredients

8 slices (¾ inch/2 cm thick) **day-old French bread**
3 tbsp **butter,** softened
2 cups **2% milk** or homogenized milk
⅔ cup **granulated sugar**
½ cup **10% cream**

3 **eggs**
1 **banana,** chopped
3 oz (85 g) **bittersweet chocolate,** chopped

method

Trim crusts from bread; spread both sides of each slice with butter. Cut into pieces; arrange in greased 8-inch (2 L) square baking dish.

In large bowl, whisk together milk, sugar, cream and eggs; stir in banana. Pour over bread; let stand for 5 minutes. Sprinkle with chocolate.

Bake in 350°F (180°C) oven until knife inserted in centre comes out clean, 40 to 45 minutes. Let cool in pan on rack for 20 minutes before serving.

MAKES 4 TO 6 SERVINGS.

PER EACH OF 6 SERVINGS: about 455 cal, 12 g pro, 19 g total fat (10 g sat. fat), 62 g carb, 3 g fibre, 121 mg chol, 380 mg sodium, 301 mg potassium. % RDI: 16% calcium, 15% iron, 14% vit A, 2% vit C, 22% folate.

Choose Good Chocolate

We use high-quality chocolate for all of our recipes. It costs more to buy premium brands, such as Lindt or Callebaut, but they work and taste better in chocolate dishes. They also contain real cocoa butter (not vegetable fat), which melts more smoothly and results in glossier glazes, candies and more.

This fudgy cake is as delicious as it is beautiful, so it's perfect for entertaining.
The variation is a wonderful kosher Passover dessert you can indulge in after a Seder.

Flourless Chocolate Truffle Cake

ingredients

½ cup **unsalted butter**

6 oz (170 g) **bittersweet chocolate,** chopped

4 **eggs**

1 cup **granulated sugar**

Pinch **salt**

⅓ cup **ground almonds**

1 tsp **instant espresso powder** or instant coffee granules

2 tbsp **cocoa powder**

CHOCOLATE ESPRESSO GLAZE:

4 oz (115 g) **bittersweet chocolate,** chopped

¼ cup **unsalted butter**

¼ cup hot **water**

¼ tsp **instant espresso powder**

method

Grease then line bottom and side of 9-inch (2.5 L) springform pan with parchment paper. Set aside.

In heatproof bowl over saucepan of hot (not boiling) water, melt butter with chocolate, stirring until smooth. Let cool.

In large bowl, beat together eggs, sugar and salt until pale and thickened, 5 minutes. Fold in chocolate mixture, almonds and espresso powder. Sift cocoa powder over top; fold in. Scrape into prepared pan, smoothing top.

Bake in 350°F (180°C) oven until crackly on top and cake tester inserted in centre comes out with a few moist crumbs clinging, 30 to 35 minutes. Let cool. Remove side of pan and paper; place cake on rack over rimmed baking sheet.

CHOCOLATE ESPRESSO GLAZE: In heatproof bowl over saucepan of hot (not boiling) water, melt together chocolate, butter, hot water and espresso powder, stirring until smooth. Pour over centre of cake; spread to within 1 inch (2.5 cm) of edge. Refrigerate until set, about 1 hour. *(Make-ahead: Cover loosely and refrigerate for up to 24 hours.)*

MAKES 12 SERVINGS.

PER SERVING: about 345 cal, 4 g pro, 24 g total fat (13 g sat. fat), 30 g carb, 3 g fibre, 93 mg chol, 25 mg sodium, 205 mg potassium. % RDI: 3% calcium, 14% iron, 14% vit A, 5% folate.

CHANGE IT UP
Passover Flourless Chocolate Truffle Cake
Substitute kosher pareve margarine for the butter, kosher pareve bittersweet chocolate (such as Lieber's) for the regular chocolate, and kosher pareve cocoa powder (such as Ghirardelli) for the regular cocoa powder.

The dark chocolaty exterior of this cookie hides a decadent surprise:
a flowy caramel and chocolate centre. Just don't dig in to them before they've cooled –
the filling stays piping hot for a long time and can burn tender tongues.

Chocolate Caramel Cookies

ingredients

4 oz (115 g) **bittersweet chocolate,** chopped
¾ cup **butter,** softened
1 cup **granulated sugar**
2 **eggs**
1 tbsp **vanilla**
2 cups **all-purpose flour**
½ cup **cocoa powder**

1 tsp **baking powder**
½ tsp each **baking soda** and **salt**
3 **chocolate-covered caramel bars** (each 52 g), such as Caramilk, chilled

method

In bowl over saucepan of hot (not boiling) water, melt bittersweet chocolate, stirring occasionally until smooth. Let cool.

In large bowl, beat butter with sugar until fluffy; beat in eggs, 1 at a time. Beat in vanilla, then melted chocolate. Whisk together flour, cocoa powder, baking powder, baking soda and salt; stir into butter mixture. Cover and refrigerate until firm enough to shape, about 30 minutes.

Break each chocolate bar into 10 pieces. Roll dough by heaping 1 tbsp into balls; flatten and place 1 piece of chocolate bar in centre of each ball. Seal dough around chocolate. Place, seam side down, on parchment paper–lined rimless baking sheet.

Bake in 375°F (190°C) oven until edges are firm and centres are still soft, about 10 minutes. Let cool on pan on rack for 2 minutes. Transfer to rack; let cool completely. *(Make-ahead: Store in airtight container for up to 1 day or freeze for up to 2 weeks.)*

MAKES 30 COOKIES.
PER COOKIE: about 146 cal, 2 g pro, 8 g total fat (5 g sat. fat), 18 g carb, 1 g fibre, 28 mg chol, 128 mg sodium. % RDI: 2% calcium, 6% iron, 5% vit A, 5% folate.

Corn Syrup Types

Corn syrup comes in various colours. In Canada, it can be golden or white; in the United States, there's also a dark (brown) version. The darker the colour, the more molasses-type flavour the syrup will have. But all corn syrup behaves the same way in cooking and baking, so you can usually use the different colours interchangeably.

Test Kitchen TIP

{ gooey }

Homemade marshmallows are light, airy and a real treat compared with commercial ones. The mixture does get very sticky, so a well-greased spreader will be your best friend. White corn syrup is the choice here, because you want the marshmallows to be snow white.

Chocolate-Covered Homemade Marshmallows

ingredients

⅓ cup **icing sugar**
1 cup **granulated sugar**
2 tbsp **white corn syrup** (see Tip, opposite)
2 pkg (each 7 g) **unflavoured gelatin**
½ cup cold **water**

2 **egg whites**
Pinch **salt**
¼ tsp **vanilla**
8 oz (225 g) **bittersweet chocolate,**
  chopped

method

Grease 9-inch (2.5 L) square cake pan; line with parchment paper. Lightly grease paper; dust with some of the icing sugar. Set aside.

In saucepan, bring granulated sugar, ⅓ cup water and corn syrup to boil over medium-high heat, stirring until sugar is dissolved. Boil, without stirring but brushing down side of pan with pastry brush dipped in cold water, until candy thermometer reaches hard-ball stage of 260°F (125°C), about 12 minutes, or 1 tsp hot syrup dropped into cold water forms hard ball. Remove from heat.

Meanwhile, in small saucepan, sprinkle gelatin over cold water; let stand for 5 minutes. Heat over low heat, stirring, until clear, 3 to 5 minutes. Whisk into hot sugar mixture. (Mixture will bubble up.)

In stand mixer, beat egg whites with salt until stiff peaks form. With machine running, gradually pour in gelatin mixture, beating on high until increased in volume and cool, about 12 minutes. Beat in vanilla.

Immediately scrape into prepared pan. Using greased palette knife or spatula, smooth top. Sprinkle with some of the remaining icing sugar. Let stand, uncovered, at room temperature until firm, about 4 hours.

Remove from pan; peel off paper. Transfer to icing sugar–dusted cutting board. Using greased knife and cleaning and greasing knife between cuts, trim edges even; cut into 40 squares.

Gently press sides and bottom of each square into remaining icing sugar to coat; dust off excess. Let stand on waxed paper–lined baking sheet until dry, about 1 hour. With dry pastry brush, brush off excess sugar.

In heatproof bowl over saucepan of hot (not boiling) water, stir two-thirds of the chocolate just until melted. Remove from heat; stir in remaining chocolate until melted. Using candy-dipping fork or fork, coat each marshmallow in chocolate, tapping fork to let excess chocolate drip back into bowl.

Place on parchment paper– or waxed paper–lined baking sheets. Refrigerate until chocolate is firm, about 30 minutes.

MAKES 40 PIECES.
PER PIECE: about 56 cal, 1 g pro, 2 g total fat (1 g sat. fat), 9 g carb, 1 g fibre, 0 mg chol, 5 mg sodium, 2 mg potassium. % RDI: 1% iron.

When you're looking for a treat to make for gift giving, look no further than this homemade homage to classic Turtles candies. The chewy, buttery caramel is worth the work.

Chocolate Caramel Pecan Clusters

ingredients

96 **pecan halves**

CARAMEL:
1 cup **granulated sugar**
1 cup **whipping cream (35%)**
½ cup **corn syrup**
3 tbsp **butter**
¼ tsp **salt**
½ tsp **vanilla**

CHOCOLATE:
3 oz (85 g) **bittersweet chocolate,** chopped

method

Arrange pecans in groups of 4 in star shape, 1 inch (2.5 cm) apart, on parchment paper–lined rimmed baking sheets. Set aside.

CARAMEL: In large saucepan, bring sugar, cream, corn syrup, butter and salt to boil over medium heat, stirring often. Boil, stirring occasionally, until candy thermometer reaches firm-ball stage of 248°F (120°C), 15 to 20 minutes, or 1 tsp hot syrup dropped into cold water forms firm but pliable ball. Remove from heat. Stir in vanilla.

Set saucepan base in cold water for 30 seconds to stop cooking. Let stand on rack until cooled to 170°F (77°C). (Mixture will thicken.) Using greased measure, spoon 1 tbsp onto centre of each pecan cluster. Let stand until cooled and firm, about 30 minutes.

CHOCOLATE: In heatproof bowl over saucepan of hot (not boiling) water, melt chocolate, stirring until smooth. Let cool to room temperature. Spoon about 1 tsp onto each caramel centre; refrigerate until set, about 15 minutes.

MAKES 24 PIECES.

PER PIECE: about 156 cal, 1 g pro, 10 g total fat (4 g sat. fat), 17 g carb, 1 g fibre, 17 mg chol, 46 mg sodium, 32 mg potassium. % RDI: 1% calcium, 2% iron, 5% vit A, 1% folate.

Called *bonet* in Italy's Piedmont region, where these individual baked custards originated, this dessert is like a gooey chocolate version of classic crème caramel.

Caramel Chocolate Custard

ingredients

3 cups **milk**

6 oz (170 g) **bittersweet chocolate,** finely chopped

2 oz (55 g) **unsweetened chocolate,** finely chopped

¾ cup crushed **amaretti cookies** (about 12)

4 **egg yolks**

2 **eggs**

¼ cup **granulated sugar**

1 tbsp **brandy** or rum

CHOCOLATE CARAMEL:

1 cup **granulated sugar**

2 oz (55 g) **bittersweet chocolate,** finely chopped

method

CHOCOLATE CARAMEL: In heavy saucepan, heat sugar with 1 cup water over medium heat, stirring, until sugar is dissolved. Bring to boil; boil vigorously, without stirring but occasionally brushing down side of pan with pastry brush dipped in cold water, until thick and clear, about 7 minutes.

Add chocolate; stir until melted. Return to boil; boil for 1 minute. Immediately divide among eight ¾-cup (175 mL) ramekins or custard cups, swirling each to coat bottom and ½ inch (1 cm) up side. Set aside.

In saucepan, bring milk to simmer over medium heat; stir in bittersweet chocolate and unsweetened chocolate until melted. Remove from heat. Add amaretti cookies; let stand for 10 minutes.

In large bowl, whisk together egg yolks, eggs, sugar and brandy; slowly whisk in milk mixture. Pour into prepared ramekins. Place in large roasting pan; pour in enough boiling water to come halfway up sides of ramekins.

Cover pan with foil; bake in 350°F (180°C) oven for 20 minutes. Uncover and bake until centres are no longer jiggly, about 30 minutes. Transfer ramekins to rack; let cool completely. *(Make-ahead: Cover loosely and refrigerate for up to 1 day.)*

Run knife around edge of each custard to loosen; invert onto dessert plate, letting excess caramel dribble down side.

MAKES 8 SERVINGS.

PER SERVING: about 436 cal, 10 g pro, 26 g total fat (15 g sat. fat), 52 g carb, 6 g fibre, 155 mg chol, 92 mg sodium. % RDI: 14% calcium, 20% iron, 11% vit A, 12% folate.

A make-ahead dish means next to no fussing in the morning. For a decadent breakfast or creative dessert, serve with Rich Double-Chocolate Sauce (page 36) instead of regular chocolate sauce.

Chocolate Hazelnut French Toast

ingredients

16 slices **egg bread** (challah),
  about 1 loaf
½ cup **chocolate hazelnut spread**
  (such as Nutella)
6 **eggs**
1½ cups **milk**
1 tbsp **granulated sugar**
1 tsp **vanilla**
2 tbsp **icing sugar**

2 tbsp **cocoa powder**
½ cup **hazelnuts,** toasted, skinned
  and chopped
¼ cup **chocolate sauce**

method

Remove crusts from bread. Spread half of the slices with chocolate hazelnut spread. Place remaining slices on top. Arrange sandwiches, just touching, on large rimmed baking sheet.

In bowl, whisk together eggs, milk, granulated sugar and vanilla; pour over sandwiches. Turn over; let soak until liquid is absorbed, about 10 minutes. *(Make-ahead: Cover and refrigerate for up to 12 hours.)*

Bake in 350°F (180°C) oven until puffed and golden, about 30 minutes.

Cut each sandwich in half diagonally. Dust half of the sandwiches with icing sugar; dust remaining sandwiches with cocoa powder. Arrange 1 of each flavour on each plate. Sprinkle with hazelnuts; drizzle with chocolate sauce.

MAKES 8 SERVINGS.
PER SERVING: about 466 cal, 15 g pro, 20 g total fat (5 g sat. fat), 57 g carb, 4 g fibre, 177 mg chol, 429 mg sodium. % RDI: 16% calcium, 26% iron, 10% vit A, 2% vit C, 39% folate.

HOW-TO

Cinnamon buns are already a huge hit: how could you make them better, right? Well, this rich chocolate dough, wrapped around chocolate chunks and a cinnamon swirl, is pretty good at making them even more irresistible.

Chocolate Cinnamon Buns

ingredients

½ cup **milk**
¼ cup **granulated sugar**
¼ cup **butter**
1 tsp **salt**
½ cup warm **water**
1 tbsp **active dry yeast**
2 **eggs,** beaten
3½ cups **all-purpose flour** (approx)
½ cup **cocoa powder**

FILLING:
¾ cup **butter**
1 cup packed **brown sugar**
½ cup **corn syrup**
¾ cup chopped **walnuts** or pecans
6 oz (170 g) **bittersweet chocolate,** chopped
1 tbsp **cinnamon**

method

In saucepan, heat together milk, all but 1 tsp of the sugar, the butter and salt until butter is melted; let cool to lukewarm.

Meanwhile, in large bowl, dissolve remaining sugar in warm water. Sprinkle in yeast; let stand until frothy, about 10 minutes. Stir in eggs and milk mixture.

Into separate bowl, sift flour with cocoa powder; sift again. Gradually beat 1½ cups of the flour mixture into egg mixture until combined; beat for 2 minutes. Stir in enough of the remaining flour mixture to make soft slightly sticky dough that comes away from side of bowl.

Lightly sprinkle some of the remaining flour mixture onto work surface; turn out dough and knead until smooth and elastic, sprinkling with more of the remaining flour mixture if sticky, about 10 minutes. Place in large greased bowl, turning to grease all over. Cover and let rise in warm draft-free place until doubled in bulk, 1 to 1½ hours.

FILLING: In saucepan, melt butter over medium heat; remove 2 tbsp and set aside. Add ¼ cup of the brown sugar and the corn syrup to pan; heat until sugar is dissolved. Pour into greased 13- x 9-inch (3 L) baking dish. Combine remaining brown sugar, walnuts, chocolate and cinnamon; set aside.

Punch down dough. Turn out onto lightly floured surface; roll out into 18- x 14-inch (45 x 35 cm) rectangle ❶. Leaving ½-inch (1 cm) border uncovered, brush with reserved butter; sprinkle with sugar mixture. Starting at long side, tightly roll up ❷, pinching seam to seal ❸. Using serrated knife, cut into 15 pieces ❹; place, cut side down, in prepared pan. Cover and let rise until doubled in bulk, about 1 hour.

Bake in 375°F (190°C) oven until golden and tops sound hollow when tapped, about 25 minutes. Let cool for 3 minutes. Place flat serving tray over pan. Wearing oven mitts, grasp pan and tray; turn over. Lift off pan, scraping out remaining filling and drizzling over buns. *(Make-ahead: Cover and store for up to 24 hours. Re-warm in 350°C/180°C oven for about 10 minutes.)*

MAKES 15 BUNS.
PER BUN: about 437 cal, 7 g pro, 24 g total fat (12 g sat. fat), 55 g carb, 4 g fibre, 64 mg chol, 313 mg sodium. % RDI: 5% calcium, 24% iron, 13% vit A, 30% folate.

{ gooey }

Everyone needs an arsenal of easy, delicious dessert sauces in their recipe box. Try the Boozy Chocolate Sauce over ice cream or a slice of chocolate cake. White Chocolate Coconut Sauce is particularly tasty over tropical fruit or fruity sorbets.

Boozy Chocolate Sauce

ingredients

1 cup **whipping cream (35%)**
2 tbsp **corn syrup**
6 oz (170 g) **bittersweet chocolate,** chopped
2 tbsp **coffee liqueur**
1 tbsp **amber rum**

method

In saucepan, bring cream and corn syrup to boil; remove from heat. Whisk in chocolate until smooth. Stir in liqueur and rum. Let stand until thickened, about 15 minutes. *(Make-ahead: Refrigerate in airtight container for up to 1 week; gently rewarm to liquefy.)*

MAKES 1¾ CUPS.
PER 1 TBSP: about 71 cal, 1 g pro, 5 g total fat (3 g sat. fat), 5 g carb, 1 g fibre, 11 mg chol, 5 mg sodium. % RDI: 1% calcium, 2% iron, 3% vit A.

White Chocolate Coconut Sauce

8 oz (225 g) **white chocolate,** chopped
⅔ cup **whipping cream (35%)**
½ cup **coconut milk**
¼ tsp **coconut extract**

Place white chocolate in heatproof bowl. In saucepan, bring cream just to boil; pour over chocolate, stirring until smooth. Let cool to room temperature.

Stir in coconut milk and coconut extract. Let cool. *(Make-ahead: Refrigerate in airtight container for up to 3 days; gently rewarm to liquefy.)*

MAKES ABOUT 2 CUPS.
PER 2 TBSP: about 123 cal, 1 g pro, 10 g total fat (6 g sat. fat), 9 g carb, 0 g fibre, 16 mg chol, 17 mg sodium. % RDI: 3% calcium, 2% iron, 3% vit A, 2% folate.

{ *gooey* }

Warm Cinnamon Chocolate Sauce is inspired by Mexican cuisine, which frequently mixes chocolate with cinnamon. Peanut Butter Caramel Sauce doesn't contain chocolate, it's true, but it's so delicious over chocolate ice cream that we just had to include it here as a bonus.

Warm Cinnamon Chocolate Sauce

Peanut Butter Caramel Sauce

ingredients

4 oz (115 g) **bittersweet chocolate**, chopped
2 oz (55 g) **milk chocolate**, chopped
½ cup **milk**
2 tbsp **butter**
2 tbsp **granulated sugar**
2 tbsp **whipping cream (35%)**
½ tsp **cinnamon**

¼ cup **unsalted butter**
½ cup packed **brown sugar**
¼ cup **granulated sugar**
¼ cup **golden corn syrup**
¼ tsp **salt**
⅓ cup **whipping cream (35%)**
½ cup **smooth peanut butter**

method

In saucepan, heat together bittersweet chocolate, milk chocolate, milk and butter over-low heat, stirring, until smooth.

Stir in sugar, cream and cinnamon; cook, stirring, until sugar is dissolved, 1 minute. Let cool for 5 minutes before serving. *(Make-ahead: Refrigerate in airtight container for up to 2 weeks; gently rewarm to liquefy.)*

MAKES 1⅓ CUPS.
PER 1 TBSP: about 67 cal, 1 g pro, 5 g total fat (3 g sat. fat), 6 g carb, 1 g fibre, 6 mg chol, 14 mg sodium, 59 mg potassium. % RDI: 2% calcium, 5% iron, 2% vit A.

In saucepan, melt butter over medium-low heat; stir in brown sugar, granulated sugar, corn syrup, 2 tbsp water and salt. Cook, stirring, until thickened, about 5 minutes.

Stir in cream; cook for 30 seconds. Remove from heat.

Stir in peanut butter; let cool. Serve warm or at room temperature. *(Make-ahead: Refrigerate in airtight container for up to 1 week; gently rewarm to liquefy.)*

MAKES ABOUT 1⅔ CUPS.
PER 2 TBSP: about 170 cal, 3 g pro, 10 g total fat (5 g sat. fat), 19 g carb, 1 g fibre, 17 mg chol, 101 mg sodium, 98 mg potassium. % RDI: 1% calcium, 2% iron, 5% vit A, 4% folate.

Make sure you're alone in the kitchen when you drizzle this creamy chocolate sauce over dessert: The best part is getting to lick the extras off the spoon all by yourself. This sauce is also delectable poured over Chocolate Hazelnut French Toast (page 31).

Rich Double-Chocolate Sauce

ingredients

1 cup **whipping cream (35%)**
2 tbsp **corn syrup**

4 oz (115 g) **bittersweet chocolate,** chopped
2 oz (55 g) **milk chocolate,** chopped

method

In small saucepan, bring whipping cream and corn syrup just to boil; remove from heat.

Add bittersweet chocolate and milk chocolate; whisk until smooth. Let cool to room temperature. *(Make-ahead: Refrigerate in airtight container for up to 1 week; gently rewarm to liquefy.)*

MAKES ABOUT 1½ CUPS.
PER 1 TBSP: about 76 cal, 1 g pro, 6 g total fat (4 g sat. fat), 5 g carb, 1 g fibre, 13 mg chol, 8 mg sodium.
% RDI: 1% calcium, 1% iron, 3% vit A.

Turn Sauces Into Gifts

Rich dessert sauces like this one and the others on pages 34, 35 and 38 make fail-safe hostess gifts. Canning jars are the easiest and most convenient choice (who doesn't have a pile of them hanging around?), but decorative bottles with tight-fitting corks or hinged lids make your gift even prettier. Just make sure that the lids are free of strong smells – it's no fun when a former pickle jar makes your chocolate sauce smell like dill!

Let sauces cool to room temperature. Pour in the sauce, using a funnel to keep it from dripping onto the mouth of the container. If some escapes, dampen a towel and wipe off the excess to prevent the container from becoming sticky. Secure the lid, then add some pretty decorations: Channel your creativity with raffia, ribbon, strings of beads or old-fashioned cloth circles cut with pinking shears.

Test Kitchen TIP

These classic chocolate sauces are all-time favourites. They're so good you might want to dispense with the ice cream and eat them straight out of the pan.

Silky Dark Chocolate Sauce

ingredients

1¼ cups **whipping cream (35%)**
3 tbsp **corn syrup**
6 oz (170 g) **bittersweet chocolate,** chopped

method

In saucepan, bring cream and corn syrup just to boil; remove from heat. Add chocolate; whisk until smooth. Let stand until thickened, about 15 minutes. *(Make-ahead: Refrigerate in airtight container for up to 5 days.)*

MAKES ABOUT 2 CUPS.
PER 2 TBSP: about 127 cal, 1 g pro, 12 g total fat (8 g sat. fat), 6 g carb, 2 g fibre, 24 mg chol, 13 mg sodium. % RDI: 2% calcium, 5% iron, 6% vit A.

CHANGE IT UP
Thick & Fudgy Dark Chocolate Sauce
Increase chocolate to 8 oz (225 g).

Mocha Fudge Sauce

ingredients

⅔ cup **cocoa powder**
⅔ cup **corn syrup**
8 oz (225 g) **semisweet chocolate,** chopped
1 tbsp **instant espresso powder**
Pinch **salt**

method

In deep saucepan, bring 1½ cups water, cocoa powder and corn syrup to boil over medium heat, whisking constantly; boil for 2 minutes. Reduce heat to low.

Add chocolate and espresso powder; cook, whisking, until melted. Remove from heat; whisk in salt. *(Make-ahead: Let cool for 30 minutes; refrigerate in airtight container for up to 2 days. Gently rewarm to liquefy.)*

MAKES 3 CUPS.
PER 2 TBSP: about 77 cal, 1 g pro, 3 g total fat (2 g sat. fat), 14 g carb, 1 g fibre, 0 mg chol, 13 mg sodium, 103 mg potassium. % RDI: 1% calcium, 5% iron.

KNOW YOUR

Chocolate

All types of chocolate are made with some combination of the same building blocks: cocoa liquor, cocoa butter, milk and sugar. Some include all the elements, while others omit one or most of them. Here's the info you need to find the right chocolate for your recipe.

Unsweetened chocolate
Also called baking chocolate, this is pure, unsweetened chocolate liquor cooled and moulded into blocks. It is bitter and cannot be used interchangeably with semisweet or bittersweet chocolate.

Bittersweet and semisweet chocolate
These chocolates contain pure chocolate liquor, cocoa butter, sugar, vanilla and lecithin. In baking, both types are interchangeable, although the bittersweet has a more pronounced chocolate flavour.

Dark chocolate
This is a catch-all term for chocolate that contains a high amount of cocoa liquor. It comes in a number of different varieties, which are described on the label in terms of cocoa percentage. Our recipes often call for dark chocolate with 70% cocoa because it has a beautiful balance between bitterness, sweetness and rich flavour.

Sweet chocolate
This chocolate contains the same ingredients as semisweet chocolate, but has a higher sugar content.

Milk chocolate
This chocolate has dry or concentrated milk added to the same ingredients as semisweet, bittersweet and sweet chocolate. It is popular for eating out of hand.

White chocolate
This type does not actually contain any chocolate liquor, just cocoa butter. Good-quality white chocolate is ivory or cream coloured; it's not the same as white chocolate confectionery coating. Real white chocolate contains cocoa butter, whereas confectionery white chocolate contains vegetable fats instead.

Cocoa powder
Made of ground, partially defatted cocoa solids, cocoa powder comes in two types: natural (usually labelled unsweetened cocoa powder) and Dutch-processed, which has been treated to neutralize its natural acidity. Cocoa powder should not be replaced with hot chocolate powders.

This recipe takes simple campfire s'mores and turns them into a decadent dessert to enjoy at home. The stretchy marshmallow filling and warm, oozy chocolate are a sweet ending to a special family meal.

S'mores Chocolate Fondue

ingredients

½ cup **unsalted butter,** softened
¼ cup **liquid honey**
2 tbsp **fancy molasses**
¼ cup **milk**
1½ cups **whole wheat flour**
¾ cup **all-purpose flour**
½ tsp each **baking soda** and **salt**
¼ tsp **cinnamon**
Pinch **ground ginger**

12 **marshmallows,** halved
2 **bananas** (optional), sliced

CHOCOLATE FONDUE:
⅓ cup each **whipping cream (35%)**
  and **milk**
2 tbsp **granulated sugar**
6 oz (170 g) **bittersweet chocolate,**
  finely chopped
1 tbsp **unsalted butter**

method

In large bowl, beat together butter, honey and molasses until light; beat in milk. Whisk together whole wheat flour, all-purpose flour, baking soda, salt, cinnamon and ginger; stir into butter mixture.

Turn out onto lightly floured surface; gently knead until combined. Divide in half and flatten into discs; wrap each and refrigerate until firm, about 30 minutes.

Between lightly floured waxed paper, roll out each disc to generous ⅛-inch (3 mm) thickness. Using 2½-inch (6 cm) fluted round cutter, cut out 24 cookies, rerolling and cutting scraps. Place on parchment paper–lined rimless baking sheet; using fork, prick each cookie 3 times.

Bake in 350°F (180°C) oven until light golden, about 12 minutes. Turn half of the cookies over; gently press marshmallows on top. Return to oven and bake until slightly melted, about 1 minute. Top with bananas (if using). Place uncovered cookies on top, pressing lightly.

CHOCOLATE FONDUE: Meanwhile, in saucepan, bring cream, milk and sugar just to boil. Place chocolate in fondue pot or heatproof bowl; whisk in cream mixture until chocolate is melted. Whisk in butter. Keep warm. Serve with cookie sandwiches for dipping.

MAKES 24 SERVINGS.
PER SERVING: about 163 cal, 2 g pro, 9 g total fat (5 g sat. fat), 21 g carb, 2 g fibre, 16 mg chol, 81 mg sodium, 75 mg potassium. % RDI: 2% calcium, 6% iron, 5% vit A, 5% folate.

creamy

White Chocolate Cherry Torte **45**

Two-Tone Mocha Cheesecake **46**

Rocky Road Cheesecake **47**

Mocha Mousse Cake **48**

Milk Chocolate Cheesecake **50**

Mini White Chocolate Cheesecake **51**

Chocolate Cappuccino Cheesecake **53**

Chocolate Hazelnut Swirl Cheesecake **54**

Grasshopper Truffle Tart **55**

No-Bake Chocolate Marble Cheesecake Pie **56**

Milk Chocolate Tart Brûlée **58**

Chocolate Coconut Cream Pie **59**

Chocolate Peanut Butter Pie **61**

Chocolate Fondue **62**

White Chocolate Pouring Custard **63**

Chocolate Banana Cream Pie **64**

Cardamom Chocolate Pots de Crème **66**

Silky Chocolate Mousse **67**

Chocolate Chestnut Mousse **69**

Mocha Mousse **70**

Two-Tone Chocolate Espresso Panna Cotta **71**

Hazelnut Chocolate Mousse **72**

White Chocolate Pomegranate Trifle **75**

Black Forest Trifle **76**

Chocolate Hazelnut Trifle **77**

Black Forest Mousse Parfaits **78**

White Chocolate Mocha Mugs **80**

Malted Hot Chocolate **81**

Marshmallow Hot Chocolate Mix **81**

Hot Chocolate **82**

Chocolate Soufflé Cakes With Sherry Cream **83**

Classic Chocolate Soufflé **85**

Chocolate Caramel Layered Pudding **86**

Amaretti White Chocolate Coffee Parfaits **87**

Double-Chocolate Éclairs **89**

This elegant torte combines luscious brandy-laced cherries, almonds and smooth white chocolate custard. If you make the components ahead of time, it's just a matter of quick assembly before serving.

White Chocolate Cherry Torte

ingredients

½ cup **butter,** softened
6 tbsp **granulated sugar**
1 **egg yolk**
1 tsp **vanilla**
1 cup **all-purpose flour**
⅔ cup **ground almonds**
Pinch **baking powder**
¼ cup **sliced almonds,** toasted

WHITE CHOCOLATE CUSTARD:
4 **egg yolks**
2 cups **milk**
⅓ cup **granulated sugar**
¼ cup **cornstarch**
2 oz (55 g) **white chocolate,** chopped

BRANDIED CHERRY COMPOTE:
2½ cups **sour cherries,** pitted
¼ cup **granulated sugar**
2 tsp **cornstarch**
2 tbsp **cherry brandy**

method

WHITE CHOCOLATE CUSTARD: In bowl, whisk together egg yolks, 1 cup of the milk, sugar and cornstarch. In heavy saucepan, heat remaining milk over medium heat just until bubbles form around edge; gradually whisk into egg mixture. Return to saucepan and cook, whisking, until thick enough to mound on spoon, about 7 minutes. Strain through fine sieve into clean bowl; stir in white chocolate until melted, about 1 minute. Place plastic wrap directly on surface. Refrigerate until cold, about 4 hours. *(Make-ahead: Refrigerate for up to 24 hours.)*

BRANDIED CHERRY COMPOTE: Meanwhile, in saucepan, stir together cherries, sugar and 2 tbsp water over medium-high heat; cook, stirring frequently, until softened, about 15 minutes. Stir cornstarch with 2 tbsp water; stir into cherry mixture and cook, stirring, until thickened, about 1 minute. Stir in cherry brandy. Let cool completely, about 3 hours. *(Make-ahead: Refrigerate in airtight container for up to 24 hours.)*

In large bowl, beat butter with sugar until fluffy; beat in egg yolk and vanilla. Whisk together flour, ground almonds and baking powder; stir into butter mixture to form soft crumbly dough.

Press dough onto bottom and up side of greased 9-inch (23 cm) round tart pan with removable bottom. Refrigerate until firm, about 30 minutes. *(Make-ahead: Cover and refrigerate for up to 24 hours.)*

Using fork, prick crust all over. Line with foil; fill with pie weights or dried beans. Bake in 350°F (180°C) oven until edge starts to turn golden, about 15 minutes. Remove weights and foil; bake until golden, about 15 minutes. Let cool completely in pan on rack.

Fill crust with custard, smoothing top. Top with cherry compote. Sprinkle with almonds.

MAKES 12 SERVINGS.
PER SERVING: about 312 cal, 6 g pro, 16 g total fat (7 g sat. fat), 37 g carb, 2 g fibre, 104 mg chol, 82 mg sodium, 185 mg potassium. % RDI: 8% calcium, 9% iron, 17% vit A, 3% vit C, 15% folate.

Coffee and chocolate are a match made in heaven. If you like, decorate this cheesecake with Piped Chocolate Trees (page 82), supporting each with a small piece of chocolate.

Two-Tone Mocha Cheesecake

ingredients

1½ cups **chocolate wafer crumbs**
3 tbsp **butter,** melted
1 tsp **instant coffee granules** or instant espresso powder

FILLING:
8 oz (225 g) **milk chocolate,** chopped
4 oz (115 g) **bittersweet chocolate,** chopped
3 pkg (each 250 g) **cream cheese,** softened
¾ cup **granulated sugar**
3 **eggs**
1 cup **whipping cream (35%)**
3 tbsp **coffee liqueur**

method

Grease 9½-inch (2.75 L) springform pan. Centre on large square of heavy-duty foil; bring foil up and press to side of pan.

Stir together chocolate wafer crumbs, butter and coffee granules until moistened; press onto bottom and ½ inch (1 cm) up side of prepared pan. Bake in 325°F (160°C) oven until firm, about 10 minutes. Let cool.

FILLING: Meanwhile, in separate heatproof bowls over saucepan of hot (not boiling) water, melt milk chocolate and bittersweet chocolate, stirring until smooth; let cool to room temperature.

In large bowl, beat cream cheese until smooth; beat in sugar, scraping down side of bowl often. Beat in eggs, 1 at a time, beating well after each. Beat in cream, coffee liqueur and milk chocolate until blended.

Transfer one-third of the batter to separate bowl; whisk in bittersweet chocolate. Pour bittersweet chocolate batter over prepared crust; smooth top. Pour remaining batter over top; smooth top.

Set pan in larger pan; pour in enough hot water to come 1 inch (2.5 cm) up side. Bake in 325°F (160°C) oven until set around edge but centre is still jiggly, about 1 hour. Turn off oven; let stand in oven for 1 hour.

Transfer springform pan to rack and remove foil; let cool completely. Cover and refrigerate until firm and chilled, about 4 hours. *(Make-ahead: Refrigerate for up to 3 days or overwrap in heavy-duty foil and freeze for up to 2 weeks.)*

MAKES 12 SERVINGS.

PER SERVING: about 592 cal, 10 g pro, 46 g total fat (27 g sat. fat), 41 g carb, 2 g fibre, 160 mg chol, 336 mg sodium. % RDI: 11% calcium, 17% iron, 40% vit A, 8% folate.

This vintage ice cream flavour – packed with chocolate and dotted with marshmallows – translates beautifully into a rich cheesecake. This is a mighty sweet dessert, so serve it with strong coffee or tea to balance the sugary hit.

Rocky Road Cheesecake

ingredients

8 oz (225 g) **bittersweet chocolate** or semisweet chocolate, chopped

2 pkg (each 250 g) **cream cheese,** softened

½ cup **granulated sugar**

2 **eggs**

¾ cup **whipping cream (35%)**

2 cups **mini marshmallows**

¼ cup **caramel sauce**

¼ cup **chocolate sauce**

CRUST:

1½ cups **chocolate wafer crumbs**

3 tbsp **butter,** melted

method

Grease 9-inch (2.5 L) springform pan; line side with parchment paper. Centre on large square of heavy-duty foil; bring foil up and press to side of pan.

CRUST: Stir chocolate wafer crumbs with butter until moistened; press onto bottom of prepared pan. Bake in 325°F (160°C) oven until firm, about 10 minutes. Let cool in pan on rack.

Meanwhile, in heatproof bowl over saucepan of hot (not boiling) water, melt bittersweet chocolate, stirring until smooth; let cool to room temperature.

In large bowl, beat cream cheese until smooth; beat in sugar. Beat in eggs; beat in cream and chocolate until smooth. Scrape over prepared crust; smooth top.

Set pan in larger pan; pour in enough hot water to come 1 inch (2.5 cm) up side. Bake in 325°F (160°C) oven until set around edge but centre is still jiggly, about 1 hour. Turn off oven; let stand in oven for 1 hour.

Transfer springform pan to rack and remove foil; let cool completely. Cover and refrigerate until firm and chilled, about 4 hours. *(Make-ahead: Refrigerate for up to 3 days.)*

Sprinkle marshmallows over cheesecake. Drizzle with caramel and chocolate sauces. *(Make-ahead: Cover with cake dome or loose plastic wrap; refrigerate for up to 4 hours.)*

MAKES 12 SERVINGS.

PER SERVING: about 487 cal, 8 g pro, 36 g total fat (21 g sat. fat), 40 g carb, 4 g fibre, 105 mg chol, 301 mg sodium. % RDI: 7% calcium, 18% iron, 25% vit A, 9% folate.

Cutting Cheesecakes

A hot, dry knife is the best tool for cutting cool, creamy cheesecakes and mousse cakes into neat slices. Dip the blade into hot water and dry well between slices.

Test Kitchen TIP

This creamy layered cake will satisfy chocolate and coffee lovers alike —
and the chocolate hearts make it perfect for an anniversary or Valentine's Day dessert.
Keep this indulgent cake cool in the fridge until you're ready to serve it.

Mocha Mousse Cake

ingredients

1½ cups **all-purpose flour**
1 cup **granulated sugar**
⅓ cup **cocoa powder**
1 tsp **baking soda**
¼ tsp **salt**
1 cup cold brewed **coffee** or water
½ cup **vegetable oil**
1 tsp **vanilla**
4 tsp **cider vinegar**
2 oz (55 g) **bittersweet chocolate, shaved**
Chocolate Hearts (page 82)

MOCHA MOUSSE:
1 pkg (7 g) **unflavoured gelatin**
⅔ cup **milk**
4 **egg yolks**
¼ cup **granulated sugar**
Pinch **salt**
4 oz (115 g) **bittersweet chocolate,** melted
2 oz (55 g) **milk chocolate,** melted
¼ cup **coffee liqueur**
1 tsp **vanilla**
2 cups **whipping cream (35%)**

CHOCOLATE GANACHE:
4 oz (115 g) **bittersweet chocolate,** chopped
½ cup **whipping cream (35%)**

method

Grease 8-inch (1.2 L) round cake pan; line with parchment paper. In bowl, whisk together flour, sugar, cocoa powder, baking soda and salt. Whisk in coffee, oil and vanilla. Stir in vinegar. Bake in 350°F (180°C) oven until cake tester inserted in centre comes out clean, 40 to 45 minutes. Let cool in pan on rack for 5 minutes. Turn out onto rack; let cool.

MOCHA MOUSSE: Meanwhile, sprinkle gelatin over 2 tbsp water; set aside. In saucepan, heat milk over medium-high heat just until bubbles form around edge. In heatproof bowl, whisk egg yolks, sugar and salt; slowly whisk in milk. Place bowl over saucepan of simmering water; cook, stirring, until thick enough to thinly coat back of spoon ❶ and instant-read thermometer reads 160°F (71°C), 8 minutes. Remove from heat. Stir in gelatin mixture until melted. Whisk in bittersweet and milk chocolates, liqueur and vanilla. Refrigerate, stirring twice, until cold and thick enough to mound on spoon ❷, 15 minutes. Whip cream; whisk one-quarter into chocolate mixture. Fold in remaining cream.

Grease 9-inch (2.5 L) springform pan; line side with parchment paper, extending 1 inch (2.5 cm) above rim. Using serrated knife, trim top of cake to level. Cut cake horizontally in half; place 1 layer in prepared pan. Pour in half of the mousse; spread to fill in space around cake ❸. Top with remaining cake layer. Pour in remaining mousse; spread to cover top and side. Refrigerate until set, 2 hours.

CHOCOLATE GANACHE: Place chocolate in heatproof bowl. In saucepan, bring cream just to boil; whisk into chocolate until smooth. Pour over mousse, smoothing top. Refrigerate until almost set, 30 minutes. *(Make-ahead: Cover; refrigerate for up to 24 hours.)*

Remove side of pan and paper; press shaved chocolate onto side of cake. Make 16 shallow 1-inch (2.5 cm) long slits in ganache around edge. Alternating white and dark, insert 1 side of chocolate heart into each slit.

MAKES 16 SERVINGS.
PER SERVING: about 485 cal, 5 g pro, 31 g total fat (15 g sat. fat), 45 g carb, 3 g fibre, 102 mg chol, 466 mg sodium, 252 mg potassium. % RDI: 6% calcium, 16% iron, 16% vit A, 15% folate.

Milk chocolate makes this chocolate cheesecake sweeter and creamier than its darker counterparts. For a kid-friendly caramel garnish, sprinkle chopped candy, such as Rolos, over the top.

Milk Chocolate Cheesecake

ingredients

3 pkg (each 250 g) **cream cheese,** softened
¾ cup **granulated sugar**
3 **eggs**
1¼ cups **whipping cream (35%)**
10 oz (280 g) **milk chocolate,** melted

CRUST:
1½ cups **chocolate wafer crumbs**
¼ cup **butter,** melted

CHOCOLATE GANACHE:
6 oz (170 g) **bittersweet chocolate,** chopped
⅓ cup **whipping cream (35%)**

method

Grease 9-inch (2.5 L) springform pan; line side with parchment paper. Centre on large square of heavy-duty foil; bring foil up and press to side of pan.

CRUST: Stir chocolate wafer crumbs with butter until moistened; press onto bottom of prepared pan. Bake in 325°F (160°C) oven until firm, about 10 minutes. Let cool.

In large bowl, beat cream cheese with sugar until smooth; beat in eggs, 1 at a time. Beat in cream; stir in milk chocolate until combined. Scrape over crust, smoothing top.

Set pan in larger pan; pour in enough hot water to come 1 inch (2.5 cm) up side. Bake in 325°F (160°C) oven until edge is set but centre is still jiggly, about 1 hour. Turn off oven; let stand in oven for 1 hour.

Transfer springform pan to rack and remove foil; let cool completely. Cover and refrigerate until firm and chilled, about 4 hours.

CHOCOLATE GANACHE: In heatproof bowl over saucepan of hot (not boiling) water, melt chocolate with cream, stirring until smooth. Let cool just until spreading consistency, about 15 minutes.

Pour ganache over cake; using small offset spatula, spread smoothly to edge. Refrigerate until firm, about 30 minutes. *(Make-ahead: Cover and refrigerate for up to 3 days or overwrap with heavy-duty foil and freeze in airtight container for up to 2 weeks.)*

MAKES 12 TO 16 SERVINGS.
PER EACH OF 16 SERVINGS: about 513 cal, 8 g pro, 39 g total fat (24 g sat. fat), 35 g carb, 2 g fibre, 130 mg chol, 263 mg sodium. % RDI: 9% calcium, 13% iron, 31% vit A, 8% folate.

This cheesecake is exquisite either unadorned or served with cubed fresh mango or pineapple (or a mix of the two). It's just the right size for an intimate dinner party.

Mini White Chocolate Cheesecake

ingredients

1 pkg (250 g) **cream cheese,** softened
¼ cup **granulated sugar**
1 **egg**
2 tsp **lemon juice**
1 tsp **vanilla**
6 oz (170 g) **white chocolate,** melted
½ cup **sour cream**

CRUST:
¾ cup **shortbread cookie crumbs**
2 tbsp **butter,** melted

method

Grease bottom of 6-inch (1.25 L) springform pan; line side with parchment paper. Centre on large square of heavy-duty foil; bring foil up and press to side of pan.

CRUST: Stir shortbread cookie crumbs with butter until moistened; press onto bottom of prepared pan. Bake in 350°F (180°C) oven until firm, about 10 minutes. Let cool.

In large bowl, beat cream cheese until fluffy; beat in sugar until smooth. Beat in egg, lemon juice and vanilla; whisk in white chocolate and sour cream. Pour over crust, smoothing top.

Set pan in larger pan; pour in enough hot water to come 1 inch (2.5 cm) up side. Bake in 325°F (160°C) oven until edge is set but centre is still jiggly, about 40 minutes. Turn off oven; let stand in oven for 45 minutes.

Transfer springform pan to rack and remove foil; let cool completely. Cover and refrigerate until firm and chilled, 2 hours. *(Make-ahead: Refrigerate for up to 2 days or overwrap in heavy-duty foil and freeze for up to 2 weeks.)*

MAKES 8 SERVINGS.
PER SERVING: about 376 cal, 6 g pro, 27 g total fat (15 g sat. fat), 30 g carb, trace fibre, 80 mg chol, 219 mg sodium. % RDI: 8% calcium, 6% iron, 17% vit A, 10% folate.

Making Cookie Crumbs

Using a food processor is the quickest way to make your own cookie crumbs for cheesecake bases. Break cookies into pieces and pulse until fine but not powdery. If you're worried the crumbs will get too fine too quickly, or you want a coarser texture, place the cookies in a resealable plastic bag and crush by hand using a rolling pin.

Chocolate and coffee make a perfect marriage in desserts. Because the filling is cooked before it's added to the crust, this cheesecake is easier than traditional versions, which require a water bath and a long time in the oven.

Chocolate Cappuccino Cheesecake

ingredients

1½ cups **chocolate wafer crumbs**
¼ cup **butter,** melted

FILLING:
4 oz (115 g) **bittersweet chocolate,** chopped
4 oz (115 g) **white chocolate,** chopped
3 pkg (each 250 g) **cream cheese,** softened
4 **eggs**
¾ cup **granulated sugar**

¼ cup **whipping cream (35%)**
1 tbsp **instant espresso powder**

TOPPING:
1 tsp **instant espresso powder**
½ cup **whipping cream (35%)**

method

Grease 9-inch (2.5 L) springform pan; line side with parchment paper. Stir chocolate wafer crumbs with butter; press onto bottom of prepared pan. Bake in 350°F (180°C) oven until firm, about 10 minutes. Let cool.

FILLING: Meanwhile, in separate heatproof bowls over saucepan of hot (not boiling) water, melt bittersweet chocolate and white chocolate, stirring until smooth; let cool to room temperature.

Beat cream cheese until fluffy; set aside. In large heatproof bowl over saucepan of simmering water, beat eggs with sugar until thickened and instant-read thermometer reads 160°F (71°C), about 7 minutes. Making 3 additions, beat in cream cheese until smooth.

Transfer half of the filling to separate bowl; beat in bittersweet chocolate and whipping cream. Pour over crust, smoothing top.

Stir espresso powder with 1 tsp hot water; beat into remaining filling along with white chocolate. Gently spoon over chocolate layer, smoothing top. Cover and refrigerate until firm and chilled, about 8 hours. *(Make-ahead: Refrigerate for up to 2 days.)*

TOPPING: Sprinkle cheesecake with espresso powder; remove side of pan. Whip cream; pipe into rosettes around top edge of cake.

MAKES 12 TO 16 SERVINGS.
PER EACH OF 16 SERVINGS: about 405 cal, 7 g pro, 31 g total fat (18 g sat. fat), 27 g carb, 1 g fibre, 120 mg chol, 246 mg sodium. % RDI: 7% calcium, 11% iron, 26% vit A, 9% folate.

This swirl-topped cheesecake looks impressive – but it's not difficult to create. The two batters have very similar textures, so they blend together easily. For an elegant finish, garnish each serving with a dollop of whipped cream and a whole hazelnut or hazelnut wafer cookie.

Chocolate Hazelnut Swirl Cheesecake

ingredients

1½ cups ground **hazelnuts**
½ cup **graham cracker crumbs**
¼ cup **unsalted butter,** melted
3 pkg (each 250 g) **cream cheese,** softened
½ cup **granulated sugar**
4 **eggs**

⅓ cup **whipping cream (35%)**
⅓ cup **hazelnut liqueur**
1 bar (100 g) **milk chocolate,** melted
¼ cup **chocolate hazelnut spread** (such as Nutella)

method

Grease 9-inch (2.5 L) springform pan; line side with parchment paper. Centre on large square of heavy-duty foil; bring foil up and press to side of pan.

Stir together hazelnuts, graham cracker crumbs and butter until moistened; press firmly onto bottom of prepared pan. Bake in 350°F (180°C) oven until firm, 10 to 12 minutes. Let cool.

In large bowl, beat cream cheese until smooth. Beat in sugar until fluffy; beat in eggs, 1 at a time. Beat in cream until combined. Transfer 1½ cups to small bowl; stir in half of the hazelnut liqueur. Set aside.

Beat milk chocolate, chocolate hazelnut spread and remaining hazelnut liqueur into remaining batter. Pour half of the chocolate batter over crust; smooth and level top. Drizzle with half of the white batter; top with remaining chocolate batter. Dot with remaining white batter. Using tip of knife, swirl batters together to create pattern. Tap gently on counter to release any air bubbles.

Set pan in larger pan; pour in enough hot water to come 1 inch (2.5 cm) up side. Bake in 325°F (160°C) oven until edge is set but centre is still jiggly, 55 to 60 minutes.

Let cool in pan in water for 15 minutes. Transfer springform pan to rack; remove foil. Let cool to room temperature. Cover and refrigerate until firm and chilled, 4 to 6 hours. *(Make-ahead: Cover and refrigerate for up to 3 days.)*

MAKES 12 TO 16 SERVINGS.
PER EACH OF 16 SERVINGS: about 398 cal, 7 g pro, 32 g total fat (16 g sat. fat), 20 g carb, 2 g fibre, 113 mg chol, 179 mg sodium, 190 mg potassium. % RDI: 7% calcium, 9% iron, 24% vit A, 10% folate.

This fancier version of retro grasshopper pie combines whipped chocolate ganache with everyone's favourite chocolate cookie crumb base. Crème de menthe does double duty, flavouring the filling and giving it a hint of green.

Grasshopper Truffle Tart

ingredients

2 cups **chocolate wafer crumbs**
½ cup **butter,** melted
½ cup shaved **dark chocolate**

FILLING:

6 oz (170 g) **white chocolate,**
 finely chopped
¾ cup **whipping cream (35%)**
3 tbsp **green crème de menthe**

method

Stir chocolate wafer crumbs with butter until moistened; press onto bottom and up side of 9-inch (23 cm) fluted round tart pan with removable bottom. Bake in 350°F (180°C) oven until firm, about 10 minutes. Let cool.

FILLING: Meanwhile, place white chocolate in large heatproof bowl. In saucepan, bring cream just to boil; pour over white chocolate, whisking until smooth. Stir in crème de menthe. Refrigerate, stirring occasionally, until consistency of thin custard, 2 hours.

In stand mixer, using whisk attachment, whip filling until soft peaks form. Scrape into prepared crust; smooth top. Refrigerate until set, about 2 hours. *(Make-ahead: Cover loosely and refrigerate for up to 2 days.)*

Garnish with shaved chocolate.

MAKES 8 TO 10 SERVINGS.
PER EACH OF 10 SERVINGS: about 364 cal, 3 g pro, 25 g total fat (15 g sat. fat), 31 g carb, 1 g fibre, 49 mg chol, 218 mg sodium, 133 mg potassium. % RDI: 5% calcium, 9% iron, 14% vit A, 7% folate.

Stand Mixer vs. Hand Mixer

The whisk attachment on a stand mixer is incredibly efficient at whipping air into liquids, such as egg whites, whipping cream or mousse mixtures. If you don't have one, use a hand mixer. It will take a little longer (and your hand might get tired), but the results will be just as fluffy.

Test Kitchen TIP

If you can't decide between chocolate and vanilla,
go with a marbled cheesecake that features both. This is a wonderful no-bake dessert
for times when the oven is busy cooking other dishes.

No-Bake Chocolate Marble Cheesecake Pie

ingredients

1½ cups **chocolate wafer crumbs**
⅓ cup **butter,** melted
¾ cup **whipping cream (35%)**
1 oz (30 g) **bittersweet chocolate,**
  finely chopped

FILLING:
4 oz (115 g) **bittersweet chocolate,**
  finely chopped
¾ cup **whipping cream (35%)**
1½ pkg (each 250 g) **cream cheese,**
  softened
⅓ cup **sweetened condensed milk**
1 tsp **vanilla**

method

Stir chocolate wafer crumbs with butter until moistened; press onto bottom and up side of 9-inch (23 cm) pie plate. Refrigerate until firm, about 30 minutes.

FILLING: Place chocolate in heatproof bowl. In small saucepan, bring half of the cream just to boil; pour over chocolate, whisking until melted and smooth. Let cool slightly.

In separate bowl, beat together cream cheese, remaining cream, sweetened condensed milk and vanilla until smooth; spoon randomly into prepared crust. Pour chocolate mixture into gaps. Using tip of knife, roughly swirl mixtures together. Tap on counter to smooth top. Cover and refrigerate until firm, about 4 hours. *(Make-ahead: Refrigerate for up to 2 days.)*

Whip cream; pipe into rosettes or spoon along edge of pie. Sprinkle chopped chocolate over whipped cream.

MAKES 8 TO 10 SERVINGS.

PER EACH OF 10 SERVINGS: about 482 cal, 7 g pro, 43 g total fat (26 g sat. fat), 24 g carb, 3 g fibre, 110 mg chol, 299 mg sodium. % RDI: 9% calcium, 15% iron, 35% vit A, 8% folate.

This tart is designed for special occasions. The crackly caramel topping encloses
a smooth milk chocolate filling that beautifully complements the hazelnuts in the pastry.
Edible gold flakes on top make the tart even more beautiful.

Milk Chocolate Tart Brûlée

ingredients

⅓ cup **hazelnuts**
1¼ cups **all-purpose flour**
½ cup **unsalted butter,** softened
½ cup **granulated sugar**
2 **egg yolks**
Pinch **salt**

FILLING:
1½ cups **milk**
8 oz (225 g) **milk chocolate,**
    chopped

2 oz (55 g) **bittersweet chocolate,**
    chopped
3 **eggs**
3 **egg yolks**
½ cup **granulated sugar**
1½ tsp **vanilla**

TOPPING:
½ cup **granulated sugar**
½ cup **whipping cream (35%)**
Edible gold flakes

method

Spread hazelnuts in single layer on rimmed baking sheet; toast in 350°F (180°C) oven until fragrant and skins crack, 10 minutes. Let cool slightly. Transfer to towel; rub briskly to remove as much of the skin as possible. In food processor, finely grind hazelnuts with 2 tbsp of the flour; set aside.

In bowl, beat butter until light, 2 minutes. Beat in sugar until fluffy; beat in egg yolks, 1 at a time, beating well after each. Whisk together hazelnut mixture, remaining flour and salt; using wooden spoon, stir into butter mixture until dough holds together, adding up to 2 tbsp water if too crumbly.

Transfer dough to work surface; knead 2 or 3 times to form ball. Press into disc; wrap in plastic wrap and refrigerate until firm, about 1 hour. *(Make-ahead: Refrigerate for up to 1 day. Let stand at room temperature for 45 minutes.)*

Press dough onto bottom and up side of greased 11-inch (28 cm) tart pan with removable bottom. Freeze until firm, about 10 minutes. Line pastry shell with foil; fill evenly with pie weights or dried beans. Bake on bottom rack in 400°F (200°C) oven for 20 minutes. Remove weights and foil; bake until golden, about 10 minutes. Let cool in pan on rack.

FILLING: Meanwhile, in saucepan, heat milk until bubbles form around edge. Remove from heat. Whisk in milk chocolate and bittersweet chocolate until smooth. In bowl, whisk together eggs, egg yolks, sugar and vanilla. Gradually whisk in chocolate mixture. Let stand at room temperature for 10 minutes. Pour through fine sieve into prepared tart shell.

Bake in 325°F (160°C) oven just until bubbles rise to surface and knife inserted in centre comes out clean, about 25 minutes. Let cool in pan on rack. Refrigerate until chilled, about 2 hours. *(Make-ahead: Cover loosely with plastic wrap and refrigerate for up to 24 hours.)*

TOPPING: Just before serving, sprinkle sugar evenly over top. Shield crust with strips of foil; using propane torch or under broiler, melt and caramelize sugar. Let stand until sugar is hardened, about 10 minutes. Whip cream; pipe into rosettes or spoon along edge of tart. Garnish with gold flakes.

MAKES 12 SERVINGS.
PER SERVING: about 505 cal, 9 g pro, 32 g total fat (14 g sat. fat), 51 g carb, 3 g fibre, 171 mg chol, 55 mg sodium. % RDI: 12% calcium, 14% iron, 19% vit A, 20% folate.

We've jazzed up a decadent coconut cream pie even more with chocolate pastry and a shower of grated chocolate on top. Look for the piña colada concentrate in the drinks aisle or the freezer section of the supermarket.

Chocolate Coconut Cream Pie

ingredients

1¼ cups **all-purpose flour**
¼ cup **cocoa powder**
2 tbsp **granulated sugar**
½ tsp **salt**
¼ cup cold **butter,** cubed
¼ cup cold **lard,** cubed
1 **egg yolk**
1 tsp **vinegar**
Ice water

FILLING:
2½ cups **milk**
½ cup **granulated sugar**
⅓ cup **cornstarch**

¼ tsp **salt**
⅓ cup **piña colada concentrate**
4 **egg yolks,** beaten
5 oz (140 g) **semisweet chocolate,** chopped
½ cup **sweetened shredded coconut,** toasted
1 tbsp **butter**
1½ tsp **vanilla**
½ cup **whipping cream (35%)**

GARNISH:
¾ cup **whipping cream (35%)**
2 tbsp grated **semisweet chocolate**

method

In large bowl, sift flour, cocoa powder, sugar and salt. Using pastry blender or 2 knives, cut in butter and lard until in fine crumbs with a few larger pieces. In liquid measure, whisk egg yolk with vinegar. Add enough ice water to make ⅓ cup. Drizzle over flour mixture; using fork, briskly stir until dough holds together. Press into disc; wrap in plastic wrap and refrigerate until chilled, 30 minutes. *(Make-ahead: Refrigerate for up to 3 days.)*

On lightly floured surface, roll out pastry to ⅛-inch (3 mm) thickness; fit into 9-inch (23 cm) pie plate, trimming to leave ½-inch (1 cm) overhang. Fold overhang under; flute edge. Prick all over with fork. Line with foil; fill evenly with pie weights or dried beans. Bake on bottom rack in 425°F (220°C) oven for 15 minutes. Remove weights and foil; bake until firm, 5 to 7 minutes. Let cool in pan on rack. *(Make-ahead: Cover and store at room temperature for up to 1 day.)*

FILLING: In heavy saucepan, whisk together ½ cup of the milk, sugar, cornstarch and salt; stir in remaining milk and piña colada concentrate. Bring to boil over medium heat,

stirring constantly. Reduce heat to medium-low; cook, stirring, until thickened, 8 minutes. Remove from heat. Stir 1 cup of the milk mixture into egg yolks; return to pan and cook, stirring, until thick enough to mound on spoon, about 4 minutes. Remove from heat. Add 4 oz (115 g) of the chocolate, the coconut, butter and vanilla; stir until chocolate is melted. Transfer to clean bowl and place plastic wrap directly on surface; refrigerate until chilled, 2 to 2½ hours.

Meanwhile, in bowl over saucepan of hot (not boiling) water, melt remaining chocolate; brush over crust. Refrigerate until set.

Whip cream; fold into filling. Pour into prepared crust; refrigerate until firm enough to slice, about 3 hours.

GARNISH: Whip cream; pipe rosettes or spoon around edge of pie. Sprinkle with chocolate. *(Make-ahead: Refrigerate for up to 8 hours.)*

MAKES 8 TO 10 SERVINGS.
PER EACH OF 10 SERVINGS: about 493 cal, 7 g pro, 32 g total fat (18 g sat. fat), 49 g carb, 2 g fibre, 160 mg chol, 291 mg sodium. % RDI: 11% calcium, 14% iron, 24% vit A, 2% vit C, 16% folate.

This irresistible combination has it all – a crunchy crust, a creamy filling, a velvety ganache and a sprinkle of peanuts. It's really rich, so just a small slice is satisfying.

Chocolate Peanut Butter Pie

ingredients

1½ cups **chocolate wafer crumbs**
⅓ cup **butter,** melted

FILLING:
½ cup **whipping cream (35%)**
1 pkg (250 g) **cream cheese,** softened
1 cup **smooth natural peanut butter**
2 tbsp **butter,** softened
1 tbsp **vanilla**
1 cup **icing sugar**

TOPPING:
2 oz (55 g) **bittersweet chocolate**
or semisweet chocolate, chopped
3 tbsp **whipping cream (35%)**
2 tbsp chopped **roasted peanuts**

method

Stir chocolate wafer crumbs with butter until moistened; press onto bottom and up side of 9-inch (23 cm) pie plate. Bake in 350°F (180°C) oven until firm, about 8 minutes. Let cool.

FILLING: Whip cream; set aside. In large bowl, beat cream cheese until smooth; beat in peanut butter, butter and vanilla. Beat in icing sugar until fluffy. Fold in one-quarter of the whipped cream; fold in remaining whipped cream. Spread over prepared crust. Cover loosely and refrigerate until firm, about 2 hours.

TOPPING: Meanwhile, in heatproof bowl set over saucepan of hot (not boiling) water, melt chocolate with cream, stirring until smooth; let cool. Drizzle over filling; sprinkle with peanuts. Cover loosely and refrigerate until set, about 2 hours. *(Make-ahead: Refrigerate for up to 2 days.)*

MAKES 10 SERVINGS.
PER SERVING: about 521 cal, 11 g pro, 42 g total fat (20 g sat. fat), 31 g carb, 3 g fibre, 75 mg chol, 391 mg sodium. % RDI: 5% calcium, 14% iron, 24% vit A, 15% folate.

Peanut Butter for Desserts

Natural peanut butter contains just nuts. We use it here and in many other recipes because it has a pure, nutty flavour – and this pie gets plenty of sweetness from the icing sugar. If you substitute regular peanut butter in recipes that call for natural, the added sugar and salt will change the flavour.

Choose fruit that's easy to spear and dip into this luscious mixture: Apple and pear slices, strawberries and pineapple chunks are ideal. Place a dish of small skewers or toothpicks alongside to make dipping easier and neater.

Chocolate Fondue

ingredients

6 oz (170 g) **bittersweet chocolate,** finely chopped

4 oz (115 g) **milk chocolate,** finely chopped

¾ cup **whipping cream (35%)**

2 tbsp **amaretto,** brandy or rum (optional)

method

Place bittersweet chocolate and milk chocolate in shallow heatproof bowl.

In saucepan, bring cream just to boil; pour over chocolate, whisking until melted. Whisk in amaretto (if using).

MAKES 2 CUPS.
PER 1 TBSP: about 64 cal, 1 g pro, 6 g total fat (4 g sat. fat), 4 g carb, 1 g fibre, 8 mg chol, 6 mg sodium. % RDI: 1% calcium, 3% iron, 2% vit A.

Fondue for a Party

You can transfer this fondue to a decorative bowl or ceramic fondue pot for entertaining. (Metal ones heat too quickly over an open flame and can scorch the chocolate.) Try making single batches rather than a double or triple batch, and refill your dish when the old one is empty – that way the mixture is always fresh and inviting. The fondue will stay soft for up to an hour; if it begins to set, microwave it on high for 15 to 20 seconds to reliquefy.

Berries and pineapple chunks will hold up well on a platter, but apple and pear slices brown quickly when exposed to air. Slice just what you need for the first part of the party, then slice more fruit and replenish platters as they run out.

Test Kitchen TIP

Pouring custard is a deliciously old-fashioned topping for cakes,
pies and other desserts. Here, white chocolate gives it a sweet accent
while orange zest and liqueur provide a citrusy zing.

White Chocolate Pouring Custard

ingredients

1 orange
2 cups **10% cream**
5 **egg yolks**
¾ cup **granulated sugar**

2 oz (55 g) **white chocolate,** chopped
1 tbsp **orange liqueur**

method

Cut strips of zest from orange; reserve orange flesh for another use. In saucepan, heat cream and orange zest over medium heat until tiny bubbles form around edge. Remove from heat; cover and let stand for 10 minutes.

Whisk egg yolks with sugar; slowly whisk in cream mixture. Return to pan; cook over medium-low heat, stirring constantly, until thick enough to coat back of spoon, about 8 minutes.

Add white chocolate and liqueur to custard; whisk until smooth. Strain through sieve into bowl. Place plastic wrap directly on surface; refrigerate until cold. *(Make-ahead: Refrigerate for up to 3 days.)*

MAKES 2½ CUPS.
PER 1 TBSP: about 45 cal, 1 g pro, 2 g total fat (1 g sat. fat), 5 g carb, 0 g fibre, 28 mg chol, 7 mg sodium, 22 mg potassium. % RDI: 2% calcium, 1% iron, 2% vit A, 2% folate.

63

Are you a banana cream pie aficionado? If you are, try this updated version featuring a surprise dark chocolate layer, chocolate-hazelnut custard filling and bourbon—whipped cream topping.

Chocolate Banana Cream Pie

ingredients

1¼ cups **all-purpose flour**
½ tsp **salt**
¼ cup cold **unsalted butter,** cubed
¼ cup cold **lard,** cubed
2 tbsp cold **water** (approx)
4½ tsp **sour cream**
1 **egg yolk**
1½ oz (45 g) **semisweet chocolate,** melted
4 **bananas,** thinly sliced

CUSTARD:
4 **egg yolks**
2 cups **milk**

⅓ cup **granulated sugar**
¼ cup **cornstarch**
¼ cup **chocolate hazelnut spread** (such as Nutella)
1 tsp **vanilla**

GARNISH:
½ cup **whipping cream (35%)**
2 tsp **granulated sugar**
2 tsp **bourbon**
1 tsp **vanilla**
1 oz (30 g) **semisweet chocolate,** shaved

method

In bowl, whisk flour with salt. Using pastry blender or 2 knives, cut in butter and lard until in coarse crumbs with a few larger pieces. Whisk together cold water, sour cream and egg yolk; drizzle over flour mixture, tossing with fork and adding up to 1 tsp more cold water if necessary, until ragged dough forms. Shape into disc; wrap and refrigerate until chilled, about 30 minutes. *(Make-ahead: Refrigerate for up to 3 days or overwrap with foil and freeze for up to 1 month.)*

On lightly floured surface, roll out pastry to generous ⅛-inch (3 mm) thickness; fit into 9-inch (23 cm) pie plate, trimming if necessary to leave ¾-inch (2 cm) overhang. Fold overhang under; crimp edge with fork. Refrigerate for 30 minutes.

Using fork, prick bottom of pastry shell. Line with parchment paper; fill evenly with pie weights or dried beans. Bake on bottom rack in 400°F (200°C) oven until rim is light golden, about 20 minutes. Remove weights and paper; bake until side is golden, about 10 minutes. Let cool in pan on rack.

CUSTARD: In bowl, whisk together egg yolks, ½ cup of the milk, sugar and cornstarch. In heavy saucepan, heat remaining milk over medium heat just until bubbles form around edge; gradually whisk into egg yolk mixture. Return to pan and cook, whisking, until thick enough to mound on spoon, about 3 minutes. Strain through fine sieve into bowl; stir in chocolate-hazelnut spread and vanilla. Place plastic wrap directly on surface; refrigerate until cold, about 1 hour. *(Make-ahead: Refrigerate for up to 24 hours.)*

Meanwhile, using pastry brush, paint melted chocolate onto inside of pie shell. Refrigerate until chocolate is firm, about 10 minutes. Layer bananas in prepared pie shell; top with custard, smoothing top. Cover and refrigerate for 4 hours.

GARNISH: Whip cream; whisk in sugar, bourbon and vanilla. Leaving 2-inch (5 cm) border, spread over custard. Sprinkle with shaved chocolate.

MAKES 8 SERVINGS.
PER SERVING: about 498 cal, 8 g pro, 28 g total fat (13 g sat. fat), 56 g carb, 3 g fibre, 153 mg chol, 155 mg sodium, 427 mg potassium. % RDI: 11% calcium, 14% iron, 21% vit A, 8% vit C, 28% folate.

Baking these puddings in a bain-marie, or water bath, gives them an incredible silky texture. If you prefer cinnamon over cardamom, try the variation.

Cardamom Chocolate Pots de Crème

ingredients

1½ cups **whipping cream (35%)**
¾ cup **milk**
10 **cardamom pods,** crushed
8 **whole cloves**
3 **whole star anise**
7 oz (210 g) **bittersweet chocolate,** finely chopped

6 **egg yolks**
5 tbsp **granulated sugar**
1 tsp **vanilla**
Pinch **salt**

method

In saucepan, heat cream, milk, cardamom, cloves and star anise over medium-high heat until steaming. Remove from heat; cover and let stand for 40 minutes. Strain through fine-mesh sieve into clean saucepan; heat over medium-low heat until steaming. Whisk in chocolate until melted and smooth.

In large bowl, whisk egg yolks with sugar until pale; whisk in about ½ cup of the chocolate mixture. Whisk in remaining chocolate mixture, vanilla and salt until smooth. Strain through fine sieve. Divide among eight ¾-cup (175 mL) ramekins or custard cups. Place in roasting pan lined with tea towel. Pour in enough boiling water to come halfway up sides of ramekins; cover pan with foil.

Bake in 325°F (160°C) oven until edges are set but centres are still jiggly, 25 to 35 minutes. Transfer ramekins to rack; let cool. Cover and refrigerate for 6 hours. *(Make-ahead: Refrigerate for up to 24 hours.)*

MAKES 8 SERVINGS.
PER SERVING: about 374 cal, 6 g pro, 30 g total fat (17 g sat. fat), 23 g carb, 3 g fibre, 212 mg chol, 31 mg sodium, 84 mg potassium. % RDI: 8% calcium, 11% iron, 22% vit A, 10% folate.

CHANGE IT UP
Cinnamon Chocolate Pots de Crème
Replace cardamom, cloves and whole star anise with 10 peppercorns, 1 cinnamon stick and 1½ tsp aniseed.

A light, airy chocolate mousse like this one is a wonderful way to end a meal when entertaining. The combination of two types of chocolate – sweet, creamy milk chocolate and deep, rich dark chocolate – brings the best qualities of both to the dessert.

Silky Chocolate Mousse

ingredients

4 oz (115 g) **milk chocolate,** chopped
2 oz (55 g) **70% dark chocolate,** chopped
1½ cups **whipping cream (35%)**
4 **egg yolks**

3 tbsp **granulated sugar**
Pinch **salt**
½ tsp **vanilla**

method

In heatproof bowl over saucepan of hot (not boiling) water, melt milk chocolate with dark chocolate, stirring until smooth. Set aside.

In small saucepan, heat ½ cup of the cream over medium-high heat just until tiny bubbles form around edge.

In separate heatproof bowl, whisk together egg yolks, sugar and salt; slowly whisk in hot cream. Place bowl over saucepan of gently simmering water; cook, stirring, until instant-read thermometer reads 160°F (71°C) and custard is thick enough to coat back of spoon, about 15 minutes. Remove from heat.

Whisk in melted chocolate and vanilla. Place plastic wrap directly on surface; let cool for 15 minutes.

Whip remaining cream; fold one-quarter into chocolate mixture. Fold in remaining whipped cream. Divide among dessert dishes; cover and refrigerate until set, about 4 hours. *(Make-ahead: Refrigerate for up to 24 hours.)*

MAKES 6 SERVINGS.
PER SERVING: about 413 cal, 5 g pro, 34 g total fat (20 g sat. fat), 24 g carb, 2 g fibre, 209 mg chol, 43 mg sodium, 201 mg potassium. % RDI: 9% calcium, 14% iron, 27% vit A, 10% folate.

CHANGE IT UP
Silky Mocha Mousse
Heat 2 tbsp instant coffee granules along with cream.

Chestnuts have a nutty, slightly earthy flavour that pairs well with chocolate.
Look for tubes or cans of sweetened chestnut purée in the baking aisle.

Chocolate Chestnut Mousse

ingredients

1⅔ cups **whipping cream (35%)**
4 **egg yolks**
3 tbsp **granulated sugar**
Pinch **salt**
3 oz (85 g) **bittersweet chocolate,**
  finely chopped

1 oz (30 g) **milk chocolate,** finely
  chopped
½ cup **sweetened chestnut purée**
2 tbsp **rum** (or 1 tsp vanilla)

method

In small saucepan, heat ⅔ cup of the cream over medium-high heat just until tiny bubbles form around edge.

Meanwhile, in heatproof bowl, whisk together egg yolks, sugar and salt; slowly whisk in hot cream. Place bowl over saucepan of simmering water; cook, stirring, until instant-read thermometer reads 160°F (71°C) and custard is thick enough to coat back of spoon, about 8 minutes. Remove from heat.

Whisk in bittersweet chocolate, milk chocolate, chestnut purée and rum. Return to heat, stirring, just until melted and combined. Place plastic wrap directly on surface; let cool until stiffened, about 1 hour.

Whip remaining cream; fold one-quarter into chocolate mixture. Fold in remaining whipped cream. Pipe or spoon mousse into dessert cups. Cover and refrigerate until firm, about 6 hours. *(Make-ahead: Refrigerate for up to 24 hours.)*

MAKES 6 TO 8 SERVINGS.

PER EACH OF 8 SERVINGS: about 333 cal, 4 g pro, 25 g total fat (15 g sat. fat), 23 g carb, 1 g fibre, 166 mg chol, 26 mg sodium. % RDI: 6% calcium, 6% iron, 22% vit A, 3% vit C, 8% folate.

This has to be the easiest chocolate recipe there is. Simply heat the cream, combine it with chocolate then chill and whip into a dense, decadent dessert. For a chic presentation, serve in demitasse or small coffee cups.

Mocha Mousse

ingredients

6 oz (170 g) **bittersweet chocolate** or semisweet chocolate, finely chopped
2 cups **whipping cream (35%)**
2 tbsp **coffee liqueur**

2 tsp **vanilla**
¼ cup **chocolate-covered espresso beans**

method

Place chocolate in large heatproof bowl. In saucepan, heat cream just until boiling; pour over chocolate, whisking until melted and smooth.

Whisk in coffee liqueur and vanilla. Place plastic wrap directly on surface. Refrigerate until chilled, about 4 hours. *(Make-ahead: Refrigerate for up to 2 days.)*

Beat chocolate mixture just until stiff peaks form. Spoon into 6 dessert dishes; top with espresso beans.

MAKES 6 SERVINGS.
PER SERVING: about 461 cal, 5 g pro, 47 g total fat (29 g sat. fat), 15 g carb, 5 g fibre, 102 mg chol, 34 mg sodium. % RDI: 7% calcium, 16% iron, 26% vit A, 2% folate.

CHANGE IT UP
Orange Chocolate Mousse
Replace coffee liqueur and espresso beans with orange liqueur and strips of orange zest.

Raspberry Chocolate Mousse
Replace coffee liqueur and espresso beans with raspberry liqueur and fresh raspberries.

Lightened-Up Mocha Mousse
Reduce chocolate to 4 oz (115 g) and cream to 1½ cups; prepare and chill as directed. In large bowl, beat ½ cup pasteurized egg whites until stiff peaks form. Fold half into prepared mousse; fold in remaining whites.

MAKES 8 SERVINGS.

Calling all java junkies! This decadent Italian "cooked cream"
is just the dessert to wake up your senses. The marbled chocolate garnish
looks great on lots of other treats too.

Two-Tone Chocolate Espresso Panna Cotta

ingredients

2 pkg (each 7 g) **unflavoured gelatin**
2 cups **milk**
6 oz (170 g) **milk chocolate,** chopped
2 cups **whipping cream (35%)**
⅔ cup **granulated sugar**
2 tsp **instant coffee granules**

VANILLA LAYER:
1 pkg (7 g) **unflavoured gelatin**
1 cup **milk**
1 cup **whipping cream (35%)**
⅓ cup **granulated sugar**
1 tsp **vanilla**

CURLY MARBLE SHARDS:
2 oz (55 g) **bittersweet chocolate**
   or semisweet chocolate, chopped
1 oz (30 g) **white chocolate,** chopped

method

In small saucepan, sprinkle gelatin over milk; let stand for 5 minutes. Warm over low heat until gelatin is dissolved; remove from heat.

Place milk chocolate in bowl. In separate saucepan, bring cream, sugar and coffee granules just to boil, stirring until sugar is dissolved; pour over chocolate, stirring until melted and smooth. Stir in gelatin mixture. Pour into eight 1-cup (250 mL) wineglasses, martini glasses or bowls. Refrigerate until firm, about 2 hours.

VANILLA LAYER: In small saucepan, sprinkle gelatin over milk; let stand for 5 minutes. Warm over low heat until gelatin is dissolved; remove from heat.

In separate saucepan, heat cream with sugar until sugar is dissolved and bubbles form around edge. Stir in gelatin mixture; stir in vanilla. Pour over chocolate mixture in glasses. Refrigerate until firm, about 2 hours. *(Make-ahead: Cover and refrigerate for up to 2 days.)*

CURLY MARBLE SHARDS: Meanwhile, in separate heatproof bowls over saucepan of hot (not boiling) water, melt bittersweet chocolate and white chocolate, stirring until smooth; set aside. Spread bittersweet chocolate as thinly as possible onto back of rimmed baking sheet. Drizzle with white chocolate; swirl with tip of knife. Refrigerate until firm, about 15 minutes.

Let chocolate stand at room temperature until slightly softened, about 1 minute. Using edge of metal spatula, firmly scrape chocolate away from you into curly shards. If chocolate is too firm, let stand at room temperature until easy to scrape. If too soft, refrigerate until firm. Arrange on waxed paper–lined baking sheet; refrigerate until firm, about 20 minutes. *(Make-ahead: Cover and refrigerate for up to 2 days.)*

Using skewer or tweezers, arrange a few of the curly marble shards upright in centre of each serving.

MAKES 8 SERVINGS.
PER SERVING: about 609 cal, 10 g pro, 45 g total fat (27 g sat. fat), 49 g carb, 2 g fibre, 127 mg chol, 105 mg sodium. % RDI: 21% calcium, 6% iron, 35% vit A, 2% vit C, 5% folate.

Just four ingredients! No one will believe how easy it is to make this rich hazelnut-scented mousse. Try it on a busy weeknight when you need something sweet to finish your day.

Hazelnut Chocolate Mousse

ingredients

½ cup **hazelnut chocolate spread** (such as Nutella)

1 tbsp **unsalted butter,** softened

¾ cup **whipping cream (35%)**

12 toasted **hazelnuts** (optional), halved

method

In heatproof bowl over saucepan of hot (not boiling) water, melt hazelnut chocolate spread with 3 tbsp water until smooth; stir in butter. Keep warm.

Whip cream; fold one-third into chocolate mixture. Fold in remaining whipped cream. Divide among four 1-cup dessert glasses. Cover and refrigerate for 2 hours. Garnish with hazelnuts (if using).

MAKES 4 SERVINGS.

PER SERVING: about 388 cal, 4 g pro, 31 g total fat (14 g sat. fat), 26 g carb, 2 g fibre, 66 mg chol, 32 mg sodium, 229 mg potassium. % RDI: 8% calcium, 7% iron, 20% vit A, 4% folate.

How to Skin Toasted Hazelnuts

Just a few hazelnuts garnish this mousse, so there's no need to go to the trouble of peeling off their papery skins. But if you're baking with a large amount of hazelnuts, you'll probably want to skin them. Toast the nuts in a single layer on a rimmed baking sheet in a 350°F (180°C) oven until they're fragrant and the skins crack, about 10 minutes. Let them cool slightly, then transfer the nuts to a tea towel. Briskly rub the towel over the nuts to remove as much of the skin as possible. Pick the skinned nuts off the towel, and they're ready to use.

Sweet white chocolate pairs perfectly with the tartness of pomegranate seeds. To make a nonalcoholic version, substitute pomegranate juice for the pomegranate liqueur. If substituting pound cake for the golden vanilla cake, add up to ⅓ cup more pomegranate liqueur.

White Chocolate Pomegranate Trifle

ingredients

1½ cups **pomegranate seeds**
   (1 pomegranate)
1 pkg (390 g) **golden vanilla cake**
   or vanilla pound cake
¾ cup **pomegranate liqueur**
   (or ¼ cup pomegranate juice
   and ½ cup vodka)
1 cup **whipping cream (35%)**
2 tsp **granulated sugar**
¼ cup shaved **white chocolate**

WHITE CHOCOLATE CUSTARD:
8 **egg yolks**
4 cups **milk**
¾ cup **granulated sugar**
½ cup **cornstarch**
4 oz (115 g) **white chocolate,**
   finely chopped

method

WHITE CHOCOLATE CUSTARD: In large bowl, whisk together egg yolks, ½ cup of the milk, the sugar and cornstarch. In heavy saucepan, heat remaining milk over medium heat just until bubbles form around edge; gradually whisk into yolk mixture. Return to pan and cook, whisking, until thick enough to mound on spoon, about 7 minutes.

Strain through fine sieve into clean bowl; stir in white chocolate until melted, about 1 minute. Place plastic wrap directly on surface. Refrigerate until cold, about 4 hours. *(Make-ahead: Refrigerate for up to 24 hours.)*

Reserve ¼ cup of the pomegranate seeds for garnish; cover and refrigerate.

Cut cake into ¾-inch (2 cm) thick slices or cubes. Line 16-cup (4 L) trifle bowl with one-third of the cake pieces; drizzle with one-third of pomegranate liqueur. Sprinkle with one-third of the remaining pomegranate seeds; spoon one-third of the custard over top. Repeat layers twice. Cover with plastic wrap and refrigerate for 12 hours. *(Make-ahead: Refrigerate for up to 24 hours.)*

Whip cream with sugar; spread over trifle. Garnish with shaved chocolate and reserved pomegranate seeds.

MAKES 12 TO 14 SERVINGS.
PER EACH OF 14 SERVINGS: about 366 cal, 6 g pro, 18 g total fat (8 g sat. fat), 42 g carb, trace fibre, 163 mg chol, 156 mg sodium, 215 mg potassium. % RDI: 12% calcium, 7% iron, 15% vit A, 2% vit C, 9% folate.

The Easy Way to Seed a Pomegranate

Submerge pomegranate, one-half at a time, in a bowl of water and use your fingers to pluck out the seeds. The seeds sink to the bottom, while the pith floats to the top.

Test Kitchen TIP

If you love retro Black Forest cake, this trifle is for you.
We love the flavour and aroma of cherry brandy, but you can also use kirsch
if you have it in your liquor cupboard.

Black Forest Trifle

ingredients

1¼ cups **cherry brandy**
½ cup **sour cherry jam**
2 cups drained **bottled pitted sour cherries in syrup**
1½ cups **whipping cream (35%)**
1 tbsp **granulated sugar**
7 **maraschino cherries**
¼ cup grated **dark chocolate**

CUSTARD:
8 **egg yolks**
4 cups **milk**
¾ cup **granulated sugar**

½ cup **cornstarch**
4 tsp **almond extract**

CHOCOLATE POUND CAKE:
¾ cup **butter,** softened
1 cup **granulated sugar**
2 **eggs**
2 tsp **vanilla**
1¾ cups **all-purpose flour**
½ cup **cocoa powder,** sifted
1 tsp **baking soda**
½ tsp **salt**
⅔ cup **buttermilk**

method

CUSTARD: In large bowl, whisk egg yolks, ½ cup of the milk, the sugar and cornstarch. In heavy saucepan, heat remaining milk over medium heat just until bubbles form around edge; gradually whisk into yolk mixture. Return to pan and cook, whisking, until thick enough to mound on spoon, about 5 minutes. Strain through fine sieve into clean bowl; stir in almond extract. Place plastic wrap directly on surface. Refrigerate until cold, 4 hours. *(Make-ahead: Refrigerate for up to 24 hours.)*

CHOCOLATE POUND CAKE: Meanwhile, in bowl, beat butter with sugar until light and fluffy; beat in eggs, 1 at a time. Beat in vanilla. Whisk flour, cocoa powder, baking soda and salt; stir into butter mixture alternately with buttermilk, making 3 additions of flour mixture and 2 of buttermilk. Spoon into lightly greased 8- x 4-inch (1.5 L) loaf pan, smoothing top.

Bake in 350°F (180°C) oven until cake tester inserted in centre comes out clean, 60 to 70 minutes.

Let cool in pan on rack for 10 minutes. Transfer to rack; let cool completely. *(Make-ahead: Cover and refrigerate for up to 3 days or overwrap in foil and freeze for up to 1 month.)*

Stir cherry brandy with jam. Cut cake into ¾-inch (2 cm) cubes. Line 16-cup (4 L) trifle bowl with one-third of the cake pieces; spoon one-third of the jam mixture over top. Top with one-third of the drained sour cherries; spoon one-third of the custard over top. Repeat layers twice. Cover with plastic wrap and refrigerate for 24 hours.

Whip cream with sugar; spread three-quarters over trifle. Using piping bag fitted with star tip, pipe remaining whipped cream into 7 rosettes around edge. Top each rosette with 1 maraschino cherry. Sprinkle with chocolate.

MAKES 12 TO 14 SERVINGS.
PER EACH OF 14 SERVINGS: about 523 cal, 9 g pro, 25 g total fat (15 g sat. fat), 64 g carb, 2 g fibre, 208 mg chol, 309 mg sodium, 295 mg potassium. % RDI: 13% calcium, 15% iron, 28% vit A, 3% vit C, 26% folate.

Chunks of chocolate cake doused in hazelnut liqueur and layered with dollops of chocolate-hazelnut pastry cream make this one of the most spectacular desserts you'll ever taste. Gold leaf adds a touch of elegance as a garnish; look for it in baking supply stores.

Chocolate Hazelnut Trifle

ingredients

1 bar (100 g) **70% dark chocolate,** cut in ¼-inch (5 mm) pieces
1½ cups **hazelnut liqueur**
1¼ cups **whipping cream (35%)**
1 tbsp **granulated sugar**
¼ cup chopped skinned toasted **hazelnuts** (see Tip, page 72)
Edible gold leaf (optional)

CUSTARD:
8 **egg yolks**
4 cups **milk**
¾ cup **granulated sugar**

½ cup **cornstarch**
½ cup **chocolate hazelnut spread** (such as Nutella)

CHOCOLATE POUND CAKE:
¾ cup **butter,** softened
1 cup **granulated sugar**
2 **eggs**
2 tsp **vanilla**
1¾ cups **all-purpose flour**
½ cup **cocoa powder,** sifted
1 tsp **baking soda**
½ tsp **salt**
⅔ cup **buttermilk**

method

CUSTARD: In large bowl, whisk together egg yolks, ½ cup of the milk, the sugar and cornstarch. In heavy saucepan, heat remaining milk over medium heat just until bubbles form around edge; gradually whisk into yolk mixture. Return to pan and cook, whisking, until thick enough to mound on spoon, about 5 minutes. Strain through fine sieve into clean bowl; stir in chocolate hazelnut spread. Place plastic wrap directly on surface. Refrigerate until cold, 4 hours. *(Make-ahead: Refrigerate for up to 24 hours.)*

CHOCOLATE POUND CAKE: Meanwhile, in bowl, beat butter with sugar until light and fluffy; beat in eggs, 1 at a time. Beat in vanilla. Whisk together flour, cocoa powder, baking soda and salt; stir into butter mixture alternately with buttermilk, making 3 additions of flour mixture and 2 of buttermilk. Spoon into lightly greased 8- x 4-inch (1.5 L) loaf pan, smoothing top.

Bake in 350°F (180°C) oven until cake tester inserted in centre comes out clean, 60 to 70 minutes.

Let cool in pan on rack for 10 minutes. Transfer to rack; let cool completely. *(Make-ahead: Cover and refrigerate for up to 3 days or overwrap in foil and freeze for up to 1 month.)*

Cut cake into ¾-inch (2 cm) cubes. Line 16-cup (4 L) trifle bowl with half of the cake pieces; sprinkle with half of the chocolate. Spoon half of the hazelnut liqueur over top; spread half of the custard over top. Repeat layers once. Cover and refrigerate for 24 hours.

Whip cream with sugar; spread over trifle. Sprinkle with hazelnuts, and gold leaf (if using).

MAKES 12 TO 14 SERVINGS.
PER EACH OF 14 SERVINGS: about 615 cal, 10 g pro, 31 g total fat (16 g sat. fat), 73 g carb, 3 g fibre, 203 mg chol, 310 mg sodium, 377 mg potassium. % RDI: 15% calcium, 18% iron, 25% vit A, 26% folate.

Dark chocolate is usually the focus of any dessert with the name Black Forest. Here, white chocolate adds a fresh dimension to the classic combination of chocolate and cherries — and who could resist when it's served in individual glasses?

Black Forest Mousse Parfaits

ingredients

½ cup **milk**
⅓ cup **cocoa powder**
2 oz (55 g) **bittersweet chocolate**, chopped
3 tbsp strong brewed **coffee** or water
⅓ cup **unsalted butter**, softened
¾ cup **granulated sugar**
2 **eggs**
1 tsp **vanilla**
1 cup **all-purpose flour**
½ tsp each **baking soda** and **baking powder**
Pinch **salt**

WHITE CHOCOLATE MOUSSE:
4 oz (115 g) **white chocolate,** chopped
2 **eggs**
¼ cup **granulated sugar**
1¼ cups **whipping cream (35%)**

SYRUP:
1 jar (19 oz/540 mL) **pitted sour red cherries in syrup**
3 tbsp **kirsch** or brandy
2 tbsp **granulated sugar**

GARNISH:
1 oz (30 g) **bittersweet chocolate,** grated

method

Whisk milk with cocoa powder until smooth; set aside. In heatproof bowl over saucepan of hot (not boiling) water, melt chocolate with coffee, whisking until smooth. In large bowl, beat butter until light, about 1 minute; gradually beat in sugar until fluffy, about 3 minutes. Beat in eggs, 1 at a time; beat in vanilla. Beat in coffee mixture.

Whisk together flour, baking soda, baking powder and salt; stir into butter mixture alternately with cocoa mixture, making 3 additions of flour mixture and 2 of cocoa mixture. Scrape into parchment paper–lined 8-inch (2 L) square cake pan.

Bake in 350°F (180°C) oven until cake tester inserted in centre comes out with a few moist crumbs clinging, 30 to 35 minutes. Let cool in pan on rack. (*Make-ahead: Wrap in plastic wrap and store for up to 24 hours.*)

WHITE CHOCOLATE MOUSSE: In heatproof bowl over saucepan of hot (not boiling) water, melt white chocolate, stirring until smooth; remove from heat. In separate heatproof bowl, whisk eggs with sugar. Place bowl over simmering water; cook, whisking constantly, until thickened and foamy, 4 minutes.

Remove from heat; stir in white chocolate. Let cool slightly. Whip cream; fold one-third into white chocolate mixture. Fold in remaining cream; refrigerate until chilled, about 2 hours.

SYRUP: Reserving 1¼ cups of the syrup, drain cherries. In saucepan over medium heat, boil syrup until reduced to ¾ cup. Remove from heat; stir in kirsch and sugar. Set aside.

Reserve 8 cherries for garnish. Halve remaining cherries; drain on towel. Fold into mousse.

Cut cake into 64 squares. Place 4 squares in each of eight 1-cup (250 mL) glasses, pressing gently; pour 2 tsp of the syrup over top. Top each with ¼ cup of the mousse. Repeat layers once.

GARNISH: Top each with reserved cherry and grated chocolate. (*Make-ahead: Cover and refrigerate for up to 24 hours.*)

MAKES 8 SERVINGS.

PER SERVING: about 618 cal, 9 g pro, 33 g total fat (19 g sat. fat), 75 g carb, 3 g fibre, 163 mg chol, 168 mg sodium, 308 mg potassium. % RDI: 10% calcium, 21% iron, 31% vit A, 3% vit C, 25% folate.

This warm, silky drink makes a luxurious start to brunch. For a tasty treat for kids on a cold morning, omit the coffee and divide the hot chocolate mixture among fewer mugs.

White Chocolate Mocha Mugs

ingredients

¾ cup **whipping cream (35%)**
4 cups **milk**
6 oz (170 g) **white chocolate,** finely chopped

2 cups double-strength brewed **coffee**
1 oz (30 g) **bittersweet chocolate,** grated

method

Whip cream; set aside. In saucepan, heat milk just until bubbles form around edge; remove from heat. Whisk in white chocolate until melted.

Pour ¼ cup coffee into each of 8 warmed mugs; top with hot chocolate mixture.

Garnish with whipped cream; sprinkle with grated chocolate.

MAKES 8 SERVINGS.

PER SERVING: about 289 cal, 7 g pro, 20 g total fat (12 g sat. fat), 22 g carb, 1 g fibre, 42 mg chol, 91 mg sodium. % RDI: 19% calcium, 4% iron, 14% vit A, 2% vit C, 5% folate.

Grating & Shaving Chocolate

Test Kitchen TIP

Sometimes you want a really finely textured chocolate garnish. Grating chocolate on the fine side of a box grater creates tiny flakes that melt incredibly quickly. Shaving the side of a chocolate bar with a vegetable peeler will give you thicker but still delicate shreds with a coarser texture than grated chocolate. Both will melt from the heat of your hands, so grate or shave over a piece of waxed paper and use a spoon or other utensil to sprinkle them over your desserts.

For an extra-special treat, top Malted Hot Chocolate with whipped cream and crushed chocolate-covered malt balls. Marshmallow Hot Chocolate Mix makes a thoughtful gift for teachers. Add instructions (stir ¼ cup mix into 1 cup very hot milk) to the gift tag.

Malted Hot Chocolate

ingredients

8 cups **milk**
¼ cup **granulated sugar**
⅓ cup **powdered chocolate malt** (such as Ovaltine)
4 oz (115 g) **bittersweet chocolate**, finely chopped

method

In saucepan, bring milk and sugar just to boil over medium-high heat, stirring often. Remove from heat.

Whisk in powdered chocolate malt and chopped chocolate until smooth. *(Make-ahead: Let cool. Refrigerate in airtight container for up to 2 days; reheat.)*

MAKES 8 SERVINGS.
PER SERVING: about 251 cal, 10 g pro, 10 g total fat (6 g sat. fat), 31 g carb, 1 g fibre, 18 mg chol, 122 mg sodium. % RDI: 28% calcium, 5% iron, 12% vit A, 2% vit C, 4% folate.

Marshmallow Hot Chocolate Mix

ingredients

2 cups **skim milk powder**
¾ cup **instant dissolving (fruit/berry) sugar**
½ cup **cocoa powder**
1 tsp **cinnamon** (optional)
2 cups **mini marshmallows**

method

In bowl, stir together skim milk powder, sugar, cocoa powder, and cinnamon (if using). Stir in marshmallows. Spoon into airtight container and seal. *(Make-ahead: Store for up to 1 month.)*

MAKES 3 CUPS.
PER ¼ CUP: about 121 cal, 5 g pro, 1 g total fat (trace sat. fat), 27 g carb, 1 g fibre, 2 mg chol, 67 mg sodium. % RDI: 13% calcium, 4% iron, 8% vit A, 2% vit C, 3% folate.

This drink is so rich and authentic that anyone will know at first sip that it's not from a mix. Garnish with whipped cream and grated chocolate if desired.

Hot Chocolate

ingredients

6 oz (170 g) **semisweet chocolate,**
    finely chopped
3 cups **milk**

method

In heatproof bowl over saucepan of hot (not boiling) water, melt chocolate with ½ cup water, stirring until smooth.

Meanwhile, in saucepan, heat milk until steaming and small bubbles form around edge. Using immersion blender or whisk, blend in chocolate. Pour into mugs.

MAKES 4 SERVINGS.
PER SERVING: about 312 cal, 8 g pro, 15 g total fat (9 g sat. fat), 37 g carb, 3 g fibre, 16 mg chol, 77 mg sodium. % RDI: 21% calcium, 9% iron, 9% vit A, 8% folate.

 **Decorate** LIKE A PRO

Cakes and tarts sometimes need a little extra something to make them look dressed up for entertaining. Piped chocolate decorations and cutouts do the job beautifully (and they're edible – a tasty bonus). Here are two ideas to get you started: Christmas trees for the holidays and hearts for Valentine's Day. For other special occasions, get inventive and customize the shapes.

Piped Chocolate Trees

In heatproof bowl over saucepan of hot (not boiling) water, melt 6 oz (170 g) bittersweet chocolate, chopped. On parchment paper– or waxed paper–lined baking sheet, draw twelve 3½-inch (9 cm) Christmas trees. Turn paper over. Spoon chocolate into pastry bag fitted with small plain tip; pipe chocolate over outlines, filling in with lacy pattern or piping back and forth within outlines. Pipe ½-inch (1 cm) trunks at bottoms for support, if desired. Refrigerate until firm, about 30 minutes. **MAKES 12 TREES.**

Chocolate Hearts

In heatproof bowl over saucepan of hot (not boiling) water, melt 2 oz (55 g) bittersweet chocolate, stirring until smooth. Line baking sheet with parchment paper; using small offset spatula, spread chocolate to ⅛-inch (3 mm) thickness on paper. Refrigerate just until firm, about 8 minutes. Using 1½-inch (4 cm) heart-shaped cookie cutter, cut out 8 hearts. Refrigerate until firm, about 20 minutes. Repeat with 2 oz (55 g) white chocolate, chopped. **MAKES 16 HEARTS.**

These delicate cakes rise while baking but fall while cooling, creating a soft, silky interior. The best part is that you can make them ahead, then reheat them in the microwave until they puff back up.

Chocolate Soufflé Cakes
WITH SHERRY CREAM

ingredients

½ cup **unsalted butter** (approx)
8 oz (225 g) **bittersweet chocolate,** chopped
3 **eggs**
1 cup **granulated sugar**
1 tsp **vanilla**
3 **egg whites**
Icing sugar (optional)

SHERRY CREAM:
½ cup **whipping cream (35%)**
1 tbsp **icing sugar**
1 tbsp **cream sherry** (or 1 tsp vanilla)

method

Brush eight ¾-cup (175 mL) custard cups with 1 tbsp of the butter; set aside. In heatproof bowl over saucepan of hot (not boiling) water, melt chocolate with remaining ½ cup butter; let cool slightly. In separate bowl, beat whole eggs with half of the granulated sugar just until pale; whisk in chocolate mixture and vanilla.

Beat egg whites until soft peaks form; gradually beat in remaining granulated sugar, 2 tbsp at a time, until stiff glossy peaks form. Fold one-quarter into chocolate mixture; fold in remaining egg whites. Spoon into prepared custard cups.

Bake on baking sheet in 350°F (180°C) oven until tops are puffed and cracked and centres are still moist, 25 to 28 minutes. Let cool on rack. *(Make-ahead: Cover and refrigerate for up to 2 days. To reheat, microwave on high, 4 at a time, until puffed, about 90 seconds.)* Dust with icing sugar (if using).

SHERRY CREAM: Whip together cream, icing sugar and sherry. Serve with cakes.

MAKES 8 SERVINGS.

PER SERVING: about 460 cal, 6 g pro, 31 g total fat (18 g sat. fat), 41 g carb, 3 g fibre, 123 mg chol, 50 mg sodium. % RDI: 4% calcium, 11% iron, 20% vit A, 5% folate.

Timing is everything when it comes to soufflé success. A few minutes either way
in the oven can matter, so keep your eyes on your timer. An optimum melt-in-your-mouth soufflé
has a slight jiggle and a centre that oozes seductively when spooned out.

Classic Chocolate Soufflé

ingredients

⅓ cup **unsalted butter,** softened
½ cup **granulated sugar**
5 oz (140 g) **bittersweet chocolate,**
  chopped
3 oz (85 g) **milk chocolate,** chopped
2 tbsp brewed **coffee** or water
Pinch **salt**
Half **vanilla bean** (or ¾ tsp vanilla)

2 tbsp **cocoa powder**
6 **egg yolks**
8 **egg whites**
¼ tsp **cream of tartar**
2 tsp **icing sugar** or cocoa powder

method

Grease 8- x 3¾-inch (2.5 L) soufflé dish with
4 tsp of the butter; sprinkle with 4 tsp of the
granulated sugar, tapping out excess. Wrap
parchment paper strip around outside of dish
to extend at least 2 inches (5 cm) above rim;
tie securely with kitchen string ❶.

In large heatproof bowl over saucepan of hot
(not boiling) water, melt together bittersweet
chocolate, milk chocolate, coffee, salt and
remaining butter, stirring occasionally.

Slit vanilla bean lengthwise; scrape out
seeds. Stir seeds into chocolate mixture.
Remove from heat; whisk in cocoa powder
until smooth. Let cool slightly.

Beat egg yolks with remaining granulated
sugar until light and thickened enough that
batter falls in ribbons when beaters are lifted,
about 2 minutes. Fold into chocolate mixture.

In clean bowl, beat egg whites until foamy;
beat in cream of tartar until stiff glossy peaks
form. Fold one-quarter into chocolate mixture;
fold in remaining egg whites until no streaks
remain ❷. Scrape into prepared dish.

Bake on bottom rack in 375°F (190°C) oven
until edge is firm and top is lightly browned
but centre is still jiggly, 30 to 35 minutes.
Sift icing sugar over top. Serve immediately.

MAKES 8 TO 10 SERVINGS.
PER EACH OF 10 SERVINGS: about 273 cal, 6 g pro,
18 g total fat (10 g sat. fat), 24 g carb, 2 g fibre, 141 mg
chol, 55 mg sodium, 202 mg potassium. % RDI: 4%
calcium, 11% iron, 10% vit A, 8% folate.

Layers of silky milk chocolate and caramel puddings come together for a taste that's out of this world. Toffee bits on top give each spoonful just a hint of crunch.

Chocolate Caramel Layered Pudding

ingredients

½ cup **whipping cream (35%)**
¼ cup **toffee bits**

CARAMEL PUDDING:
⅓ cup **granulated sugar**
2 tbsp **unsalted butter**
¼ cup **whipping cream (35%)**
1 cup **homogenized milk**
1 **egg yolk**
Pinch **salt**
1 tbsp **cornstarch**

MILK CHOCOLATE PUDDING:
1 tbsp **cornstarch**
1 tbsp **granulated sugar**
1 tbsp **cocoa powder**
Pinch **salt**
1 cup **homogenized milk**
¼ cup **whipping cream (35%)**
2 oz (55 g) **milk chocolate**, chopped

method

CARAMEL PUDDING: In saucepan, melt sugar with butter over medium-low heat until dissolved and bubbly. Boil, stirring occasionally, until deep amber colour, 3 to 4 minutes. Remove from heat. Whisk in cream until smooth, about 1 minute.

Whisk together ¾ cup of the milk, egg yolk and salt; whisk into sugar mixture and cook over medium heat, stirring, until slightly thickened and just beginning to steam, 4 to 6 minutes.

Whisk cornstarch with remaining milk; whisk into milk mixture and cook, whisking constantly, until thickened, about 1 minute. Strain through fine sieve into clean bowl.

MILK CHOCOLATE PUDDING: In saucepan, whisk together cornstarch, sugar, cocoa powder and salt. Whisk in milk, cream and chocolate; cook over medium heat, whisking constantly, until thickened, 4 to 6 minutes. Strain through fine sieve into clean bowl.

In 6 small glass dessert dishes, layer caramel and milk chocolate puddings. Place plastic wrap directly on surface. Refrigerate until chilled, about 2 hours. (*Make-ahead: Refrigerate for up to 24 hours.*)

Whip cream; spoon over pudding. Sprinkle with toffee bits.

MAKES 6 SERVINGS.

PER SERVING: about 372 cal, 5 g pro, 27 g total fat (16 g sat. fat), 31 g carb, 1 g fibre, 109 mg chol, 88 mg sodium, 216 mg potassium. % RDI: 13% calcium, 4% iron, 23% vit A, 5% folate.

Almondy amaretti cookies and fragrant, strong coffee complement a creamy white chocolate ganache in this pretty-enough-for-company treat.

Amaretti White Chocolate Coffee Parfaits

ingredients

2 tsp **instant coffee granules**
1 tsp **vanilla**
8 oz (225 g) **white chocolate,** finely chopped
3 cups **whipping cream (35%)**
2½ cups coarsely crumbled **amaretti cookies** or almond biscotti (about 23 cookies)

¼ cup cold strong **coffee**
2 tbsp **almond liqueur** or coffee liqueur
1 oz (30 g) **bittersweet chocolate,** finely grated

method

Dissolve coffee granules in vanilla; set aside. Place white chocolate in large heatproof bowl. In saucepan, heat 1½ cups of the cream over medium heat just until bubbles form around edge, about 4 minutes. Pour over white chocolate along with vanilla mixture, whisking until smooth. Whisk in remaining cream. Cover and refrigerate until thoroughly chilled, about 8 hours.

Place cookies in separate bowl; toss with coffee and liqueur. Let stand until slightly softened, about 15 minutes.

Meanwhile, beat white chocolate mixture until very stiff peaks form; spoon into piping bag fitted with star tip, or use spoon. Pipe or spoon one-third of the white chocolate mixture into 6 martini glasses. Sprinkle with half of the cookies. Repeat layers once. Pipe or spoon remaining white chocolate mixture over top; sprinkle with grated chocolate. *(Make-ahead: Cover and refrigerate for up to 24 hours.)*

MAKES 6 SERVINGS.

PER SERVING: about 819 cal, 7 g pro, 65 g total fat (39 g sat. fat), 56 g carb, 3 g fibre, 161 mg chol, 91 mg sodium. % RDI: 15% calcium, 6% iron, 42% vit A, 2% vit C, 8% folate.

Chill Out

Thoroughly chilling a white chocolate ganache before beating, as in this recipe, helps prevent separating. Make sure to beat the ganache just until stiff peaks form – anything more will make it grainy.

Éclairs are an impressive bakeshop treat that look hard to make. But they're not once you get the hang of piping the dough. The chocolaty spiced cream in the middle is a delicious surprise.

Double-Chocolate Éclairs

ingredients

½ cup **milk**
⅓ cup **unsalted butter**
1 tsp **granulated sugar**
¼ tsp **salt**
1 cup **all-purpose flour**
4 **eggs**

CHOCOLATE SPICE PASTRY CREAM:
4 **egg yolks**
⅓ cup **granulated sugar**
¼ cup **cornstarch**
1¾ cups **milk**

¾ tsp **cinnamon**
¼ tsp each **ground ginger** and **cayenne pepper**
4 oz (115 g) **bittersweet chocolate,** finely chopped
3 tbsp **unsalted butter,** softened

CHOCOLATE GLAZE:
2 oz (55 g) **bittersweet chocolate,** finely chopped
2 tbsp **unsalted butter**
2 tsp **corn syrup**

method

In saucepan, bring ½ cup water, milk, butter, sugar and salt to boil over medium-high heat, stirring until butter is melted. With wooden spoon, stir in flour until mixture forms ball and film forms on bottom of pan, about 2 minutes. Cook, stirring, for 1 minute.

Transfer to stand mixer or bowl. Beat for 30 seconds to cool. Beat in 3 of the eggs, 1 at a time, beating well after each until smooth and shiny.

Using piping bag fitted with ¾-inch (2 cm) plain tip, pipe dough into 4- x 1-inch (10 x 2.5 cm) logs, 1 inch (2.5 cm) apart, onto parchment paper–lined baking sheets.

Whisk remaining egg with 1 tbsp water; brush over logs, gently smoothing tops if necessary.

Bake in 425°F (220°C) oven until puffed, 20 minutes. Reduce heat to 375°F (190°C); bake until crisp and golden, about 10 minutes. Turn off oven; let stand in oven for 25 minutes to dry. Transfer to rack; let cool completely. *(Make-ahead: Store in airtight container for up to 24 hours. Recrisp in 350°F/180°C oven for 5 minutes; let cool before filling.)*

CHOCOLATE SPICE PASTRY CREAM: In bowl, whisk egg yolks, sugar and cornstarch; whisk in ¼ cup of the milk. In saucepan, heat remaining milk, cinnamon, ginger and cayenne until bubbles form around edge; whisk into egg yolk mixture. Whisk in chocolate until melted. Return to pan; cook over medium heat, whisking constantly, until thickened, 5 minutes. Remove from heat; whisk in butter until smooth. Scrape into bowl. Place plastic wrap directly on surface; refrigerate until cool, 1 hour. *(Make-ahead: Refrigerate in airtight container for up to 24 hours.)*

CHOCOLATE GLAZE: In heatproof bowl over saucepan of hot (not boiling) water, melt together chocolate, butter and corn syrup, stirring until smooth. Keep warm.

Push chopstick through each éclair, end to end, to make channel. Using piping bag fitted with ¼-inch (5 mm) plain tip, pipe in pastry cream. Dip tops into glaze. Let stand until set, 20 minutes. *(Make-ahead: Refrigerate in airtight container for up to 4 hours.)*

MAKES 14 ÉCLAIRS.

PER ÉCLAIR: about 266 cal, 6 g pro, 17 g total fat (10 g sat. fat), 23 g carb, 2 g fibre, 137 mg chol, 80 mg sodium, 95 mg potassium. % RDI: 7% calcium, 10% iron, 14% vit A, 15% folate.

crunchy

Double–Chocolate Chip Waffles With Bananas & Strawberry Coulis 93
Sour Cherry & Almond Chocolate Bar 94
Fruit & Nut Clusters 95
Chocolate Hazelnut Baklava 96
English Toffee 98
Bittersweet Amaretti Bark 99
Marbled Almond Bark 99
Tropical Fruit Bark 101
No-Bake Fudge Crispies 102
Chocolate Gingerbread Pretzels 103
Matzo Chocolate Almond Buttercrunch 104
Hazelnut Chocolate Pizzelle 106
Dairy-Free Chocolate Meringues 107
Cranberry White Chocolate Biscotti 109
Itty-Bitty Hazelnut Cioccolata Biscotti 110
Cherry Almond White Chocolate Biscotti 111
Chocolate, Star Anise & Orange Biscotti 112
Mostaccioli 114
Chocolate Cigar Cookies 115
Chocolate Hazelnut Palmiers 117
Chocolate Gingersnap Hearts 118
Scoop & Freeze Double-Chocolate Cookies 119
Toffee Chocolate Chip Toonies 120
Chocolate Overload Cookies 122
Cocoa Sugar Cookies 122
Big Chocolate Chip Orange Cookies 125
Chocolate Macarons 126
White Chocolate, Cranberry & Pistachio Cookies 127
Triple-Chocolate Cookies 128
Chocolate Chestnut Fingers 130
Mocha Chocolate Crackles 131

Chocolate waffles are a decadent way to start the day.
A dollop of whipped cream or plain yogurt both make excellent toppings.

Double-Chocolate Chip Waffles
WITH BANANAS & STRAWBERRY COULIS

ingredients

2 **bananas,** sliced

WAFFLES:
1¼ cups **all-purpose flour**
¼ cup **cocoa powder**
2 tbsp **granulated sugar**
1 tsp **baking powder**
½ tsp **baking soda**
¼ tsp **salt**
2 **eggs**
1¼ cups **buttermilk**

2 tbsp **butter,** melted
⅓ cup **mini semisweet chocolate chips**
1 tbsp **vegetable oil**

STRAWBERRY COULIS:
2 cups **frozen strawberries,** thawed
3 tbsp **granulated sugar**
1 tsp **lime juice** or lemon juice

method

STRAWBERRY COULIS: In food processor, purée together strawberries, sugar and lime juice until smooth; set aside. *(Make-ahead: Refrigerate in airtight container for up to 24 hours.)*

WAFFLES: In large bowl, whisk together flour, cocoa powder, sugar, baking powder, baking soda and salt. Whisk together eggs, buttermilk and butter; pour over flour mixture. Sprinkle with chocolate chips; stir just until combined.

Heat waffle iron; brush lightly with some of the vegetable oil. Using about ½ cup batter per waffle (or enough to spread to edges), pour onto waffle iron.

Close lid and cook until waffle is crisp and steam stops, about 8 minutes. *(Make-ahead: Let cool. Wrap individually and freeze in airtight container for up to 2 weeks.)* Keep warm in single layer on rack on baking sheet in 200°F (100°C) oven.

To serve, top each waffle with bananas; drizzle with coulis.

MAKES 4 TO 6 SERVINGS.
PER EACH OF 6 SERVINGS: about 353 cal, 9 g pro, 12 g total fat (6 g sat. fat), 55 g carb, 4 g fibre, 77 mg chol, 338 mg sodium, 480 mg potassium. % RDI: 11% calcium, 20% iron, 7% vit A, 40% vit C, 38% folate.

Sometimes all you need is a piece of chocolate to make everything better.
Made with fruit, nuts and high-quality dark chocolate, this bar is just the right mix
of crunchy, chewy and creamy.

Sour Cherry & Almond Chocolate Bar

ingredients

1 bar (100 g) **70% dark chocolate,** chopped

⅓ cup **dried sour cherries**

⅓ cup toasted **slivered almonds**

method

In small heatproof bowl over saucepan of hot (not boiling) water, melt chocolate, stirring until smooth. Stir in cherries and almonds.

Spread in parchment paper–lined 9- x 5-inch (2 L) loaf pan, pushing into corners and smoothing top. Refrigerate until firm, about 1½ hours. Cut into pieces.

MAKES 12 TO 16 PIECES.
PER EACH OF 16 PIECES: about 52 cal, 1 g pro, 3 g total fat (2 g sat. fat), 6 g carb, 1 g fibre, 0 mg chol, 6 mg sodium. % RDI: 1% calcium, 7% iron, 1% vit A.

Melting Chocolate

With its high ratio of cocoa butter, chocolate must be handled gently when melting so that it doesn't curdle, scorch or lose its shine. Here is how to melt any type of chocolate successfully.

- **Chop finely.** Pieces a bit smaller than almonds will melt quickly. Place them in a heatproof glass or stainless-steel bowl with a rim just slightly larger than the rim of the saucepan that will be underneath it. (If the bowl is too large, the burner may heat it and burn the chocolate.) Make sure the bottom of the bowl doesn't touch the water.

- **Simmer gently.** Pour enough water into the pan to come 1 inch (2.5 cm) up the side. Place over medium heat; heat the water just until steaming (not boiling). Place the bowl over the pan. Let stand just until three-quarters of the chocolate is melted.

- **Stir well.** Remove the bowl from the saucepan and stir with a metal spoon until the remaining chocolate is melted.

- **Do not cover.** Moisture droplets can accumulate on the lid and drop into the chocolate, causing it to seize, or clump into an unusable mass.

These morsels are the perfect bite-size sweets to end a meal, dress up a cookie platter or package in a gift box. Make all three varieties to create a pretty presentation.

Fruit & Nut Clusters

ingredients

3 bars (each 100 g) **milk chocolate,** chopped and tempered (see Tempering Chocolate, below)

½ cup **dry-roasted peanuts**

½ cup **raisins**

method

Stir together chocolate, peanuts and raisins. Drop by 1 tbsp, about 1 inch (2.5 cm) apart, onto parchment paper– or waxed paper–lined rimmed baking sheets. Refrigerate until firm, about 1 hour.

Cut into pieces.

MAKES ABOUT 25 PIECES.
PER PIECE: about 88 cal, 2 g pro, 5 g total fat (2 g sat. fat), 10 g carb, 1 g fibre, 3 mg chol, 34 mg sodium, 87 mg potassium. % RDI: 2% calcium, 2% iron, 1% vit A, 2% folate.

CHANGE IT UP
Pistachio Apricot Clusters
Replace milk chocolate with white chocolate, peanuts with pistachios and raisins with chopped dried apricots.

Sour Cherry Almond Clusters
Replace milk chocolate with dark chocolate, peanuts with toasted slivered almonds and raisins with dried sour cherries.

Tempering Chocolate

Tempering gives chocolate a beautiful sheen and a satisfying snappy texture. Here's how.

- In heatproof bowl over saucepan of hot (not boiling) water, melt chopped chocolate, stirring often, until smooth and instant-read thermometer reads 115°F (46°C).

- Remove bowl from saucepan. Place over bowl of cold water; stir constantly until temperature falls to 80°F (27°C).

- Replace bowl over hot water or place on heating pad; stir constantly until temperature reaches 88°F (31°C). Hold between 88 and 92°F (31 and 33°C) while using.

- When tempering milk and white chocolates, reduce each of the temperatures listed (left) by 2°F (1.7°C).

- Improperly tempered chocolate may develop a bloom (white or grey film on the surface); it's harmless. Just retemper the chocolate to remove it.

Step it up a notch with a milk chocolate–laced version of the classic honey-nut Greek pastry.
An offset spatula makes removing the pieces from the pan effortless.

Chocolate Hazelnut Baklava

ingredients

2⅓ cups **hazelnuts**
2 tbsp **granulated sugar**
½ tsp **cinnamon**
¼ tsp **nutmeg**
6 oz (170 g) **milk chocolate,** chopped
⅔ cup **butter,** melted
12 sheets **phyllo pastry**

SYRUP:
1 cup **granulated sugar**
½ cup **liquid honey**
1 tbsp **lemon juice**

method

Toast hazelnuts on large rimmed baking sheet in 350°F (180°C) oven until fragrant and skins are loose, about 10 minutes. Transfer to tea towel; rub briskly to remove most of the skins. Let cool.

In food processor, chop together hazelnuts, sugar, cinnamon and nutmeg until in coarse crumbs; transfer to bowl. Stir in chocolate; set aside.

Generously brush 13- x 9-inch (3.5 L) cake pan with some of the butter; set aside. Lay phyllo on work surface with short end facing you.

Cut stack in half crosswise; stack halves together and cover with damp towel to prevent drying out. Place 1 sheet of phyllo on work surface; brush lightly with some of the butter. Top with second sheet of phyllo; brush with butter. Repeat layers with 4 more sheets.

Place buttered phyllo stack in prepared pan; sprinkle with 1 cup of the hazelnut mixture ❶. Stack 4 more phyllo sheets, brushing each lightly with some of the butter; place on hazelnut mixture in pan. Sprinkle with 1 cup of the remaining hazelnut mixture.

Repeat layers twice, using 8 sheets buttered phyllo and remaining hazelnut mixture. Stack remaining 6 phyllo sheets, brushing each with some of the remaining butter. Place on top of layers in pan; press gently to compact slightly.

Using tip of sharp knife and without cutting all the way through to filling, score top into squares or diamonds ❷. Bake in 350°F (180°C) oven until phyllo is golden, crisp and flaky, 40 to 45 minutes.

SYRUP: Meanwhile, in small saucepan, whisk together sugar, honey, ⅓ cup water and lemon juice. Bring to boil over medium-high heat; boil, stirring, for 1 minute. Pour over hot baklava ❸. Let cool in pan on rack. Cut along score lines into pieces. *(Make-ahead: Store in airtight container for up to 24 hours.)*

MAKES 30 PIECES.
PER PIECE: about 207 cal, 3 g pro, 13 g total fat (4 g sat. fat), 22 g carb, 2 g fibre, 14 mg chol, 94 mg sodium. % RDI: 3% calcium, 6% iron, 4% vit A, 7% folate.

HOW-TO

Buttery, rich and totally yummy, this chocolate-and-nut-covered confection is pretty easy to make. It makes a delectable holiday gift, but make sure you hold back a couple of shards for yourself.

English Toffee

ingredients

¾ cup **natural almonds**
⅔ cup **unsalted butter**
1⅓ cups **granulated sugar**
1 tbsp **corn syrup**

½ tsp **salt**
½ tsp **vanilla**
5 oz (140 g) **bittersweet chocolate,** finely chopped

method

On baking sheet, toast almonds in 350°F (180°C) oven until golden and fragrant, 8 to 10 minutes. Let cool; chop.

Spread ½ cup of the almonds in parchment paper–lined 13- x 9-inch (3.5 L) cake pan. Set aside.

In heavy 12-cup (3 L) saucepan, melt butter over medium heat. Stir in sugar, 3 tbsp water, corn syrup and salt. Bring to boil; boil, without stirring but brushing down side of pan with pastry brush dipped in cold water, for 7 minutes.

Continue cooking, stirring occasionally as colour deepens, until candy thermometer reaches hard-crack stage of 300 to 309°F (149 to 154°C), about 3 minutes, or 1 tsp hot syrup dropped into cold water forms separate hard brittle threads.

Remove from heat. Stir in vanilla. Immediately pour over almonds in pan, spreading with greased spatula almost to edges. Let stand until slightly cooled but still hot, 2 minutes.

Sprinkle with chocolate; let stand until melted, 2 minutes. Spread chocolate evenly over toffee; sprinkle with remaining almonds.

Refrigerate until firm, about 1 hour. Using small mallet or hammer, or tip of butter knife, break into shards. *(Make-ahead: Layer between waxed paper in airtight container and refrigerate for up to 2 weeks.)*

MAKES ABOUT 20 PIECES.
PER PIECE: about 180 cal, 2 g pro, 11 g total fat (6 g sat. fat), 19 g carb, 1 g fibre, 16 mg chol, 59 mg sodium, 41 mg potassium. % RDI: 2% calcium, 4% iron, 5% vit A, 1% folate.

If you love almonds, these two confections are for you. Chunks of amaretti cookies give Bittersweet Amaretti Bark a nice bite, while whole natural almonds give the Marbled Almond Bark a satisfying nutty crunch.

Bittersweet Amaretti Bark

Marbled Almond Bark

ingredients

Bittersweet Amaretti Bark
1 lb (450 g) **bittersweet chocolate,** melted
1 cup quartered **amaretti cookies**
1 tsp **vanilla**

Marbled Almond Bark
8 oz (225 g) **semisweet chocolate,** chopped
2 cups **natural almonds,** toasted
8 oz (225 g) **white chocolate,** chopped

method

Bittersweet Amaretti Bark

Line 15- x 10-inch (38 x 25 cm) rimmed baking sheet with foil; grease foil. Set aside.

In large bowl, stir together chocolate, amaretti cookies and vanilla. Spread to about ¼-inch (5 mm) thickness over two-thirds of prepared pan. Refrigerate until firm, about 30 minutes.

Break bark into chunks. *(Make-ahead: Layer between waxed paper in airtight container and refrigerate for up to 2 weeks.)*

MAKES ABOUT 16 PIECES.
PER PIECE: about 176 cal, 2 g pro, 11 g total fat (6 g sat. fat), 18 g carb, 2 g fibre, 0 mg chol, 9 mg sodium. % RDI: 2% calcium, 9% iron.

Marbled Almond Bark

Line rimmed baking sheet with parchment paper; draw 12- x 8-inch (30 x 20 cm) rectangle on paper. Turn paper over.

In bowl over saucepan of hot (not boiling) water, melt semisweet chocolate, stirring occasionally until smooth. Remove from heat; stir in almonds. Spread evenly onto rectangle on paper.

In bowl over saucepan of hot (not boiling) water, melt white chocolate, stirring occasionally until smooth. Spoon over semisweet chocolate; swirl with tip of knife. Refrigerate until firm, about 1 hour. Break into pieces. *(Make-ahead: Layer between waxed paper in airtight container and refrigerate for up to 2 weeks.)*

MAKES ABOUT 50 PIECES.
PER PIECE: about 79 cal, 2 g pro, 6 g total fat (2 g sat. fat), 7 g carb, 1 g fibre, 0 mg chol, 5 mg sodium, 71 mg potassium. % RDI: 2% calcium, 3% iron, 1% folate.

Cutting Amaretti Neatly

Use a sharp chef's knife to keep the cookies from crumbling as you cut them.

This sweet candy treat is another wonderful option to make as a gift.
Enclose it (with or without the Black Forest variation) in a clear cellophane bag and tie
with a pretty ribbon for a delicious present chocoholics will gobble up.

Tropical Fruit Bark

ingredients

1 lb (450 g) **white chocolate,** chopped

½ cup chopped **macadamia nuts**

½ cup diced **dried mango**

½ cup diced **dried papaya**

½ cup diced **candied pineapple**

method

Line rimmed baking sheet with parchment paper; draw 12- x 8-inch (30 x 20 cm) rectangle on paper. Turn paper over.

In bowl over saucepan of hot (not boiling) water, melt white chocolate, stirring occasionally until smooth. Remove from heat; stir in macadamia nuts, mango, papaya and pineapple. Spread evenly onto rectangle on paper.

Refrigerate until firm, about 1 hour. Break into pieces. *(Make-ahead: Layer between waxed paper in airtight container and refrigerate for up to 2 weeks.)*

MAKES ABOUT 50 PIECES.
PER PIECE: about 73 cal, 1 g pro, 4 g total fat (2 g sat. fat), 9 g carb, trace fibre, 2 mg chol, 9 mg sodium. % RDI: 2% calcium, 1% iron, 2% vit A, 7% vit C, 1% folate.

CHANGE IT UP
Black Forest Bark
Omit white chocolate. Melt 1 lb (450 g) semisweet chocolate or bittersweet chocolate as directed. Omit macadamia nuts and dried fruit; add 2 cups dried sour cherries or cranberries.

Buying White Chocolate

Check the ingredient list when buying white chocolate. It should include cocoa butter, sugar, dry milk solids and vanilla. Avoid less-expensive white chocolate, which is usually whiter than good-quality cream-coloured white chocolate, because vegetable fats have replaced some or all of the cocoa butter.

Test Kitchen TIP

Cereal is a simple base for any number of crunchy treats.
This recipe skips the typical melted marshmallows and uses a combination of
melted chocolate and sweetened condensed milk to "glue" the clusters together.

No-Bake Fudge Crispies

ingredients

1¼ cups **semisweet chocolate chips**
½ cup **sweetened condensed milk**
2 tbsp **butter**

2 cups **rice crisp cereal** or other
crisp cereal (such as cornflakes)
2 oz (55 g) **white chocolate,** finely
chopped

method

In large microwaveable bowl, combine chocolate chips, sweetened condensed milk and butter. Microwave on medium (50%) for 1 minute; stir well. Microwave on medium (50%) until melted and smooth, about 30 seconds. (Or, in large saucepan, combine chocolate chips, sweetened condensed milk and butter; heat over medium-low heat, stirring often, until melted and smooth, about 5 minutes.)

Using greased spoon, stir cereal with chocolate mixture until coated. Using greased 1 tbsp measure, scoop mounds onto waxed paper– or foil-lined baking sheets. Press to flatten slightly; set aside.

In small microwaveable bowl, microwave white chocolate on medium (50%), stirring 3 or 4 times, just until melted, 1 to 2 minutes. (Or, in heatproof bowl set over saucepan of hot, not boiling, water, melt chocolate, stirring until smooth.) Using fork, drizzle white chocolate over mounds.

Refrigerate until firm, about 1 hour. *(Make-ahead: Layer between waxed paper in airtight container and refrigerate for up to 1 day.)*

MAKES ABOUT 40 COOKIES.
PER COOKIE: about 58 cal, 1 g pro, 3 g total fat (2 g sat. fat), 8 g carb, trace fibre, 3 mg chol, 28 mg sodium. % RDI: 1% calcium, 3% iron, 1% vit A, 1% folate.

Sticky Issues

Test
Kitchen
TIP

The key to working with a sticky mixture like this is to grease whatever touches it, such as spoons, bowls and even your hands. Greasing them means you'll be able to work more quickly with the mixture without it hardening into cement on your tools.

Salty pretzels are nice, but this ginger-and-chocolate cookie version –
twisted into the traditional shape – is a sweet surprise.

Chocolate Gingerbread Pretzels

ingredients

½ cup **unsalted butter,** softened
½ cup **granulated sugar**
1 **egg**
¼ cup **fancy molasses**
2 cups **all-purpose flour**
¼ cup **cocoa powder**
1 tsp **ground ginger**
½ tsp **baking soda**

½ tsp **salt**
½ tsp each **ground cloves**
   and **cinnamon**

GLAZE:
1½ cups **icing sugar**
2 tbsp **milk**

method

In large bowl, beat butter with sugar until fluffy; beat in egg and molasses. Whisk together flour, cocoa powder, ginger, baking soda, salt, cloves and cinnamon; stir into molasses mixture in 2 additions, using hands if dough is too stiff to stir. Press into disc; wrap and refrigerate until firm, about 1 hour.

Divide dough into quarters; roll each into 10-inch (25 cm) log. Cut 1 log into 1-inch (2.5 cm) thick slices. Roll each slice into 8-inch (20 cm) rope. Curve each to create horseshoe shape; cross ends over each other twice. Bring ends to curve to create pretzel shape; press ends down to adhere. Repeat with remaining logs.

Place pretzels, about 1 inch (2.5 cm) apart, on parchment paper–lined rimless baking sheets. Bake in 350°F (180°C) oven until firm and darkened on bottoms, about 12 minutes. Let cool on pans on racks for 5 minutes.

GLAZE: In bowl, stir together icing sugar, milk and 1½ tbsp water. Dip tops of warm pretzels into glaze. Let stand on racks until dry and cool, about 30 minutes; use spatula to loosen.

MAKES ABOUT 40 COOKIES.
PER COOKIE: about 77 cal, 1 g pro, 3 g total fat (2 g sat. fat), 13 g carb, trace fibre, 11 mg chol, 48 mg sodium, 55 mg potassium. % RDI: 1% calcium, 4% iron, 2% vit A, 6% folate.

103

Matzo is usually a side with a meal or a base for savoury dishes.
Here, it's a confection so irresistible you don't need to celebrate Passover to enjoy it.
Many people take credit for the original, but this is the version perfected by The Test Kitchen.

Matzo Chocolate Almond Buttercrunch

ingredients

4½ sheets **unsalted matzos**
1 cup **butter**
1 cup packed **brown sugar**
1¼ cups **semisweet chocolate chips**

½ cup chopped toasted **natural almonds**
Pinch **sea salt** or kosher salt

method

Lay matzos on foil-lined rimmed baking sheet, breaking to cover sheet completely. Set aside.

In saucepan, bring butter and brown sugar to boil over medium-high heat; boil until slightly thickened, 2 to 3 minutes. Pour over matzos, spreading evenly with offset spatula.

Bake in 325°F (160°C) oven until bubbly and golden, about 7 minutes. Let cool for 5 minutes.

Sprinkle with chocolate chips; let stand until melted, about 2 minutes. Using offset spatula, spread chocolate over matzos. Sprinkle with almonds and salt. Refrigerate until chocolate is firm, about 1 hour. Break into shards. *(Make-ahead: Refrigerate in airtight container for up to 3 days.)*

MAKES 16 PIECES.
PER PIECE: about 267 cal, 2 g pro, 17 g total fat (10 g sat. fat), 29 g carb, 1 g fibre, 31 mg chol, 89 mg sodium, 132 mg potassium. % RDI: 3% calcium, 8% iron, 10% vit A, 5% folate.

Pizzelle are crisp, waferlike Italian cookies. To make them, you need a pizzelle iron, which is available in specialty kitchen shops. Sure, you can buy ready-made pizzelle in Italian bakeries and fine food stores, but these homemade hazelnut-chocolate ones are definitely worth the work.

Hazelnut Chocolate Pizzelle

ingredients

⅓ cup **hazelnuts**
⅓ cup **butter**
½ cup **granulated sugar**
2 **eggs**
1 tbsp **hazelnut liqueur**

1 cup **all-purpose flour**
½ cup **cocoa powder**
1 tsp **baking powder**

method

On rimmed baking sheet, toast hazelnuts in 350°F (180°C) oven until fragrant and skins are loose, about 15 minutes. Transfer to tea towel; rub briskly to remove as much of the skins as possible. Let cool. In food processor or using knife, chop finely. Set aside.

In saucepan over medium heat or in microwave, melt butter. Whisk in sugar, then eggs, 1 at a time; whisk in hazelnut liqueur.

Whisk together flour, cocoa powder and baking powder. Add to egg mixture; stir until smooth. Stir in hazelnuts to form stiff but sticky batter.

Preheat pizzelle iron over medium heat. Spoon heaping 2 tbsp batter into centre; close lid and lock handles. Cook, turning iron once, until pizzelle is crisp and pulls away easily from iron, about 45 seconds.

Using fork to lift edge, transfer to rack. Let cool; trim excess from around edge. Repeat with remaining batter. *(Make-ahead: Let cool completely. Divide in 2 stacks; wrap each in plastic wrap. Store in airtight container for up to 3 days or freeze for up to 3 weeks.)*

MAKES 12 COOKIES.
PER COOKIE: about 165 cal, 3 g pro, 9 g total fat (4 g sat. fat), 20 g carb, 2 g fibre, 47 mg chol, 85 mg sodium. % RDI: 2% calcium, 9% iron, 6% vit A, 10% folate.

Recrisping Pizzelle

If pizzelle are soft after thawing, place in single layer on rimmed baking sheet; bake in 300°F (150°C) oven until crisp, about 5 minutes.

Cookies can be a landmine for people with a dairy allergy or sensitivity. But these sumptuous, light-as-a-feather meringues are just the ticket to satisfy a sweet tooth. Check the label on your chocolate to make sure the ingredient list is free of milk solids and other dairy ingredients.

Dairy-Free Chocolate Meringues

ingredients

4 **egg whites**
1 cup **granulated sugar**
3 tbsp **all-purpose flour**

1 tsp **vanilla**
2 cups coarsely chopped **dark chocolate** (10 oz/280 g)

method

In large heatproof bowl over saucepan of hot (not boiling) water, cook egg whites with sugar, whisking occasionally, until opaque, about 10 minutes. Remove from heat. Beat until cool, thick and glossy, about 7 minutes. Fold in flour and vanilla. Fold in chocolate.

Drop by 1 tbsp onto parchment paper–lined rimless baking sheets. Bake in 350°F (180°C) oven until light brown, 25 to 30 minutes.

Let cool on pans on racks. *(Make-ahead: Store in airtight container for up to 3 days.)*

MAKES ABOUT 45 COOKIES.
PER COOKIE: about 53 cal, 1 g pro, 2 g total fat (1 g sat. fat), 9 g carb, 1 g fibre, 0 mg chol, 5 mg sodium. % RDI: 1% iron.

What's not to like about a cookie you can have with your morning coffee?
The chocolate sets even more quickly in the refrigerator, which is a great place to store these
gems, especially if your kitchen is warm from a lot of baking.

Cranberry White Chocolate Biscotti

ingredients

½ cup **butter,** softened
1 cup **granulated sugar**
2 **eggs**
1 tsp **vanilla**
2½ cups **all-purpose flour**
2 tsp **baking powder**
¼ tsp **salt**

1 cup shelled **pistachios**
1 cup **dried cranberries**
1 **egg white**
10 oz (280 g) **white chocolate,**
  melted

method

In large bowl, beat butter with sugar until fluffy; beat in eggs, 1 at a time. Beat in vanilla. Whisk together flour, baking powder and salt; add to butter mixture in 2 additions, stirring just until combined. Stir in pistachios and cranberries.

Divide dough in half. On lightly floured surface, shape each half into 12-inch (30 cm) long rectangle. Place, 2 inches (5 cm) apart, on parchment paper–lined rimless baking sheet; press to flatten slightly. Stir egg white with 1 tsp water; liberally brush over tops of biscotti.

Bake in 325°F (160°C) oven until light golden and just firm to the touch, about 30 minutes. Let cool on pan on rack for 10 minutes.

Transfer logs to cutting board. Using chef's knife, cut diagonally into ½-inch (1 cm) thick slices. Stand slices upright, about ½ inch (1 cm) apart, on baking sheet. Bake in 300°F (150°C) oven until almost dry, 35 minutes. Transfer to rack; let cool completely.

Dip 1 end of each biscotti in white chocolate, letting excess drip off. Place on waxed paper– or parchment paper–lined baking sheet; refrigerate until chocolate is set, about 20 minutes.

MAKES ABOUT 36 COOKIES.
PER COOKIE: about 130 cal, 2 g pro, 5 g total fat (3 g sat. fat), 19 g carb, 1 g fibre, 17 mg chol, 64 mg sodium, 38 mg potassium. % RDI: 2% calcium, 4% iron, 3% vit A, 9% folate.

109

CANADIAN LIVING • THE COMPLETE CHOCOLATE BOOK

This is a miniature version of the ever-popular twice-baked crisp Italian favourite.
To make them extra special, dip one end of the finished biscotti into melted white or dark
chocolate, then let them dry for about two hours before storing.

Itty-Bitty Hazelnut Cioccolata Biscotti

ingredients

1 cup **hazelnuts**
½ cup **butter,** softened
1 cup **granulated sugar**
3 **eggs**
2 tsp **vanilla**

2¾ cups **all-purpose flour**
½ cup **cocoa powder**
1½ tsp **baking powder**
¼ tsp **salt**
4 oz (115 g) **semisweet chocolate** or
      bittersweet chocolate, chopped

method

Toast hazelnuts on rimmed baking sheet in 350°F (180°C) oven until fragrant and skins crack, about 8 minutes. Transfer to tea towel; rub briskly to remove as much of the skins as possible. Let cool.

In large bowl, beat butter with sugar until fluffy; beat in eggs, 1 at a time. Beat in vanilla. Sift together flour, cocoa powder, baking powder and salt; add to butter mixture, stirring until combined. Stir in hazelnuts and chocolate.

Divide dough into quarters; with floured hands, shape each quarter into 15-inch (38 cm) long log. Place, 4 inches (10 cm) apart, on 2 parchment paper–lined rimless baking sheets. Flatten each until about 1½ inches (4 cm) wide, leaving top slightly rounded.

Bake on top and bottom racks in 325°F (160°C) oven, switching and rotating pans halfway through, until firm and tops are dry, about 30 minutes. Let cool on pans on racks for 10 minutes.

Transfer logs to cutting board. With serrated knife, cut into ½-inch (1 cm) thick slices. Stand slices upright, about ½-inch (1 cm) apart, on baking sheets; bake until dry and crisp and nuts just start to colour, about 30 minutes. Transfer to racks; let cool. *(Make-ahead: Layer between waxed paper in airtight container and store for up to 1 week or freeze for up to 1 month.)*

MAKES 72 COOKIES.
PER COOKIE: about 64 cal, 1 g pro, 3 g total fat (1 g sat. fat), 8 g carb, 1 g fibre, 12 mg chol, 29 mg sodium. % RDI: 1% calcium, 4% iron, 2% vit A, 5% folate.

In North America, biscotti are inevitably dunked in cups of coffee or tea. But in Italy, they make a nice partner to a glass of Vin Santo or other dessert wine – a custom so delicious that it should be more common here. Blanched or natural almonds will work well in this recipe.

Cherry Almond White Chocolate Biscotti

ingredients

¾ cup coarsely chopped **dried sour cherries**
2 tbsp **kirsch,** brandy or water
½ cup **butter,** softened
1 cup **granulated sugar**
2 **eggs**
2 tsp **almond extract**
2½ cups **all-purpose flour**
2 tsp **baking powder**

¼ tsp **salt**
¾ cup **whole almonds,** coarsely chopped
12 oz (340 g) **white chocolate,** chopped

method

In microwaveable bowl, microwave cherries, kirsch and 2 tbsp water on high for 45 seconds. Stir; let stand until most of the liquid is absorbed, about 20 minutes.

Meanwhile, in bowl, beat butter with sugar until fluffy; beat in eggs, 1 at a time. Beat in almond extract. Whisk together flour, baking powder and salt; add to butter mixture in 2 additions, stirring just until combined. Drain cherries, if necessary. Add cherries, almonds and one-third of the white chocolate to dough; mix well.

Divide dough into thirds. On lightly floured surface, roll each third into 12-inch (30 cm) long log. Place, 2 inches (5 cm) apart, on parchment paper–lined or greased rimless baking sheet; press to flatten logs slightly.

Bake in 325ºF (160ºC) oven until light golden and just firm to the touch, about 30 minutes. Let cool on pan on rack for 10 minutes.

Transfer logs to cutting board. Using chef's knife, cut into ½-inch (1 cm) thick slices. Stand slices up, about ½ inch (1 cm) apart, on baking sheet. Bake in 325ºF (160ºC) oven until almost dry, about 30 minutes. Transfer to rack; let cool completely.

In bowl over saucepan of hot (not boiling) water, melt remaining white chocolate, stirring until smooth. Dip 1 end of each cookie into chocolate. Place on waxed paper– or parchment paper–lined baking sheet; let stand until set, about 1 hour. *(Make-ahead: Layer between waxed paper in airtight container and store for up to 1 week or freeze for up to 1 month.)*

MAKES ABOUT 72 COOKIES.
PER COOKIE: about 80 cal, 1 g pro, 4 g total fat (2 g sat. fat), 10 g carb, trace fibre, 9 mg chol, 32 mg sodium. % RDI: 2% calcium, 2% iron, 2% vit A, 5% folate.

The unique flavour trinity of chocolate, star anise and orange makes these biscotti sing.
They're so delicious that they will vanish before your eyes, so
make sure you save a few for yourself.

Chocolate, Star Anise & Orange Biscotti

ingredients

½ cup **unsalted butter,** softened
1 cup **granulated sugar**
3 tbsp grated **orange zest**
2 **eggs**
1 tsp **vanilla**
2½ cups **all-purpose flour**

2 tsp **baking powder**
1½ tsp **ground star anise**
¼ tsp **salt**
4 oz (115 g) **dark chocolate,** chopped
1 **egg white**

method

In large bowl, beat together butter, sugar and orange zest until fluffy; beat in eggs, 1 at a time. Beat in vanilla. Whisk together flour, baking powder, star anise and salt; add to butter mixture in 2 additions, stirring just until combined. Add chocolate; mix well.

Divide dough in half. On lightly floured surface, shape each half into 12-inch (30 cm) long rectangle. Place, 2 inches (5 cm) apart, on parchment paper–lined rimless baking sheet; press to flatten slightly. Stir egg white with 1 tsp water; liberally brush over top of dough.

Bake in 325ºF (160ºC) oven until light golden and just firm to the touch, about 30 minutes. Let cool on pan on rack for 10 minutes.

Transfer logs to cutting board. Using chef's knife, cut diagonally into ½-inch (1 cm) thick slices. Stand slices upright, about ½ inch (1 cm) apart, on baking sheet. Bake in 300ºF (150ºC) oven until almost dry, 35 minutes. Transfer to rack; let cool completely.

MAKES ABOUT 36 COOKIES.
PER COOKIE: about 100 cal, 2 g pro, 4 g total fat (2 g sat. fat), 14 g carb, 1 g fibre, 17 mg chol, 38 mg sodium, 36 mg potassium. % RDI: 1% calcium, 5% iron, 3% vit A, 2% vit C, 9% folate.

The Right Knife

Biscotti dough can be a bit crumbly for slicing. Here, we tested a sharp chef's knife and it was perfect for the job. Use the knife specified in the recipe method for the smoothest, straightest cuts.

In Roman times, these cookies were sweetened with grape must,
or *mosto* (as the name indicates), the leftover grape skins and seeds from wine production.
This modern version gets it sweetness from good old sugar.

Mostaccioli

ingredients

¼ cup **unsalted butter**
½ cup **granulated sugar**
1 **egg**
1¼ cups **all-purpose flour**
¼ cup **cocoa powder**
1 tsp **cinnamon**
½ tsp each **baking soda** and **baking powder**
¼ tsp each **ground cloves** and **salt**
⅓ cup **milk**

1 cup **semisweet chocolate chips**
⅓ cup chopped **walnuts**

GLAZE:
1¼ cups **icing sugar**
¼ cup brewed **coffee**
½ tsp **vanilla**

method

In bowl, beat butter with granulated sugar until light and fluffy; beat in egg. Whisk together flour, cocoa powder, cinnamon, baking soda, baking powder, cloves and salt; stir into butter mixture alternately with milk, making 2 additions of each and scraping down bowl between additions.

Stir in chocolate chips and walnuts. Cover and refrigerate until firm, about 2 hours.

Roll by generous 1 tbsp into 1-inch (2.5 cm) balls. Place, 2 inches (5 cm) apart, on parchment paper–lined rimless baking sheets.

Bake on top and bottom racks in 350°F (180°C) oven, rotating and switching pans halfway through, until tops begin to crack, about 12 minutes.

Let cool on pan on rack for 2 minutes. Transfer to rack; let cool completely.

GLAZE: Place rack on baking sheet. In bowl, whisk together icing sugar, coffee and vanilla; spoon 1 tsp over each cookie. Let stand until set. *(Make-ahead: Layer between waxed paper in airtight container and store for up to 5 days.)*

MAKES ABOUT 34 COOKIES.
PER COOKIE: about 95 cal, 1 g pro, 4 g total fat (2 g sat. fat), 15 g carb, 1 g fibre, 9 mg chol, 43 mg sodium. % RDI: 1% calcium, 4% iron, 2% vit A, 6% folate.

Easy to whip up and fancy looking, these cookies make deliciously simple desserts.
Add them to bowls of ice cream or pudding for a crunchy accent.

Chocolate Cigar Cookies

ingredients

2 tbsp **butter,** softened
⅓ cup **icing sugar**
1 **egg white**
¼ tsp **vanilla**

3 tbsp **all-purpose flour**
2 oz (55 g) **bittersweet chocolate,** melted
¼ cup finely chopped **hazelnuts**

method

Line rimless baking sheet with parchment paper. Trace three 4-inch (10 cm) circles on paper; turn over. Set aside.

In bowl, beat butter with icing sugar until fluffy; beat in egg white and vanilla. Stir in flour. Drop by level 1 tbsp onto centre of each circle; spread with offset spatula to fill circle. Bake in 350°F (180°C) oven until pale golden, about 6 minutes.

One at a time, remove cookies from pan and turn over; quickly roll around ⅓-inch (8 mm) thick handle of wooden spoon. Slip cookie off handle; let cool on rack. Repeat with remaining batter.

Dip half of each cookie into melted chocolate; roll chocolate in hazelnuts. Refrigerate until set, about 10 minutes. *(Make-ahead: Store in airtight container for up to 3 days.)*

MAKES 12 COOKIES.
PER COOKIE: about 78 cal, 1 g pro, 6 g total fat (3 g sat. fat), 7 g carb, 1 g fibre, 5 mg chol, 19 mg sodium. % RDI: 1% calcium, 4% iron, 2% vit A, 3% folate.

Tracing on Parchment Paper

A No. 2 pencil works well to trace or draw shapes on parchment paper. Turning the paper over before you spread dough or batter on it ensures none of the pencil lead will transfer to your baked goods. The parchment is translucent, so the marks will still be clear enough to work with.

Test Kitchen TIP

Flaky, crunchy and chocolaty – is there a better combination?
If you don't have time to make homemade puff pastry, thaw 1 package (1 lb/450 g)
frozen butter puff pastry and skip ahead to the filling and forming steps.

Chocolate Hazelnut Palmiers

ingredients

½ cup **hazelnuts**
4 oz (115 g) **semisweet chocolate,**
   melted
1 **egg yolk**

QUICK PUFF PASTRY:
1 cup cold **unsalted butter,** cubed
1⅔ cups **all-purpose flour**
¾ tsp **salt**
⅓ cup cold **water**

117

method

QUICK PUFF PASTRY: Set aside three-quarters of the butter in refrigerator. In food processor, blend flour with salt. Sprinkle remaining butter over top; pulse until indistinguishable, 10 seconds. Sprinkle with reserved butter; pulse 4 or 5 times or until in pea-size pieces.

Pour cold water evenly over mixture (not through feed tube). Pulse 6 to 8 times until loose ragged dough forms (do not let form ball). Transfer to floured waxed paper; gather and press into rectangle. Dust with flour; top with waxed paper. Roll out into 15- x 12-inch (38 x 30 cm) rectangle.

Remove top paper. Starting at long edge and using bottom paper to lift pastry, fold over one-third; fold opposite long edge over top, bringing flush with edge of first fold to make 15- x 4-inch (38 x 10 cm) rectangle. Starting from 1 short end, roll up firmly; flatten into 5-inch (12 cm) square. Wrap and refrigerate until firm, about 1 hour. *(Make-ahead:*

Refrigerate in airtight container for up to 5 days or freeze for up to 2 weeks.)

In cake pan, toast hazelnuts in 350°F (180°C) oven until fragrant and skins crack, about 10 minutes. Transfer to tea towel; rub briskly to remove as much of the skin as possible. Finely chop hazelnuts.

Divide pastry in half. On lightly floured surface, roll out each half into 10-inch (25 cm) square. Leaving ½-inch (1 cm) border on all sides, brush with chocolate. Sprinkle with nuts. Starting at 1 end, roll up to centre of square; roll up opposite end to meet in centre ❶. Arrange rolls, seam side down, on parchment paper–lined baking sheets. Cover and freeze until firm, about 15 minutes.

Transfer rolls to cutting board. In bowl, beat egg yolk with 1 tbsp water; brush over rolls. Using serrated knife, trim ends even; cut each roll into twenty-four ¼-inch (5 mm) thick slices ❷. *(Make-ahead: Layer between waxed paper in airtight container; freeze for up to 2 weeks. Bake from frozen, adding 5 minutes to baking time.)* Return, cut sides down, to baking sheets.

Bake in 450°F (230°C) oven until puffed and golden, about 12 minutes.

MAKES 48 PIECES.
PER PIECE: about 73 cal, 1 g pro, 6 g total fat (3 g sat. fat), 5 g carb, trace fibre, 15 mg chol, 37 mg sodium. % RDI: 2% iron, 4% vit A, 5% folate.

HOW-TO

Thin, crisp and sturdy, these spicy hearts are the perfect cookies to mail to someone you love. Fancy molasses has a lighter taste than cooking molasses, and doesn't overpower the other flavours in this recipe.

Chocolate Gingersnap Hearts

ingredients

⅔ cup **butter,** softened
½ cup **granulated sugar**
¼ cup **fancy molasses**
3 oz (85 g) **milk chocolate,** melted
2¼ cups **all-purpose flour**
¼ cup **cocoa powder**

1 tbsp **ground ginger**
1 tsp **cinnamon**
½ tsp each **baking soda** and **ground cloves**
Pinch **salt**

method

In bowl, beat butter with sugar until fluffy; beat in molasses and chocolate. Whisk together flour, cocoa powder, ginger, cinnamon, baking soda, cloves and salt; stir into butter mixture in 2 additions. Divide in half; shape into discs. Wrap and refrigerate until firm, about 30 minutes. *(Make-ahead: Refrigerate for up to 3 days.)*

Between sheets of lightly floured waxed paper, roll out each disc to ⅛-inch (3 mm) thickness. Using floured 1½-inch (4 cm) heart-shaped cutter, cut out shapes, rerolling and cutting scraps. Place, 1 inch (2.5 cm) apart, on parchment paper–lined or greased rimless baking sheets. Refrigerate until firm, about 30 minutes.

Bake on top and bottom racks in 375°F (190°C) oven, rotating and switching pans halfway through, until bottoms are lightly browned and tops are firm to the touch, about 7 minutes.

Let cool on pans on racks for 5 minutes. Transfer to racks; let cool completely.

MAKES ABOUT 100 COOKIES.
PER COOKIE: about 33 cal, trace pro, 2 g total fat (1 g sat. fat), 4 g carb, trace fibre, 3 mg chol, 16 mg sodium. % RDI: 1% iron, 1% vit A, 3% folate.

There's nothing better than having ready-to-bake cookies standing by in the freezer.
Serve the cookies as is or use them to sandwich vanilla ice cream or roasted marshmallows.

Scoop & Freeze Double-Chocolate Cookies

ingredients

8 oz (225 g) **bittersweet chocolate,** chopped
½ cup **unsalted butter**
1½ cups **granulated sugar**
2 **eggs**
1 tsp **vanilla**

1½ cups **all-purpose flour**
½ tsp **baking soda**
¼ tsp **salt**

119

method

In large heatproof bowl over saucepan of hot (not boiling) water, melt half of the chocolate with butter; let cool to lukewarm. Stir in sugar, eggs and vanilla.

Whisk together flour, baking soda and salt; stir into chocolate mixture. Stir in remaining chopped chocolate. Cover and refrigerate for 30 minutes.

Drop by 2 tbsp or by 1-oz ice cream scoop onto parchment paper–lined baking sheets. *(Make-ahead: Freeze until firm. Transfer to airtight container and freeze for up to 2 weeks. Bake from frozen, adding 2 minutes to baking time.)*

Bake in 350°F (180°C) oven until tops are cracked and no longer glossy, 12 to 15 minutes.

Let cool on pan on rack for 2 minutes. Transfer to rack; let cool completely.

MAKES ABOUT 30 COOKIES.

PER COOKIE: about 136 cal, 2 g pro, 6 g total fat (4 g sat. fat), 19 g carb, 1 g fibre, 21 mg chol, 45 mg sodium, 12 mg potassium. % RDI: 1% calcium, 5% iron, 3% vit A, 6% folate.

Just the right shape for popping into your mouth in a single bite, these coin-size cookies are loaded with toffee and chocolate. They're guaranteed to please kids and adults alike.

Toffee Chocolate Chip Toonies

ingredients

⅔ cup **unsalted butter,** softened
¾ cup packed **brown sugar**
¼ cup **granulated sugar**
1 **egg**
1 tsp **vanilla**
1⅔ cups **all-purpose flour**
½ tsp **baking soda**

¼ tsp **salt**
½ cup **toffee bits**
½ cup **mini semisweet chocolate chips**

method

In large bowl, beat together butter, brown sugar and granulated sugar until fluffy; beat in egg and vanilla.

Whisk together flour, baking soda and salt; stir into butter mixture until combined. Stir in toffee bits and chocolate chips.

Drop by rounded 1 tsp, about 2 inches (5 cm) apart, onto parchment paper–lined rimless baking sheets. Bake in 350ºF (180ºC) oven until golden, 10 to 12 minutes.

Let cool on pan on rack for 5 minutes. Transfer to rack; let cool completely.

MAKES ABOUT 75 COOKIES.
PER COOKIE: about 47 cal, trace pro, 2 g total fat (2 g sat. fat), 6 g carb, trace fibre, 8 mg chol, 23 mg sodium, 16 mg potassium. % RDI: 1% iron, 2% vit A, 3% folate.

Try a Scoop

A scoop with a pusher in it (like an ice cream scoop) is a handy tool for cookie baking. Scoops come in a wide range of sizes – from small enough for dainty cookies or truffles to extra-large for muffins – and speed up the dough-dropping process nicely.

Test Kitchen TIP

Is there any such thing as too much chocolate? No, definitely not.
But with these two cookies, there's enough to satisfy even the most outrageous chocoholic.

Chocolate Overload Cookies

ingredients

¾ cup **unsalted butter**, softened
⅓ cup each **granulated sugar** and packed **brown sugar**
1 tsp **vanilla**
1 **egg**
1½ cups **all-purpose flour**
½ cup **cocoa powder**
½ tsp **baking powder**
¼ tsp each **baking soda** and **salt**
⅓ cup each chopped **bittersweet chocolate**, **milk chocolate** and **white chocolate**

method

In large bowl, beat butter, granulated sugar and brown sugar; beat in vanilla and egg.

Sift together flour, cocoa powder, baking powder, baking soda and salt; stir into butter mixture. Stir in bittersweet chocolate, milk chocolate and white chocolate. Form into 10-inch (25 cm) long log; wrap and refrigerate until firm, about 2 hours.

Using sawing motion with sharp knife, cut log into generous ¼-inch (5 mm) thick slices. Place, 1 inch (2.5 cm) apart, on parchment paper–lined rimless baking sheets.

Bake in 350°F (180°C) oven until firm, 10 to 11 minutes. Let cool on pans on racks for 5 minutes. Transfer to racks; let cool completely.

MAKES ABOUT 30 COOKIES.
PER COOKIE: about 48 cal, 1 g pro, 3 g total fat (2 g sat. fat), 5 g carb, trace fibre, 8 mg chol, 18 mg sodium, 13 mg potassium. % RDI: 1% calcium, 1% iron, 2% vit A, 3% folate.

Cocoa Sugar Cookies

ingredients

¾ cup **unsalted butter**, softened
1 cup **granulated sugar**
1 **egg**
1 tsp **vanilla**
2¼ cups **all-purpose flour**
⅓ cup **cocoa powder**
½ tsp **baking powder**
¼ tsp **salt**

method

In large bowl, beat butter with sugar until fluffy; beat in egg and vanilla. Whisk together flour, cocoa powder, baking powder and salt; stir into butter mixture in 2 additions to make smooth dough. Divide in half and flatten into discs; wrap each and refrigerate until firm, about 1 hour. (Make-ahead: Refrigerate for up to 24 hours.)

On floured surface, roll out each disc to ¼-inch (5 mm) thickness. Using cookie cutter, cut out desired shapes, rerolling scraps and chilling dough before cutting again. Place, 1 inch (2.5 cm) apart, on parchment paper–lined rimless baking sheets. Freeze for 15 minutes or refrigerate for 30 minutes until firm.

Bake in 350°F (180°C) oven until edges begin to darken, 20 to 25 minutes. Let cool on pans on racks for 2 minutes. Transfer to racks; let cool completely. (Make-ahead: Store in airtight container for up to 1 month.)

MAKES ABOUT 24 COOKIES.
PER COOKIE: about 132 cal, 2 g pro, 6 g total fat (4 g sat. fat), 18 g carb, 1 g fibre, 23 mg chol, 34 mg sodium. % RDI: 1% calcium, 6% iron, 5% vit A, 11% folate.

FANCY

Cookie Decorating

Sugar cookies, like our cocoa version (opposite), make an excellent palette for decorating. Start by making a batch of Royal Icing Paint (below), then decorate using any of the techniques below.

Royal Icing Paint

In large bowl, beat ¼ cup meringue powder with ½ cup water until foamy, about 2 minutes. Beat in 4½ cups icing sugar until stiff, about 9 minutes. Tint icing with paste food colouring if desired. Cover with damp cloth to prevent drying out.

MAKES 2⅔ CUPS.

Piping

Spoon Royal Icing Paint into piping bag fitted with small plain tip. Pipe outline around cookies and details as desired. Let dry for 1 hour. Enjoy as is or continue with other decorative effects.

Flooding

Mix water into Royal Icing Paint, 1 tsp at a time, until thinned to consistency of whipping cream.

- **Wet-on-Wet Decorating:** Spoon thinned icing onto centre of desired area. Using small offset spatula, spread to piped edges. Burst any air bubbles with toothpick. If adding second colour, add while first colour is still wet, making designs, such as dots and stripes. To make hearts, using skewer, drop dots of thinned icing onto surface, then draw toothpick through middle of each to create heart shape.

- **Wet-on-Dry Decorating:** Spread first colour of thinned icing as per wet-on-wet decorating. Let dry for 2 hours before using contrasting colour of thicker Royal Icing Paint to pipe on outlines, details and decorations. Let dry completely.

Flocking

Spoon Royal Icing Paint into piping bag fitted with small plain tip. Pipe desired design on uniced or dried flooded cookies. While piping is wet, sprinkle with coarse or sanding sugar. Let dry; shake off excess.

Let iced cookies dry and set for 24 hours before storing them.

From top: Chocolate Overload Cookies (page 122)
and Big Chocolate Chip Orange Cookies (opposite)

Who doesn't love a coffee shop–style giant cookie? Studded with chocolate
and flavoured with orange, these big treats are destined to become a cookie jar staple.

Big Chocolate Chip Orange Cookies

ingredients

¾ cup **unsalted butter,** softened
⅓ cup each **granulated sugar** and
  packed **brown sugar**
1 tsp grated **orange zest**
1 tsp **vanilla**

1½ cups **all-purpose flour**
½ tsp **baking powder**
¼ tsp each **baking soda** and **salt**
½ cup **mini semisweet chocolate chips**
½ cup chopped **walnuts**

method

In large bowl, beat together butter, granulated sugar and brown sugar until light; beat in orange zest and vanilla. Whisk together flour, baking powder, baking soda and salt; beat into butter mixture. Stir in chocolate chips and walnuts.

Form into 10-inch (25 cm) long log. Wrap and refrigerate until firm, about 2 hours.

Slice into ⅓-inch (8 mm) thick rounds. Place, 1 inch (2.5 cm) apart, on parchment paper–lined rimless baking sheets.

Bake in 350°F (180°C) oven until golden and firm, about 12 minutes. Let cool on pans on racks for 5 minutes. Transfer to racks; let cool completely.

MAKES ABOUT 26 COOKIES.
PER COOKIE: about 126 cal, 1 g pro, 8 g total fat
(4 g sat. fat), 13 g carb, 1 g fibre, 14 mg chol, 42 mg
sodium, 41 mg potassium. % RDI: 1% calcium,
4% iron, 5% vit A, 8% folate.

125

These darlings of every French pastry shop are worth the effort and fuss for which they are famous. For best results, make them when the weather is clear and dry to avoid soft or sticky macarons.

Chocolate Macarons

ingredients

1 cup **icing sugar**
½ cup **ground almonds**
2 tbsp **cocoa powder**
2 **egg whites**
2 tbsp **granulated sugar**
1½ tsp **meringue powder**

BLACK CURRANT FILLING:
1 cup **black currant jam**

method

In food processor, pulse together icing sugar, almonds and cocoa powder until fine. Sift through fine sieve into bowl; set aside. In large bowl, beat egg whites until foamy. Beat in granulated sugar and meringue powder until soft peaks form. Fold in almond mixture, one-third at a time, until blended.

Using piping bag fitted with ¼-inch (5 mm) plain tip, pipe meringue into 1-inch (2.5 cm) rounds, 1 inch (2.5 cm) apart, on parchment paper–lined rimless baking sheets. Let stand for 15 minutes.

Bake in 325ºF (160ºC) oven until puffed, smooth on top and cracked around bottom edges, 12 to 14 minutes. Let cool on pans on racks. (Make-ahead: Store in airtight container for up to 3 days.)

BLACK CURRANT FILLING: Meanwhile, press jam through fine sieve into small saucepan. Bring to boil over medium heat; reduce heat and simmer until thickened slightly, about 5 minutes. Transfer to bowl; let cool, stirring occasionally, until thickened and spreadable.

Spread about ¼ tsp filling onto bottom of each of half of the macarons. Sandwich with remaining macarons, bottom side down. (Make-ahead: Layer between waxed paper in airtight container and store for up to 24 hours.)

MAKES ABOUT 30 COOKIES.

PER COOKIE: about 59 cal, 1 g pro, 1 g total fat (trace sat. fat), 12 g carb, trace fibre, 0 mg chol, 7 mg sodium, 23 mg potassium. % RDI: 1% calcium, 1% iron, 2% vit C, 2% folate.

CHANGE IT UP
Chocolate Ganache Macarons

Omit black currant filling. In saucepan, heat ¼ cup whipping cream (35%) over medium heat until small bubbles form around edge. Stir in 2 oz (55 g) bittersweet chocolate, finely chopped, until melted. Stir in 1 tbsp unsalted butter until smooth. Transfer to bowl. Let cool until thick enough to spread. Fill and sandwich cookies as directed.

Crunchy and chewy, with a sweet hit of white chocolate, these cookies are perfect with tea or coffee at the end of a meal or as a mid-afternoon pick-me-up.

White Chocolate, Cranberry & Pistachio Cookies

ingredients

⅔ cup **unsalted butter,** softened
¾ cup packed **brown sugar**
⅓ cup **granulated sugar**
1 **egg**
½ tsp **vanilla**
1½ cups **all-purpose flour**
½ tsp **baking soda**

¼ tsp **salt**
6 oz (170 g) **white chocolate,** chopped
⅔ cup shelled **pistachios**
½ cup **dried cranberries**

method

In large bowl, beat together butter, brown sugar and granulated sugar until fluffy. Beat in egg; beat in vanilla.

Whisk together flour, baking soda and salt; stir into butter mixture. Stir in white chocolate, pistachios and cranberries.

Drop by heaping 1 tsp onto parchment paper–lined rimless baking sheets. Bake in 350°F (180°C) oven until golden, 10 to 12 minutes. Let cool on pans on racks.

MAKES ABOUT 80 COOKIES.
PER COOKIE: about 54 cal, 1 g pro, 3 g total fat (2 g sat. fat), 7 g carb, trace fibre, 6 mg chol, 19 mg sodium, 28 mg potassium. % RDI: 1% calcium, 1% iron, 2% vit A, 3% folate.

127

These cookies are dark and delicious with an intense chocolate flavour.
You can substitute 1 cup each milk chocolate chips and semisweet chocolate chips for both the chopped chocolates if you have them in your pantry.

Triple-Chocolate Cookies

ingredients

1 cup **butter,** softened
1 cup **granulated sugar**
½ cup packed **brown sugar**
2 **eggs**
1 tsp **vanilla**
2¼ cups **all-purpose flour**
½ cup **cocoa powder**
1 tsp **baking soda**
¼ tsp **salt**

6 oz (170 g) **bittersweet chocolate,** chopped
4 oz (115 g) **milk chocolate,** chopped
1 cup coarsely chopped **walnuts** (optional)

method

In large bowl, beat together butter, granulated sugar and brown sugar until fluffy. Beat in eggs, 1 at a time; beat in vanilla. Sift together flour, cocoa powder, baking soda and salt; stir into butter mixture. Stir in bittersweet and milk chocolates, and walnuts (if using).

Drop by heaping 1 tbsp, about 2 inches (5 cm) apart, onto parchment paper–lined rimless baking sheets. Bake on top and bottom racks in 350°F (180°C) oven, rotating and switching pans halfway through, until firm to the touch and no longer glossy, about 12 minutes.

Let cool on pans on racks for 2 minutes. Transfer to racks; let cool completely. *(Make-ahead: Layer between waxed paper in airtight container and store for up to 3 days or freeze for up to 2 weeks.)*

MAKES ABOUT 48 COOKIES.

PER COOKIE: about 117 cal, 2 g pro, 6 g total fat (4 g sat. fat), 15 g carb, 1 g fibre, 18 mg chol, 71 mg sodium. % RDI: 1% calcium, 5% iron, 4% vit A, 6% folate.

From left: Hot Chocolate (page 82)
and Triple-Chocolate Cookies (opposite)

Canned chestnut purée adds European chic to elegant finger cookies.
If you want to freeze the fingers, do so before dipping them in chocolate.

Chocolate Chestnut Fingers

ingredients

½ cup **canned chestnut purée**
⅓ cup **butter,** softened
¼ cup **granulated sugar**
1 **egg yolk**
1 oz (30 g) **bittersweet chocolate,** melted
1 cup **all-purpose flour**
¼ tsp **cinnamon**

GARNISH:
2 oz (55 g) **bittersweet chocolate,** melted
2 tbsp **sliced almonds**

method

In large bowl, beat together chestnut purée, butter and sugar until light and fluffy; beat in egg yolk and chocolate until combined.

In separate bowl, whisk flour with cinnamon; add to butter mixture, about one-third at a time, stirring to make smooth dough. Cover and refrigerate for 1 hour.

Using scant 1 tbsp for each, roll dough into 2½-inch (6 cm) long fingers; place, about 1 inch (2.5 cm) apart, on 2 parchment paper–lined rimless baking sheets.

Bake on top and bottom racks in 350°F (180°C) oven, rotating and switching pans halfway through, until firm and pale brown on bottoms, about 20 minutes. Let cool on pans on racks.

GARNISH: Dip 1 end of each cookie in chocolate; place on parchment paper–lined baking sheets. Sprinkle with almonds; refrigerate until firm, about 30 minutes. *(Make-ahead: Layer between waxed paper in airtight container and store for up to 1 week.)*

MAKES ABOUT 36 COOKIES.
PER COOKIE: about 57 cal, 1 g pro, 3 g total fat (2 g sat. fat), 7 g carb, 1 g fibre, 11 mg chol, 19 mg sodium. % RDI: 1% calcium, 3% iron, 2% vit A, 3% folate.

These rich morsels have a gorgeous crackle topping. French roast coffee is strong and dark, and will give these cookies a lovely java flavour.

Mocha Chocolate Crackles

ingredients

¼ cup **butter**
2 oz (55 g) **bittersweet chocolate,** chopped
3 tbsp strong brewed **coffee**
1 **egg**
¼ cup packed **brown sugar**
¾ cup **all-purpose flour**

¼ cup **cocoa powder**
½ tsp **baking powder**
¼ tsp **salt**
⅓ cup **icing sugar**

method

In heatproof bowl over saucepan of hot (not boiling) water, melt butter with chocolate, stirring occasionally until smooth. Stir in coffee. Set aside.

In large bowl, beat egg with brown sugar until pale and thickened; beat in chocolate mixture. Whisk together flour, cocoa powder, baking powder and salt; add to chocolate mixture in 2 additions, stirring just until blended. Cover and refrigerate until firm, about 1 hour.

Pour icing sugar into shallow dish. Roll dough by scant 1 tbsp into balls; roll each in icing sugar to coat generously. Arrange, 2 inches (5 cm) apart, on parchment paper–lined or greased rimless baking sheets.

Bake in 325°F (160°C) oven until cracked, 12 to 14 minutes.

Let cool on pans on racks for 2 minutes. Transfer to racks; let cool completely. *(Make-ahead: Layer between waxed paper in airtight container and store for up to 5 days or freeze for up to 3 weeks.)*

MAKES ABOUT 30 COOKIES.
PER COOKIE: about 50 cal, 1 g pro, 3 g total fat (2 g sat. fat), 6 g carb, 1 g fibre, 11 mg chol, 42 mg sodium. % RDI: 1% calcium, 3% iron, 2% vit A, 2% folate.

131

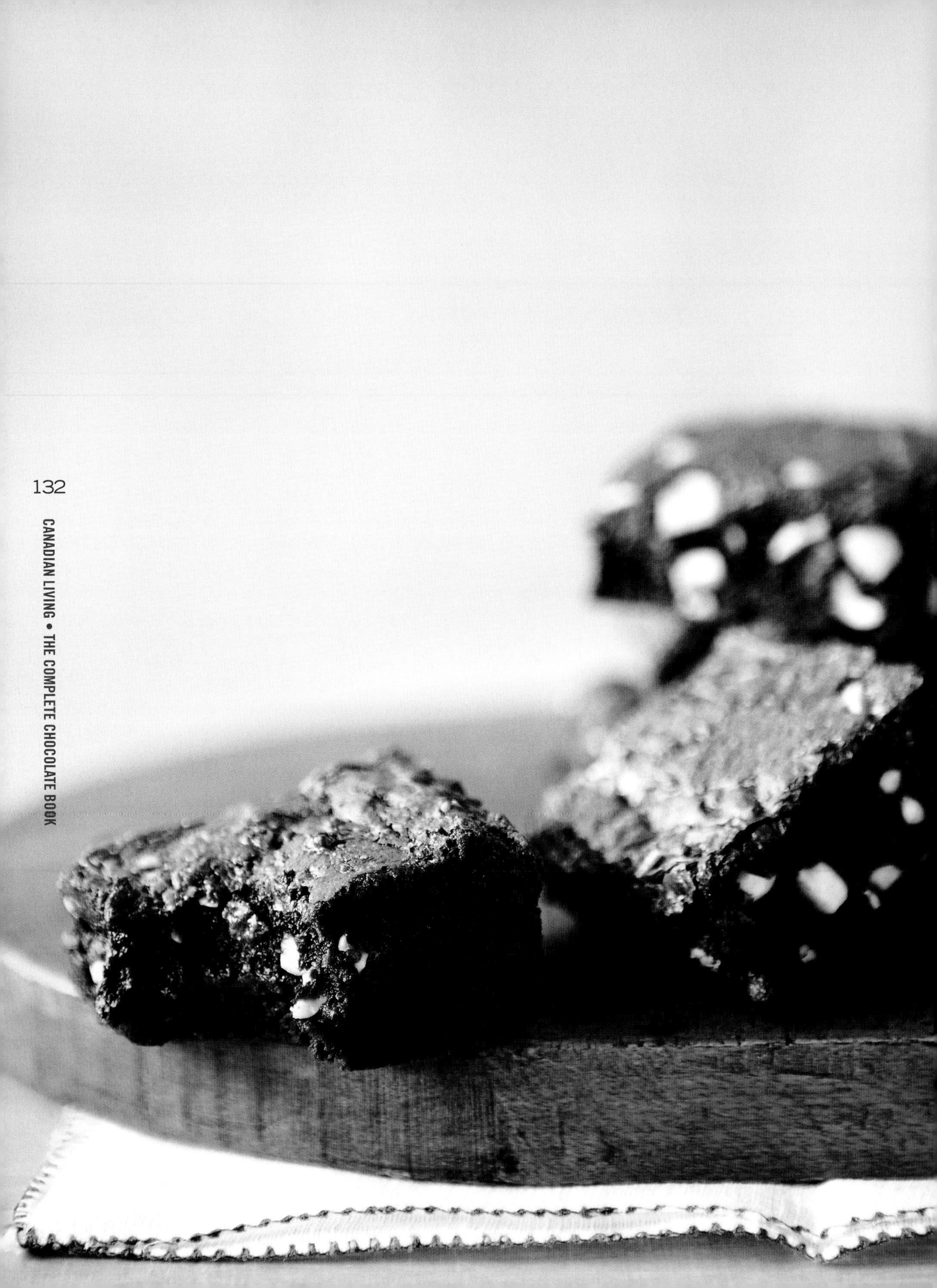

chewy

Chocolate Babka 134

Chocolate Breakfast Braid 135

Chocolate Monkey Bread 137

Banana Brownies 138

Gluten-Free Super Fudgy Chocolate Brownies 139

Chocolate Bar Brownies 140

White Chocolate Cranberry Blondies 142

Chocolate Caramel Bites 143

The Best Chocolate Brownies 145

Chocolate Coconut Mounds 146

Cocoa Pecan Macaroons 147

Irish Cream Brownie Bites 148

Gluten-Free Chocolate Glitter Cookies 150

Gluten-Free White Chocolate Pistachio Cookies 151

Peanut Butter Brownies 153

German Chocolate Brownies 154

Chewy Caramel Pecan Squares 156

Ginger Macadamia Blondies 157

Rocky Road Blondies 159

Candied Ginger & White Chocolate Hermits 160

Chocolate Hazelnut Rugalach 161

Monkey Bars 162

Oatmeal Chocolate Chip Cookies 164

Surprise Peanut Butter Cookies 165

Ginger Butterscotch Squares 167

White Chocolate Butterscotch Oatmeal Chippers 168

Classic Chocolate Chip Cookies 169

Double-Chocolate Minties 170

Dark & Dangerous Triple-Chocolate Cookies 172

Toffee, Macadamia & White Chocolate Chunk Cookies 173

Double-Chocolate Walnut Chunks 175

This yeast coffee cake, named after the Yiddish or Polish word *baba,* or grandmother, is often found in Jewish bakeries and delis.

Chocolate Babka

ingredients

¾ cup **2% milk** or homogenized milk
1 pkg (8 g) **active dry yeast** (or 2¼ tsp)
⅓ cup **granulated sugar**
⅓ cup **unsalted butter,** softened
¾ tsp **salt**
3 **eggs**
3¼ cups **all-purpose flour** (approx)

FILLING:
¼ cup **unsalted butter,** softened
½ cup **granulated sugar**
½ cup **cocoa powder**

STREUSEL:
⅓ cup **all-purpose flour**
¼ cup **granulated sugar**
3 tbsp **unsalted butter**

method

In saucepan, heat milk over medium-low heat just until warm to the touch (100°F/38°C); pour into large bowl. Sprinkle in yeast; let stand until frothy, about 10 minutes.

Transfer to stand mixer. Whisk in sugar, butter, salt and 2 of the eggs. Add 3 cups of the flour; mix, adding remaining flour, 1 tbsp at a time, if necessary, until dough is smooth, elastic and comes away from side of bowl, about 10 minutes. Transfer to lightly floured surface; knead into ball. Place in large greased bowl, turning to grease all over. Cover and let rise in warm place until doubled in bulk, about 1½ hours.

Punch down dough; divide in half. Roll out each half into 18- x 7-inch (45 x 18 cm) rectangle.

FILLING: Leaving ½-inch (1 cm) border on 1 long side of each, spread butter over rectangles. Mix sugar with cocoa powder; sprinkle over butter. Starting at long buttered side, roll up tightly into log; pinch edge to seal, brushing with water if necessary. Fold each log in half; twist twice and pinch open ends together to seal. Fit into 2 greased 8- x 4-inch (1.5 L) loaf pans.

Cover with greased plastic wrap; let rise in warm place until doubled in bulk, 1 to 1½ hours. Whisk remaining egg with 2 tsp water. Brush over loaves.

STREUSEL: Stir flour with sugar. Using pastry blender or 2 knives, cut in butter until in coarse crumbs. Sprinkle over loaves.

Bake in 350°F (180°C) oven until browned and bottoms sound hollow when tapped, 35 to 40 minutes. Transfer to racks; let cool.

MAKES 2 LOAVES, 8 SLICES EACH.

PER SLICE: about 257 cal, 5 g pro, 11 g total fat (6 g sat. fat), 37 g carb, 2 g fibre, 59 mg chol, 126 mg sodium, 138 mg potassium. % RDI: 3% calcium, 14% iron, 10% vit A, 33% folate.

Checking Yeast Strength

To keep yeast working at its peak, store it, tightly sealed, in the refrigerator. Check the expiry date and buy fresh yeast if it's past its prime. You can proof the yeast to test if it's still active: Mix ¼ tsp granulated sugar with 1 cup warm water; sprinkle in ½ tsp yeast and let stand for 10 minutes. If it's frothy and bubbles up, the yeast is ready for baking.

The chocolate nugget in the centre of this bread makes the loaf reminiscent of *pain au chocolat*. It's a decadent breakfast or teatime snack.

Chocolate Breakfast Braid

ingredients

1½ cups chopped **bittersweet chocolate** or milk chocolate (about 7 oz/210 g)

1 **egg,** beaten

SWEET YEAST DOUGH:

¼ cup **granulated sugar**

¼ cup warm **water**

1 pkg (8 g) **active dry yeast** (or 2¼ tsp)

½ cup **milk**

¼ cup **butter**

1 tsp **salt**

2 **eggs,** beaten

4 cups **all-purpose flour** (approx)

method

SWEET YEAST DOUGH: In large bowl, stir 2 tsp of the sugar with warm water until dissolved. Sprinkle in yeast; let stand until frothy, about 10 minutes.

Meanwhile, in saucepan, heat milk, remaining sugar, butter and salt until butter is melted; let cool to lukewarm. Stir into yeast mixture along with eggs. Stir in 3¼ cups of the flour, about 1 cup at a time, to form shaggy dough.

Turn out onto lightly floured surface; knead, adding as much of the remaining flour as necessary, until smooth and elastic, about 10 minutes. Transfer to large greased bowl, turning to grease all over. Cover and let rise in warm draft-free place until doubled in bulk, about 1½ hours.

Punch down dough; divide in half. Working with half at a time, divide dough into thirds. Press or roll each third into 8- x 4-inch (20 x 10 cm) rectangle. Leaving 1-inch (2.5 cm) border all around, sprinkle ¼ cup of the chocolate onto centre of each. Fold long sides of dough together, pinching to enclose chocolate. Roll each gently into rope about 12 inches (30 cm) long.

Pinch 3 ropes together at 1 end. Braid ropes, pinching ends and tucking under. Repeat with remaining dough to make second loaf.

Place loaves, 3 inches (8 cm) apart, on parchment paper–lined or greased large baking sheet. *(Make-ahead: Cover and refrigerate for up to 12 hours; let come to room temperature before continuing, about 40 minutes.)* Cover and let rise in warm draft-free place until doubled in bulk, about 1 hour.

Brush tops with egg. Bake in 375°F (190°C) oven until golden and loaves sound hollow when tapped on bottoms, about 20 minutes. Let cool on pan on rack for 5 minutes. Transfer to rack; let cool completely. *(Make-ahead: Wrap in plastic wrap and overwrap in heavy-duty foil; freeze for up to 2 weeks.)*

MAKES 2 LOAVES, 12 SLICES EACH.

PER SLICE: about 157 cal, 4 g pro, 7 g total fat (4 g sat. fat), 21 g carb, 2 g fibre, 29 mg chol, 121 mg sodium. % RDI: 2% calcium, 11% iron, 3% vit A, 25% folate.

CHANGE IT UP

Bread Machine Chocolate Breakfast Braid Dough

Into pan of 1½ to 2 lb (675 to 900 g) bread machine, add (in order): warm water, milk, eggs, melted butter, sugar, salt, 4 cups flour and bread machine yeast. (Do not let yeast touch liquid.) Choose dough setting. Shape, fill and bake as directed.

HOW-TO

1

2

Monkey bread is so named because you're supposed to pull apart the buns like a monkey pulls a banana from the bunch. Requested over and over since it first appeared in *Canadian Living* magazine in 1999, this sweet bread will become one of your family's most requested recipes too.

Chocolate Monkey Bread

ingredients

⅓ cup **granulated sugar**
¼ cup warm **water**
2 tsp **active dry yeast**
¾ cup **milk**
¼ cup **butter,** melted
2 **eggs**
2 tsp **vanilla**
¾ tsp **salt**
4½ cups **all-purpose flour** (approx)
1 cup **mini semisweet chocolate chips**

CHOCOLATE TOPPING:
3 tbsp **butter,** melted
½ cup **granulated sugar**
2 tbsp **cocoa powder**

ICING:
½ cup **icing sugar**

method

In large bowl, dissolve 1 tsp of the sugar in warm water. Sprinkle in yeast; let stand until frothy, about 10 minutes.

Whisk in remaining sugar, milk, butter, eggs, vanilla and salt. Whisk in 2 cups of the flour. With wooden spoon, stir in enough of the remaining flour, ½ cup at a time, to make soft slightly sticky dough.

Turn out dough onto lightly floured surface; knead, adding as much of the remaining flour as necessary, until smooth and elastic, about 10 minutes. Knead in chocolate chips.

Place in greased bowl, turning to grease all over. Cover and let rise in warm draft-free place until doubled in bulk, about 1 hour.

CHOCOLATE TOPPING: Punch down dough. Divide into 24 portions; shape each into ball. Place butter in small bowl. In separate bowl, combine sugar with cocoa powder. Roll balls first in butter, then in cocoa mixture ❶.

Arrange in greased 10-inch (4 L) tube pan with removable bottom ❷. Cover and let rise in warm draft-free place until doubled in bulk, about 40 minutes.

Bake in 350°F (180°C) oven until golden, about 45 minutes. Let cool in pan on rack for 10 minutes. Remove outside of pan; let cool completely.

ICING: Stir icing sugar with 1 tbsp water until smooth; drizzle over bread.

MAKES 24 BUNS.
PER BUN: about 195 cal, 4 g pro, 6 g total fat (4 g sat. fat), 32 g carb, 1 g fibre, 26 mg chol, 114 mg sodium. % RDI: 2% calcium, 9% iron, 4% vit A, 17% folate.

CHANGE IT UP

Nutty Caramel Monkey Bread
Substitute toasted chopped pecans for chocolate chips. Omit chocolate topping. Dip balls into ½ cup packed brown sugar mixed with 2 tsp cinnamon.

Bread Machine Chocolate Monkey Bread Dough
Into pan of 1½ to 2 lb (675 to 900 g) machine, add (in order): milk, warm water, butter, eggs, vanilla, sugar, salt, flour and yeast. (Do not let yeast touch liquid.) Choose dough setting. Turn out onto work surface; knead in chocolate chips. Shape and bake as directed.

Bananas take these dense brownies – made with both bittersweet and unsweetened chocolate – to the next dimension of deliciousness.

Banana Brownies

ingredients

⅓ cup **butter**

4 oz (115 g) **bittersweet chocolate** or semisweet chocolate, chopped

2 oz (55 g) **unsweetened chocolate,** chopped

¾ cup **granulated sugar**

2 **eggs**

½ cup mashed **banana**

2 tsp **vanilla**

⅔ cup **all-purpose flour**

1 tsp **baking powder**

Pinch **salt**

1 cup **semisweet chocolate chips**

16 **banana chips**

method

In saucepan, melt together butter, bittersweet chocolate and unsweetened chocolate over medium heat, stirring until smooth; let cool for 10 minutes. Whisk in sugar.

Whisk together eggs, banana and vanilla; whisk into chocolate mixture in 2 additions. Whisk together flour, baking powder and salt; stir into saucepan just until combined. Scrape into parchment paper–lined 8-inch (2 L) square cake pan.

Bake in 350°F (180°C) oven until cake tester inserted in centre comes out with a few moist crumbs clinging, about 35 minutes.

Transfer pan to rack. Sprinkle brownies with chocolate chips; let stand for 5 minutes. Spread chocolate evenly over top. With tip of knife, score into 16 squares; top each with 1 banana chip. Let cool. (*Make-ahead: Store in airtight container for up to 3 days or freeze for up to 2 weeks.*)

MAKES 16 SQUARES.

PER SQUARE: about 225 cal, 3 g pro, 12 g total fat (7 g sat. fat), 29 g carb, 2 g fibre, 35 mg chol, 64 mg sodium. % RDI: 2% calcium, 8% iron, 5% vit A, 2% vit C, 7% folate.

Bananas for Baking

Ripe bananas have the most potent flavour in baked goods, so let them sit on the counter until they're lightly speckled and fragrant. If the peel is a little bit on the black side, it won't hurt – the flavour will be even more concentrated.

Test Kitchen TIP

These brownies are so rich and chocolaty that there's no need for icing. White rice flour (such as Bob's Red Mill) is available in Asian stores and health food stores, and some supermarkets.

Gluten-Free Super Fudgy Chocolate Brownies

ingredients

3 bars (each 100 g) **70% dark chocolate,** chopped
1 cup **unsalted butter,** cubed
¼ cup **whipping cream (35%)**
4 **eggs**
1 cup **granulated sugar**

¼ cup **cocoa powder,** sifted
¼ cup **white rice flour**
1 tsp **vanilla**
1 cup chopped **walnuts**

method

In heatproof bowl over saucepan of hot (not boiling) water, melt together chocolate, butter and cream, stirring, until smooth. Let cool slightly.

In large bowl, whisk together eggs, sugar, cocoa powder, rice flour and vanilla; stir in chocolate mixture and walnuts. Scrape into parchment paper–lined 9-inch (2.5 L) square cake pan.

Bake in 350°F (180°C) oven until puffed and cracked at edges, about 35 minutes. Let cool in pan on rack. Refrigerate until cold, about 1 hour.

Wiping knife with damp cloth between cuts, cut into squares. *(Make-ahead: Refrigerate in airtight container for up to 1 week.)*

MAKES 25 SQUARES.
PER SQUARE: about 226 cal, 3 g pro, 17 g total fat (9 g sat. fat), 16 g carb, 2 g fibre, 53 mg chol, 14 mg sodium, 143 mg potassium. % RDI: 2% calcium, 13% iron, 8% vit A, 4% folate.

Topping rich brownies with candy is just gilding the lily, isn't it?
But it's so good you'll never want to go back! Experiment to find your favourite topping —
especially around Halloween, when there's lots of leftover candy around the house.

Chocolate Bar Brownies

ingredients

⅔ cup **butter**

7 oz (210 g) **bittersweet chocolate,**
  chopped

5 oz (140 g) **unsweetened chocolate,**
  chopped

1½ cups **granulated sugar**

2 tsp **vanilla**

4 **eggs**

1 cup **all-purpose flour**

1 tsp **salt**

TOPPING:

5 oz (140 g) **bittersweet chocolate,**
  chopped

⅔ cup **whipping cream (35%)**

1 cup chopped **chocolate-covered
  candy** (such as Turtles, Maltesers,
  After Eights or Rolos)

method

In saucepan, melt together butter, bittersweet
chocolate and unsweetened chocolate over
medium-low heat, stirring until smooth; let
cool for 10 minutes.

Whisk in sugar and vanilla; whisk in eggs,
1 at a time. Stir in flour and salt. Spread in
parchment paper–lined 13- x 9-inch (3.5 L)
cake pan; smooth top.

Bake in 350°F (180°C) oven until cake tester
inserted in centre comes out with a few moist
crumbs clinging, about 25 minutes. Let cool
in pan on rack.

TOPPING: Place chocolate in heatproof bowl.
In saucepan, bring cream just to boil; pour
over chocolate, whisking until smooth. Let
cool for 3 minutes. Spread over brownies;
sprinkle with candy. Cut into bars.

MAKES ABOUT 40 BARS.

PER BAR: about 182 cal, 2 g pro, 11 g total fat
(7 g sat. fat), 18 g carb, 1 g fibre, 37 mg chol, 103 mg
sodium. % RDI: 2% calcium, 6% iron, 6% vit A,
4% folate.

Buying Vanilla Extract

The real stuff is worth the money. Pure vanilla extract –
not artificial – is a must in most Canadian Living
Test Kitchen recipes. It's made by percolating vanilla beans
with ethyl alcohol and water, and its pure flavour is vital in
custards and delicate, fresh desserts. Artificial, or imitation,
vanilla extract does have its uses, though. It works well in high
heat and can taste just fine in longer-baked cakes or loaves.

These rich, chewy blondies have a cracked brownie-style top, with tangy cranberries and orange zest to complement the sweet white chocolate.

White Chocolate Cranberry Blondies

ingredients

1 cup **butter,** softened
10 oz (280 g) **white chocolate,** chopped
1¼ cups **granulated sugar**
4 **eggs**
2 cups **all-purpose flour**
1 cup **dried cranberries**

1 tbsp grated **orange zest**
1 tbsp **vanilla**
½ tsp **salt**

method

In saucepan over low heat, melt butter with white chocolate, stirring occasionally, until smooth. Let cool for 10 minutes.

Using wooden spoon, stir in sugar; stir eggs, 1 at a time, stirring well after each. Stir in flour, cranberries, orange zest, vanilla and salt. Spread in parchment paper–lined 13- x 9-inch (3.5 L) cake pan.

Bake in 325°F (160°C) oven until cake tester inserted in centre comes out clean, 30 to 35 minutes.

Cut into bars.

MAKES 40 BARS.
PER BAR: about 142 cal, 2 g pro, 7 g total fat (4 g sat. fat), 17 g carb, trace fibre, 33 mg chol, 88 mg sodium. % RDI: 2% calcium, 2% iron, 5% vit A, 2% vit C, 5% folate.

This toothsome caramel requires a watchful eye and constant stirring.
But it's worth all the elbow grease when you bite into one of these delightful buttery candies.

Chocolate Caramel Bites

ingredients

1 cup **pecan halves**
Pinch **salt**
⅔ cup **sweetened condensed milk**
½ cup packed **dark brown sugar**
½ cup **unsalted butter**
2 tbsp **corn syrup**
½ tsp **vanilla**

2 oz (55 g) **bittersweet chocolate,** chopped
2 tbsp **whipping cream (35%)**

method

Spread pecans on rimmed baking sheet; sprinkle with salt. Bake in 350°F (180°C) oven until fragrant and golden, about 7 minutes. Let cool.

Remove 24 halves and set aside. Chop remaining pecans; divide evenly among 24 greased mini muffin or tart cups.

In small saucepan over medium heat, melt together sweetened condensed milk, brown sugar, butter and corn syrup, stirring until smooth. Simmer over medium-low heat, stirring constantly, until thickened, deep caramel colour and candy thermometer reads 215 to 220°F (102 to 104°C), 25 to 27 minutes. Remove from heat. Immediately stir in vanilla. Spoon 1 tbsp into each cup; tap pans to spread evenly. Let cool in pans on rack.

Meanwhile, in bowl over saucepan of hot (not boiling) water, melt chocolate with cream. Remove from heat; stir until smooth.

Spoon scant ½ tsp chocolate mixture onto centre of each candy. Top each with 1 of the reserved pecan halves. Refrigerate until firm, about 30 minutes. *(Make-ahead: Layer between waxed paper in airtight container and refrigerate for up to 2 weeks.)*

MAKES 24 PIECES.
PER PIECE: about 130 cal, 1 g pro, 9 g total fat (4 g sat. fat), 12 g carb, 1 g fibre, 15 mg chol, 16 mg sodium. % RDI: 3% calcium, 2% iron, 5% vit A, 1% folate.

Yes, these really are the best brownies ever! For a fancy plated dessert, cut cooled brownies with a round cutter, dust with icing sugar or cocoa powder, and serve with a dollop of whipped cream.

The Best Chocolate Brownies

ingredients

8 oz (225 g) **bittersweet chocolate,** chopped
2 oz (55 g) **unsweetened chocolate,** chopped
1 cup **butter**
2 cups **granulated sugar**
1 tbsp **vanilla**

4 **eggs**
1 cup **all-purpose flour**
¼ tsp **salt**

method

In saucepan, melt together bittersweet chocolate, unsweetened chocolate and butter over medium-low heat, stirring occasionally; let cool for 10 minutes.

Whisk in sugar and vanilla; whisk in eggs, 1 at a time. With wooden spoon, stir in flour and salt. Spread in greased or parchment paper–lined 13- x 9-inch (3 L) baking dish; smooth top.

Bake in 350°F (180°C) oven until cake tester inserted in centre comes out with a few moist crumbs clinging, 35 to 40 minutes.

Let cool in pan on rack. Cut into bars. *(Make-ahead: Layer between waxed paper in airtight container and refrigerate for up to 3 days or freeze for up to 2 weeks.)*

MAKES 48 BARS.
PER BAR: about 115 cal, 1 g pro, 7 g total fat (4 g sat. fat), 13 g carb, 1 g fibre, 26 mg chol, 45 mg sodium, 46 mg potassium. % RDI: 1% calcium, 5% iron, 4% vit A, 4% folate.

LINING PANS WITH
Parchment Paper

Square and rectangular pans pose a challenge when it comes to lining them with parchment paper. Here's how to do it with no tears.

1. Place pan on parchment paper; cut paper 3 inches (8 cm) larger on each side.
2. Grease pan lightly to give the paper something to stick to.
3. At each corner, make 3-inch (8 cm) long cut from corner of paper toward centre.
4. Place paper in pan, pressing bottom to adhere.
5. At each corner, tuck one piece of paper behind the other; add batter.

Dense and packed with coconut, these little mounds – perched on
delicious chocolate bases – are a terrific match with afternoon tea or coffee.

Chocolate Coconut Mounds

ingredients

2 **egg whites,** at room temperature
Pinch **salt**
1 tsp **vanilla**
¾ cup **granulated sugar**

3½ cups **sweetened shredded
 coconut**
4 oz (115 g) **bittersweet chocolate,**
 melted

method

In bowl, beat egg whites with salt until foamy; beat in vanilla. Beat in sugar, 2 tbsp at a time, until stiff peaks form. Fold in coconut.

Drop by 1 tbsp, 1 inch (2.5 cm) apart, onto parchment paper–lined rimless baking sheet. Bake in 325°F (160°C) oven until edges are golden, about 18 minutes. Let cool on pan on rack for 5 minutes. Transfer to racks; let cool completely.

Line baking sheet with parchment paper. Place melted chocolate in bowl. Dip bottoms of cookies into chocolate; place on pan. Refrigerate until hardened, about 10 minutes.

MAKES ABOUT 36 COOKIES.
PER COOKIE: about 80 cal, 1 g pro, 4 g total fat (4 g sat. fat), 10 g carb, 1 g fibre, 0 mg chol, 27 mg sodium. % RDI: 2% iron.

Which Type of Coconut?

There are two types of coconut in the baking aisle (sweetened and unsweetened), in a variety of textures. For these cookies, sweetened shredded coconut is the right choice. It gives them an airier texture than flaked, which would pack down more tightly when moulded, and the sugar balances the enticing bitterness of the chocolate.

Test Kitchen TIP

Different brands of cocoa are different colours, so these cookies can range from
pale to dark brown. But whatever colour they are, they're chewy with a delicious pecan crunch.
And they're not calorific as far as cookies go, which is a nice bonus.

Cocoa Pecan Macaroons

ingredients

1¾ cup **pecan halves,** chopped
2½ cups **icing sugar**
¾ cup **cocoa powder**
Pinch **salt**
4 **egg whites**

1 tbsp **vanilla**
½ cup **semisweet chocolate chips**

method

In small cake pan, toast pecans in 350°F
(180°C) oven until fragrant, about 6 minutes.
Let cool.

Into large bowl, sift together icing sugar,
cocoa powder and salt. Add egg whites and
vanilla; beat until thickened and beaters leave
trails in batter, about 10 minutes. Stir in
pecans and chocolate chips.

Drop by heaping 1 tsp onto 2 parchment
paper–lined rimless baking sheets. Bake in
350°F (180°C) oven until glossy, about
12 minutes.

Let cool on pans on racks for 5 minutes.
Angling spatula slightly downward, slide under
cookies to loosen. Transfer to racks; let cool
completely. *(Make-ahead: Layer between
waxed paper in airtight container and store for
up to 2 weeks.)*

MAKES ABOUT 56 COOKIES.
PER COOKIE: about 54 cal, 1 g pro, 3 g total fat
(1 g sat. fat), 7 g carb, 1 g fibre, 0 mg chol, 5 mg sodium.
% RDI: 1% calcium, 2% iron.

147

These little mouthfuls are topped with a decadent Irish cream–flavoured ganache.
For a kid-friendly version, substitute 1½ tsp vanilla for the liqueur. Adorn the tops with
coarse sugar, or silver or gold sprinkles, if desired.

Irish Cream Brownie Bites

ingredients

4 oz (115 g) **bittersweet chocolate,** chopped
1 oz (30 g) **unsweetened chocolate,** chopped
½ cup **unsalted butter,** cubed
1 cup **granulated sugar**
2 tsp **vanilla**
2 **eggs**

½ cup **all-purpose flour**
2 tsp **instant espresso powder**
Pinch **salt**

IRISH CREAM GANACHE:
2 oz (55 g) **bittersweet chocolate,** chopped
3 tbsp **whipping cream (35%)**
1 tbsp **butter,** softened
1 tbsp **Irish cream liqueur**

method

In saucepan, melt together bittersweet chocolate, unsweetened chocolate and butter over medium-low heat, stirring occasionally until smooth; let cool for 10 minutes.

Whisk in sugar and vanilla; whisk in eggs, 1 at a time. With wooden spoon, stir in flour, espresso powder and salt. Spoon by 1 tbsp into paper-lined mini muffin cups.

Bake in 350°F (180°C) oven until cake tester inserted in centre comes out with a few moist crumbs clinging, 18 to 22 minutes. Let cool in pan on rack.

IRISH CREAM GANACHE: In small saucepan, melt chocolate with cream over low heat, stirring occasionally, until smooth. Whisk in butter and liqueur; let cool for 15 minutes.

Spread scant ½ tsp ganache over each brownie. Cover loosely and refrigerate until set, about 30 minutes. *(Make-ahead: Layer between waxed paper in airtight container and refrigerate for up to 3 days or freeze for up to 2 weeks.)*

MAKES 24 PIECES.
PER PIECE: about 141 cal, 2 g pro, 9 g total fat (5 g sat. fat), 15 g carb, 1 g fibre, 30 mg chol, 11 mg sodium, 66 mg potassium. % RDI: 1% calcium, 6% iron, 5% vit A, 4% folate.

{ chewy }

Coarse sugar gives these cookies a frosted look that's lovely during the holidays.
They're a pretty, chocolaty option for people with gluten allergies and intolerances.

Gluten-Free Chocolate Glitter Cookies

ingredients

6 oz (170 g) **bittersweet chocolate,**
  chopped
3 tbsp **butter**
2 **eggs**
¼ cup **granulated sugar**
¼ cup **liquid honey**

2 cups **ground almonds**
Pinch **salt**
¼ cup **coarse sugar**

method

In heatproof bowl over saucepan of hot
(not boiling) water, melt bittersweet chocolate
with butter, stirring until smooth. Let cool to
room temperature.

In bowl, beat together eggs, granulated sugar
and honey until foamy; fold in chocolate
mixture. Whisk almonds with salt; fold into
chocolate mixture. Cover and refrigerate until
firm, about 1 hour. *(Make-ahead: Refrigerate
for up to 24 hours.)*

Roll dough by rounded 1 tbsp into balls; roll
each in coarse sugar. Place, 2 inches (5 cm)
apart, on 2 parchment paper–lined or greased
rimless baking sheets. Freeze until firm,
about 15 minutes.

Bake on top and bottom racks in 325°F
(160°C) oven, rotating and switching pans
halfway through, until bottoms are darkened,
about 16 minutes.

Let cool on pans on racks for 5 minutes.
Transfer to racks; let cool completely.

MAKES 36 COOKIES.
PER COOKIE: about 88 cal, 2 g pro, 6 g total fat (2 g
sat. fat), 8 g carb, 1 g fibre, 13 mg chol, 10 mg sodium.
% RDI: 2% calcium, 4% iron, 1% vit A, 1% folate.

Storing Cookies

Unless otherwise noted, you can layer
cookies between waxed paper in an
airtight container and store them for up to
5 days or freeze them for up to 1 month.

{ chewy }

Letting this batter stand allows the pretty green tint of the pistachios to develop.
If you don't have a piping bag, use a small plastic bag with a corner snipped off.

Gluten-Free White Chocolate Pistachio Cookies

ingredients

3 **egg whites**
½ cup **granulated sugar**
2 cups ground **pistachios**
½ cup **gluten-free all-purpose baking flour** (such as Bob's Red Mill)
¼ tsp **ground cardamom**

Pinch **salt**
3 oz (85 g) **white chocolate,** chopped

method

In large bowl, beat egg whites until soft peaks form; beat in sugar, 2 tbsp at a time, until stiff glossy peaks form. Whisk together 1¾ cups of the pistachios, flour, cardamom and salt; fold into egg whites. Let stand for 5 minutes.

With damp hands, roll by rounded 1 tbsp into balls. Place, 2 inches (5 cm) apart, on parchment paper–lined rimless baking sheets; press into 1½-inch (4 cm) rounds. Bake in 325°F (160°C) oven until firm to the touch and bottoms are golden, 15 to 18 minutes. Let cool on pan on rack.

In heatproof bowl over saucepan of hot (not boiling) water, melt white chocolate. Using piping bag fitted with small plain tip, pipe white chocolate over cooled cookies. Sprinkle with remaining pistachios. Let stand on rack until set. *(Make-ahead: Layer between waxed paper in airtight container and store for up to 5 days.)*

MAKES 32 COOKIES.

PER COOKIE: about 61 cal, 2 g pro, 3 g total fat (1 g sat. fat), 7 g carb, 1 g fibre, 0 mg chol, 7 mg sodium. % RDI: 1% calcium, 1% iron, 1% folate.

HOW-TO

1

2

3

Peanut butter is stiff, so an offset spatula is the best utensil to use for spreading. Different brands of regular peanut butter contain varying amounts of salt and sugar, so for this recipe, we've used natural peanut butter to ensure the brownies have a perfect salty-sweet balance.

Peanut Butter Brownies

ingredients

6 oz (170 g) **bittersweet chocolate,** chopped

4 oz (115 g) **unsweetened chocolate,** chopped

⅓ cup **butter**

⅓ cup **smooth natural peanut butter,** at room temperature

2 cups **granulated sugar**

1 tsp **vanilla**

4 **eggs**

1⅔ cups **all-purpose flour**

1 cup chopped **unsalted peanuts**

Pinch **salt**

TOPPING:

⅓ cup **butter,** softened

¼ cup **smooth natural peanut butter,** at room temperature

½ tsp **vanilla**

2 cups **icing sugar**

1 tbsp **milk**

3 oz (85 g) **bittersweet chocolate,** melted

method

In saucepan, melt together bittersweet chocolate, unsweetened chocolate, butter and peanut butter over medium-low heat, stirring until smooth; let cool for 10 minutes. Whisk in sugar and vanilla. Whisk in eggs, 1 at a time, whisking well after each. Stir in flour, peanuts and salt. Spread in parchment paper–lined or greased 13- x 9-inch (3.5 L) cake pan.

Bake in 350°F (180°C) oven until cake tester inserted in centre comes out with a few moist crumbs clinging ❶, about 25 minutes. Let cool in pan on rack.

TOPPING: In bowl, beat together butter, peanut butter and vanilla until creamy. Beat in icing sugar in 2 additions; beat in milk. Using paper as handles, transfer brownies to cutting board; peel off paper. Spread peanut butter mixture over brownies ❷. Drizzle with melted chocolate ❸.

Wrap in plastic wrap and refrigerate until firm, about 1 hour. *(Make-ahead: Refrigerate for up to 5 days or overwrap in heavy-duty foil and freeze for up to 1 month.)*

Cut into bars.

MAKES 60 BARS.

PER BAR: about 139 cal, 3 g pro, 7 g total fat (3 g sat. fat), 17 g carb, 1 g fibre, 18 mg chol, 20 mg sodium. % RDI: 1% calcium, 4% iron, 2% vit A, 5% folate.

The nut-studded coconut ganache topping on these brownies was inspired by the icing on a traditional German chocolate cake. Fun fact: The original cake was named for a chocolate inventor by the name of Samuel German — it's not from Germany at all.

German Chocolate Brownies

ingredients

8 oz (225 g) **bittersweet chocolate,** chopped
2 oz (55 g) **unsweetened chocolate,** chopped
1 cup **butter**
2 cups **granulated sugar**
1 tbsp **vanilla**
4 **eggs**
1 cup **all-purpose flour**
¼ tsp **salt**
1⅓ cups **sweetened shredded coconut**
1 cup chopped **pecans**

GERMAN CHOCOLATE ICING:
12 oz (340 g) **white chocolate,** chopped
⅓ cup **whipping cream (35%)**
1 cup **sweetened shredded coconut,** toasted
½ cup chopped **pecans,** toasted
¼ cup **butter**
2 tsp **vanilla**

method

In saucepan, melt together bittersweet chocolate, unsweetened chocolate and butter over medium-low heat, stirring occasionally until smooth; let cool for 10 minutes.

Whisk in sugar and vanilla; whisk in eggs, 1 at a time. With wooden spoon, stir in flour and salt. Fold in coconut and pecans; scrape into parchment paper–lined 13- x 9-inch (3 L) baking dish; smooth top.

Bake in 350°F (180°C) oven until cake tester inserted in centre comes out with a few moist crumbs clinging, about 30 minutes. Let cool in pan on rack.

GERMAN CHOCOLATE ICING: Meanwhile, place white chocolate in heatproof bowl. In saucepan, bring cream just to boil; pour over chocolate, whisking until smooth. Whisk in half of the coconut, the pecans, butter and vanilla. Let cool for 15 minutes. Spread over brownies; sprinkle with remaining coconut. Cover loosely and refrigerate until set, about 1 hour.

Using paper as handles, transfer brownies to cutting board; peel off paper. Cut into bars. *(Make-ahead: Layer between waxed paper in airtight container and refrigerate for up to 3 days or freeze for up to 2 weeks.)*

MAKES 48 BARS.
PER BAR: about 213 cal, 2 g pro, 15 g total fat (8 g sat. fat), 20 g carb, 1 g fibre, 31 mg chol, 71 mg sodium, 97 mg potassium. % RDI: 2% calcium, 6% iron, 5% vit A, 5% folate.

Grinding pecans in a food processor and adding them to the crust gives
these squares a rich and nutty base. You'll need to start with about 2½ cups of vanilla wafers
to make the necessary amount of crumbs.

Chewy Caramel Pecan Squares

ingredients

1¼ cups finely ground **vanilla wafers**
⅓ cup **butter,** melted
¼ cup coarsely ground **pecans**
2 cups **semisweet chocolate chips**

1½ cups chopped **pecans**
1 can (300 mL) **sweetened condensed milk**

method

Stir together ground vanilla wafers, butter and ground pecans until moistened; press into parchment paper–lined 9-inch (2.5 L) square cake pan.

Sprinkle with chocolate chips and chopped pecans; pour condensed milk over top.

Bake in 350°F (180°C) oven until set in centre, about 30 minutes. Let cool in pan on rack for 30 minutes.

Cover and refrigerate until completely cooled, about 1 hour. *(Make-ahead: Remove from pan; wrap in plastic wrap and refrigerate for up to 5 days or overwrap in foil and freeze for up to 1 month.)*

Cut into squares.

MAKES 25 SQUARES.
PER SQUARE: about 203 cal, 3 g pro, 9 g total fat (4 g sat. fat), 21 g carb, 1 g fibre, 12 mg chol, 60 mg sodium, 147 mg potassium. % RDI: 6% calcium, 6% iron, 4% vit A, 2% vit C, 2% folate.

Blondies are similar to brownies but don't usually include chocolate. This recipe adds some white chocolate, ginger and macadamia nuts to the mix to give the squares a decadent edge over plain blondies.

Ginger Macadamia Blondies

ingredients

9 oz (255 g) **white chocolate,** chopped
⅓ cup **butter**
½ cup **granulated sugar**
¼ cup **fancy molasses**
2 **eggs**
1 tsp **vanilla**
1⅓ cups **all-purpose flour**
1½ tsp **ground ginger**

½ tsp each **cinnamon** and **baking soda**
¼ tsp **ground cloves**
Pinch **salt**
½ cup chopped **macadamia nuts**

method

In saucepan over low heat, melt 1 cup of the white chocolate with butter, stirring until smooth. Remove from heat; whisk in sugar and molasses. Whisk in eggs, 1 at a time, whisking well after each; whisk in vanilla.

Whisk together flour, ginger, cinnamon, baking soda, cloves and salt; whisk into chocolate mixture. Stir in nuts and remaining white chocolate. Spread in parchment paper–lined 9-inch (2.5 L) square cake pan.

Bake in 325ºF (160ºC) oven until cake tester inserted in centre comes out clean, about 45 minutes.

Let cool in pan on rack. Cover and refrigerate until chilled, about 2 hours.

Cut into bars.

MAKES ABOUT 32 BARS.
PER BAR: about 119 cal, 2 g pro, 6 g total fat (3 g sat. fat), 14 g carb, trace fibre, 17 mg chol, 46 mg sodium. % RDI: 2% calcium, 4% iron, 2% vit A, 6% folate.

Grinding Spices

Whole spices keep their potency much longer than ground spices, so it pays to grind just the amount you need before adding it to a recipe. You can use a mortar and pestle, but it takes some elbow grease to get a finely textured result. Electric spice grinders and coffee grinders are very efficient at this job, so it's handy to have one in your kitchen. If your coffee grinder is doing double duty, make sure to clean out any pungent spice smells (such as the cloves for this recipe) before you grind your coffee beans. Throw a handful or two of white rice into the grinder and whizz it around until it's powdery. It may take a couple of tries, but the rice should soak up any fragrant oils.

Test Kitchen TIP

Marshmallows become an ooey, gooey topping in this chocolate chip–studded twist on blondies. To cut into squares easily, use a greased knife and make sure the blondies are fridge cold. They make a nice change of pace at a bake sale.

Rocky Road Blondies

ingredients

1 cup **butter,** softened
2½ cups packed **brown sugar**
4 **eggs**
1 tbsp **vanilla**
2½ cups **all-purpose flour**

1¼ tsp **salt**
1¼ cups **semisweet chocolate chips**
2 cups **marshmallows**

method

In large bowl, beat butter with brown sugar until fluffy; beat in eggs, 1 at a time. Beat in vanilla. Whisk flour with salt; stir into butter mixture in 2 additions. Stir in 1 cup of the chocolate chips just until combined. Spread in parchment paper–lined or greased 13- x 9-inch (3.5 L) cake pan; smooth top.

Bake in 350°F (180°C) oven until cake tester inserted in centre comes out with a few moist crumbs clinging, about 25 minutes.

Sprinkle with remaining chocolate chips. Leaving ½-inch (1 cm) border to prevent sticking to sides of pan, sprinkle with marshmallows. Bake until marshmallows are puffed, about 3 minutes.

Let cool in pan on rack. *(Make-ahead: Wrap in plastic wrap and refrigerate for up to 3 days or overwrap in heavy-duty foil and freeze for up to 2 weeks.)*

With greased sharp knife, cut into squares.

MAKES 48 SQUARES.
PER SQUARE: about 134 cal, 1 g pro, 6 g total fat (3 g sat. fat), 21 g carb, 1 g fibre, 26 mg chol, 98 mg sodium, 69 mg potassium. % RDI: 1% calcium, 5% iron, 4% vit A, 7% folate.

The humble look of these easy drop cookies belies their luscious flavour.
You can freeze the unbaked cookies, then bake them fresh when friends drop in.

Candied Ginger & White Chocolate Hermits

ingredients

½ cup **butter,** softened
½ cup **shortening,** softened
⅔ cup packed **brown sugar**
½ cup **granulated sugar**
2 **eggs**
2¼ cups **all-purpose flour**
1 tsp **baking powder**
¾ tsp **ground ginger**
½ tsp **baking soda**

½ tsp each **ground nutmeg**
and **ground allspice**
1 cup finely chopped **crystallized ginger**
6 oz (170 g) **white chocolate,** chopped
1 cup chopped **dried apricots**

method

In large bowl, beat together butter, shortening, brown sugar and granulated sugar until fluffy; beat in eggs, 1 at a time. Whisk together flour, baking powder, ground ginger, baking soda, nutmeg and allspice; stir into butter mixture in 2 additions. Stir in crystallized ginger, white chocolate and apricots.

Drop by 1 tbsp, 2 inches (5 cm) apart, onto greased or parchment paper–lined rimless baking sheets. *(Make-ahead: Freeze on baking sheets until solid. Layer between waxed paper in airtight container and freeze for up to 1 month. Bake from frozen.)*

Bake on top and bottom racks in 350°F (180°C) oven, rotating and switching pans halfway through, until bottoms are golden, 10 to 12 minutes. (Or bake from frozen in 325°F/160°C oven for 20 minutes.)

Let cool on pans on racks for 5 minutes. Transfer to racks; let cool completely. *(Make-ahead: Layer between waxed paper in airtight container and store for up to 5 days or freeze for up to 1 month.)*

MAKES ABOUT 72 COOKIES.
PER COOKIE: about 80 cal, 1 g pro, 4 g total fat (2 g sat. fat), 11 g carb, trace fibre, 9 mg chol, 32 mg sodium. % RDI: 2% calcium, 6% iron, 3% vit A, 2% vit C, 2% folate.

CHANGE IT UP
Pecan Cherry Chocolate Hermits
Omit crystallized ginger, white chocolate and apricots. Add 1¼ cups each toasted chopped pecans, dried cherries and chocolate chips.

Cream cheese makes this traditional Jewish cookie dough tender and toothsome.
Rugalach are often filled with jam, but this one has a luscious combination
of chocolate and hazelnuts wrapped inside.

Chocolate Hazelnut Rugalach

ingredients

1 pkg (250 g) **cream cheese**, softened

1 cup **butter**, softened

¼ cup **granulated sugar**

1 tsp **vanilla**

1¾ cups **all-purpose flour**

⅓ cup **cocoa powder**

¼ tsp **salt**

1 cup **chocolate hazelnut spread** (such as Nutella)

1 cup **sliced hazelnuts**

1 **egg**, beaten

method

In large bowl, beat cream cheese with butter until fluffy; beat in sugar and vanilla. Whisk together flour, cocoa powder and salt; stir into cream cheese mixture in 2 additions. Form dough into rectangle; cut into quarters and shape each into rectangle. Wrap each and refrigerate until firm, about 30 minutes.

On floured surface, roll 1 of the quarters into 12- x 8-inch (30 x 20 cm) rectangle. Spread with one-quarter of the chocolate hazelnut spread; sprinkle with one-quarter of the hazelnuts. Starting at long side, roll into tight log.

Cut log into twelve 1-inch (2.5 cm) thick slices. Arrange slices upright, ¼ inch (5 mm) apart, on 2 parchment paper–lined or greased rimless baking sheets; refrigerate for 30 minutes. Repeat with remaining dough. *(Make-ahead: Freeze until firm, about 30 minutes. Layer between waxed paper in airtight container and freeze for up to 1 month. Thaw before baking.)*

Brush tops with egg. Bake on top and bottom racks in 350°F (180°C) oven, rotating and switching pans halfway through, until darkened and firm to the touch, 20 minutes. Transfer to racks; let cool completely.

MAKES ABOUT 44 COOKIES.
PER COOKIE: about 141 cal, 2 g pro, 10 g total fat (5 g sat. fat), 10 g carb, 1 g fibre, 22 mg chol, 54 mg sodium. % RDI: 1% calcium, 4% iron, 6% vit A, 7% folate.

161

These squares are loaded with banana chips and peanuts for maximum crunchiness.
Breaking the banana chips into small chunks makes it easier to cut the bars later on.
For a twist, replace the peanuts with cashews or toasted unsweetened coconut.

Monkey Bars

ingredients

1½ cups **chocolate wafer crumbs**
⅓ cup **butter,** melted
1½ cups **banana chips,** broken in pieces
1 cup **semisweet chocolate chips**
1 cup **salted roasted peanuts**

¾ cup **peanut butter chips**
1 can (300 mL) **sweetened condensed milk**

method

Stir chocolate wafer crumbs with butter until moistened; press into parchment paper–lined 9-inch (2.5 L) square cake pan.

Sprinkle with banana chips, chocolate chips, peanuts and peanut butter chips; pour sweetened condensed milk over top.

Bake in 350°F (180°C) oven until set in centre, about 30 minutes. Let cool in pan on rack for 30 minutes.

Cover and refrigerate until completely cool, about 1 hour. *(Make-ahead: Remove from pan; wrap in plastic wrap and refrigerate for up to 5 days or overwrap in foil and freeze for up to 1 month.)*

Cut into bars.

MAKES 25 BARS.
PER BAR: about 216 cal, 5 g pro, 13 g total fat (6 g sat. fat), 23 g carb, 2 g fibre, 12 mg chol, 112 mg sodium, 176 mg potassium. % RDI: 5% calcium, 5% iron, 3% vit A, 2% vit C, 6% folate.

Oatmeal cookies are something every cook should have in his or her recipe box.
And this version, dressed up with chocolate chips, is a surefire hit with both kids and adults.

Oatmeal Chocolate Chip Cookies

ingredients

⅔ cup **butter,** softened
1 cup packed **brown sugar**
1 **egg**
2 tsp **vanilla**
1½ cups **large-flake rolled oats**
1 cup **all-purpose flour**

½ tsp each **baking powder** and
  baking soda
¼ tsp **salt**
1½ cups **semisweet chocolate chips**

method

In large bowl, beat butter with brown sugar until fluffy; beat in egg and vanilla. Whisk together oats, flour, baking powder, baking soda and salt; stir into butter mixture until combined. Stir in chocolate chips.

Drop by heaping 1 tbsp, about 2 inches (5 cm) apart, onto parchment paper–lined rimless baking sheets. Bake on top and bottom racks in 375°F (190°C) oven, rotating and switching pans halfway through, until golden, about 12 minutes.

Let cool on pans on racks for 2 minutes. Transfer to racks; let cool completely. *(Make-ahead: Layer between waxed paper in airtight container and store for up to 5 days or freeze for up to 2 weeks.)*

MAKES ABOUT 36 COOKIES.
PER COOKIE: about 119 cal, 1 g pro, 6 g total fat (3 g sat. fat), 16 g carb, 1 g fibre, 16 mg chol, 75 mg sodium. % RDI: 1% calcium, 5% iron, 4% vit A, 4% folate.

Oats come in a variety of textures that are intended for different purposes. All oats – from the simple groat to the smallest rolled variety – are whole grains. They contain all the healthy germ and bran in the kernel, so they're a nutritious addition to all sorts of foods. So what type do you need?

Steel-cut oats: These are whole oat groats (kernels) cut roughly in thirds. They make great porridge but aren't used in baking.

Large-flake rolled oats: All rolled oats are groats that have been steamed and rolled to a specific thickness. Large-flake oats are great for baking when you need a thick, chewy result (like the cookies above).

Quick-cooking rolled oats: These are thinner and suit some baking recipes where a less chewy result is desirable.

Instant oatmeal: These oats are cut into tiny flecks and are designed for making lightning-fast porridge in the morning – not baking.

This chocolaty cookie hides a delicious surprise in the centre: creamy, sweet peanut butter. It's one of the most harmonious flavour pairings in the cookie world.

Surprise Peanut Butter Cookies

ingredients

1 cup **icing sugar**
1 cup **smooth peanut butter**
½ cup **butter,** softened
½ cup each **granulated sugar** and packed **brown sugar**
1 **egg**
1 tsp **vanilla**

1¼ cups **all-purpose flour**
½ cup **cocoa powder**
½ tsp **baking soda**
¼ cup chopped **peanuts**

method

Stir icing sugar with ¾ cup of the peanut butter until smooth. Roll by 1 tsp into 50 balls; place on rimmed baking sheets. Refrigerate until firm, about 30 minutes.

Meanwhile, in large bowl, beat together butter, remaining peanut butter, granulated sugar and brown sugar until fluffy; beat in egg and vanilla. Whisk together flour, cocoa powder and baking soda; stir into butter mixture until combined.

Roll by 1 tbsp into 50 balls; flatten each to make 2-inch (5 cm) round. Place chilled peanut butter ball in centre of each; bring dough up over ball to cover. Roll into smooth ball; place, 2 inches (5 cm) apart, on 2 parchment paper–lined or greased rimless baking sheets. With bottom of round glass or measuring cup, press until about ½ inch (1 cm) thick and edges are cracked. Lightly press peanuts into tops.

Bake on top and bottom racks in 375°F (190°C) oven, rotating and switching pans halfway through, just until set, about 7 minutes.

Let cool on pans on racks for 5 minutes. Transfer to racks; let cool completely. *(Make-ahead: Layer between waxed paper in airtight container and store for up to 5 days or freeze for up to 3 weeks.)*

MAKES 50 COOKIES.
PER COOKIE: about 90 cal, 2 g pro, 5 g total fat (2 g sat. fat), 10 g carb, 1 g fibre, 10 mg chol, 60 mg sodium. % RDI: 1% calcium, 3% iron, 2% vit A, 4% folate.

165

CANADIAN LIVING • THE COMPLETE CHOCOLATE BOOK

Sweet butterscotch squares hide a layer of crystallized ginger and velvety milk chocolate. They make a pretty gift in a clear-topped box tied with ribbon, or a delicious addition to a bake-sale lineup.

Ginger Butterscotch Squares

ingredients

2 cups **gingersnap cookie crumbs**
⅓ cup **butter,** melted
4 oz (115 g) **milk chocolate,** chopped
½ cup **butterscotch chips**
¼ cup chopped **crystallized ginger**
¾ cup packed **dark brown sugar**
2 **eggs**
1 tsp **vanilla**
1 cup **all-purpose flour**
¼ tsp **salt**

TOPPING:
3 oz (85 g) **milk chocolate,** melted
2 tbsp finely chopped **crystallized ginger**

method

Stir gingersnap crumbs with butter until moistened; press into parchment paper–lined 9-inch (2.5 L) square cake pan. Bake in 350°F (180°C) oven until firm, 12 to 15 minutes. Let cool in pan on rack.

Sprinkle milk chocolate, butterscotch chips and ginger over base.

In bowl, whisk together brown sugar, eggs and vanilla until pale and fluffy, about 3 minutes. Stir in flour and salt. Spread over base.

Bake in 375°F (190°C) oven until golden and firm to the touch, 20 to 23 minutes. Let cool in pan on rack. Cut into squares.

TOPPING: Drizzle squares with chocolate; sprinkle with ginger. Let stand until chocolate is set, about 30 minutes. *(Make-ahead: Refrigerate in airtight container for up to 4 days or freeze for up to 2 weeks.)*

MAKES 36 SQUARES.
PER SQUARE: about 122 cal, 2 g pro, 5 g total fat (3 g sat. fat), 17 g carb, 1 g fibre, 16 mg chol, 99 mg sodium, 122 mg potassium. % RDI: 3% calcium, 9% iron, 2% vit A, 2% vit C, 7% folate.

167

CANADIAN LIVING • THE COMPLETE CHOCOLATE BOOK

Coconut and oatmeal lend a crunchy texture to these irresistible drop cookies.
For a nut-free variation, omit the pecans or walnuts.

White Chocolate Butterscotch Oatmeal Chippers

ingredients

½ cup chopped **pecans** or
   walnut halves
1 cup **butter,** softened
1 cup packed **brown sugar**
2 **eggs**
2 tsp **vanilla**
2½ cups **large-flake rolled oats**
1¼ cups **all-purpose flour**

½ cup **sweetened shredded coconut**
1 tsp **baking soda**
½ tsp **salt**
1 cup **white chocolate chips**
½ cup **butterscotch chips**

method

Spread pecans on small rimmed baking sheet; toast in 350°F (180°C) oven until fragrant and golden, about 5 minutes. Let cool.

In large bowl, beat butter with brown sugar until fluffy. Beat in eggs, 1 at a time; beat in vanilla. Whisk together oats, flour, coconut, baking soda and salt. Stir into butter mixture; stir in white chocolate chips, butterscotch chips and pecans.

Drop by heaping 1 tbsp, about 2 inches (5 cm) apart, onto parchment paper–lined or greased rimless baking sheets. Bake on top and bottom racks in 350°F (180°C) oven, rotating and switching pans halfway through, until golden on bottoms, about 12 minutes.

Let cool on pans on racks for 2 minutes. Transfer to racks; let cool completely. *(Make-ahead: Layer between waxed paper in airtight container and store for up to 5 days or freeze for up to 2 weeks.)*

MAKES ABOUT 48 COOKIES.
PER COOKIE: about 124 cal, 2 g pro, 7 g total fat (4 g sat. fat), 14 g carb, 1 g fibre, 21 mg chol, 101 mg sodium. % RDI: 2% calcium, 4% iron, 4% vit A, 4% folate.

This easy-as-pie recipe has been in *Canadian Living*'s recipe archive for decades.
For a larger cookie, simply double the amount of dough per cookie and increase the baking time
by a couple of minutes. They're so tasty you'll want to make them all the time.

Classic Chocolate Chip Cookies

ingredients

1 cup **butter,** softened
1 cup packed **brown sugar**
½ cup **granulated sugar**
2 **eggs**
1 tbsp **vanilla**
2⅓ cups **all-purpose flour**

1 tsp **baking soda**
½ tsp **salt**
2 cups **semisweet chocolate chips**

method

In large bowl, beat together butter, brown sugar and granulated sugar until fluffy. Beat in eggs, 1 at a time; beat in vanilla. Whisk together flour, baking soda and salt; stir into butter mixture until combined. Stir in chocolate chips.

Drop by rounded 1 tbsp, about 2 inches (5 cm) apart, onto parchment paper–lined or greased rimless baking sheets. With fork, flatten to ½-inch (1 cm) thickness. Bake in 375°F (190°C) oven until edges are golden but centres are slightly soft, 8 to 10 minutes.

Let cool on pans on racks for 5 minutes. Transfer to racks; let cool completely. *(Make-ahead: Layer between waxed paper in airtight container and store for up to 5 days.)*

MAKES ABOUT 50 COOKIES.
PER COOKIE: about 113 cal, 1 g pro, 6 g total fat (4 g sat. fat), 15 g carb, 1 g fibre, 17 mg chol, 79 mg sodium, 50 mg potassium. % RDI: 1% calcium, 4% iron, 3% vit A, 6% folate.

These fudgy cookies have a super chocolaty and extremely minty flavour without being overwhelming. To help the cookies keep their round shape, chill the dough well before slicing.

Double-Chocolate Minties

ingredients

8 oz (225 g) **semisweet chocolate,** chopped
¾ cup **unsalted butter,** cubed
1¼ cups **granulated sugar**
2 **eggs**
1¾ cups **all-purpose flour**
½ tsp **baking powder**
Pinch **salt**

PEPPERMINT GANACHE:
½ cup **whipping cream (35%)**
8 oz (225 g) **70% dark chocolate,** finely chopped
2 tsp **peppermint extract**

method

In large heatproof bowl over saucepan of hot (not boiling) water, melt chocolate with butter, stirring occasionally until smooth. Remove from heat. Beat in sugar; beat in eggs, 1 at a time. Whisk together flour, baking powder and salt; stir into chocolate mixture. Refrigerate until firm, about 1 hour.

Roll by rounded 1 tsp into balls; place, about 2 inches (5 cm) apart, on parchment paper–lined rimless baking sheets. Bake in 350°F (180°C) oven until firm to the touch and no longer shiny, 8 to 10 minutes.

Let cool on pans on racks for 5 minutes. Transfer to racks; let cool completely. *(Make-ahead: Layer between waxed paper in airtight container and store for up to 5 days.)*

PEPPERMINT GANACHE: In saucepan, bring cream just to boil. Remove from heat; stir in chocolate until smooth. Stir in peppermint extract; let cool to room temperature.

Spoon or pipe about 1 tsp of the ganache onto flat side of half of the cookies; sandwich with remaining cookies, pressing lightly to bring ganache to edge. Refrigerate on baking sheets until ganache is set, about 10 minutes. *(Make-ahead: Refrigerate in airtight container for up to 5 days. Let come to room temperature before serving.)*

MAKES ABOUT 55 COOKIES.
PER COOKIE: about 109 cal, 1 g pro, 7 g total fat (4 g sat. fat), 12 g carb, 1 g fibre, 16 mg chol, 7 mg sodium, 54 mg potassium. % RDI: 1% calcium, 6% iron, 3% vit A, 4% folate.

These dark, delicious, intensely chocolaty cookies are just the thing when you need a chocolate fix. Team them up with your beverage of choice: milk, tea, chai or cappuccino.

Dark & Dangerous Triple-Chocolate Cookies

ingredients

1 cup **butter,** softened
1 cup **granulated sugar**
½ cup packed **brown sugar**
2 **eggs**
1 tsp **vanilla**
2 cups **all-purpose flour**
½ cup **cocoa powder**
1 tsp **baking soda**

¼ tsp **salt**
1 cup **semisweet chocolate chips**
1 cup **white chocolate chips** or milk chocolate chips

method

In large bowl, beat together butter, granulated sugar and brown sugar until fluffy. Beat in eggs, 1 at a time; beat in vanilla. Whisk together flour, cocoa powder, baking soda and salt; stir into butter mixture. Stir in semisweet chocolate chips and white chocolate chips.

Drop by heaping 1 tbsp, about 2 inches (5 cm) apart, onto parchment paper–lined or greased rimless baking sheets. Bake on top and bottom racks in 350°F (180°C) oven, rotating and switching pans halfway through, until firm to the touch and no longer glossy, about 12 minutes.

Let cool on pans on racks for 2 minutes. Transfer to racks; let cool completely. *(Make-ahead: Layer between waxed paper in airtight container and store for up to 5 days or freeze for up to 2 weeks.)*

MAKES 48 COOKIES.
PER COOKIE: about 120 cal, 1 g pro, 6 g total fat (4 g sat. fat), 15 g carb, 1 g fibre, 21 mg chol, 82 mg sodium. % RDI: 1% calcium, 4% iron, 4% vit A, 4% folate.

{ chewy }

The buttery-rich flavour of macadamia nuts complements the sweetness of these easy, classic drop cookies. Try salted nuts for a salty-sweet version.

TOFFEE, MACADAMIA &
White Chocolate Chunk Cookies

ingredients

1 cup **butter**, softened
1 cup packed **brown sugar**
½ cup **granulated sugar**
2 **eggs**
1 tsp **vanilla**
2⅓ cups **all-purpose flour**
1 tsp **baking soda**
¼ tsp **salt**

12 oz (340 g) **white chocolate**, coarsely chopped
¾ cup **macadamia nuts**, toasted and coarsely chopped
½ cup **toffee bits**

method

In large bowl, beat together butter, brown sugar and granulated sugar until fluffy; beat in eggs, 1 at a time, beating well after each. Beat in vanilla. Whisk together flour, baking soda and salt; stir into butter mixture. Stir in white chocolate, macadamia nuts and toffee bits.

Drop by rounded 1 tbsp onto greased or parchment paper–lined rimless baking sheets. Bake in 350°F (180°C) oven until edges are golden, about 12 minutes.

Let cool on pans on racks for 5 minutes. Transfer to racks; let cool completely. *(Make-ahead: Store in airtight container for up to 5 days.)*

MAKES ABOUT 45 COOKIES.
PER COOKIE: about 157 cal, 2 g pro, 9 g total fat (5 g sat. fat), 18 g carb, trace fibre, 21 mg chol, 90 mg sodium, 58 mg potassium. % RDI: 2% calcium, 4% iron, 4% vit A, 7% folate.

Freshly Baked Cookies, Anytime

This simple drop cookie dough freezes really well. Scoop portions of dough onto a baking sheet and freeze until firm. Transfer the portions to a resealable freezer bag and freeze for up to 1 month. Thaw and bake them any day you need a batch of fresh cookies, even when you're short on time.

Chunks of walnuts make these cookies delightfully crunchy, while the shredded coconut gives them a slight tropical flavour that's so nice with the bittersweet and milk chocolates.

Double-Chocolate Walnut Chunks

ingredients

1 cup chopped **walnuts**
6 oz (170 g) **bittersweet chocolate,** chopped
¼ cup **unsalted butter,** cubed
2 **eggs**
¾ cup **granulated sugar**
1 tsp **vanilla**
⅓ cup **all-purpose flour**

¼ cup **cocoa powder,** sifted
½ tsp **baking powder**
¼ tsp **salt**
¾ cup **sweetened shredded coconut**
3 oz (85 g) **milk chocolate,** chopped

method

On baking sheet, toast walnuts in 350°F (180°C) oven until fragrant, about 8 minutes. Set aside.

In heatproof bowl over saucepan of hot (not boiling) water, melt bittersweet chocolate with butter, stirring occasionally. Let cool slightly.

In large bowl, beat eggs with sugar until pale, about 2 minutes. Stir in vanilla and bittersweet chocolate mixture. Whisk together flour, cocoa powder, baking powder and salt; stir into bittersweet chocolate mixture. Stir in walnuts, coconut and milk chocolate.

Drop by heaping 1 tbsp, about 2 inches (5 cm) apart, onto parchment paper–lined or greased rimless baking sheets. Bake in 350°F (180°C) oven until no longer shiny and tops begin to crack, about 10 minutes.

Let cool on pans on racks for 2 minutes; if desired, flatten slightly with spatula. Transfer to racks; let cool completely.

MAKES ABOUT 36 COOKIES.
PER COOKIE: about 107 cal, 2 g pro, 7 g total fat (3 g sat. fat), 11 g carb, 1 g fibre, 14 mg chol, 31 mg sodium, 50 mg potassium. % RDI: 1% calcium, 4% iron, 2% vit A, 3% folate.

Test Kitchen TIP

Keeping Walnuts Fresh

For the best flavour, choose California walnut halves and chop them yourself. Packaged prechopped nuts tend to go rancid at room temperature on store shelves. If you stock up on walnuts when they're on sale, freeze them in a resealable freezer bag for up to 6 months.

melty

Terrine au Chocolat 179

Boca Negra With Rum-Soaked Cherries 180

Two-Tone Peppermint Bark 181

Candied Orange & Ginger Bark 182

Really Good Rum Balls 184

Mocha Rosettes 185

Brazilian Brigadeiros 187

Gluten-Free Chocolate-Dipped Peanut Butter Balls 188

Cocoa Orange Truffles 189

Dark Chocolate Truffles 190

Irish Cream Chocolate Truffles 192

White Chocolate Praline Truffles 193

Ganache-Filled Chocolates 195

Scotch on the Rocks Truffle Cups 196

Gingerbread Truffles 197

Earl Grey Chocolate Truffles 198

White Chocolate Cinnamon Butter Truffles 200

Coconut Rum Truffles 201

Chocolate Cherry Cups 202

Chocolate Goat's Milk Fudge 204

Cranberry Jewel Fudge 205

Crispy Coffee Truffle Slice 206

White Chocolate Chai Fudge 208

Triple-Nut Chocolate Fudge 209

Classic Nanaimo Bars 210

Easy Chocolate Walnut Fudge 212

Hazelnut Mochaccino Fudge 213

Reverse Nanaimo Bars 215

Chocolate Mint Nanaimo Bars 216

Peanut Butter Cups 217

Chocoholics might be satisfied with just a small sliver of this rich, nut-topped pâté.
It makes a sophisticated end to a special-occasion meal. Add a handful of fresh strawberries
and raspberries for a pretty (and delicious) garnish.

Terrine au Chocolat

ingredients

½ cup **granulated sugar**
½ cup strong brewed **coffee**
1 cup **butter**
8 oz (225 g) **bittersweet chocolate,**
  chopped

4 **eggs**
1 tbsp **all-purpose flour**
½ cup chopped **pistachios**

method

Line 8- x 4-inch (1.5 L) loaf pan with parchment paper; trim paper even with rim. Set aside.

In heatproof bowl over saucepan of hot (not boiling) water, stir sugar with coffee until dissolved. Add butter and chocolate; melt, stirring occasionally, until smooth. Set aside.

In large bowl, whisk eggs until pale; sift flour over top and whisk in. Fold in chocolate mixture until no streaks remain; pour into prepared pan.

Place pan in larger pan; pour in enough hot water into larger pan to come halfway up sides of loaf pan. Bake in 350°F (180°C) oven until top is set, edges are puffed and centre is still slightly jiggly, about 45 minutes.

Transfer loaf pan to rack; let cool completely. Cover with plastic wrap and refrigerate until firm, about 12 hours. *(Make-ahead: Refrigerate for up to 2 days. Let stand at room temperature for 1 hour before serving.)*

Run knife around sides of pan to loosen paper. Invert serving platter over top; turn over. Remove pan; peel off paper. Sprinkle pistachios over top.

MAKES 12 SERVINGS.

PER SERVING: about 331 cal, 5 g pro, 26 g total fat (14 g sat. fat), 21 g carb, 2 g fibre, 110 mg chol, 177 mg sodium. % RDI: 3% calcium, 9% iron, 17% vit A, 5% folate.

These moist little cakes, each with a texture like that of a dense
chocolate pâté, will thrill chocolate lovers. The rum-soaked cherries also make a
heavenly topping for plain cheesecake.

Boca Negra
WITH RUM-SOAKED CHERRIES

ingredients

4½ oz (130 g) **bittersweet chocolate**,
   finely chopped
½ cup **granulated sugar**
3 tbsp **dark rum** or coffee
⅓ cup **butter**, softened
2 **eggs**
2 tsp **all-purpose flour**

RUM-SOAKED CHERRIES:
2 tbsp packed **brown sugar**
2 tbsp **dark rum**
1 cup drained **bottled pitted sour cherries**
   in syrup

method

RUM-SOAKED CHERRIES: In bowl, stir brown sugar with rum until dissolved; stir in cherries. Let stand for 1 hour. *(Make-ahead: Cover and refrigerate for up to 2 days. Gently rewarm to serve.)*

Grease eight ¾-cup (175 mL) ramekins or mini soufflé dishes; line bottoms with parchment paper. Place in roasting pan.

Place chocolate in heatproof bowl. In small saucepan over medium heat, stir together sugar, rum and 1 tbsp water just until sugar is dissolved and bubbles appear at edge. Pour over chocolate, whisking until smooth. Whisk in butter in 2 additions.

In separate bowl, whisk eggs until foamy; whisk in flour, then chocolate mixture. Pour into prepared ramekins. Pour enough boiling water into roasting pan to come 1 inch (2.5 cm) up sides of ramekins.

Bake in 350°F (180°C) oven until shiny and slightly puffed, about 22 minutes. Remove from pan; let cool for 10 minutes. *(Make-ahead: Let cool completely. Cover and refrigerate for up to 2 days. To unmould, dip each ramekin into pan of hot water for 20 seconds; turn out as directed below.)*

Run tip of small knife around side of each cake to loosen. Invert serving plate over dish. Turn over; lift off ramekin and peel off paper. Spoon cherries over top. Serve warm or at room temperature

MAKES 8 SERVINGS.
PER SERVING: about 262 cal, 4 g pro, 18 g total fat (10 g sat. fat), 25 g carb, 3 g fibre, 67 mg chol, 74 mg sodium. % RDI: 2% calcium, 10% iron, 9% vit A, 5% folate.

Package this delightful gift in cellophane bags and tie with festive ribbon to make the holidays bright. Of course, for peppermint and chocolate lovers, this is an easy year-round treat.

Two-Tone Peppermint Bark

ingredients

12 oz (340 g) **bittersweet chocolate,** chopped

¾ tsp **peppermint extract**

12 oz (340 g) **white chocolate,** chopped

2 tbsp coarsely crushed **candy canes** or hard peppermint candies

method

Line 15- x 10-inch (38 x 25 cm) rimmed baking sheet with foil; grease foil. Set aside.

In heatproof bowl over saucepan of hot (not boiling) water, melt bittersweet chocolate, stirring until smooth. Stir in peppermint extract. Spread into 10-inch (25 cm) square on prepared pan. Let stand just until set but not hard, about 15 minutes at room temperature, or 8 minutes in refrigerator.

In clean heatproof bowl over saucepan of hot (not boiling) water, melt white chocolate, stirring until smooth. Spread over bittersweet chocolate; sprinkle with crushed candy. Refrigerate until firm, about 1 hour.

Break into chunks. *(Make-ahead: Layer between waxed paper in airtight container and refrigerate for up to 2 weeks.)*

MAKES 24 SERVINGS.
PER SERVING: about 162 cal, 2 g pro, 10 g total fat (6 g sat. fat), 17 g carb, 1 g fibre, 1 mg chol, 13 mg sodium. % RDI: 4% calcium, 4% iron.

181

Crushing Candy

To keep things tidy, place candy canes or candies in a resealable plastic bag and pound them with the flat side of a meat mallet or rolling pin until coarse but not powdery. Bigger chunks are tastier in this bark.

Test Kitchen TIP

Adding candied orange slices to this milk chocolate bark gives it a pretty, crystalline finish. You'll have a few orange slices left over; they make a tasty garnish for cakes and other desserts.

Candied Orange & Ginger Bark

ingredients

1½ lb (675 g) **bittersweet chocolate,** chopped
⅔ cup shelled **pistachios,** coarsely chopped
⅓ cup **crystallized ginger,** chopped
⅓ cup **dried cranberries**

CANDIED ORANGE:
1 **orange**
2½ cups **granulated sugar**

method

CANDIED ORANGE: Cut orange in half from stem to blossom end. Place, cut sides down, on work surface; cut crosswise into ¼-inch (5 mm) thick half-moons.

In saucepan, cover orange slices with cold water and bring to gentle boil; immediately drain, discarding water. With fresh water, repeat boiling and draining twice.

In saucepan, stir 2 cups of the sugar with 2 cups water over medium heat until sugar is dissolved. Add orange slices; reduce heat to low and simmer for 45 minutes.

Using slotted spoon, transfer orange slices to rack over baking sheet; let stand until dry, about 12 hours. *(Make-ahead: Let stand for up to 24 hours.)* Dredge slices in remaining sugar, pressing to coat. Cut each slice into 3 triangles.

In heatproof bowl over saucepan of hot (not boiling) water, melt chocolate, stirring until smooth. Mix together pistachios, ginger and cranberries; stir half into chocolate. Scrape into parchment paper–lined 13- x 9-inch (3.5 L) cake pan, smoothing top. Sprinkle evenly with remaining ginger mixture.

Arrange 18 candied orange pieces on top. Refrigerate until firm, about 45 minutes. Cut into chunks. *(Make-ahead: Refrigerate in airtight container for up to 2 days.)*

MAKES ABOUT 18 SERVINGS.
PER SERVING: about 285 cal, 3 g pro, 17 g total fat (9 g sat. fat), 35 g carb, 4 g fibre, 2 mg chol, 6 mg sodium, 376 mg potassium. % RDI: 4% calcium, 25% iron, 1% vit A, 8% vit C, 1% folate.

There are rum ball recipes galore, but none better than this one. Chocolate shot is another name for chocolate sprinkles (the sort you'd find on top of a doughnut). You'll find them in the baking aisle of the grocery store or in bulk food stores. They may also go by the name Chocolate Décors.

Really Good Rum Balls

ingredients

1 cup **icing sugar**
1 cup **ground almonds**
3 oz (85 g) **bittersweet chocolate,**
  grated

⅓ cup **dark rum**
1 tsp **vanilla**
½ cup **chocolate shot**

method

In large bowl, whisk together icing sugar, almonds and bittersweet chocolate. Stir in ¼ cup of the rum and vanilla until mixture forms solid moist mass; press together. Chill until firm enough to roll, about 15 minutes.

Roll by rounded 1 tsp into balls, moistening and wiping hands with damp cloth as needed. Place on waxed paper–lined baking sheets.

Pour remaining rum into shallow bowl. Pour chocolate shot into separate shallow bowl. Roll balls in rum then in chocolate shot, pressing lightly to adhere. Let dry on baking sheet, about 1 hour.

Refrigerate until firm, about 2 hours. *(Make-ahead: Layer between waxed paper in airtight container and refrigerate for up to 1 month or freeze for up to 2 months.)*

MAKES ABOUT 36 BALLS.
PER BALL: about 57 cal, 1 g pro, 3 g total fat (1 g sat. fat), 6 g carb, 1 g fibre, 0 mg chol, 1 mg sodium.
% RDI: 1% calcium, 2% iron, 1% folate.

The Best Rum for the Job

Rum balls should taste strongly and unapologetically of rum. The dark type has the richest flavour and will shine through the chocolate and other flavourings. You can use amber rum in a pinch, but save your white rum for cocktails – it's just too mild for this treat.

Full of flavour but lower in fat than many traditional cookies, these meringues melt in your mouth. The touch of coffee really makes the chocolate flavour pop.

Mocha Rosettes

ingredients

¼ cup **cocoa powder**
1 oz (30 g) **unsweetened chocolate**
¼ cup **icing sugar**
2 tbsp **cornstarch**

3 **egg whites**
2 tsp **instant coffee granules**
⅔ cup **granulated sugar**

method

In food processor, chop together cocoa powder, chocolate, icing sugar and cornstarch until powdery.

In bowl, stir egg whites with coffee granules; let stand until granules are dissolved, about 5 minutes. Beat until soft peaks form. Beat in sugar, 2 tbsp at a time, until stiff glossy peaks form. Sprinkle with half of the cocoa mixture; fold in. Repeat with remaining cocoa mixture.

Spoon into piping bag fitted with ½-inch (1 cm) star tip; pipe rosettes, 1 inch (2.5 cm) apart, onto 2 parchment paper–lined or greased rimless baking sheets (or drop by 1 tbsp).

Bake on top and bottom racks in 300°F (150°C) oven, rotating and switching pans halfway through, until firm to light touch, 20 to 25 minutes.

Let cool on pans on racks for 3 minutes. Transfer to racks; let cool completely. *(Make-ahead: Store in airtight container for up to 2 weeks or freeze for up to 1 month.)*

MAKES 40 COOKIES.
PER COOKIE: about 24 cal, trace pro, 1 g total fat (trace sat. fat), 5 g carb, trace fibre, 0 mg chol, 8 mg sodium. % RDI: 1% iron.

185

These Brazilian candy treats are said to be named for a brigadier general.
They look like truffles but are made with sweetened condensed milk,
a South American pantry staple.

Brazilian Brigadeiros

ingredients

3 tbsp **cocoa powder,** sifted
1 can (300 mL) **sweetened
condensed milk**

1 tbsp **unsalted butter**
½ cup **chocolate shot**
 (see Tip, page 265)

method

In bowl, stir cocoa powder with ¼ cup of the sweetened condensed milk until smooth. Stir in remaining sweetened condensed milk.

In small saucepan, melt butter over medium heat. Using heatproof spatula, stir in milk mixture; cook, stirring constantly and scraping bottom of pan to prevent scorching, until thickened, glossy and mixture holds wide trail after spatula is pulled through centre, 12 to 14 minutes. Immediately scrape into buttered shallow dish. Let cool enough to handle, about 20 minutes.

Place chocolate shot in small shallow bowl. With well-buttered hands, roll milk mixture by 1 tsp into balls; immediately roll each in chocolate shot. *(Make-ahead: Layer between waxed paper in airtight container and store for up to 24 hours.)*

Nestle into paper candy cups, if desired.

MAKES 36 PIECES.
PER PIECE: about 46 cal, 1 g pro, 1 g total fat (1 g sat. fat), 8 g carb, trace fibre, 5 mg chol, 14 mg sodium, 52 mg potassium. % RDI: 3% calcium, 1% iron, 1% vit A.

187

Sifting Cocoa Powder

Some containers of cocoa powder are lumpier than others. Sifting cocoa before adding it to other ingredients removes the lumps and ensures that it will seamlessly incorporate into the recipe. It's a step you can do anytime you're baking, whether the recipe calls for it specifically or not.

Gluten-free icing sugar is available at health food and bulk food stores. While you're at the store, look for natural peanut butter that's made from peanuts only or for brands that have no icing sugar added. Stir the peanut butter well before using because the oil rises to the top.

GLUTEN-FREE

Chocolate-Dipped Peanut Butter Balls

ingredients

1½ cups **smooth natural peanut butter**
¼ cup **butter,** softened
½ tsp **vanilla**
2 cups **gluten-free icing sugar**
5 oz (140 g) **semisweet chocolate** or
  bittersweet chocolate, chopped

2 tsp **shortening**
¼ cup **peanut butter chips**

method

In heatproof bowl over saucepan of hot (not boiling) water, melt peanut butter with butter, stirring until smooth. Stir in vanilla. Stir in icing sugar until smooth and thickened. Let stand until cool enough to handle, about 5 minutes.

Roll dough by rounded 1 tsp into balls; place on parchment paper– or waxed paper–lined large rimmed baking sheet. Refrigerate until firm, about 30 minutes.

Meanwhile, in clean heatproof bowl over saucepan of hot (not boiling) water, melt semisweet chocolate with shortening. Skewer each peanut butter ball with toothpick; dip into chocolate mixture. Place on parchment paper– or waxed paper–lined baking sheet; refrigerate until firm, about 30 minutes.

In microwaveable dish or saucepan, melt peanut butter chips, stirring until smooth; drizzle over balls. Let stand until set. *(Make-ahead: Layer between waxed paper in airtight container and refrigerate for up to 1 week or freeze for up to 2 weeks.)*

MAKES ABOUT 54 PIECES.
PER PIECE: about 84 cal, 2 g pro, 6 g total fat (2 g sat. fat), 7 g carb, 1 g fibre, 3 mg chol, 44 mg sodium. % RDI: 1% iron, 1% vit A, 3% folate.

These cocoa-dusted truffles hold a velvety orange-scented chocolate ganache.
For a kid-friendly version, substitute orange juice for the liqueur.

Cocoa Orange Truffles

ingredients

8 oz (225 g) **semisweet chocolate**, finely chopped
½ cup **whipping cream (35%)**
4 tsp **orange liqueur** (such as Grand Marnier)
1 tbsp grated **orange zest**

COATING:
8 oz (225 g) **semisweet chocolate**, chopped
½ cup **cocoa powder**

method

Place chocolate in heatproof bowl. In small saucepan, heat cream over medium heat just until bubbles form around edge; pour over chocolate, whisking until smooth. Fold in liqueur and orange zest. Cover and refrigerate until thickened and cold, about 2 hours.

Using melon baller or small spoon, drop by rounded 1 tsp onto waxed paper–lined rimmed baking sheet. Refrigerate for 30 minutes. Gently roll each ball between fingertips to round off. Freeze until hardened and almost solid, about 1 hour.

COATING: In heatproof bowl over saucepan of hot (not boiling) water, melt chocolate, stirring until smooth; let cool slightly. Sift cocoa powder into pie plate. Using 2 forks, dip each ball into chocolate, letting excess drip off. (If chocolate thickens, rewarm gently.) Place balls in cocoa powder. Using 2 clean forks, roll in cocoa; refrigerate on waxed paper–lined rimmed baking sheet until hardened.

Place in candy cups; refrigerate in airtight container until serving. *(Make-ahead: Refrigerate for up to 1 week or freeze for up to 3 months.)*

MAKES ABOUT 42 TRUFFLES.

PER TRUFFLE: about 65 cal, 1 g pro, 4 g total fat (3 g sat. fat), 8 g carb, 1 g fibre, 4 mg chol, 2 mg sodium, 68 mg potassium. % RDI: 1% calcium, 4% iron, 1% vit A.

CHANGE IT UP
Hazelnut Truffles
Replace orange liqueur with hazelnut liqueur (such as Frangelico). Replace cocoa powder with crushed hazelnuts.

Cool Down

If the chocolate filling gets too soft and sticky when you're shaping it into balls, refrigerate it for a few minutes to return it to the proper texture.

Test Kitchen TIP

These sinfully rich chocolates simply melt in your mouth. The dark chocolate main recipe is just a place to start — there are also two gorgeous variations. Truffles freeze beautifully, so you can make them well ahead for holiday parties and gifts.

Dark Chocolate Truffles

ingredients

8 oz (225 g) **semisweet chocolate** or bittersweet chocolate, finely chopped
⅔ cup **whipping cream (35%)**
¼ cup **butter,** cubed
1 tbsp **vanilla**

COATING:
8 oz (225 g) **semisweet chocolate** or bittersweet chocolate, chopped

method

Place chocolate in heatproof bowl. In saucepan, heat cream with butter just until butter is melted and bubbles form around edge. Pour over chocolate; whisk until smooth. Whisk in vanilla. Cover and refrigerate until firm, about 2 hours.

Using melon baller or teaspoon, drop by rounded 1 tsp onto waxed paper–lined rimmed baking sheets. Gently roll each ball between fingertips to round off. Freeze until hard, about 1 hour. *(Make-ahead: Cover and freeze for up to 24 hours.)*

COATING: In heatproof bowl over saucepan of hot (not boiling) water, melt half of the chocolate at a time, stirring often. Remove from heat and let cool slightly.

Working with 1 pan of truffles at a time and using 2 forks, dip each into chocolate, tapping forks on edge of bowl to remove excess. Return to waxed paper–lined baking sheet. Refrigerate until coating is hardened, about 2 hours. *(Make-ahead: Layer between waxed paper in airtight container and refrigerate for up to 1 week or freeze for up to 3 months.)*

Place in candy cups, if desired.

MAKES ABOUT 32 TRUFFLES.
PER TRUFFLE: about 93 cal, 1 g pro, 7 g total fat (4 g sat. fat), 9 g carb, 1 g fibre, 10 mg chol, 13 mg sodium, 53 mg potassium. % RDI: 1% calcium, 3% iron, 3% vit A.

CHANGE IT UP
Cinnamon Pistachio Truffles
Add ½ tsp cinnamon along with vanilla. After dipping truffles in coating, roll in 1½ cups finely chopped toasted natural pistachios.

Hazelnut Truffles
Reduce whipping cream to ½ cup; replace vanilla with 3 tbsp hazelnut liqueur (such as Frangelico). After dipping truffles in coating, roll in 1½ cups finely chopped toasted hazelnuts.

From left: Hazelnut Truffles, Dark Chocolate Truffles and Cinnamon Pistachio Truffles

Irish cream liqueur is a popular flavouring in coffee, so why not add it to rich truffles? The cocoa powder dusting gives the first bite a hint of bitterness that then gives way to the creamy, sweet ganache below.

Irish Cream Chocolate Truffles

ingredients

8 oz (225 g) **milk chocolate,** chopped

4 oz (115 g) **bittersweet chocolate,** chopped

⅓ cup **whipping cream (35%)**

2 tbsp **unsalted butter**

Pinch **salt**

¼ cup **Irish cream liqueur** (such as Baileys Original liqueur)

⅓ cup **cocoa powder,** sifted

method

In food processor, chop milk chocolate with bittersweet chocolate until in fine pieces.

In saucepan, bring cream, butter and salt just to boil. Pour over chocolate in food processor; process until smooth. Add liqueur; process to combine. Scrape into shallow dish; cover and chill until firm, about 2 hours.

Using melon baller or teaspoon, drop by heaping 1 tsp onto waxed paper–lined rimmed baking sheets to make 36 pieces. Gently roll each ball between fingertips to round off. Refrigerate until firm, about 1 hour.

Place cocoa powder in small shallow dish; roll truffle centres in cocoa powder until coated.

MAKES 36 TRUFFLES.

PER TRUFFLE: about 69 cal, 1 g pro, 5 g total fat (3 g sat. fat), 6 g carb, 1 g fibre, 6 mg chol, 8 mg sodium, 32 mg potassium. % RDI: 1% calcium, 2% iron, 2% vit A.

The crisp praline coating makes each bite of these white chocolate truffles crunchy and divine. Praline is usually made with pecans, but this one is more like a brittle made with toasted hazelnuts and almonds.

White Chocolate Praline Truffles

ingredients

12 oz (340 g) **white chocolate,** finely chopped
⅓ cup **whipping cream (35%)**
¼ cup **butter,** cubed
1 tbsp **vanilla**
1 tbsp **hazelnut liqueur** (such as Frangelico)

PRALINE:
2 tsp **vegetable oil**
½ cup each **natural almonds** and **hazelnuts**
1 cup **granulated sugar**
⅛ tsp **cream of tartar**

method

PRALINE: Brush oil over rimmed baking sheet; set aside. Spread almonds and hazelnuts on separate rimmed baking sheets; toast in 350°F (180°C) oven until fragrant, about 10 minutes. Transfer hazelnuts to clean tea towel; rub briskly to remove as much of the skin as possible. Let cool.

In heavy saucepan, stir together sugar, ½ cup water and cream of tartar; bring to boil over medium-high heat. Cook, without stirring but brushing down side of pan occasionally with pastry brush dipped in cold water, until light tea colour, about 15 minutes. Stir in nuts.

Spread nut mixture on prepared pan; let cool to room temperature. Break into small pieces. In food processor, grind to make about 1½ cups praline. Set aside.

In large heatproof bowl over saucepan of hot (not boiling) water, heat white chocolate, stirring, until about half is melted. Remove from heat.

Meanwhile, in separate saucepan, heat cream with butter just until butter is melted and bubbles form around edge; pour over chocolate, whisking until smooth. Whisk in vanilla and liqueur. Stir in ½ cup of the praline. Cover and refrigerate until firm, about 2 hours.

Using melon baller or teaspoon, drop chocolate mixture by rounded 1 tsp onto waxed paper–lined rimmed baking sheets. Gently roll each ball between fingertips to round off. Freeze until solid, about 1 hour. *(Make-ahead: Cover and freeze for up to 24 hours.)*

Spread remaining praline in shallow dish. Roll each truffle in praline until coated. Refrigerate until hardened, about 2 hours. *(Make-ahead: Layer between waxed paper in airtight container and refrigerate for up to 1 week or freeze for up to 1 month.)*

MAKES ABOUT 36 TRUFFLES.
PER TRUFFLE: about 118 cal, 1 g pro, 7 g total fat (3 g sat. fat), 12 g carb, trace fibre, 9 mg chol, 23 mg sodium. % RDI: 3% calcium, 1% iron, 2% vit A, 2% folate.

How to Use Up Leftover Praline

Any leftover ground praline is delicious as a topping for ice cream or sprinkled over plain cheesecake.

Tempering chocolate takes time, patience and a candy thermometer,
but it gives beautiful results. The finished chocolates are smooth and shiny, and yield with a
satisfying snap when you bite into them.

Ganache-Filled Chocolates

ingredients

8 oz (225 g) **70% dark chocolate,** grated

GANACHE:
2 oz (55 g) **70% dark chocolate,** grated
1 oz (30 g) **milk chocolate,** grated
¼ cup **whipping cream (35%)**
2 tbsp **liqueur** (such as Frangelico, Kahlúa, Tia Maria or amaretto)

method

GANACHE: Place dark chocolate and milk chocolate in heatproof bowl. In small saucepan, heat cream until steaming and small bubbles form around edge. Pour over chocolate; stir until melted and smooth. Stir in liqueur. Let cool to room temperature.

Polish chocolate moulds with soft dry cloth or cotton batting; set aside.

In heatproof bowl over saucepan of hot (not boiling) water, melt chocolate, stirring often, until smooth and candy thermometer reads 115°F (46°C). Remove bowl from saucepan. Place over bowl of cold water; stir constantly until temperature falls to 80°F (27°C). Replace bowl over hot water or place on heating pad; stir constantly until temperature reaches 88°F (31°C). Hold between 88 and 92°F (31 and 33°C) while moulding.

Place rack over waxed paper– or parchment paper–lined baking sheet; set aside.

Spoon tempered chocolate into moulds, filling each to top. Using metal spatula, scrape across top of mould to remove excess; return excess to bowl.

Turn moulds upside down over bowl; tap moulds to remove excess. Let stand upside down on rack for 30 seconds, allowing excess to drip out, leaving thin coating on moulds. Scrape to level top of moulds. Refrigerate for 5 minutes.

Using pastry bag fitted with ¼-inch (5 mm) plain tip, pipe ganache into each mould until ⅛ inch (3 mm) from top. Tap mould gently. Refrigerate for 10 minutes.

If necessary, reheat remaining tempered chocolate to between 88 and 92°F (31 and 33°C). Pour over ganache in moulds. Using metal spatula, scrape across top of mould to remove excess; return excess to bowl. Refrigerate until chocolate is set and has shrunk away from sides of moulds, about 20 minutes. Unmould onto tray. *(Make-ahead: Store in airtight container at room temperature for up to 2 weeks.)*

MAKES 24 PIECES.
PER PIECE: about 90 cal, 1 g pro, 6 g total fat (4 g sat. fat), 7 g carb, 1 g fibre, 4 mg chol, 6 mg sodium, 86 mg potassium. % RDI: 1% calcium, 10% iron, 1% vit A.

Little truffle cups are as decadent as rolled truffles but simpler to prepare –
just mix, pour and enjoy. Try an assortment of flavours for a party or make them to give as gifts.

Scotch on the Rocks Truffle Cups

ingredients

8 oz (225 g) **bittersweet chocolate,** chopped
⅔ cup **whipping cream (35%)**
2 tbsp **unsalted butter**
1 tbsp **corn syrup**

2 tbsp **Scotch whisky**
1 tbsp **coarse sugar**

method

Place chocolate in 4-cup (1 L) glass measure. In small saucepan, heat together cream, butter and corn syrup just until butter is melted and bubbles form around edge; pour over chocolate, whisking until smooth. Whisk in Scotch whisky.

Line mini muffin cups with paper or foil candy cups. Pour about 1 tbsp chocolate mixture into each; tap tray on counter to settle mixture. Sprinkle with sugar. Refrigerate until set and firm, about 1 hour. *(Make-ahead: Refrigerate in airtight container for up to 1 week.)*

MAKES ABOUT 40 PIECES.
PER PIECE: about 52 cal, 1 g pro, 5 g total fat (3 g sat. fat), 2 g carb, 1 g fibre, 7 mg chol, 3 mg sodium.
% RDI: 1% calcium, 3% iron, 2% vit A.

CHANGE IT UP

Dry Gin Martini Truffle Cups
Substitute gin for Scotch whisky. Omit sugar. Top each cup with shelled pistachio.

Dark & Stormy Truffle Cups
Substitute ginger liqueur or dark rum for Scotch whisky. Omit sugar. Sprinkle each cup with chopped crystallized ginger.

Orange Blossom Truffle Cups
Substitute orange liqueur for Scotch whisky. Omit sugar. Sprinkle each cup with thinly sliced candied orange.

Test Kitchen TIP

Where to Find Coarse Sugar

You'll find this decorating staple in the baking section of the supermarket (especially during the holidays), in bulk stores and in the cake decorating sections of craft stores. It's sometimes labelled "decorating sugar" and comes in a rainbow of colours. Plain untinted is the sophisticated choice for these fancy truffle cups.

Ginger, cinnamon and nutmeg infuse these truffles with subtle gingerbread flavours.
Grated fresh nutmeg has the best fragrance; keep whole nutmegs in your spice drawer and
grate on a palm-size nutmeg grater whenever you need some in a recipe.

Gingerbread Truffles

ingredients

¾ cup **whipping cream (35%)**
1 **cinnamon stick,** broken in pieces
2 slices **fresh ginger**
¼ tsp grated **nutmeg**
¼ cup **unsalted butter,** cubed
2 bars (each 100 g) **milk chocolate,**
  finely chopped
1 bar (100 g) **70% dark chocolate,**
  finely chopped

COATING:
8 oz (225 g) **70% dark chocolate,**
  finely chopped

GARNISH:
36 small pieces **crystallized ginger**

method

In saucepan, heat together cream, cinnamon,
ginger and nutmeg until bubbles form around
edge; remove from heat. Cover and let steep
for 1 hour. Strain through cheesecloth-lined
sieve into clean saucepan. Add butter; heat
until melted and bubbles form around edge.

Place milk chocolate and dark chocolate in
heatproof bowl; whisk in cream mixture,
stirring until chocolate is melted and smooth.
Cover and refrigerate until firm, 3 hours.
(Make-ahead: Refrigerate for up to 24 hours.)

Using melon baller or teaspoon, drop by
heaping 1 tsp onto waxed paper–lined
rimmed baking sheets to make 36 pieces.
Gently roll each ball between fingertips to
round off. Refrigerate until hard, about
1 hour. Reroll to smooth edges; refrigerate.
*(Make-ahead: Cover and refrigerate for up
to 24 hours.)*

COATING: In heatproof bowl over saucepan
of hot (not boiling) water, melt chocolate,
stirring occasionally, until no large pieces
remain and candy thermometer reads 115°F
(46°C). Remove bowl from saucepan. Place
over bowl of cold water; stir constantly until
temperature falls to 80°F (27°C). Replace
bowl over hot water or place on heating pad;
stir until temperature reaches 88°F (31°C).
Hold between 88 and 92°F (31 and 33°C)
while using.

Using candy-dipping fork or 2 forks, dip each
truffle centre into chocolate, tapping fork on
edge of bowl to remove excess. Place on
waxed paper–lined rimmed baking sheet.

GARNISH: Using skewer or toothpick, dab
small amount of remaining melted chocolate
onto each piece of crystallized ginger. Centre
on top of each truffle. Refrigerate until
coating is hardened, about 2 hours. *(Make-
ahead: Layer between waxed paper in airtight
container and refrigerate for up to 2 weeks or
freeze for up to 1 month.)*

MAKES 36 TRUFFLES.
PER TRUFFLE: about 103 cal, 1 g pro, 8 g total fat (5 g
sat. fat), 9 g carb, 1 g fibre, 11 mg chol, 14 mg sodium.
% RDI: 2% calcium, 11% iron, 3% vit A.

Infusing cream with loose tea leaves gives these chocolates a subtle floral flavour, thanks to the citrusy bergamot in the Earl Grey blend. You'll have some chocolate left over after dipping the truffles; just let it harden, then store and reuse another time.

Earl Grey Chocolate Truffles

ingredients

⅔ cup **whipping cream (35%)**
2 tsp **loose leaf Earl Grey tea**
1 strip **orange zest**
¼ cup **unsalted butter,** cubed
8 oz (225 g) **milk chocolate,**
  finely chopped

COATING:
6 oz (170 g) each **milk chocolate** and **bittersweet chocolate,** finely chopped

PIPING:
1 oz (30 g) **white chocolate,** milk chocolate or bittersweet chocolate, finely chopped

method

In saucepan, heat cream until bubbles form around edge; remove from heat. Stir in tea and orange zest; cover and let steep for 1 hour. Strain though cheesecloth-lined sieve into clean saucepan. Add butter; heat until melted and bubbles form around edge.

Place chocolate in heatproof bowl. Pour in cream mixture, whisking until chocolate is melted and smooth. Cover and refrigerate until firm, about 1 hour.

Using melon baller or teaspoon, drop by heaping 1 tsp onto waxed paper–lined rimmed baking sheets to make 36 pieces. Gently roll each ball between fingertips to round off ❶. Freeze until hard, about 1 hour. Reroll to smooth edges; freeze. (Make-ahead: Cover and freeze for up to 24 hours.)

COATING: In heatproof bowl over saucepan of hot (not boiling) water, melt milk chocolate with bittersweet chocolate, stirring, until no large pieces remain and candy thermometer reads 113°F (45°C). Remove bowl from saucepan. Place over bowl of cold water; stir constantly until temperature falls to 78°F (26°C). Replace bowl over hot water or place on heating pad; stir constantly until temperature reaches 86°F (30°C); hold between 86 and 90°F (30 and 32°C) while using.

Using candy-dipping fork or 2 forks, dip each truffle centre into chocolate ❷, tapping fork on edge of bowl to remove excess. Place on waxed paper–lined rimmed baking sheet. Refrigerate until coating is hardened, about 2 hours.

PIPING: In heatproof bowl over saucepan of hot (not boiling) water, melt chocolate, stirring until smooth. Spoon into piping bag fitted with writing tip. Pipe swirl or monogram onto top of each truffle ❸. Refrigerate until hardened, about 30 minutes. (Make-ahead: Layer between waxed paper in airtight container and refrigerate for up to 1 week.) Place in paper candy cups.

MAKES 36 TRUFFLES.
PER TRUFFLE: about 105 cal, 1 g pro, 8 g total fat (5 g sat. fat), 9 g carb, 1 g fibre, 11 mg chol, 10 mg sodium. % RDI: 2% calcium, 2% iron, 3% vit A.

CHANGE IT UP
Chai Tea Chocolate Truffles
Replace Earl Grey with Darjeeling or Assam tea. To hot cream, add 1 slice fresh ginger; 1 tsp each aniseed and whole cloves; ½ tsp black peppercorns; and half cinnamon stick, broken. Steep as directed. Continue with recipe. Omit piping. Garnish just-dipped chocolate with slices of candied orange peel.

From left: Chai Tea Chocolate Truffles
and Earl Grey Chocolate Truffles

HOW-TO

① ② ③

Steeping cinnamon sticks in cream gives a warm and surprisingly sophisticated cinnamon toast flavour to these luscious chocolates. Tempering the coating makes it shiny and beautiful.

White Chocolate Cinnamon Butter Truffles

ingredients

½ cup **whipping cream (35%)**
2 **cinnamon sticks,** broken in pieces
3 bars (each 100 g) **white chocolate,**
    finely chopped
¼ cup **unsalted butter,** softened

COATING:
1 bar (100 g) each **70% dark chocolate**
    and **milk chocolate,** finely chopped
½ tsp **cinnamon**

method

In saucepan, heat cream with cinnamon until bubbles form around edge; remove from heat. Cover and let steep for 1 hour. Strain into clean saucepan; set aside.

In heatproof bowl over saucepan of hot (not boiling) water, melt white chocolate, stirring until smooth. Reheat cream mixture just until bubbles form around edge; stir into white chocolate along with butter until smooth. Cover and chill until firm, about 2 hours.

Using melon baller or teaspoon, drop by heaping 1 tsp onto waxed paper–lined rimmed baking sheets to make 36 pieces. Gently roll each ball between fingertips to round off. Refrigerate until firm, about 1 hour. Reroll to smooth edges; refrigerate. (Make-ahead: Cover and refrigerate for up to 24 hours.)

COATING: In heatproof bowl over saucepan of hot (not boiling) water, melt dark chocolate with milk chocolate, stirring occasionally, until no large pieces remain and candy thermometer reads 113°F (45°C). Remove bowl from saucepan. Place over bowl of cold water; stir constantly until temperature falls to 78°F (26°C). Replace bowl over hot water or place on heating pad; stir constantly until temperature

reaches 86°F (30°C); hold between 86 and 90°F (30 and 32°C) while using.

Using candy-dipping fork or 2 forks, dip each truffle centre into chocolate, tapping fork on edge of bowl to remove excess. Place on waxed paper–lined rimmed baking sheet.

Sift cinnamon over top. Refrigerate until coating is hardened, about 2 hours. (Make-ahead: Layer between waxed paper in airtight container and refrigerate for up to 2 weeks or freeze for up to 1 month.)

MAKES 36 TRUFFLES.
PER TRUFFLE: about 95 cal, 1 g pro, 7 g total fat (4 g sat. fat), 8 g carb, trace fibre, 9 mg chol, 13 mg sodium, 38 mg potassium. % RDI: 2% calcium, 4% iron, 2% vit A.

What Is Bloom?

Easiest to see on dark chocolate, a greyish coating on a chocolate bar indicates bloom, or that fat or sugar has risen to the surface. This can be caused by storing chocolate at extreme temperatures, excessive humidity or poor tempering. While it may not look attractive, it's perfectly fine to eat.

Test Kitchen TIP

Just a bite of these truffles sweeps your taste buds away to a tropical island.
For simple rum truffles, omit the coating and roll the centres in cocoa powder.

Coconut Rum Truffles

ingredients

4 oz (115 g) each **milk chocolate** and
   bittersweet chocolate, finely chopped
⅔ cup **whipping cream (35%)**
¼ cup **unsalted butter,** cubed
2 tbsp **amber rum**

COATING:
1½ cups **sweetened shredded coconut**
8 oz (225 g) **70% bittersweet chocolate,**
   finely chopped

method

Place milk chocolate and bittersweet chocolate in heatproof bowl. In saucepan, heat cream with butter until butter is melted and bubbles form around edge; pour over chocolate, whisking until smooth. Whisk in rum. Cover and refrigerate until firm, about 3 hours.

Using melon baller or teaspoon, drop by heaping 1 tsp onto 2 waxed paper–lined rimmed baking sheets to make 36 pieces. Gently roll each ball between fingertips to round off. Refrigerate until hard, about 1 hour. Reroll to smooth edges; refrigerate. *(Make-ahead: Refrigerate for up to 24 hours.)*

COATING: Meanwhile, on baking sheet, toast coconut in 300°F (150°C) oven, stirring often, until golden and fragrant, 6 to 7 minutes. Transfer to shallow dish; let cool. In heatproof bowl over saucepan of hot (not boiling) water, melt chocolate, stirring until smooth.

Using candy-dipping fork or 2 forks, dip each truffle centre into chocolate, tapping fork on edge of bowl to remove excess. Roll in coconut.

Return to waxed paper–lined rimmed baking sheet. Refrigerate until coating is hardened, about 2 hours. *(Make-ahead: Layer between waxed paper in airtight container and refrigerate for up to 2 weeks or freeze for up to 1 month.)*

MAKES 36 TRUFFLES.
PER TRUFFLE: about 97 cal, 1 g pro, 8 g total fat (5 g sat. fat), 7 g carb, 1 g fibre, 10 mg chol, 15 mg sodium. % RDI: 1% calcium, 6% iron, 3% vit A.

Getting the marzipan cherry filling into the centre of these delightful chocolates is surprisingly simple, but no need to tell people as they wonder at the look – and taste – of them.

Chocolate Cherry Cups

ingredients

10 oz (280 g) **70% dark chocolate,** chopped
6 oz (170 g) **milk chocolate,** chopped
1 pkg (200 g) **marzipan**
½ cup **glacé cherries**

GARNISH:
10 **glacé cherries,** cut in thirds

method

In heatproof bowl over saucepan of hot (not boiling) water, melt together half each of the dark chocolate and milk chocolate, stirring until smooth. Pour about 1 tsp into each of thirty 1¾-inch (4.5 cm) wide candy cups. Refrigerate until firm, about 30 minutes.

Meanwhile, in food processor, pulse marzipan with cherries until smooth paste forms. Roll by fully rounded 1 tsp into balls. Gently press balls into candy cups, flattening tops almost but not all the way to edge.

In heatproof bowl over saucepan of hot (not boiling) water, melt together remaining dark and milk chocolates; pour 1 tsp over each filling to cover, smoothing top. Refrigerate for 10 minutes.

GARNISH: Top each chocolate with 1 cherry piece. Refrigerate until firm, about 1 hour. *(Make-ahead: Layer between waxed paper in airtight container and refrigerate for up to 1 week.)*

MAKES 30 PIECES.
PER PIECE: about 131 cal, 2 g pro, 8 g total fat (4 g sat. fat), 15 g carb, 2 g fibre, 2 mg chol, 8 mg sodium, 123 mg potassium. % RDI: 2% calcium, 9% iron, 1% folate.

Marzipan vs. Almond Paste

Both of these ingredients are made from almonds and sugar, but they aren't interchangeable in recipes. Marzipan contains more sugar than almond paste (up to three times more in some brands). It's designed for moulding into shapes and use in confections like these cherry cups. You can even shape marzipan into fruits or figurines and paint on designs with food-safe colourings.

While goat's milk is not dairy-free, some people with lactose intolerance
(or milk allergies) can tolerate it. Be sure to ask before serving this to anyone you
suspect might be sensitive to dairy.

Chocolate Goat's Milk Fudge

ingredients

2 cups **granulated sugar**
1 cup **whole goat's milk**
¼ cup **unsalted goat's butter**

2 oz (55 g) **70% dark chocolate,**
  chopped
Pinch **salt**

method

In heavy saucepan, stir together sugar, milk, butter, chocolate and salt over medium heat until sugar is dissolved and butter is melted. Bring to boil; cover and boil for 2 minutes.

Uncover and boil until candy thermometer reads soft-ball stage of 234ºF (112ºC), 10 to 20 minutes, or 1 tsp hot syrup dropped in cold water forms soft ball that flattens when removed from water.

Remove from heat; dip bottom of pan in cold water for 30 seconds. Let cool on rack until temperature falls to 110ºF (43ºC), 30 to 45 minutes.

Beat until thick, creamy, no longer as glossy and mixture forms distinct ridges when beaten, 3 to 5 minutes. (Do not overbeat; if fudge starts to seize up, stop beating.) Spread in parchment paper–lined 9- x 5-inch (2 L) loaf pan; let cool.

Using paper as handles, transfer fudge to cutting board. With hot dry knife, cut into ¾-inch (2 cm) squares. (Make-ahead: Refrigerate in airtight container for up to 1 week.)

MAKES ABOUT 40 PIECES.
PER PIECE: about 60 cal, trace pro, 2 g total fat (1 g sat. fat), 11 g carb, trace fibre, 4 mg chol, 8 mg sodium, 13 mg potassium. % RDI: 1% calcium, 1% iron, 1% vit A.

Where to Find Goat's Milk

It used to be tough to find goat's milk products, but their increasing popularity means you don't have to look far and wide for them anymore. Look for goat's milk and goat's butter in the dairy section of health food stores and the organic or natural foods section of supermarkets.

Test Kitchen TIP

Since fudge is always a favourite, this makes a delicious gift that will please just about anyone. The "jewels" in the fudge are the glistening dried cranberries.

Cranberry Jewel Fudge

ingredients

12 oz (340 g) **bittersweet chocolate,** chopped
1 can (300 mL) **sweetened condensed milk**
2 tsp **vanilla**

CRANBERRY TOPPING:
5 oz (140 g) **white chocolate,** coarsely chopped
¾ cup **dried cranberries**

method

Line 8-inch (2 L) square cake pan with parchment paper or foil, leaving 1 inch (2.5 cm) extending above sides; set aside.

In heatproof bowl over saucepan of hot (not boiling) water, melt bittersweet chocolate with sweetened condensed milk, stirring occasionally until smooth, about 5 minutes. Stir in vanilla. Spread evenly in prepared pan. Refrigerate until firm, about 1 hour.

CRANBERRY TOPPING: In heatproof bowl over saucepan of hot (not boiling) water, melt white chocolate; spread over bittersweet chocolate layer. Sprinkle with cranberries, pressing lightly to adhere. Refrigerate until firm, about 3 hours.

Using paper as handles, transfer fudge to cutting board; peel off paper. With hot dry knife, cut into 48 pieces. *(Make-ahead: Layer between waxed paper in airtight container and refrigerate for up to 1 week or freeze for up to 1 month.)*

MAKES 48 PIECES.
PER PIECE: about 84 cal, 2 g pro, 6 g total fat (3 g sat. fat), 10 g carb, 1 g fibre, 3 mg chol, 14 mg sodium. % RDI: 3% calcium, 4% iron, 1% vit A, 2% vit C, 1% folate.

CHANGE IT UP
Snowball Chocolate Fudge
Omit cranberry topping. Stir in 2 cups mini marshmallows.

Candy-Covered Fudge
Omit cranberry topping. Sprinkle ¾ cup candy-coated chocolate pieces onto hot fudge; press lightly.

Nut Fudge
Omit cranberry topping. Score fudge into 48 pieces. Place toasted pecan piece or walnut half on each piece.

Test Kitchen TIP

Cutting Fudge

Fudge is creamy and can get a little messy when you're cutting it into squares. To keep your slices neat, dip a sharp chef's knife into hot water and wipe it dry before making each slice. You'll have tidy corners and no gooey bits stuck to the knife.

Three layers of creamy chocolate ganache meld beautifully in this stunning candy. It gives you the melt-in-your-mouth texture of truffles without the effort of rolling and coating.

Crispy Coffee Truffle Slice

ingredients

8 oz (225 g) **white chocolate,** finely chopped
¼ cup **whipping cream (35%)**
2 tbsp **unsalted butter**

MILK CHOCOLATE COFFEE GANACHE:
8 oz (225 g) **milk chocolate,** finely chopped
½ cup **whipping cream (35%)**
2 tbsp **unsalted butter**
1 tbsp **instant coffee granules**
1 tsp **vanilla**

CRISPY DARK CHOCOLATE GANACHE:
8 oz (225 g) **70% dark chocolate,** finely chopped
⅓ cup **whipping cream (35%)**
2 tbsp **unsalted butter**
1 cup **rice crisp cereal**

method

In heatproof bowl over saucepan of hot (not boiling) water, melt together white chocolate, cream and butter, stirring occasionally until smooth. Pour into parchment paper–lined 8-inch (2 L) square cake pan; using small offset spatula, smooth to edge. Refrigerate until firm, about 1½ hours.

MILK CHOCOLATE COFFEE GANACHE: In heatproof bowl over saucepan of hot (not boiling) water, melt together milk chocolate, cream, butter, coffee granules and vanilla, stirring occasionally, until melted and smooth.

Pour over white chocolate ganache; using small offset spatula, smooth to edge. Refrigerate until firm, about 1½ hours.

CRISPY DARK CHOCOLATE GANACHE: In heatproof bowl over saucepan of hot (not boiling) water, melt together dark chocolate, cream and butter, stirring occasionally until smooth. Remove from heat; stir in cereal.

Pour over milk chocolate coffee ganache; using small offset spatula, smooth to edge. Refrigerate until firm, about 2 hours.

Using paper as handles, invert onto cutting board and peel off paper. Wiping thin sharp knife with damp cloth between slices, trim edges to even; cut into 36 pieces. *(Make-ahead: Layer between waxed paper in airtight container and refrigerate for up to 1 week.)* Place in candy cups if desired.

MAKES 36 PIECES.
PER PIECE: about 146 cal, 2 g pro, 11 g total fat (7 g sat. fat), 11 g carb, 1 g fibre, 16 mg chol, 19 mg sodium, 100 mg potassium. % RDI: 3% calcium, 6% iron, 4% vit A.

Above: Crispy Coffee Truffle Slice (opposite).
Left: Triple-Nut Chocolate Fudge (page 209)

Chai spices are so warm and inviting. Why not add them to a simple, creamy white chocolate fudge? Top with sparkly gold leaf to give the squares a touch of sophistication.

White Chocolate Chai Fudge

ingredients

1 lb (450 g) **white chocolate,** chopped

1 can (300 mL) **sweetened condensed milk**

½ tsp each **cinnamon** and **ground allspice**

¼ tsp **ground cardamom**

1½ cups chopped **cashews** (about 8 oz/225 g)

method

In bowl over saucepan of hot (not boiling) water, melt together chocolate, sweetened condensed milk, cinnamon, allspice and cardamom, stirring until smooth, about 5 minutes. Remove from heat. Stir in chopped cashews.

Scrape into parchment paper–lined 9-inch (2.5 L) square cake pan; smooth top. Refrigerate until firm, about 3 hours.

Using paper as handles, transfer to cutting board; peel off paper. Cut into squares. *(Make-ahead: Layer between waxed paper in airtight container and refrigerate for up to 2 weeks.)*

MAKES 36 PIECES.
PER PIECE: about 139 cal, 3 g pro, 8 g total fat (4 g sat. fat), 15 g carb, trace fibre, 4 mg chol, 26 mg sodium, 117 mg potassium. % RDI: 5% calcium, 3% iron, 1% vit A, 2% folate.

Fudge Secret Weapon

So why are most of our foolproof fudge recipes based on sweetened condensed milk? The old-fashioned way of making fudge – starting with a caramel cooked to the soft-ball stage – is trickier than this method. A mixture of hot caramel and plain milk can seize up on you, ruining all of your hard work.

Sweetened condensed milk is thick, and the sugar in it is very stable when heated, so it will never curdle or clump. That means more delicious fudge and fewer headaches.

This dark, dense fudge is so easy to make — with only a few ingredients. Best of all, you don't have to fuss with any special equipment, such as a candy thermometer. We use a combination of cashews, pecans and walnuts, but you can substitute any chopped nuts.

Triple-Nut Chocolate Fudge

ingredients

1 lb (450 g) **semisweet chocolate** or 70% dark chocolate, chopped

1 can (300 mL) **sweetened condensed milk**

1 tsp **vanilla**

½ cup chopped **roasted cashews**

½ cup chopped **pecans**

½ cup chopped **walnuts**

method

In bowl over saucepan of hot (not boiling) water, melt chocolate with sweetened condensed milk, stirring frequently, until smooth, about 5 minutes. Stir in vanilla. Stir in cashews, pecans and walnuts.

Pour into parchment paper–lined 9-inch (2.5 L) square cake pan; smooth top. Refrigerate until firm, about 3 hours.

Using paper as handles, transfer fudge to cutting board; peel off paper. Cut into 36 pieces. *(Make-ahead: Layer between waxed paper in airtight container and refrigerate for up to 2 weeks.)*

MAKES 36 PIECES.

PER PIECE: about 127 cal, 2 g pro, 8 g total fat (3 g sat. fat), 15 g carb, 1 g fibre, 4 mg chol, 15 mg sodium, 111 mg potassium. % RDI: 3% calcium, 4% iron, 1% vit A, 2% folate.

CHANGE IT UP
S'mores Fudge
Substitute 1½ cups mini marshmallows and 1 cup coarsely broken graham crackers for the chopped nuts.

The pride of Nanaimo, B.C., these bars have a crumb base layered with a creamy custard filling and a chocolaty topping. Best served at room temperature, the bars stand by patiently in the refrigerator or freezer.

Classic Nanaimo Bars

ingredients

1 cup **graham cracker crumbs**
½ cup **sweetened shredded coconut**
⅓ cup finely chopped **walnuts**
¼ cup **cocoa powder**
¼ cup **granulated sugar**
⅓ cup **butter,** melted
1 **egg,** lightly beaten

FILLING:
¼ cup **butter,** softened
2 tbsp **custard powder**
½ tsp **vanilla**
2 cups **icing sugar**
2 tbsp **milk** (approx)

TOPPING:
4 oz (115 g) **semisweet chocolate,** chopped
1 tbsp **butter**

method

In bowl, stir together graham cracker crumbs, coconut, walnuts, cocoa and sugar. Drizzle with butter and egg; stir until moistened.

Press into parchment paper–lined 9-inch (2.5 L) square cake pan. Bake in 350°F (180°C) oven until firm, about 10 minutes. Let cool in pan on rack.

FILLING: In bowl, beat together butter, custard powder and vanilla. Beat in icing sugar alternately with milk, making 3 additions of sugar and 2 of milk and adding up to 1 tsp more milk if too thick to spread. Spread over cooled base. Refrigerate until firm, about 1 hour.

TOPPING: In heatproof bowl over saucepan of hot (not boiling) water, melt chocolate with butter, stirring until smooth; spread over filling. Refrigerate until chocolate is almost set, about 30 minutes.

With tip of sharp knife, score into 25 bars; refrigerate until chocolate is completely set, about 30 minutes. *(Make-ahead: Remove from pan. Wrap in plastic wrap and refrigerate for up to 4 days or overwrap in foil and freeze for up to 2 weeks.)*

Cut into bars.

MAKES 25 BARS.

PER BAR: about 150 cal, 1 g pro, 9 g total fat (5 g sat. fat), 19 g carb, 1 g fibre, 20 mg chol, 65 mg sodium, 62 mg potassium. % RDI: 1% calcium, 4% iron, 4% vit A, 2% folate.

This is a classic fudge that tastes like the one our grandmothers used to make. Sweetened condensed milk gives it a creamy texture and doesn't require long boiling and testing with a candy thermometer to achieve the proper texture. It couldn't be simpler to make.

Easy Chocolate Walnut Fudge

ingredients

1 cup coarsely chopped **walnuts**
10 oz (280 g) **bittersweet chocolate**
   or semisweet chocolate, chopped
1 can (300 mL) **sweetened**
   condensed milk

1 tsp **vanilla**
¼ tsp **baking soda**
Pinch **salt**

method

On baking sheet, toast walnuts in 350°F (180°C) oven until fragrant, about 6 minutes. Let cool.

In heatproof bowl over saucepan of hot (not boiling) water, melt bittersweet chocolate, stirring until smooth. Remove from heat. Stir in sweetened condensed milk, vanilla, baking soda and salt until smooth. Stir in walnuts.

Immediately spread in parchment paper–lined 8-inch (2 L) square cake pan. Refrigerate until set, about 2 hours.

Using paper as handles, transfer fudge to cutting board. Using hot dry knife, cut into 64 pieces.

MAKES 64 PIECES.

PER PIECE: about 57 cal, 1 g pro, 3 g total fat (1 g sat. fat), 6 g carb, 1 g fibre, 2 mg chol, 13 mg sodium, 31 mg potassium. % RDI: 2% calcium, 2% iron, 1% vit A, 1% folate.

Buying & Storing Nuts

Nuts aren't cheap, so you don't want to waste them. Buy them from a store with a regular high turnover so you're getting the freshest ones possible. To prevent their natural oils from going rancid, store nuts in a tightly sealed plastic freezer bag in the freezer. There's no need to thaw the nuts for long before you use them. Just take them out a couple of minutes ahead and they'll be fresh and ready to use.

Test Kitchen TIP

If you like the fancy java drinks at your local coffeehouse, then this fudge
will be right up your alley. Coffee and hazelnuts are excellent partners to chocolate,
on their own or paired together.

Hazelnut Mochaccino Fudge

ingredients

1 cup **hazelnuts**
1 tbsp **instant coffee granules**
2 tsp **vanilla**
10 oz (280 g) **bittersweet chocolate,**
   chopped
1 can (300 mL) **sweetened**
   condensed milk

½ tsp **cinnamon**
¼ tsp **baking soda**
Pinch **salt**

method

Toast hazelnuts on rimmed baking sheet in
350°F (180°C) oven until fragrant and skins
crack, about 6 minutes. Transfer to clean tea
towel; rub briskly to remove as much of the
skin as possible. Chop hazelnuts; set aside.

In small bowl, dissolve coffee granules in
vanilla. Set aside.

In heatproof bowl over saucepan of hot
(not boiling water), melt together chocolate,
sweetened condensed milk, coffee mixture,
cinnamon, baking soda and salt, stirring until
chocolate is almost melted but a few small
pieces remain.

Remove from heat. Stir until smooth; stir in
hazelnuts. Spread in parchment paper–lined
8-inch (2 L) square cake pan. Refrigerate
until set, about 2 hours.

Using paper as handles, transfer fudge to
cutting board. Using hot dry knife, cut into
1-inch (2.5 cm) squares. *(Make-ahead: Layer
between waxed paper in airtight container and
refrigerate for up to 5 days or freeze for up to
3 weeks.)*

MAKES 64 PIECES.
PER PIECE: about 58 cal, 1 g pro, 3 g total fat (1 g
sat. fat), 6 g carb, 1 g fibre, 2 mg chol, 13 mg sodium.
% RDI: 2% calcium, 2% iron, 1% vit A, 1% folate.

213

CANADIAN LIVING • THE COMPLETE CHOCOLATE BOOK

The inside-out version of this classic square offers a classy white chocolate top with a rich dark chocolate centre. Use a vegetable peeler to make the chocolate shavings.

Reverse Nanaimo Bars

ingredients

1½ cups **graham cracker crumbs**
½ cup **sweetened shredded coconut**
¼ cup finely chopped **almonds**
1 oz (30 g) **white chocolate,** chopped
¼ cup **butter,** melted
1 **egg,** lightly beaten

FILLING:
⅓ cup **butter**
⅔ cup **cocoa powder**

1⅓ cups **icing sugar**
3 tbsp **milk**
2 tbsp **custard powder**
1 tsp **vanilla**

TOPPING:
8 oz (225 g) **white chocolate,** coarsely chopped
½ tsp **butter**
⅓ oz (10 g) **dark chocolate,** shaved

method

In bowl, stir together graham cracker crumbs, coconut, almonds and chocolate. Drizzle with butter and egg; stir until moistened.

Press into parchment paper–lined 9-inch (2.5 L) square cake pan. Bake in 350°F (180°C) oven until firm, about 10 minutes. Let cool in pan on rack.

FILLING: In heavy saucepan, melt butter over low heat; stir in cocoa powder until smooth. Pour into bowl; beat in icing sugar, milk, custard powder and vanilla until smooth. Spread over cooled base; refrigerate until firm, about 1 hour.

TOPPING: In heatproof bowl over saucepan of hot (not boiling) water, melt white chocolate with butter, stirring until smooth; spread over filling. Refrigerate until chocolate is almost set, about 30 minutes.

With tip of sharp knife, score into bars; sprinkle with shaved chocolate. Refrigerate until chocolate is completely set, about 30 minutes. *(Make-ahead: Remove from pan. Wrap in plastic wrap and refrigerate for up to 4 days or overwrap in foil and freeze for up to 2 weeks.)*

Cut into bars.

MAKES 25 BARS.
PER BAR: about 164 cal, 2 g pro, 10 g total fat (6 g sat. fat), 18 g carb, 1 g fibre, 20 mg chol, 82 mg sodium, 116 mg potassium. % RDI: 3% calcium, 5% iron, 4% vit A, 3% folate.

Who needs after-dinner mints when you have a dessert like this? The food colouring gives the filling a zippy green colour, but you can omit it if you prefer.

Chocolate Mint Nanaimo Bars

ingredients

1 cup **butter,** melted
2 tbsp **granulated sugar**
2 **eggs**
3 cups **chocolate wafer crumbs**
1 pkg (200 g) **sweetened desiccated coconut**

FILLING:
⅓ cup **butter,** melted
¼ cup **milk**
1 tbsp **peppermint extract**
4 cups **icing sugar**
Green food colouring

TOPPING:
8 oz (225 g) **semisweet chocolate,** chopped
2 tbsp **butter**

method

Grease 13- x 9-inch (3.5 L) cake pan; line with parchment paper. Set aside.

In large bowl, whisk together butter, sugar and eggs; stir in chocolate wafer crumbs and coconut until moistened. Press into prepared pan. Bake in 350°F (180°C) oven until firm, about 20 minutes. Let cool completely in pan on rack.

FILLING: Meanwhile, in bowl, stir together butter, milk and peppermint extract; beat in icing sugar until smooth. Beat in food colouring to create desired shade. Spread evenly over base. Refrigerate until firm, about 45 minutes.

TOPPING: In bowl over saucepan of hot (not boiling) water, melt chocolate with butter, stirring until smooth; spread over filling. Let stand for 5 minutes.

With tip of sharp knife, score into 40 bars; refrigerate until chocolate is completely set, about 30 minutes.

Cut into bars. *(Make-ahead: Layer between waxed paper in airtight container and refrigerate for up to 1 week or freeze for up to 1 month.)*

MAKES 40 BARS.
PER BAR: about 195 cal, 1 g pro, 12 g total fat (7 g sat. fat), 23 g carb, 1 g fibre, 29 mg chol, 135 mg sodium. % RDI: 1% calcium, 5% iron, 7% vit A, 1% folate.

Desiccated Coconut

Shredded and flaked coconut contain more moisture than desiccated coconut. The name merely means "dried up" and the result is a dry, feathery ingredient that's great for bases like the one for these bars. Desiccated coconut comes in unsweetened and sweetened varieties.

Test Kitchen TIP

Always popular with both kids and grown-ups, these treats are made even more luscious with a blend of milk chocolate and bittersweet chocolate.

Peanut Butter Cups

ingredients

2 bars (each 100 g) **milk chocolate,** chopped
1 bar (100 g) **70% dark chocolate,** chopped

FILLING:
6 tbsp **smooth peanut butter**
3 tbsp **icing sugar**
½ tsp **vanilla**

GARNISH:
1 oz (30 g) **70% dark chocolate,** melted
10 **dry-roasted peanuts,** halved

217

method

FILLING: Stir together peanut butter, icing sugar and vanilla until smooth. Roll by level 1 tsp into balls. Cover and refrigerate on waxed paper–lined rimmed baking sheet for 30 minutes.

In heatproof bowl over saucepan of hot (not boiling) water, melt milk chocolate with dark chocolate, stirring occasionally, until no large pieces remain and candy thermometer reads 113°F (45°C). Remove bowl from saucepan. Place over bowl of cold water; stir constantly until temperature falls to 78°F (26°C). Replace bowl over hot water or place on heating pad; stir constantly until temperature reaches 86°F (30°C); hold between 86 and 90°F (30 and 32°C) while using.

Spoon 1 tsp chocolate mixture into each of 20 foil candy cups. Refrigerate on baking sheet just until set, about 15 minutes.

Place 1 peanut butter ball in centre of each chocolate cup. Using icing sugar–dusted finger, flatten slightly, making sure peanut butter filling does not touch edge of cup.

Spoon about 2 tsp of the remaining chocolate over each filling to cover completely; tap baking sheet gently on counter to release any air bubbles. Refrigerate until coating is hardened, about 1 hour.

GARNISH: Dab centre of each peanut butter cup top with some of the remaining melted chocolate; attach peanut half, flat side up. Refrigerate until hardened, about 15 minutes.

MAKES 20 PIECES.

PER PIECE: about 119 cal, 3 g pro, 8 g total fat (4 g sat. fat), 12 g carb, 1 g fibre, 2 mg chol, 39 mg sodium, 78 mg potassium. % RDI: 2% calcium, 7% iron, 1% vit A, 3% folate.

crumbly

White Chocolate Tartlets With Strawberries **220**

Chocolate Almond Tartlets **221**

Chocolate Silk Tartlet Trio **223**

White Chocolate Lemon Tart **224**

Chocolate Cream Pear Tart **225**

Cranberry White Chocolate Tarts **226**

Chocolate Fruit & Nut Tart **228**

Chocolate Mousse Pie **229**

Chocolate Key Lime Tarts **231**

White Chocolate Hazelnut Pie **232**

Chocolate Shortbread Fingers **233**

Triple-Berry Chocolate Tart **234**

Double-Chocolate Almond Shortbread **236**

Oatmeal Chocolate Chip Shortbread **237**

Chocolate Ricotta Tart **239**

Chocolate Stripe Shortbread **240**

Spicy Chocolate Cinnamon Shortbread **241**

Chocolate Walnut Tart **242**

Giant Swiss Chocolate Chunk Shortbread **244**

Cherry White Chocolate Scones **245**

Milk Chocolate Scones **247**

Dark Chocolate & Dried Cherry Scones **248**

Chocolate Hazelnut Tassies **249**

Chocolate Walnut Fudge Scones **250**

Chocolate Pecan Mounds **252**

Checkerboard Cookies **253**

Chocolate Cherry Rounds **255**

Double-Chocolate Ice Box Cookies **256**

Sparkly Chocolate Blossoms **257**

Basler Brunsli **258**

Dainty tarts like these are a must-have at showers and other celebrations. The delicate white chocolate ganache is a perfect match for strawberries and fresh mint.

White Chocolate Tartlets
WITH STRAWBERRIES

ingredients

6 whole strawberries
2 tbsp strained **strawberry jam** or jelly
12 sprigs **fresh mint**

PASTRY:
1½ cups **all-purpose flour**
¼ tsp **salt**
Pinch **nutmeg**
¼ cup cold **butter**, cubed
¼ cup cold **lard**, cubed

1 **egg yolk**
1 tsp **vinegar**
Ice **water**

WHITE CHOCOLATE GANACHE FILLING:
6 oz (170 g) **white chocolate**, chopped
½ cup **whipping cream (35%)**

method

PASTRY: In bowl, whisk together flour, salt and nutmeg. With pastry blender or 2 knives, cut in butter and lard until in fine crumbs. In liquid measure, whisk egg yolk with vinegar; add enough ice water to make ⅓ cup. Sprinkle over flour mixture, stirring briskly with fork until pastry holds together. Gather into ball; press into disc. Wrap in plastic wrap; refrigerate until chilled, 1 hour. (*Make-ahead: Refrigerate for up to 3 days.*) Let stand at room temperature for 10 minutes.

On lightly floured surface, roll out pastry to ⅛-inch (3 mm) thickness. Using 4-inch (10 cm) fluted round cookie cutter, cut out 12 circles, rerolling and cutting scraps if necessary. Fit into 2¾ - x 1¼-inch (7 x 3 cm) tartlet or muffin cups; prick bottoms all over with fork. Freeze for 30 minutes. Bake on bottom rack in 400°F (200°C) oven until golden, 20 minutes. Let cool in pan on rack.

WHITE CHOCOLATE GANACHE FILLING:
Meanwhile, in heatproof bowl over saucepan of hot (not boiling) water, melt white chocolate with cream, stirring occasionally until smooth. Let cool slightly, 10 minutes. Divide among tartlet shells. Refrigerate until set, about 2 hours. (*Make-ahead: Refrigerate for up to 24 hours. Let stand at room temperature for 1 hour before serving.*)

Cut each strawberry in half lengthwise; thinly slice each half lengthwise almost but not all the way through to top. Press slightly to fan slices; place 1 on each tartlet. In saucepan or in microwave, melt jam with 1 tsp water; brush over tartlets. Garnish with mint.

MAKES 12 TARTLETS.

PER TARTLET: about 253 cal, 3 g pro, 17 g total fat (9 g sat. fat), 23 g carb, 1 g fibre, 45 mg chol, 106 mg sodium. % RDI: 4% calcium, 7% iron, 9% vit A, 8% vit C, 13% folate.

What Is Seizing?

Test Kitchen TIP

Moisture and high heat are chocolate's mortal enemies. If any liquid gets into it or it's cooked over too-high heat, chocolate will clump, or seize, into an unusable mass. To prevent this, make sure all bowls and utensils are perfectly dry and that your heatproof bowl completely covers the lip of the saucepan so that steam doesn't touch the mixture. Keeping the water hot but not boiling reduces steam and ensures success.

These tartlets may be tiny, but they have mighty big chocolate flavour in the pastry and the filling. Instead of fluted tart pans, you can also use mini (1¼- x ¾-inch/3 x 2 cm) muffin cups.

Chocolate Almond Tartlets

ingredients

12 oz (340 g) **bittersweet chocolate,** chopped
⅔ cup **whipping cream (35%)**
2 tbsp **almond liqueur** (such as amaretto)
⅓ cup **almonds,** toasted

CHOCOLATE PASTRY:
⅓ cup **butter,** softened
¼ cup **granulated sugar**
1 **egg yolk**
½ tsp **vanilla**
¾ cup **all-purpose flour** (approx)
3 tbsp **cocoa powder**
Pinch **salt**

method

CHOCOLATE PASTRY: In large bowl, beat butter with sugar until fluffy; beat in egg yolk and vanilla. Into separate bowl, sift together flour, cocoa powder and salt; sift again. Stir into butter mixture in 2 additions. Gather into ball; press into disc. Wrap in plastic wrap; refrigerate until chilled, about 1 hour.

On lightly floured surface, roll out pastry to ⅛-inch (3 mm) thickness. Using 2½-inch (6 cm) round cutter, cut out 24 circles; gently press into 1½- x ¾-inch (4 x 2 cm) fluted tart pans. Place on baking sheet; refrigerate until firm, about 20 minutes. Prick bottoms of each tart shell twice with fork. Bake in 375°F (190°C) oven until firm and no longer shiny, about 15 minutes. Let cool on pan on rack.

Meanwhile, place half of the chocolate in heatproof bowl. In saucepan, bring cream just to boil; pour over chocolate, whisking until smooth. Whisk in liqueur. Cover and refrigerate until mixture is thick enough to mound on spoon, about 1 hour.

Chop almonds to about size of lemon seeds; remove 3 tbsp and set aside for garnish. Sprinkle ½ tsp of the remaining almonds into each tart shell. Set aside.

Beat chocolate mixture until thick and fluffy. Spoon mousse by rounded 1 tbsp into shells, rounding and smoothing tops with small palette knife. Refrigerate until firm, about 15 minutes.

Meanwhile, in separate heatproof bowl over saucepan of hot (not boiling) water, melt remaining chocolate. Let cool to room temperature. Spoon enough over mousse to cover just to edge of crust. Sprinkle reserved almonds around edge. Refrigerate until set, about 5 minutes. *(Make-ahead: Refrigerate in single layer in shallow airtight container for up to 2 days.)*

MAKES 24 TARTS.
PER TART: about 167 cal, 3 g pro, 15 g total fat (8 g sat. fat), 11 g carb, 3 g fibre, 25 mg chol, 32 mg sodium. % RDI: 2% calcium, 9% iron, 5% vit A, 4% folate.

Tiny tartlets – each just a mouthful – showcase ultrasmooth, ultrarich whipped chocolate ganache, known as "silk," in three luscious flavours. Have the cream at room temperature before you begin for the best results. Garnish with a little whipped cream or fresh mint leaves, if desired.

Chocolate Silk Tartlet Trio

ingredients

1 cup **all-purpose flour**
½ cup **icing sugar**
⅓ cup cold **butter,** cubed
1 **egg yolk**

WHITE CHOCOLATE SILK:

1½ oz (45 g) **white chocolate,** finely chopped
¾ tsp **bourbon** or rum
3 tbsp **whipping cream (35%)**
2 tbsp toasted chopped **pecans**

MILK CHOCOLATE MOCHA SILK:

¾ tsp **instant coffee granules**
3 tbsp **whipping cream (35%)**
2 oz (55 g) **milk chocolate,** finely chopped
½ oz (15 g) **semisweet chocolate,** shaved

DARK CHOCOLATE SILK:

1½ oz (45 g) **semisweet chocolate** or bittersweet chocolate, finely chopped
1 tsp **butter**
¼ cup **whipping cream (35%)**
8 **raspberries**

method

In bowl, whisk flour with sugar; using pastry blender, cut in butter until in fine crumbs. Whisk egg yolk with 1 tbsp water; stir into flour mixture just until dough begins to clump. On floured surface, knead dough a few times to form ball; press into disc. Cover and refrigerate until firm, 1 hour. Between waxed paper, roll out dough to scant ⅛-inch (3 mm) thickness ❶. Using 2-inch (5 cm) round cutter, cut out 24 rounds. Press into 2¾ - x 1¼-inch (7 x 3 cm) tartlet or muffin cups ❷; freeze for 1 hour. Prick bottoms all over with tip of knife. Bake in 350°F (180°C) oven, gently pressing with back of spoon if puffing, until golden, 20 minutes. Let cool in pan on rack. (Make-ahead: Store in airtight container for up to 3 days or freeze for up to 2 weeks.)

WHITE CHOCOLATE SILK: In heatproof bowl over saucepan of hot (not boiling) water, heat chocolate with bourbon until three-quarters is melted. Remove from heat; stir until melted. Stir in cream until smooth. Place over bowl of ice water; beat just until thickness of icing (do not overbeat). Scatter some of the pecans in 8 of the tart shells. Using piping bag fitted with medium star tip, pipe silk into shells. Garnish with remaining pecans.

MILK CHOCOLATE MOCHA SILK: Dissolve coffee in ¼ tsp water; add cream. Melt milk and semisweet chocolates as directed for white chocolate silk (left); stir in cream mixture until smooth. Beat and pipe as directed. Garnish with shaved chocolate.

DARK CHOCOLATE SILK: Melt semisweet chocolate with butter as directed for white chocolate silk (left); stir in cream until smooth. Beat and pipe as directed. Garnish with raspberries. (Make-ahead: Refrigerate tartlets in airtight container for up to 24 hours.)

MAKES 24 TARTLETS.

PER WHITE CHOCOLATE SILK TARTLET: about 189 cal, 2 g pro, 12 g total fat (6 g sat. fat), 19 g carb, 1 g fibre, 44 mg chol, 51 mg sodium. % RDI: 2% calcium, 5% iron, 8% vit A, 13% folate.

PER MILK CHOCOLATE MOCHA SILK TARTLET: about 191 cal, 2 g pro, 11 g total fat (7 g sat. fat), 21 g carb, 1 g fibre, 46 mg chol, 54 mg sodium. % RDI: 2% calcium, 6% iron, 9% vit A, 13% folate.

PER DARK CHOCOLATE SILK TARTLET: about 186 cal, 2 g pro, 11 g total fat (7 g sat. fat), 20 g carb, 1 g fibre, 48 mg chol, 51 mg sodium. % RDI: 1% calcium, 6% iron, 9% vit A, 2% vit C, 14% folate.

Straight-up white chocolate can be too sweet for some palates, but when cut with a tart fruit – such as lemon, orange or cranberry – it's nothing short of ethereal.

White Chocolate Lemon Tart

ingredients

2 **eggs**
2 **egg yolks**
⅔ cup **granulated sugar**
2 tsp grated **lemon zest**
½ cup **lemon juice**
3 oz (85 g) **white chocolate,** chopped
2 oz (55 g) **semisweet chocolate,** chopped
⅔ cup **whipping cream (35%)**

PASTRY:
1½ cups **all-purpose flour**
4 tsp **cornstarch**
1 tbsp **icing sugar**
¾ cup cold **butter,** cubed
1 tbsp **vinegar**

method

In heatproof bowl over saucepan of hot (not boiling) water, whisk together eggs, egg yolks, sugar, lemon zest and lemon juice; cook, whisking frequently, until translucent and thickened to consistency of pudding, about 10 minutes.

Remove from heat; add white chocolate, stirring until melted. Pour into clean bowl; place plastic wrap directly on surface. Refrigerate until chilled, about 1 hour. *(Make-ahead: Refrigerate for up to 3 days.)*

PASTRY: In large bowl, whisk together flour, cornstarch and icing sugar. With pastry blender or 2 knives, cut in butter until in fine crumbs with a few larger pieces. With fork, lightly stir in vinegar until mixture is moistened; let stand for 20 minutes.

With floured hands, squeeze together small handfuls of dough just until mixture holds together. Press evenly into ¼-inch (5 mm) thick layer on bottom and up side of 9-inch (23 cm) tart pan with removable bottom. Cover and refrigerate until chilled, about 1 hour. *(Make-ahead: Refrigerate for up to 3 days.)*

Prick bottom of pastry shell all over with fork; bake in 350°F (180°C) oven until golden, 35 to 40 minutes. Let cool in pan on rack.

In bowl over saucepan of hot (not boiling) water, melt semisweet chocolate, stirring until smooth. Using pastry brush, brush chocolate over inside of pastry shell. Let cool.

Whip cream. Fold half into lemon mixture; fold in remaining whipped cream just until combined. Pour into shell, swirling top. Refrigerate until set, 1 hour. *(Make-ahead: Cover and refrigerate for up to 24 hours.)*

MAKES 8 SERVINGS.
PER SERVING: about 505 cal, 6 g pro, 33 g total fat (19 g sat. fat), 49 g carb, 1 g fibre, 181 mg chol, 214 mg sodium. % RDI: 6% calcium, 11% iron, 29% vit A, 10% vit C, 17% folate.

What do you get when you combine buttery pastry, rich chocolate pastry cream and vanilla-poached pears? One divine dessert. Look for ripe but firm pears because they keep their shape after poaching.

Chocolate Cream Pear Tart

ingredients

1 cup **all-purpose flour**
1 tsp **granulated sugar**
Pinch **salt**
⅓ cup **butter,** cubed
1 **egg yolk**

CHOCOLATE PASTRY CREAM:
2 **egg yolks**
¼ cup **granulated sugar**
2 tbsp **cornstarch**
Pinch **salt**

1 cup **homogenized milk** or 2% milk
3 oz (85 g) **bittersweet chocolate,** chopped
1 tbsp **butter**
¼ tsp **vanilla**

VANILLA-POACHED PEARS:
3 **Bartlett pears**
1 cup **granulated sugar**
1 **vanilla bean,** split
1 strip **lemon zest**

method

In food processor, pulse together flour, sugar and salt. Pulse in butter until in fine crumbs with a few larger pieces. Whisk egg yolk with 2 tbsp water. With motor running, add egg mixture all at once; pulse just until dough starts to clump together. Remove and press into disc. Wrap in plastic wrap; refrigerate until chilled, about 30 minutes.

On floured surface, roll out pastry to scant ¼-inch (5 mm) thickness. Fit into 14- x 4-inch (35 x 10 cm) rectangular or 9-inch (23 cm) round tart pan with removable bottom. Fold overhang inside, leaving ¼ inch (5 mm) above rim. Prick all over with fork. Freeze until firm, about 10 minutes.

Line tart shell with greased foil, greased side down; fill with pie weights or dried beans. Bake on bottom rack in 400°F (200°C) oven for 15 minutes. Remove weights and foil. Bake until firm and golden, about 15 minutes. Let cool in pan on rack.

CHOCOLATE PASTRY CREAM: Meanwhile, in bowl, whisk together egg yolks, sugar, cornstarch and salt; whisk in ¼ cup of the milk. In small saucepan, heat remaining milk until small bubbles appear around edge; whisk into egg yolk mixture. Pour back into saucepan; cook over medium heat, stirring constantly, until thickened, about 6 minutes.

Remove from heat. Stir in chocolate, butter and vanilla until smooth; scrape into bowl. Place plastic wrap directly on surface; refrigerate until cool, about 1 hour.

VANILLA-POACHED PEARS: Peel, halve and core pears; set aside. In large skillet, bring 2 cups water, sugar, vanilla bean and lemon zest to boil; reduce heat and simmer for 5 minutes. Add pears, turning to coat. Press circle of parchment paper over pears; simmer until tender but still firm, 15 to 20 minutes. With slotted spoon, remove pears; reserve syrup for another use. Refrigerate pears on paper towel–lined rack for 30 minutes.

Whisk pastry cream to loosen; spread over tart shell. Pat pears dry; cut lengthwise into scant ¼-inch (5 mm) thick slices, discarding smallest slices. Fan pears; arrange over pastry cream.

MAKES 8 TO 10 SERVINGS.

PER EACH OF 10 SERVINGS: about 261 cal, 4 g pro, 13 g total fat (8 g sat. fat), 33 g carb, 2 g fibre, 84 mg chol, 67 mg sodium. % RDI: 4% calcium, 9% iron, 10% vit A, 2% vit C, 17% folate.

Using Up Pear Poaching Liquid

Pour ¾ cup poaching liquid over 12 cups mixed chopped fruit for a tasty fruit salad.

These flaky pastry cups full of tangy cranberries and sweet white chocolate are party-perfect. The pastry is a recipe box essential that's lovely with all sorts of fillings – it makes enough for 24 tarts or a single-crust pie.

Cranberry White Chocolate Tarts

ingredients

¼ cup **unsweetened dried cranberries**
2 tbsp **orange liqueur** (such as Grand Marnier) or orange juice
2 tbsp **whipping cream (35%)**
2 oz (55 g) **white chocolate,** finely chopped
2 tsp **butter,** softened

SINGLE-CRUST ALL-PURPOSE PASTRY:
1½ cups **all-purpose flour**
½ tsp **salt**
¼ cup each cold **butter** and **lard,** cubed
1 **egg yolk**
1 tsp **vinegar** or lemon juice
Ice **water**

method

SINGLE-CRUST ALL-PURPOSE PASTRY:
In bowl, whisk flour with salt. Using pastry blender, cut in butter and lard until mixture is in fine crumbs with a few larger pieces. In liquid measure, whisk egg yolk with vinegar; add enough ice water to make ⅓ cup. Drizzle over dry ingredients, stirring briskly with fork until ragged dough forms. Press into disc; wrap in plastic wrap and refrigerate until chilled, about 30 minutes. *(Make-ahead: Refrigerate for up to 3 days.)*

On lightly floured surface, roll out pastry to ⅛-inch (3 mm) thickness. Using 2½-inch (6 cm) round cutter, cut out 24 circles, rerolling and cutting scraps. Fit into ¾-inch (2 cm) deep mini tart or mini muffin tins. Prick all over with fork; cover and freeze until firm. Bake in 350°F (180°C) oven until golden, about 25 minutes. Let cool in pans on rack.

Meanwhile, in saucepan, cover and heat cranberries with liqueur over medium-low heat until steaming. Remove from heat; let stand until softened. Finely chop.

In small saucepan, bring cream just to boil. Remove from heat; whisk in white chocolate and butter until melted.

Divide cranberries among tart shells; top with chocolate mixture. Refrigerate until set, about 2 hours. *(Make-ahead: Cover and refrigerate for up to 2 days.)*

MAKES 24 TARTS.

PER TART: about 84 cal, 1 g pro, 5 g total fat (3 g sat. fat), 8 g carb, trace fibre, 17 mg chol, 63 mg sodium. % RDI: 1% calcium, 2% iron, 3% vit A, 7% folate.

Buying Dried Cranberries

For this recipe, look for natural unsweetened dried cranberries at your local health food or bulk food store. They have the puckery flavour that's necessary to balance the sweetness of the white chocolate filling. Sweetened dried cranberries are better for eating out of hand.

Test Kitchen TIP

If you love the flavours and textures of chocolate bars studded with dried fruit and nuts, this tart will make your taste buds sing. Serve with strong espresso or tea.

Chocolate Fruit & Nut Tart

ingredients

⅓ cup **dried currants**
⅓ cup chopped **pitted prunes**
¼ cup **brandy**
⅓ cup each **walnut halves** and **natural almonds**
⅓ cup **unsalted butter**, softened
½ cup **granulated sugar**
2 **eggs**
3 tbsp **all-purpose flour**

4 oz (115 g) **bittersweet chocolate**, finely chopped

SWEET PASTRY:
1¼ cups **all-purpose flour**
¾ cup **icing sugar**
1 tsp grated **orange zest**
Pinch **salt**
½ cup **unsalted butter**, softened
2 **egg yolks**

method

In small bowl, stir together currants, prunes and brandy; cover and let stand for 1 hour.

On baking sheet, toast walnuts and almonds in 350°F (180°C) oven until fragrant, 8 to 10 minutes. Let cool; coarsely chop.

SWEET PASTRY: Meanwhile, in food processor, pulse together flour, sugar, orange zest and salt. Pulse in butter until mixture resembles coarse meal. Pulse in egg yolks until pastry clumps together. Gather into ball; press into disc. Wrap in plastic wrap; refrigerate until firm, about 1 hour. (Make-ahead: Refrigerate for up to 24 hours.)

On lightly floured surface, roll out pastry into 12-inch (30 cm) circle; place in 9-inch (23 cm) round tart pan with removable bottom, pressing to inside edge and leaving overhang. Using rolling pin, roll across rim to trim off overhang.

With fork, prick bottom of pastry all over; refrigerate for 20 minutes. Line with foil; fill with pie weights or dried beans. Bake on bottom rack in 400°F (200°C) oven for 20 minutes. Remove weights and foil; bake until centre is golden, 3 to 7 minutes.

In bowl, beat butter until fluffy; gradually beat in sugar. Beat in eggs, 1 at a time. Stir in flour, chocolate, brandy-soaked fruit and nuts; pour into baked crust.

Bake in 350°F (180°C) oven until centre jiggles slightly and edge is browned, 20 to 25 minutes. Let cool in pan on rack. (Make-ahead: Let stand at room temperature for up to 8 hours.)

MAKES 12 SERVINGS.

PER SERVING: about 345 cal, 5 g pro, 21 g total fat (10 g sat. fat), 36 g carb, 3 g fibre, 89 mg chol, 15 mg sodium, 140 mg potassium. % RDI: 3% calcium, 11% iron, 13% vit A, 17% folate.

Docking Dough

Certain doughs – like the one for this tart – shouldn't puff up or bubble during baking. To prevent this, the dough is docked, or pricked with a fork, a skewer or the tip of a knife. This allows steam to escape and keeps the dough flat. This technique is often used for blind-baking pie crusts, which are then lined with foil and filled with pie weights or dried beans to further discourage air bubbles from popping up. Shortbread doughs are often pricked before baking, but that's just for looks.

Regular flaky pie pastry is, of course, delicious. But add some cocoa powder and it takes on a new level of richness, especially when paired with a silky hazelnut-scented mousse.

Chocolate Mousse Pie

ingredients

8 oz (225 g) **semisweet chocolate**, finely chopped
1⅔ cups **whipping cream (35%)**
¼ cup **hazelnut liqueur** (such as Frangelico)

CHOCOLATE PASTRY:
½ cup **butter**, softened
¼ cup **granulated sugar**
1 **egg yolk**
½ tsp **vanilla**

1 cup **all-purpose flour**
3 tbsp **cocoa powder**
Pinch each **baking powder** and **salt**

GARNISH:
¾ cup **whipping cream (35%)**
1 tbsp sliced **hazelnuts**, toasted

method

CHOCOLATE PASTRY: In bowl, beat butter with sugar until light; beat in egg yolk and vanilla. Sift together flour, cocoa powder, baking powder and salt; stir into butter mixture in 2 additions to make soft dough. With wet or floured hands, press onto bottom and up side of 9-inch (23 cm) round tart pan with removable bottom; prick all over with fork. Freeze until firm, about 20 minutes.

Line pie shell with greased foil, greased side down; fill with pie weights or dried beans. Bake on bottom rack in 400°F (200°C) oven for 15 minutes. Remove weights and foil. Bake until firm and edges are darkened, about 8 minutes. Let cool in pan on rack.

Meanwhile, place chocolate in heatproof bowl. In small saucepan, bring ⅔ cup of the cream just to boil; pour over chocolate, whisking until smooth. Whisk in hazelnut liqueur. Let stand, stirring occasionally, until slightly thickened and cooled, 15 to 20 minutes.

Whip remaining cream; fold one-third into chocolate mixture. Fold in remaining whipped cream. Scrape into cooled crust, swirling top. Refrigerate until set, about 2 hours. *(Make-ahead: Cover loosely and refrigerate for up to 24 hours.)*

GARNISH: Whip cream; pipe or spoon around edge of tart. Sprinkle hazelnuts over cream.

MAKES 16 SERVINGS.
PER SERVING: about 305 cal, 3 g pro, 23 g total fat (14 g sat. fat), 22 g carb, 2 g fibre, 75 mg chol, 55 mg sodium. % RDI: 3% calcium, 7% iron, 19% vit A, 11% folate.

Freshen It Up

Whenever you want a new and delicious take on this tart, substitute almond liqueur (such as amaretto) and almonds for the hazelnut liqueur and nuts.

Key lime pie is a delicious combination of tart citrus and sweet custard. The filling often tops a plain pastry or graham cracker crumb crust, but these tarts up the ante with a luscious homemade chocolate pastry.

Chocolate Key Lime Tarts

ingredients

1 each **egg** and **egg yolk**
¼ cup **granulated sugar**
1 tsp grated **lime zest**
¼ cup **lime juice** or Key lime juice
¼ cup **sweetened condensed milk**

CHOCOLATE PASTRY:
1 cup **all-purpose flour**
3 tbsp **cocoa powder**
1 tbsp **granulated sugar**
Pinch **salt**

¼ cup cold **butter,** cubed
¼ cup cold **lard,** cubed
2 tbsp ice **water** (approx)
4 tsp **sour cream**

TOPPING:
¼ cup **whipping cream (35%)**
1 tsp **granulated sugar**
½ tsp grated **lime zest**
1 **lime,** quartered and thinly sliced

method

CHOCOLATE PASTRY: In bowl, whisk together flour, cocoa powder, sugar and salt. Using pastry blender, cut in butter and lard until in fine crumbs with a few larger pieces. Whisk ice water with sour cream; drizzle over dry ingredients, stirring briskly with fork to form ragged dough and adding up to 1 tbsp more ice water if needed. Press into disc; wrap and refrigerate until chilled, about 30 minutes. *(Make-ahead: Refrigerate for up to 2 days.)*

In heatproof bowl, whisk together egg, egg yolk, sugar, lime zest and lime juice; cook over saucepan of simmering water, stirring, until thick enough to mound on spoon, about 8 minutes. Strain through fine sieve into bowl. Place plastic wrap directly on surface; refrigerate until cold, about 45 minutes. Stir in sweetened condensed milk.

Meanwhile, on floured surface, roll out pastry to ⅛-inch (3 mm) thickness. Using 2½-inch (6 cm) round cutter, cut out 24 circles, rerolling scraps. Fit into ¾-inch (2 cm) deep mini tart or mini muffin tins. Prick with fork; cover and freeze until firm, about 30 minutes. Bake in 350°F (180°C) oven until golden, about 25 minutes. Let cool in pans on rack.

TOPPING: In bowl, whip cream with sugar; fold in lime zest. Set aside.

Remove tart shells from pan. Spoon filling into shells; pipe or spoon dollop of topping over filling. Garnish each with lime slice. *(Make-ahead: Refrigerate in airtight container for up to 24 hours.)*

MAKES 24 TARTS.

PER TART: about 83 cal, 1 g pro, 5 g total fat (3 g sat. fat), 9 g carb, trace fibre, 27 mg chol, 20 mg sodium, 43 mg potassium. % RDI: 2% calcium, 3% iron, 3% vit A, 3% vit C, 5% folate.

Key Limes vs. Regular Limes

Key limes are tiny and full of intense flavour, so they make the most authentic and robust version of this pie. If you can't find them, regular limes will work just fine. Look for bags of Key limes in the produce aisle – you'll often see them in late summer or fall, though they are grown year-round.

Hazelnuts are often partnered with dark chocolate, but here white chocolate takes centre stage. The hazelnut liqueur deepens the nuttiness of the filling; if you substitute vanilla for the liqueur, the nuts will have a more subtle influence on the overall flavour of the pie.

White Chocolate Hazelnut Pie

ingredients

1¼ cups **all-purpose flour**
1 tbsp **icing sugar**
¼ tsp **salt**
⅓ cup cold **butter,** cubed
⅓ cup **whipping cream (35%)**
⅓ cup **chocolate hazelnut spread**
   (such as Nutella)

FILLING:
½ cup **hazelnuts**
2 **eggs**
⅓ cup **granulated sugar**
2 tbsp **hazelnut liqueur** (or 1 tsp vanilla)
6 oz (170 g) **white chocolate,**
   finely chopped
1 cup **whipping cream (35%)**

method

In bowl, whisk together flour, sugar and salt. Using pastry blender or 2 knives, cut in butter until in fine crumbs with a few larger pieces. Drizzle in cream, tossing with fork until dough clumps together. Press onto bottom and up side of 9-inch (23 cm) round tart pan with removable bottom. Refrigerate for 30 minutes.

Prick bottom of pastry all over with fork; bake in 375°F (190°C) oven until golden, about 25 minutes. Let cool in pan on rack. Spread chocolate-hazelnut spread over pie shell. Cover and refrigerate for 1 hour.

FILLING: On baking sheet, toast hazelnuts in 350°F (180°C) oven until fragrant and skins crack, about 10 minutes. Transfer to clean tea towel; rub briskly to remove as much of the skins as possible. Coarsely chop nuts; set aside.

In heatproof bowl over saucepan of simmering water, whisk together eggs, sugar and liqueur, whisking constantly until thick enough to coat back of spoon and instant-read thermometer reads 140°F (60°C), about 7 minutes. Whisk in white chocolate until melted and smooth. Remove bowl from heat; let cool.

Whip cream; fold one-third into white chocolate mixture. Fold in remaining whipped cream. Fold in all but 2 tbsp of the hazelnuts; spoon into prepared crust. Sprinkle with remaining hazelnuts. Freeze until firm, about 4 hours. *(Make-ahead: Cover with plastic wrap and overwrap with heavy-duty foil; freeze for up to 1 month. Thaw in refrigerator for 30 minutes before serving.)*

MAKES 8 SERVINGS.

PER SERVING: about 577 cal, 8 g pro, 39 g total fat (19 g sat. fat), 49 g carb, 2 g fibre, 126 mg chol, 204 mg sodium. % RDI: 10% calcium, 13% iron, 24% vit A, 2% vit C, 20% folate.

Melt-in-your-mouth shortbread is the perfect treat with your afternoon cuppa.
These delicate fingers make an easy, tasty gift for any chocoholics on your list.

Chocolate Shortbread Fingers

ingredients

¾ cup **unsalted butter,** softened
½ cup **granulated sugar**
1 oz (30 g) **bittersweet chocolate,**
  melted and cooled
½ tsp **vanilla**
1⅓ cups **all-purpose flour**
¼ cup **cocoa powder,** sifted
¼ cup **cornstarch**
¼ tsp **salt**

TOPPING:
1 oz (30 g) **bittersweet chocolate,**
  melted

method

In bowl, beat butter with sugar until fluffy; stir in chocolate and vanilla. Whisk together flour, cocoa powder, cornstarch and salt; stir into butter mixture. Turn out onto lightly floured surface; knead until smooth, 5 to 10 times.

Press dough into parchment paper–lined 9-inch (2.5 L) square cake pan. Refrigerate until chilled, about 30 minutes. Score into 24 bars. Using fork or wooden skewer, prick each bar once or twice.

Bake in 325ºF (160ºC) oven until firm, about 40 minutes. Let cool in pan on rack for 5 minutes.

TOPPING: Using sharp knife and leaving bars in pan, cut through score lines; let cool completely. Drizzle with melted chocolate.

MAKES 24 BARS.
PER BAR: about 113 cal, 1 g pro, 7 g total fat (4 g sat. fat), 12 g carb, 1 g fibre, 15 mg chol, 25 mg sodium, 32 mg potassium. % RDI: 4% iron, 5% vit A, 7% folate.

This gorgeous and decadent tart comes together in a snap. The truffle-like centre is a simple ganache, which allows the flavours of the ripe, fresh berries to shine.

Triple-Berry Chocolate Tart

ingredients

6 oz (170 g) each **blackberries, raspberries** and **blueberries**
¼ cup **seedless raspberry jam**

GANACHE:
8 oz (225 g) **dark chocolate,** chopped
1½ cups **whipping cream (35%)**

CHOCOLATE CRUST:
½ cup **butter,** softened
⅓ cup **granulated sugar**
1 **egg yolk**
½ tsp **vanilla**
1 cup **all-purpose flour**
⅓ cup **cocoa powder**
¼ tsp **baking powder**
Pinch **salt**

method

CHOCOLATE CRUST: In bowl, beat butter with sugar until fluffy; beat in egg yolk and vanilla. Whisk together flour, cocoa powder, baking powder and salt; stir into butter mixture. Press onto bottom and up side of greased 9-inch (23 cm) round tart pan with removable bottom. Refrigerate for 30 minutes. Bake on baking sheet in 350°F (180°C) oven until surface appears dry, about 30 minutes. Let cool in pan on rack.

GANACHE: Place chocolate in heatproof bowl. In small saucepan, bring cream just to boil; pour over chocolate. Let stand for 2 minutes; whisk until chocolate is melted and smooth. Pour into prepared crust; refrigerate for 2 hours. *(Make-ahead: Cover loosely and refrigerate for up to 24 hours.)*

Arrange blackberries around edge of tart; place 1 in centre. Arrange raspberries inside blackberries; place 5 around centre blackberry. Fill empty space with blueberries.

In small microwaveable dish, microwave raspberry jam with 1 tbsp water on high until liquid, about 40 seconds; brush over berries. Let stand at room temperature for 45 minutes before serving.

MAKES 8 SERVINGS.
PER SERVING: about 579 cal, 6 g pro, 40 g total fat (24 g sat. fat), 54 g carb, 7 g fibre, 115 mg chol, 116 mg sodium, 408 mg potassium.% RDI: 7% calcium, 25% iron, 26% vit A, 15% vit C, 21% folate.

Easy Slicing

To keep the ganache from getting everywhere when you're slicing this tart, run hot water over a sharp chef's knife and dry it before cutting. Wipe it clean after every slice for the tidiest results.

Rich and chocolaty but very delicate, these shortbread drop cookies
are anything but your grandma's shortbread. The chocolate-covered almonds give each
bite a wonderful crunch.

Double-Chocolate Almond Shortbread

ingredients

¾ cup **unsalted butter,** softened
1 bar (100 g) **70% dark chocolate,**
   melted
½ cup **granulated sugar** (approx)
½ tsp **salt**
¼ cup **cornstarch**

½ tsp **vanilla**
1¾ cups **all-purpose flour,** sifted
1 pkg (400 g) **chocolate-covered
   almonds**

method

In bowl and using wooden spoon, beat together butter, melted chocolate, sugar and salt until light; stir in cornstarch and vanilla until smooth. Stir in flour just until combined. Fold in almonds.

Dip 1 tbsp measure into more granulated sugar to coat; scoop dough by rounded 1 tbsp, ½ inch (1 cm) apart, onto parchment paper–lined rimless baking sheet. Repeat with remaining dough. Refrigerate until chilled, about 1 hour. *(Make-ahead: Cover and refrigerate for up to 24 hours.)*

Bake in 275°F (140°C) oven until firm and bottoms are slightly darker, 40 to 45 minutes.

Let cool on pans on racks for 30 minutes. Roll each in more granulated sugar to lightly coat. *(Make-ahead: Layer between waxed paper in airtight container and store for up to 1 week or freeze for up to 1 month.)*

MAKES ABOUT 36 COOKIES.
PER COOKIE: about 146 cal, 2 g pro, 9 g total fat (4 g sat. fat), 16 g carb, 2 g fibre, 10 mg chol, 36 mg sodium, 8 mg potassium. % RDI: 9% calcium, 8% iron, 3% vit A, 5% vit C, 13% folate.

Butter FOR BAKING

Some cooks swear by unsalted butter in all baked goods and use it no matter what the recipe says. The Canadian Living Test Kitchen, however, develops and tests many of its baking recipes with salted butter. So if the ingredient list says simply "butter," we mean salted. We do specify unsalted in the ingredient list when that's what we've used in testing and perfecting the recipe.

Different brands of butter contain different amounts of salt, so using unsalted butter does give you more control over the saltiness of the resulting dish. Both of these shortbreads call for unsalted butter to ensure the delicate, sweet flavour of the cookies.

This shortbread marries two favourite cookie flavours (old-fashioned oatmeal and chocolate chip) in a crumbly, rich cookie that's guaranteed to satisfy your sweet tooth.

Oatmeal Chocolate Chip Shortbread

ingredients

1 cup **unsalted butter,** softened
3 tbsp **granulated sugar**
3 tbsp packed **brown sugar**
¼ tsp **salt**
½ tsp **vanilla**
1¼ cups **all-purpose flour**

¾ cup **quick-cooking rolled oats** (not instant)
¼ cup **cornstarch**
¾ cup **semisweet chocolate chips**

method

In bowl and using wooden spoon, beat together butter, granulated sugar, brown sugar and salt until light; stir in vanilla. Stir in flour, oats and cornstarch just until combined. Gently fold in chocolate chips.

Divide dough in half; place each on waxed paper; using paper to lift and cover, roll each into 9-inch (23 cm) long log. Refrigerate until chilled, about 1 hour. *(Make-ahead: Twist ends of paper around roll to seal; refrigerate for up to 24 hours.)*

Using serrated knife, cut each roll into 18 pieces; place, about ½ inch (1 cm) apart, on parchment paper–lined rimless baking sheet. Bake in 275°F (140°C) oven until firm and bottoms are lightly browned, 40 to 45 minutes.

Let cool on pans on racks. *(Make-ahead: Layer between waxed paper in airtight container and store for up to 1 week or freeze for up to 1 month.)*

MAKES 36 COOKIES.
PER COOKIE: about 98 cal, 1 g pro, 6 g total fat (4 g sat. fat), 10 g carb, 1 g fibre, 14 mg chol, 18 mg sodium, 29 mg potassium. % RDI: 3% iron, 5% vit A, 5% folate.

HOW-TO

①

Ricotta cheese is the base of the dense, not-too-sweet filling in this Italian-inspired tart. It delivers a pleasant creaminess without making the tart heavy and overly filling.

Chocolate Ricotta Tart

ingredients

1¼ cups **all-purpose flour**
¼ cup **cocoa powder**
2 tbsp **granulated sugar**
½ tsp **salt**
¼ cup each cold **butter** and **lard,** cubed
2 **egg yolks**
1 tsp **vinegar**
Ice **water**

FILLING:
½ cup **hazelnuts**
2 **egg yolks**
½ cup **granulated sugar**
1 tub (475 g) **ricotta cheese,** softened
1 oz (30 g) **semisweet chocolate** or bittersweet chocolate, finely chopped
1 tbsp grated **orange zest**
1 tsp **vanilla**

method

In large bowl, sift together flour, cocoa powder, sugar and salt. Using pastry blender or 2 knives, cut in butter and lard until in fine crumbs with a few larger pieces. In liquid measure, whisk 1 of the egg yolks with vinegar. Add enough ice water to make ⅓ cup. Drizzle over flour mixture; using fork, briskly stir until dough holds together. Gather dough and press into disc. Wrap in plastic wrap and refrigerate until chilled, about 30 minutes. *(Make-ahead: Refrigerate for up to 3 days.)*

On lightly floured surface, roll out three-quarters of the pastry to ⅛-inch (3 mm) thickness. Fit into 9-inch (23 cm) tart pan with removable bottom. Trim off excess and press onto remaining pastry. Press into disc; wrap in plastic wrap and refrigerate until chilled, about 30 minutes.

FILLING: Toast hazelnuts on rimmed baking sheet in 350°F (180°C) oven until fragrant and skins crack, about 8 minutes. Transfer to clean tea towel; rub briskly to remove as much of the skin as possible. Let cool; coarsely chop nuts.

In bowl, beat egg yolks with sugar until pale and thickened; beat in ricotta until smooth. Stir in hazelnuts, chocolate, orange zest and vanilla. Scrape into tart shell; smooth top.

On lightly floured surface, roll out reserved pastry to ⅛-inch (3 mm) thickness. Using fluted pastry wheel or knife, cut into ¾-inch (2 cm) wide strips, rerolling and cutting scraps. Brush pastry rim with water. Weave strips over filling, ½ inch (1 cm) apart, to make lattice top, pressing ends firmly to rim ❶. Trim pastry at rim. Whisk remaining egg yolk with 1 tbsp water. Brush over lattice.

Bake on bottom rack in 425°F (220°F) oven for 15 minutes. Reduce heat to 350°F (180°C); bake until filling is firm, about 30 minutes. Let cool in pan on rack. *(Make-ahead: Cover and refrigerate for up to 8 hours. Let stand at room temperature for 30 minutes before serving.)*

MAKES 8 SERVINGS.
PER SERVING: about 456 cal, 12 g pro, 30 g total fat (12 g sat. fat), 38 g carb, 2 g fibre, 147 mg chol, 257 mg sodium. % RDI: 15% calcium, 16% iron, 17% vit A, 2% vit C, 22% folate.

If you're torn between dark and milk chocolate, you don't have to choose.
This shortbread unites them in one delicious, crumbly package.

Chocolate Stripe Shortbread

ingredients

2 oz (55 g) **bittersweet chocolate,** chopped

1 oz (30 g) **milk chocolate,** chopped

1 cup **butter,** softened

½ cup **instant dissolving (fruit/berry) sugar**

1 tsp **vanilla**

2 cups **all-purpose flour**

Pinch **salt**

method

In heatproof bowl over saucepan of hot (not boiling) water, melt bittersweet chocolate, stirring until smooth. In separate heatproof bowl, melt milk chocolate, stirring until smooth. Let cool to room temperature.

In bowl, beat butter with sugar until fluffy; stir in vanilla. Stir in flour and salt. Scrape half into separate bowl; stir in bittersweet chocolate. Remove one-third of the remaining vanilla dough; set aside. Stir milk chocolate into remaining two-thirds.

On plastic wrap, shape half of the bittersweet chocolate dough into 9- x 2-inch (23 x 5 cm) rectangle. Shape half of the milk chocolate dough into 9- x 1¾-inch (23 x 4.5 cm) rectangle; place in centre of bittersweet chocolate dough. Roll half of the remaining vanilla dough into 9-inch (23 cm) log; place in centre of milk chocolate dough. Using plastic wrap to lift and shape, press doughs together to form triangular log. Repeat with remaining dough. Refrigerate until firm, about 2 hours. (Make-ahead: Freeze in airtight container for up to 3 weeks.)

Cut each triangular log into ¼-inch (5 mm) thick slices. If straight edges are desired, trim edges to straighten. Arrange, 1 inch (2.5 cm) apart, on 2 parchment paper–lined or greased rimless baking sheets. Bake on top and bottom racks in 300°F (150ºC) oven, rotating and switching pans halfway through, until firm to the touch and bottoms are slightly golden, 20 minutes.

Let cool on pans on racks for 2 minutes. Transfer to racks; let cool completely. (Make-ahead: Layer between waxed paper in airtight container and store for up to 1 week or freeze for up to 1 month.)

MAKES ABOUT 40 COOKIES.
PER COOKIE: about 84 cal, 1 g pro, 6 g total fat (4 g sat. fat), 8 g carb, trace fibre, 12 mg chol, 34 mg sodium. % RDI: 3% iron, 4% vit A, 6% folate.

Instant Dissolving Fruit/Berry Sugar

Test Kitchen TIP ★★★

This sugar with the long name is simply very finely ground granulated sugar. It dissolves well in liquids, leaving no grittiness. If you don't have any, scoop granulated sugar into a blender or food processor and whizz until very finely ground, about 1 minute.

Chili and chocolate have been a hot pairing for years now. This cookie uses a bit of fiery cayenne pepper to add spice to the simple chocolate base.

Spicy Chocolate Cinnamon Shortbread

ingredients

3 oz (85 g) **bittersweet chocolate,** chopped
1 cup **unsalted butter,** softened
⅓ cup **granulated sugar**
½ tsp **vanilla**

2¼ cups **all-purpose flour**
¼ cup **cocoa powder**
2 tbsp **cornstarch**
1 tsp **cinnamon**
¼ tsp each **nutmeg, salt** and **pepper**
⅛ tsp **cayenne pepper**

TOPPING:
5 oz (140 g) **bittersweet chocolate,** chopped

method

In heatproof bowl over saucepan of hot (not boiling) water, melt chocolate, stirring occasionally until smooth. Remove from heat; let cool.

In bowl, beat butter with sugar until fluffy; beat in melted chocolate and vanilla until smooth. Sift flour, cocoa powder, cornstarch, cinnamon, nutmeg, salt, pepper and cayenne pepper over butter mixture; stir to make smooth dough.

Between lightly floured waxed paper, roll out dough to ¼-inch (5 mm) thickness. With 2-inch (5 cm) teardrop-shaped cutter, cut out shapes, rerolling and cutting scraps. Place, about 1 inch (2.5 cm) apart, on parchment paper–lined rimless baking sheets. Refrigerate until firm, about 20 minutes.

Bake in 325°F (160°C) oven until firm, about 20 minutes. Let cool on pans on racks for 5 minutes. Transfer cookies to racks; let cool completely.

TOPPING: In heatproof bowl over saucepan of hot (not boiling) water, melt chocolate, stirring until smooth. Dip half of each cookie into chocolate on diagonal, shaking off excess. Place on waxed paper–lined baking sheets. Refrigerate until set, about 30 minutes.

MAKES ABOUT 70 COOKIES.
PER COOKIE: about 62 cal, 1 g pro, 4 g total fat (2 g sat. fat), 6 g carb, 1 g fibre, 7 mg chol, 9 mg sodium, 13 mg potassium. % RDI: 3% iron, 2% vit A, 4% folate.

241

Top off this rich tart simply, with vanilla ice cream or whipped cream and a chocolate curl or two (see page 297 for our easy how-tos). Since nuts are the focus here, choose California walnuts to ensure freshness and the richest flavour.

Chocolate Walnut Tart

ingredients

½ cup packed **brown sugar**
½ cup **corn syrup**
1 tbsp **butter**
1 tsp **cornstarch**
1 **egg**
1 tsp **vanilla**
2 cups **walnut halves**
⅓ cup chopped **dried sour cherries** or raisins
1 **egg yolk**

CHOCOLATE PASTRY:
¾ cup **butter,** softened
½ cup **granulated sugar**
1 **egg**
1 tsp **vanilla**
1¾ cups **all-purpose flour**
⅓ cup **cocoa powder**
¼ tsp **baking powder**
Pinch **salt**

method

CHOCOLATE PASTRY: In large bowl, beat butter with sugar until fluffy; beat in egg and vanilla. Into separate bowl, sift together flour, cocoa powder, baking powder and salt; sift again. Stir into butter mixture in 2 additions to make soft dough. Working with small handfuls, press about two-thirds onto bottom and up side of 9-inch (23 cm) fluted tart pan with removable bottom.

Form remaining pastry into disc; between waxed paper, roll out to 9-inch (23 cm) circle. Using fluted pastry wheel or sharp knife, cut into 1-inch (2.5 cm) wide strips. Refrigerate strips and shell until firm, about 2 hours. (*Make-ahead: Cover and refrigerate for up to 24 hours.*)

In bowl, beat together brown sugar, corn syrup, butter and cornstarch until combined; beat in egg and vanilla. Stir in walnuts and cherries. Scrape into pastry shell.

Whisk egg yolk with 1 tbsp water; brush over pastry rim. Arrange pastry strips over filling, leaving ¼-inch (5 mm) space between each. Trim ends of strips even with rim of pan; press to adhere to rim. Brush strips with egg mixture. Bake on bottom rack in 375°F (190°C) oven until pastry is firm and edges are darkened, about 40 minutes.

Let cool in pan on rack. (*Make-ahead: Cover and store for up to 24 hours.*)

Cut into wedges.

MAKES 8 TO 12 SERVINGS.
PER EACH OF 12 SERVINGS: about 438 cal, 7 g pro, 26 g total fat (9 g sat. fat), 49 g carb, 3 g fibre, 87 mg chol, 166 mg sodium. % RDI: 5% calcium, 15% iron, 15% vit A, 22% folate.

So what do you do when you get one of those giant chocolate bars as a present?
Sure, you could just eat it. But instead, why not transform it into the gooey molten centres
of a batch of these yummy shortbread cookies?

Giant Swiss Chocolate Chunk Shortbread

ingredients

1 bar (400 g) **Swiss milk chocolate with honey and almond nougat** (such as Toblerone)
2 cups **unsalted butter,** softened
⅔ cup **superfine sugar**
1½ tsp **vanilla**

½ tsp **salt**
3¾ cups **all-purpose flour**
¼ cup **cornstarch**

method

Cut chocolate bar between triangles into 15 large pieces; set aside.

In large bowl, beat butter with superfine sugar until fluffy; beat in vanilla and salt. Stir in flour and cornstarch; knead gently to bring dough together.

On lightly floured surface, roll dough into 15-inch (38 cm) long log. Cut into 1-inch (2.5 cm) thick rounds. Place, 2 inches (5 cm) apart, on parchment paper–lined rimless baking sheets. Press 1 chocolate piece, flat side down, into each round. Press dough up to surround and overlap chocolate edges. Bake in 325°F (160°C) oven until golden, 22 to 25 minutes.

Let cool on pans on racks for 10 minutes. Transfer to racks; let cool completely.

MAKES 15 LARGE COOKIES.
PER COOKIE: about 513 cal, 5 g pro, 33 g total fat (20 g sat. fat), 51 g carb, 2 g fibre, 72 mg chol, 97 mg sodium, 41 mg potassium. % RDI: 5% calcium, 14% iron, 23% vit A, 30% folate.

CHANGE IT UP
Swiss Chocolate Chunk Shortbread
Reduce chocolate to 6 oz (170 g) and cut into sixty ¼-inch (5 mm) chunks. Roll dough by rounded 1 tbsp into balls; press chocolate chunk into each. Bake for 20 to 22 minutes.

MAKES 60 COOKIES.

Stay Cool

As tempting as these molten chocolate cookies are right out of the oven, let them cool completely before digging in. The centres are extremely hot and the sugary core can really burn your tongue if you indulge in them too soon.

Sweet and tangy at the same time, these scones are an indulgence any time of the day, but they make an especially decadent breakfast or brunch option.

Cherry White Chocolate Scones

ingredients

2½ cups **all-purpose flour**
2 tbsp **granulated sugar**
2½ tsp **baking powder**
½ tsp each **baking soda** and **salt**
½ cup cold **butter,** cubed

1 cup **buttermilk**
1 **egg**
1 cup **dried sour cherries** or dried cranberries, halved
3 oz (85 g) **white chocolate,** chopped

TOPPING:
2 oz (55 g) **white chocolate,** melted

method

In large bowl, whisk together flour, sugar, baking powder, baking soda and salt. Using pastry blender or 2 knives, cut in butter until in coarse crumbs. Whisk buttermilk with egg; add to flour mixture. Sprinkle with cherries and white chocolate; stir with fork to make soft dough.

With lightly floured hands, press dough into ball. On floured surface, knead dough gently 10 times. Pat out into 10- x 7-inch (25 x 18 cm) rectangle; trim edges to straighten.

Cut rectangle into 6 squares; cut each diagonally in half. Place on parchment paper–lined large rimless baking sheet. Bake in 400°F (200°C) oven until golden, 18 to 20 minutes. Transfer to rack; let cool.

TOPPING: Place rack over waxed paper–lined baking sheet; drizzle chocolate over scones. Let stand until set, about 1 hour. *(Make-ahead: Store in airtight container for up to 24 hours or wrap individually in plastic wrap and freeze in airtight container for up to 2 weeks.)*

MAKES 12 SCONES.
PER SCONE: about 291 cal, 5 g pro, 13 g total fat (7 g sat. fat), 40 g carb, 2 g fibre, 43 mg chol, 317 mg sodium. % RDI: 10% calcium, 11% iron, 10% vit A, 17% folate.

CHANGE IT UP
Apricot Almond Scones
Replace cherries and chocolate with ¾ cup chopped dried apricots. Omit topping. Whisk together 1 cup icing sugar, 2 tbsp milk, dash almond extract and up to 1 tsp water if necessary to make spreadable. Drizzle over scones; sprinkle with ¼ cup toasted sliced almonds.

Lemon Poppy Seed Scones
Replace cherries and chocolate with 2 tbsp grated lemon zest and 4 tsp poppy seeds. Omit topping. Whisk together 1 cup icing sugar, 2 tbsp lemon juice, and up to 1 tsp water if necessary to make spreadable; drizzle over scones.

These not-too-sweet treats are a nice change of pace from regular fruity scones.
They're delicious on their own and don't really need any butter or jam to make them divine.

Milk Chocolate Scones

ingredients

¾ cup **whipping cream (35%)**
2 **eggs**
1 tsp **vanilla**
2½ cups **all-purpose flour**
2 tbsp **granulated sugar**
4 tsp **baking powder**
¼ tsp **salt**

⅓ cup cold **unsalted butter,** cubed
2 bars (each 100 g) **milk chocolate,**
  chopped
1 **egg yolk**

method

Whisk together cream, eggs and vanilla; set aside. In large bowl, whisk together flour, sugar, baking powder and salt. Using pastry blender or 2 knives, cut in butter until in coarse crumbs with a few larger pieces. Stir in chocolate. With fork, stir in cream mixture to form soft dough.

Turn out onto lightly floured surface; knead once or twice until dough comes together. Roll out or pat into 9-inch (23 cm) square; cut into 9 squares. Cut each square in half diagonally. Place, 1 inch (2.5 cm) apart, on parchment paper–lined rimless baking sheet. *(Make-ahead: Cover with plastic wrap and refrigerate for up to 24 hours.)*

Whisk egg yolk with 1 tsp water; brush over scones. Bake in 450°F (230°C) oven until tops are golden, 11 to 12 minutes. Serve warm.

MAKES 18 SCONES.
PER SCONE: about 201 cal, 4 g pro, 11 g total fat (7 g sat. fat), 22 g carb, 1 g fibre, 56 mg chol, 120 mg sodium, 81 mg potassium. % RDI: 6% calcium, 8% iron, 8% vit A, 19% folate.

The dark chocolate and tart cherry bits in these scones make them a little more like dessert than breakfast. Indulge in them while they're still warm – the scones don't keep very long, so make the most of them while they're fresh.

Dark Chocolate & Dried Cherry Scones

ingredients

¾ cup **whipping cream (35%)**
2 **eggs**
1 tbsp **granulated sugar**
2½ cups **all-purpose flour**
4 tsp **baking powder**
¼ tsp **salt**
⅓ cup cold **butter,** cubed
½ cup **dried sour cherries**
½ cup **dark chocolate chips**

TOPPING:
1 tbsp **whipping cream (35%)**
1 tbsp **granulated sugar**

method

Whisk together cream, eggs and sugar. Set aside. In large bowl, whisk together flour, baking powder and salt. Using pastry blender or 2 knives, cut in butter until in coarse crumbs with a few larger pieces. Stir in cherries and chocolate chips. Using fork, stir in cream mixture to form soft dough.

Turn out onto lightly floured surface; knead gently once or twice until dough comes together. Pat out to scant ¾-inch (2 cm) thickness. Using floured 3-inch (8 cm) round cutter, cut out rounds, rerolling and cutting scraps once. Place, 1 inch (2.5 cm) apart, on parchment paper–lined rimless baking sheet.

TOPPING: Brush scones with cream; sprinkle with sugar. Bake in 450°F (230°C) oven until tops are light golden, about 12 minutes. Serve warm.

MAKES 10 SCONES.

PER SCONE: about 324 cal, 6 g pro, 17 g total fat (10 g sat. fat), 37 g carb, 2 g fibre, 77 mg chol, 201 mg sodium, 136 mg potassium. % RDI: 9% calcium, 16% iron, 14% vit A, 31% folate.

Cubing Cold Butter or Lard

To ensure crumbly or flaky results in pastries, it's vital that the fat stay cold and unmelted as it's cut into the flour mixture. These crumbs of solid flour-coated butter or lard melt in the oven, producing steam and lifting the layers apart. Handle the fat as little as possible when you're cubing it – the heat from your hands can melt it, so use a spoon or knife to scrape the cubes into the flour mixture.

Test Kitchen TIP

These tiny tarts feature tender pastry and a rich chocolate filling,
which make them just as tasty (and addictive) as candy. They look pretty on a dessert
tray for a party, especially during the holidays.

Chocolate Hazelnut Tassies

ingredients

½ cup **butter,** softened

Half pkg (250 g pkg) **cream cheese,**
  softened

1¼ cups **all-purpose flour**

½ cup finely chopped **hazelnuts**

GANACHE FILLING:

4 oz (115 g) **semisweet chocolate** or
  bittersweet chocolate, chopped

½ cup **whipping cream (35%)**

2 tsp **hazelnut liqueur** (such as
  Frangelico), optional

12 **whole hazelnuts** (approx)

method

In large bowl, beat butter with cream cheese
until fluffy; stir in flour and hazelnuts until
combined. Place 1 tbsp in each of 24 greased
mini muffin cups. Press evenly over bottom
and up side of each cup. Freeze until firm,
about 1 hour. *(Make-ahead: Wrap in heavy-
duty foil and freeze for up to 2 weeks.)*

Bake in 325°F (160°C) oven until golden,
about 30 minutes. Let cool in pan on rack.

GANACHE FILLING: Meanwhile, place
chocolate in heatproof bowl. In small
saucepan, bring cream, and hazelnut liqueur
(if using) just to boil; pour over chocolate,
whisking until melted and smooth. Pour into
pastry shells.

Cut each hazelnut in half; place 1 half in
centre of each tart. Let stand until filling is
firm, about 30 minutes. *(Make-ahead:
Refrigerate in airtight container for up to
5 days.)*

MAKES 24 TARTS.

PER TART: about 135 cal, 2 g pro, 11 g total fat (6 g
sat. fat), 8 g carb, 1 g fibre, 22 mg chol, 56 mg sodium.
% RDI: 2% calcium, 4% iron, 7% vit A, 5% folate.

249

Didn't think scones came in a death-by-chocolate variety? Think again.
These iced ones are so decadent but so simple, and they make an elegant dessert.

Chocolate Walnut Fudge Scones

ingredients

2 cups **all-purpose flour**
½ cup **cocoa powder**
¼ cup packed **brown sugar**
2½ tsp **baking powder**
½ tsp each **baking soda** and **salt**
½ cup cold **butter,** cubed
1 cup **buttermilk**
1 **egg**
1 tsp **vanilla**
¾ cup chopped toasted **walnuts**

FUDGE ICING:
1 cup **icing sugar**
2 tbsp **cocoa powder**
2 tbsp **milk** (approx)
1 tsp **vanilla**

method

In large bowl, whisk together flour, cocoa powder, brown sugar, baking powder, baking soda and salt. Using pastry blender or 2 knives, cut in butter until in coarse crumbs. Whisk together buttermilk, egg and vanilla; add to flour mixture. Sprinkle with walnuts; stir with fork to make soft dough.

With lightly floured hands, press dough into ball. On floured surface, knead gently 10 times. Pat into 10- x 7-inch (25 x 18 cm) rectangle; trim edges to straighten. Cut into 6 squares; cut each diagonally in half. Place on parchment paper–lined large rimless baking sheet. Bake in 400°F (200°C) oven until tops are firm to the touch, 18 to 20 minutes. Transfer to rack; let cool.

FUDGE ICING: In bowl, whisk icing sugar with cocoa powder. Add milk and vanilla; whisk until smooth, adding up to 1 tsp more milk if necessary to make spreadable. Spread over scones; let stand until set, about 1 hour. *(Make-ahead: Store in airtight container for up to 24 hours or wrap individually in plastic wrap and freeze in airtight container for up to 2 weeks.)*

MAKES 12 SCONES.
PER SCONE: about 270 cal, 5 g pro, 14 g total fat (6 g sat. fat), 34 g carb, 2 g fibre, 41 mg chol, 307 mg sodium. % RDI: 7% calcium, 15% iron, 8% vit A, 17% folate.

Buttery pecans make an appearance in both the dough and the garnish for these cookies. Pecan halves taste freshest, so chop them yourself rather than buying pieces or prechopped nuts.

Chocolate Pecan Mounds

ingredients

6 oz (170 g) **bittersweet chocolate,** chopped
1 cup **unsalted butter,** softened
⅓ cup packed **brown sugar**
1 tsp **vanilla**
¼ cup chopped toasted **pecans**
2¼ cups **all-purpose flour**

¼ cup **cornstarch**
¼ tsp **salt**
18 **pecan halves**

method

In heatproof bowl over saucepan of hot (not boiling) water, melt chocolate, stirring until smooth. Let cool.

In bowl, beat butter with brown sugar until fluffy. Stir in chocolate, vanilla then chopped pecans. Whisk together flour, cornstarch and salt; stir into chocolate mixture in 2 additions until smooth.

Scoop by rounded 1 tbsp, 1 inch (2.5 cm) apart, onto parchment paper–lined rimless baking sheets. Halve pecan halves lengthwise; press 1 pecan piece into top of each cookie, pressing dough around pecan gently to adhere. Chill until firm, about 1 hour.

Bake in 325°F (160°C) oven until darkened on bottoms, about 20 minutes.

Let cool on pans on racks for 5 minutes. Transfer to racks; let cool completely.

MAKES 36 COOKIES.
PER COOKIE: about 122 cal, 1 g pro, 8 g total fat (4 g sat. fat), 12 g carb, 1 g fibre, 14 mg chol, 18 mg sodium. % RDI: 1% calcium, 4% iron, 5% vit A, 7% folate.

The Right Size

When you're chopping chocolate for melting, use a sharp, heavy chef's knife. Chop the chocolate into pieces the size of almonds or smaller. The tinier the pieces, the more quickly and smoothly they will melt.

The cute checkerboard pattern on these cookies looks challenging, but it couldn't be simpler to make. But don't tell anyone how you did it — just let them think you're a wizard in the kitchen.

Checkerboard Cookies

ingredients

4 oz (115 g) **unsweetened chocolate,** chopped
1 cup **butter,** softened
2 cups **granulated sugar**
3 **eggs**
2 tbsp **vanilla**

4 cups **all-purpose flour**
1 tsp **baking soda**
1 tsp **salt**

method

In heatproof bowl over saucepan of hot (not boiling) water, melt chocolate, stirring often. Let cool to room temperature.

In large bowl, beat butter with sugar until fluffy; beat in 2 of the eggs, 1 at a time. Beat in vanilla. Whisk together flour, baking soda and salt; stir into butter mixture in 3 additions, using hands if too stiff to stir.

Remove half of the dough to make vanilla dough. Stir chocolate into remaining dough, using hands to blend thoroughly.

Divide vanilla dough in half; flatten each half into square. Place dough, 1 square at a time, between waxed paper; roll out to 7-inch (18 cm) square. Straighten edges with ruler. Repeat with chocolate dough. Refrigerate until firm, about 30 minutes. Using ruler and sharp knife, cut each square into nine ¾-inch (2 cm) wide strips.

Place 12-inch (30 cm) long piece of plastic wrap on work surface. Alternating vanilla and chocolate strips, place 3 strips of dough side by side (close but not touching) on plastic wrap. Whisk remaining egg; brush over sides and tops of strips. Gently press long edges of

strips together to adhere. Repeat, forming second and third layers and alternating flavours of strips, to create checkerboard pattern. Repeat to make 3 more logs, reversing colour pattern on 2 of the logs. Fold plastic wrap up to enclose logs; refrigerate for 30 minutes. *(Make-ahead: Refrigerate for up to 4 days. Or overwrap in heavy-duty foil and freeze for up to 1 month.)*

Using serrated knife, trim ends of each log; cut logs into ¼-inch (5 mm) thick slices. Arrange, about 1 inch (2.5 cm) apart, on 2 parchment paper–lined rimless baking sheets. Bake, 1 sheet at a time, in 350°F (180°C) oven until firm to the touch, about 12 minutes.

Let cool on pans on racks for 3 minutes. Transfer to racks; let cool completely. *(Make-ahead: Layer between waxed paper in airtight container and store at room temperature for up to 2 weeks or freeze for up to 1 month.)*

MAKES ABOUT 80 COOKIES.
PER COOKIE: about 73 cal, 1 g pro, 3 g total fat (2 g sat. fat), 10 g carb, trace fibre, 14 mg chol, 69 mg sodium. % RDI: 3% iron, 3% vit A, 4% folate.

Studded with sweet glacé cherries and surrounded by a rich chocolaty layer, these cookies are the perfect snack for dipping into a glass of ice cold milk.

Chocolate Cherry Rounds

ingredients

2 oz (55 g) **bittersweet chocolate,** chopped
⅔ cup **unsalted butter,** softened
¾ cup **granulated sugar**
1 **egg**
½ tsp **almond extract**
2 cups **all-purpose flour**

¼ tsp each **baking soda** and **salt**
⅓ cup chopped **glacé cherries**
1 **egg white**

method

In heatproof bowl over saucepan of hot (not boiling) water, melt chocolate, stirring until smooth. Remove from heat; let cool to room temperature.

In large bowl, beat butter with sugar until fluffy; beat in egg and almond extract. Whisk together flour, baking soda and salt; stir into butter mixture to make stiff dough.

Divide dough in half. Into one half, stir melted chocolate to form smooth dough. Set aside.

Into remaining half, mix cherries. Divide cherry dough in half. Roll each into 9-inch (23 cm) log. Wrap each in plastic wrap and refrigerate for 30 minutes.

Roll half of the chocolate dough into 9- x 4½-inch (23 x 11 cm) rectangle; brush with some of the egg white. Place 1 chilled log of the cherry dough lengthwise along centre of rectangle. Bring edges of chocolate dough over log to meet; press edges together and roll log to reshape if necessary. Repeat with remaining dough. Wrap each in plastic wrap and refrigerate until firm, about 1 hour.

Cut each log into generous ¼-inch (5 mm) thick slices. Arrange, 1 inch (2.5 cm) apart, on parchment paper–lined rimless baking sheets. Bake in 300°F (150°C) oven until firm and bottoms are light golden, about 15 minutes.

Let cool on pans on racks for 2 minutes. Transfer to racks; let cool completely.

MAKES ABOUT 50 COOKIES.
PER COOKIE: about 64 cal, 1 g pro, 3 g total fat (2 g sat. fat), 8 g carb, trace fibre, 10 mg chol, 21 mg sodium, 11 mg potassium. % RDI: 2% calcium, 2% iron, 5% folate.

Finding Glacé Cherries

These supersweet confections are easy to find during the holidays in any supermarket; look for tubs of them in the baking aisle. If they're not on supermarket shelves the rest of the year, look for them in bulk stores. They're sometimes labelled "candied cherries" or "glazed cherries."

Similar to French shortbread cookies called sablés, these treats have a slightly sandy texture and rich flavour. They may crumble a bit when sliced, but that's no problem — just pinch the bits back together.

Double-Chocolate Ice Box Cookies

ingredients

9 tbsp **unsalted butter,** softened
⅔ cup **granulated sugar**
1 tsp **vanilla**
1 cup **all-purpose flour**
⅓ cup **cocoa powder**
½ tsp **baking powder**

¼ tsp **kosher salt**
3 oz (85 g) **bittersweet chocolate,**
  cut in small chunks

method

In bowl, beat butter with sugar until fluffy; stir in vanilla. Whisk together flour, cocoa powder, baking powder and salt; stir into butter mixture in 2 additions. Stir in chocolate to make crumbly dough. On plastic wrap, form dough into 1½-inch (4 cm) diameter log; wrap in plastic wrap and refrigerate for 1½ hours.

Using sharp chef's knife, slice log into ½-inch (1 cm) thick rounds. Place, 1 inch (2.5 cm) apart, on parchment paper–lined rimless baking sheets. Bake, 1 sheet at a time, in 325°F (160°C) oven until edges appear dry but centre is still slightly moist, 12 minutes.

Let cool on pan on rack for 5 minutes. Transfer to rack; let cool completely. *(Make-ahead: Store in airtight container for up to 1 week or freeze for up to 1 month.)*

MAKES ABOUT 30 COOKIES.
PER COOKIE: about 82 cal, 1 g pro, 5 g total fat (3 g sat. fat), 10 g carb, 1 g fibre, 9 mg chol, 19 mg sodium, 46 mg potassium. % RDI: 1% calcium, 4% iron, 3% vit A, 4% folate.

These bite-size cookies just melt in your mouth. It may require a bit of practice to master the piping technique, but never fear: The dough is so easy to handle that you can scoop it back into the piping bag and try again if your first attempt isn't perfect.

Sparkly Chocolate Blossoms

ingredients

1 cup **unsalted butter,** softened
⅔ cup **icing sugar**
½ tsp **vanilla**
1 cup **all-purpose flour**
⅔ cup **cocoa powder**

¼ tsp **salt**
1 tbsp **coarse sugar**

method

In bowl, beat butter with icing sugar until fluffy; stir in vanilla. Stir in flour, cocoa powder and salt.

Spoon dough into piping bag fitted with ½-inch (1 cm) star tip; pressing tip against pan, pipe 1-inch (2.5 cm) round cookies, about 1 inch (2.5 cm) apart, onto parchment paper–lined rimless baking sheets. Sprinkle with coarse sugar.

Bake in 325°F (160°C) oven until tops are dry yet cookies are soft to the touch, about 18 minutes.

Let cool on pans on racks for 4 minutes. Transfer to racks; let cool completely. *(Make-ahead: Store in airtight container for up to 5 days.)*

MAKES ABOUT 150 COOKIES.
PER COOKIE: about 17 cal, trace pro, 1 g total fat (1 g sat. fat), 2 g carb, trace fibre, 3 mg chol, 4 mg sodium, 11 mg potassium. % RDI: 1% iron, 1% vit A, 1% folate.

257

This traditional Swiss cookie, which originated in Basel,
is a lovely combination of bittersweet chocolate and spices. Bonus: It is gluten-free.

Basler Brunsli

ingredients

8 oz (225 g) **bittersweet chocolate,** chopped
⅓ cup **cocoa powder**
2 tsp **cinnamon**
¼ tsp **ground cloves**
2 **egg whites**
¼ cup **superfine sugar**
3 cups **ground almonds**

3 tbsp **kirsch** or brandy
¼ cup **granulated sugar**
2 tbsp **coarse sugar**

method

In food processor, pulse together chocolate, cocoa powder, cinnamon and cloves until finely ground. Set aside.

In large bowl, beat egg whites until foamy; beat in superfine sugar, 1 tbsp at a time, until stiff peaks form. Fold in chocolate mixture, almonds and kirsch just until combined. Divide dough in half and shape into rectangles; wrap in plastic wrap and refrigerate until firm, about 30 minutes.

Sprinkle work surface with half of the granulated sugar. Working with 1 piece of dough, turn 2 or 3 times to coat with sugar. Roll out to scant ½-inch (1 cm) thickness. Using 2-inch (5 cm) heart-shaped cookie cutter, cut into hearts. Repeat with remaining dough. Place on waxed paper; sprinkle with coarse sugar. Let dry for 1 hour.

Arrange cutouts, about 1 inch (2.5 cm) apart, on parchment paper–lined rimless baking sheets. Bake in 325°F (160°C) oven just until firm, about 20 minutes.

Let cool on pans on racks for 2 minutes. Transfer to racks; let cool completely. *(Make-ahead: Store in airtight container for up to 4 days or freeze for up to 1 month.)*

MAKES ABOUT 45 COOKIES.
PER COOKIE: about 74 cal, 2 g pro, 5 g total fat (1 g sat. fat), 6 g carb, 1 g fibre, 0 mg chol, 3 mg sodium. % RDI: 2% calcium, 4% iron, 1% folate.

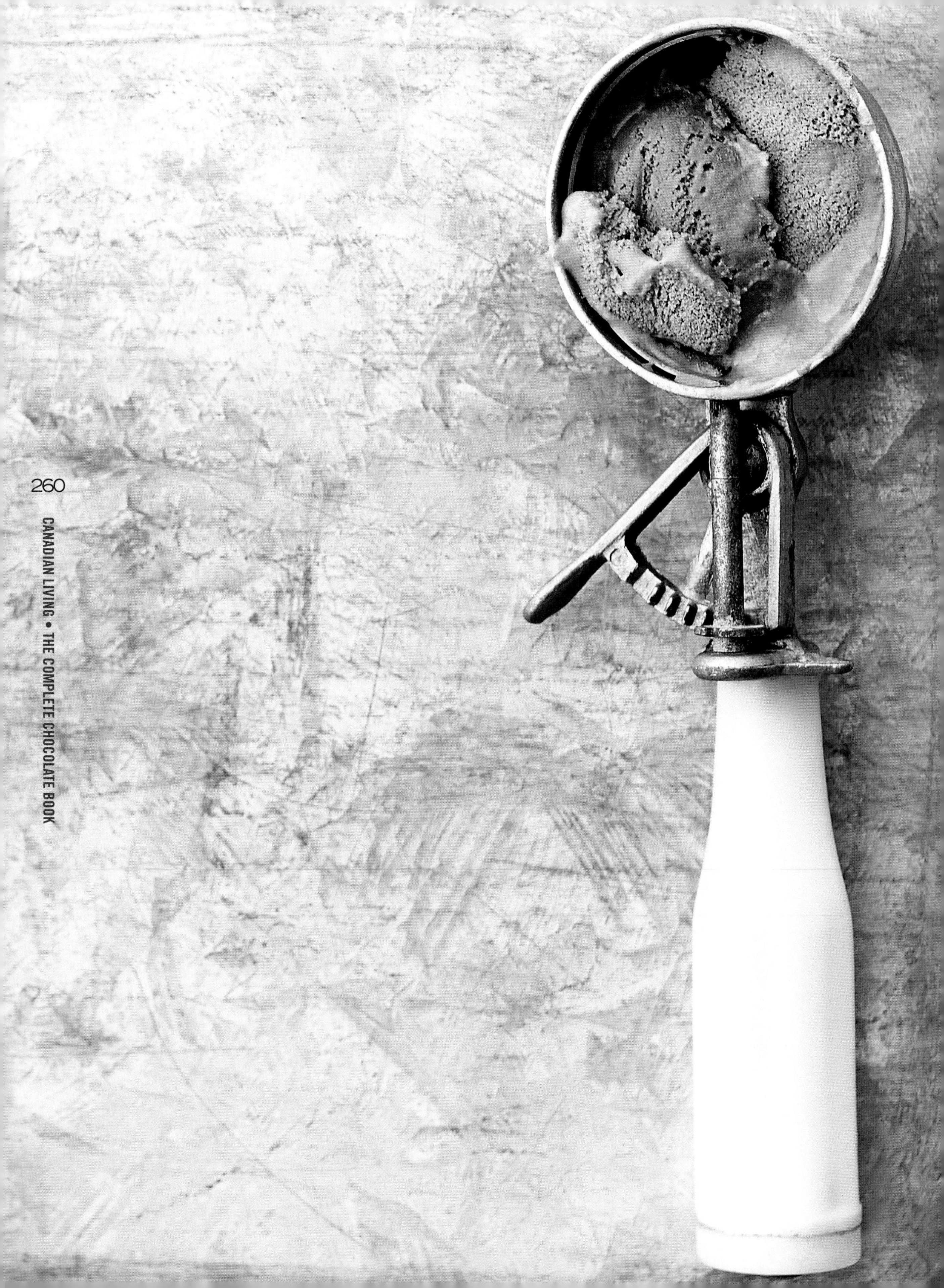

chilly

Chocolate & Salted Caramel Swirl Ice Cream 263
Chocolate Sorbet 264
Ice Cream Truffles 265
White Chocolate Ice Cream With Blueberry Swirl 268
Triple-Decker Ice Cream Stacks 268
Mocha Ice Cream Squares 269
Sublime Brownies & Bourbon Sauce Sundaes 271
Chocolate Chip Ice Cream Sandwiches 272
Triple-Chocolate Cookie Ice Cream Sandwiches 273
Three–Ice Cream Terrine 274
Mint Chocolate Sandwich Cookies 276
Nanaimo Bar Ice Cream Cake 277
Mini Baked Alaskas 279
Chocolate Raspberry Pistachio Baked Alaska 280
Tunnel of Ice Cream Cake 281
Neapolitan Pistachio Frozen Bombe 282
Frozen Chocolate Praline Meringue Torte 284
Chocolate Caramel Ice Cream Pie 285
Mint Chocolate Chip Ice Cream Pie 287
Double-Chocolate Semifreddo 288
Mocha Semifreddo 289
Frozen Banana Bites 290
Mocha Frappé 292
Raspberry Chocolate Smoothie 292
Old-Fashioned Milkshakes 293
Chocolate Soy Banana Smoothie 293
Neapolitan Milkshake 295
Moustache Straw Cookies 295
Chocolate Brownie Martini 296
Chocolate Mint Martini 296

Salty-sweet caramel and rich chocolate — what more could a chocoholic ask for? To use an ice cream machine, make the caramel sauce while the ice cream mixture is chilling and freezing, then follow the manufacturer's instructions and swirl it in during the last few minutes of freezing.

Chocolate & Salted Caramel Swirl Ice Cream

ingredients

2 cups **milk**
4 tsp **cornstarch**
1½ cups **whipping cream (35%)**
2 oz (55 g) **70% dark chocolate,** chopped
¾ cup **granulated sugar**
½ cup **cocoa powder**
1 tsp **vanilla**

SALTED CARAMEL SAUCE:
½ cup **granulated sugar**
½ cup **whipping cream (35%)**
½ tsp **salt**

method

Stir ¼ cup of the milk with cornstarch until dissolved; set aside.

In small saucepan, heat ½ cup of the cream with chocolate over low heat, stirring occasionally, just until melted and smooth, 5 minutes. Remove from heat; set aside.

Meanwhile, in heavy-bottom saucepan, whisk together remaining milk and cream, sugar, cocoa powder and vanilla. Bring to boil over medium-high heat, stirring often; reduce heat to medium and cook, stirring, for 4 minutes. Stir in cornstarch mixture; cook, stirring, until thickened, 2 to 3 minutes.

Stir in chocolate mixture until smooth. Pour into 9-inch (2.5 L) square cake pan; place plastic wrap directly on surface. Refrigerate until chilled, about 1½ hours. *(Make-ahead: Transfer to airtight container; place plastic wrap directly on surface and refrigerate for up to 24 hours.)*

Transfer to freezer container and freeze until firm but not solid, 2 to 3 hours.

SALTED CARAMEL SAUCE: Meanwhile, in small deep saucepan over medium-high heat, stir sugar with ¼ cup water until dissolved, brushing down side of pan with pastry brush dipped in cold water. Bring to boil; boil vigorously, without stirring but brushing down side of pan often, until dark amber, about 6 minutes.

Standing back and averting face, add cream and salt; cook, stirring, until smooth and slightly thickened, about 2 minutes. Transfer to heatproof bowl; let stand until at room temperature, about 1½ hours.

Scrape ice cream into food processor; purée until smooth. Spoon alternating layers of puréed ice cream and caramel sauce into freezer container, swirling with tip of knife or skewer. Cover and freeze until firm, about 4 hours.

MAKES ABOUT 4 CUPS.
PER ½ CUP: about 406 cal, 5 g pro, 26 g total fat (16 g sat. fat), 43 g carb, 2 g fibre, 82 mg chol, 192 mg sodium, 327 mg potassium. % RDI: 11% calcium, 12% iron, 22% vit A, 2% folate.

This sorbet tastes as rich as ice cream but doesn't contain eggs or cream.
Chocolate bars with 65 to 72 percent pure cocoa give the smoothest, creamiest texture.
For dairy-free sorbet, use all dark chocolate instead of the blend of dark and milk.

Chocolate Sorbet

ingredients

¾ cup **granulated sugar**
¼ cup **cocoa powder**
1 slice **fresh ginger**

7 oz (210 g) **dark chocolate,** chopped
2 oz (55 g) **milk chocolate,** chopped

method

In saucepan, bring sugar, cocoa powder, ginger and 2 cups water to boil over medium-high heat; boil, uncovered, for 5 minutes. Remove from heat; discard ginger.

Add dark and milk chocolates; whisk until smooth. Strain into 9-inch (2.5 L) square cake pan. Cover and refrigerate until cold, about 1½ hours.

Freeze until almost solid, about 1½ hours. Break up and purée in food processor until smooth. Scrape into airtight container; freeze until firm, about 4 hours. Or freeze in ice-cream machine according to manufacturer's instructions. *(Make-ahead: Freeze for up to 1 week.)*

MAKES 3 CUPS.

PER ½ CUP: about 325 cal, 5 g pro, 22 g total fat (13 g sat. fat), 42 g carb, 6 g fibre, 2 mg chol, 16 mg sodium. % RDI: 4% calcium, 20% iron, 1% vit A, 2% folate.

These bite-size ice cream confections are terrific for summer parties. We recommend chocolate ice cream (of course), but change it up with any of your other favourite flavours.

Ice Cream Truffles

ingredients

1½ cups **chocolate ice cream**

⅓ cup crushed **amaretti cookies**

⅓ cup finely chopped **almonds**, toasted

⅓ cup **chocolate shot** or coloured sprinkles

⅓ cup **sweetened flaked coconut**, toasted

method

Using small scoop or tablespoon, scoop chocolate ice cream into twenty-four 1-inch (2.5 cm) balls. Freeze on parchment paper–lined rimmed baking sheet for 2 hours.

Spread cookies, almonds, chocolate shot and coconut on 4 separate small plates. Working with a few ice cream balls at a time, roll 6 in each topping.

Return to baking sheet; freeze for 30 minutes. *(Make-ahead: Freeze in airtight container for up to 5 days.)*

Place in paper candy cups.

MAKES 24 TRUFFLES.

PER AMARETTI ICE CREAM TRUFFLE: about 37 cal, trace pro, 2 g total fat (1 g sat. fat), 6 g carb, 0 g fibre, 4 mg chol, 19 mg sodium. % RDI: 1% calcium, 1% vit A.

PER ALMOND ICE CREAM TRUFFLE: about 52 cal, 2 g pro, 4 g total fat (1 g sat. fat), 3 g carb, 1 g fibre, 4 mg chol, 8 mg sodium. % RDI: 2% calcium, 1% iron, 1% vit A, 1% folate.

PER CHOCOLATE SHOT ICE CREAM TRUFFLE: about 67 cal, 1 g pro, 3 g total fat (2 g sat. fat), 8 g carb, 1 g fibre, 4 mg chol, 7 mg sodium. % RDI: 1% calcium, 2% iron, 1% vit A, 1% folate.

PER COCONUT ICE CREAM TRUFFLE: about 36 cal, trace pro, 2 g total fat (2 g sat. fat), 4 g carb, trace fibre, 4 mg chol, 17 mg sodium. % RDI: 1% calcium, 1% iron, 1% vit A.

What Is Chocolate Shot?

Also known by the names "chocolate sprinkles" or "Chocolate Décors," chocolate shot are thin, dark brown sprinkles about ¼ inch (5 mm) long – not the tiny round balls. They're easy to find in bulk food stores and in the baking aisle of the supermarket.

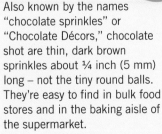

A delicate swirl of blueberry jam adds elegance to sweet, rich white chocolate
ice cream. Other contrasting jams, such as raspberry or strawberry, look pretty too.
Use jams that have a double or higher ratio of fruit to sugar.

White Chocolate Ice Cream
WITH BLUEBERRY SWIRL

ingredients

1½ cups **milk**
1½ cups **whipping cream (35%)**
1 strip (about 2 inches/5 cm long)
 orange zest
4 **egg yolks**
⅓ cup **granulated sugar**
Pinch **salt**
4 bars (each 100 g) **white chocolate,**
 chopped
¼ tsp **vanilla**

BLUEBERRY SWIRL:
¼ cup **blueberry jam**
1 tsp **orange liqueur** or water

method

In saucepan, heat together milk, cream and orange zest over medium heat until tiny bubbles form around edge. Remove from heat; cover and steep for 10 minutes. Discard orange zest.

In large bowl, whisk together egg yolks, sugar and salt; slowly whisk in cream mixture. Return to pan; cook over medium-low heat, stirring constantly, until thick enough to coat back of spoon, about 8 minutes.

Add white chocolate and vanilla; whisk until smooth and melted. Strain into 9-inch (2.5 L) square cake pan. Place plastic wrap directly on surface; refrigerate until cold, about 1½ hours.

Freeze until almost solid, about 1½ hours. Break up and purée in food processor until smooth. (Or freeze in ice cream machine according to manufacturer's instructions.)

BLUEBERRY SWIRL: Press jam through fine sieve into small bowl; stir in orange liqueur. Scrape one-quarter of the ice cream into airtight container; drizzle with one-third of the blueberry mixture, swirling slightly with spoon ❶. Repeat twice with remaining ice cream and blueberry mixture. Cover with remaining ice cream. Freeze until firm, at least 4 hours. *(Make-ahead: Freeze for up to 1 week.)*

MAKES 4 CUPS.

PER ½ CUP: about 531 cal, 7 g pro, 35 g total fat (21 g sat. fat), 48 g carb, 0 g fibre, 173 mg chol, 91 mg sodium. % RDI: 18% calcium, 4% iron, 21% vit A, 2% vit C, 13% folate.

Cutting Citrus Zest Strips

To ensure you get only the zest – and none of the bitter white pith – when cutting strips of citrus zest, use a sharp vegetable peeler. You can use a paring knife too, but be sure to trim off any pith if your slices are on the thicker side.

HOW-TO

The name may not make them sound elegant, but these little sandwiches make a dainty ending to a fancy dinner party. For a more chocolaty result, replace the strawberry sauce with chocolate sauce (for a homemade one, see the first variation below).

Triple-Decker Ice Cream Stacks

ingredients

24 **chocolate wafer cookies**

4 cups **strawberry ice cream,**
   softened

STRAWBERRY SAUCE:

1 cup hulled **strawberries** or
   frozen strawberries

2 tbsp **granulated sugar**

1 tbsp **lemon juice**

GARNISH:

8 **strawberries** (optional)

8 oz (225 g) **bittersweet chocolate,**
   finely chopped

method

Place 8 of the cookies on work surface. Spread ¼ cup of the ice cream on each. Top each with another cookie, remaining ice cream then remaining cookie. Tightly wrap each stack in plastic wrap; freeze until firm, about 4 hours. *(Make-ahead: Freeze in airtight container for up to 2 weeks.)*

STRAWBERRY SAUCE: In food processor or blender, purée together strawberries, sugar and lemon juice; press through sieve into bowl. *(Make-ahead: Cover and refrigerate for up to 2 days.)*

GARNISH: Starting at tip end of each strawberry (if using), thinly slice almost but not all the way through to stem end; fan out slices. Roll side of each ice cream stack in chocolate; place on dessert plate. Drizzle plate with strawberry sauce. Top stack with strawberry fan.

MAKES 8 SERVINGS.

PER SERVING: about 371 cal, 6 g pro, 24 g total fat (13 g sat. fat), 44 g carb, 6 g fibre, 20 mg chol, 149 mg sodium. % RDI: 10% calcium, 19% iron, 6% vit A, 27% vit C, 10% folate.

CHANGE IT UP

Double-Chocolate Coffee Ice Cream Stacks

Replace chocolate wafer cookies with chocolate chip cookies, and strawberry ice cream with coffee ice cream. Replace strawberry sauce with chocolate sauce: In small saucepan, bring 1 cup whipping cream (35%) and 2 tbsp corn syrup to boil. Add 6 oz (170 g) bittersweet chocolate, chopped; whisk until smooth. Let stand until thickened, about 15 minutes. Omit garnish. Drizzle chocolate sauce over stacks.

Ginger Vanilla Ice Cream Stacks

Replace chocolate wafer cookies with ginger cookies, and strawberry ice cream with vanilla ice cream. Replace strawberry sauce with chocolate sauce (variation, above) or store-bought butterscotch sauce. Omit garnish. Sprinkle with 1 cup finely chopped crystallized ginger.

Three of the most popular flavours — coffee, chocolate and toffee — combine in this easy dessert that's great to keep tucked away in the freezer for last-minute guests.

Mocha Ice Cream Squares

ingredients

1½ cups **chocolate wafer crumbs**
¼ cup **butter,** melted
4 cups **coffee ice cream,**
  softened

4 bars (each 39 g) **chocolate-covered
  toffee** (such as Skor), chopped
½ cup **chocolate sauce**

method

Line 8-inch (2 L) square cake pan with plastic wrap, leaving 1-inch (2.5 cm) overhang for handles. Stir chocolate wafer crumbs with butter until moistened; press onto bottom of prepared pan. Freeze for 10 minutes.

Spread half of the ice cream over crumb mixture; sprinkle with chopped chocolate bars. Spread with remaining ice cream. Freeze until firm, about 3 hours. *(Make-ahead: Place plastic wrap directly on surface; wrap in heavy-duty foil and freeze for up to 1 week.)*

Using plastic wrap as handles, transfer to cutting board; cut into 6 pieces. Serve each drizzled with chocolate sauce.

MAKES 6 SERVINGS.
PER SERVING: about 611 cal, 8 g pro, 33 g total fat (13 g sat. fat), 76 g carb, 3 g fibre, 52 mg chol, 455 mg sodium. % RDI: 14% calcium, 17% iron, 20% vit A, 2% vit C, 8% folate.

Softening Ice Cream

Working with ice cream in cake and pie recipes is easy if the ice cream is soft enough to spread. Remove it from the freezer and let it stand in the refrigerator for about 20 minutes. Check if it's easy to scoop and swirl around. If it is, then it's ready to use. If not, let it stand for another 10 minutes and check it again. Don't let it get runny, though, as the texture can change when you refreeze it.

Test Kitchen TIP

Sundaes are such deliciously guilty pleasures. This one combines a host of scrumptious elements in one sweet dessert: brownies, ice cream and a luscious bourbon sauce.

Sublime Brownies & Bourbon Sauce Sundaes

ingredients

3 oz (85 g) **bittersweet chocolate,** chopped

2 oz (55 g) **unsweetened chocolate,** chopped

⅓ cup **butter**

¾ cup **granulated sugar**

2 **eggs**

2 tsp **vanilla**

½ cup **all-purpose flour**

Pinch **salt**

¾ cup **Bourbon Sauce** (below)

3 cups **butter pecan ice cream**

method

In heavy saucepan, melt together bittersweet chocolate, unsweetened chocolate and butter, stirring until smooth. Scrape into large bowl; let cool slightly.

Whisk in sugar; whisk in eggs, 1 at a time. Whisk in vanilla. With wooden spoon, stir in flour and salt. Divide among 8 greased or paper-lined muffin cups, smoothing tops.

Bake in 350°F (180°C) oven just until cake tester inserted in centre of several comes out with a few moist crumbs clinging, about 25 minutes.

Let cool in pan on rack for 2 minutes. Transfer to rack; let cool slightly. *(Make-ahead: Let cool completely. Store in airtight container for up to 24 hours. To serve, place brownies on plate; cover and microwave on medium until softened and warm, about 1 minute.)*

Pour bourbon sauce on dessert plates; top each with brownie. Spoon ice cream over top.

MAKES 8 SERVINGS.

PER SERVING: about 540 cal, 6 g pro, 30 g total fat (16 g sat. fat), 66 g carb, 2 g fibre, 105 mg chol, 182 mg sodium. % RDI: 10% calcium, 10% iron, 16% vit A, 8% folate.

MAKE YOUR OWN
Bourbon Sauce

In heavy saucepan over medium heat, stir 1½ cups granulated sugar with ⅓ cup water until dissolved, brushing down side of pan with pastry brush dipped in cold water. Bring to boil; boil vigorously, without stirring but brushing down side of pan often, until dark amber, about 6 minutes. Standing back and averting face, add ⅔ cup whipping cream (35%); whisk until smooth. Whisk in ¼ cup bourbon and 1 tsp lemon juice. Return pan to heat; simmer for 4 minutes. *(Make-ahead: Let cool; refrigerate in airtight container for up to 1 week. Gently rewarm to liquefy.)*

MAKES 1¼ CUPS.

Reheating Dessert Sauces

Sticky sauces, like this bourbon-laced one, and chocolate sauces need to be handled gently when reheating to keep them from gumming up and burning. The easiest way to reheat them is in the microwave on medium, stirring and checking every 15 to 30 seconds until they're warm and liquid enough to pour. The gentlest method is to put them in a heatproof bowl over a saucepan of hot (not boiling) water, stirring until they're warm and liquefied.

Fudgy ice cream and mini chocolate chips pack a punch for serious chocolate lovers, while the variation with vanilla ice cream and coloured chocolate chips appeals to the young at heart.

Chocolate Chip Ice Cream Sandwiches

ingredients

4 cups **chocolate ice cream,** softened
1 cup **mini semisweet chocolate chips**

CHOCOLATE CHIP COOKIES:
1 cup **butter,** softened
1¼ cups packed **brown sugar**
1 **egg**
1 tsp **vanilla**
2 cups **all-purpose flour**

1 tsp **baking soda**
¼ tsp **salt**
2 cups **semisweet chocolate chips**
1 cup chopped toasted **pecans** (optional)

method

CHOCOLATE CHIP COOKIES: In large bowl, beat butter with brown sugar until fluffy; beat in egg and vanilla. Whisk together flour, baking soda and salt. Stir into butter mixture. Stir in chocolate chips, and pecans (if using).

Drop by ¼ cup, about 2 inches (5 cm) apart, onto 2 parchment paper–lined or greased rimless baking sheets to make 16 cookies. Bake on top and bottom racks in 350°F (180°C) oven, rotating and switching pans halfway through, until bottoms are golden, about 15 minutes.

Let cool on pans on racks for 3 minutes. Transfer to racks; let cool completely. *(Make-ahead: Layer between waxed paper in airtight container and store for up to 5 days or freeze for up to 2 weeks.)*

Spread ½ cup ice cream on bottom of each of half of the cookies. Top with remaining cookies, pressing gently to spread ice cream to edge.

Roll edge of each sandwich in chocolate chips. Wrap individually in plastic wrap and freeze in airtight container until firm, about 4 hours. *(Make-ahead: Freeze for up to 5 days.)*

MAKES 8 SERVINGS.
PER SERVING: about 928 cal, 10 g pro, 48 g total fat (29 g sat. fat), 118 g carb, 6 g fibre, 118 mg chol, 526 mg sodium. % RDI: 12% calcium, 34% iron, 31% vit A, 32% folate.

CHANGE IT UP
Vanilla Candy Ice Cream Sandwiches
Replace chocolate ice cream with vanilla ice cream; replace mini chocolate chips with mini coloured chocolate chips.

Ice cream sandwiches make excellent fare for backyard barbecues, and summer birthday or pool parties. You can make them well ahead, and they're super easy finger food. No utensils required!

Triple-Chocolate Cookie Ice Cream Sandwiches

ingredients

2½ cups **strawberry ice cream** or **chocolate ice cream**, softened
½ cup **chocolate shot** (optional), see Tip, page 265

TRIPLE-CHOCOLATE COOKIES:
½ cup **butter,** softened
⅓ cup packed **brown sugar**
2 tbsp **corn syrup**
1 **egg**
1½ tsp **vanilla**

1 cup **all-purpose flour**
¼ cup **cocoa powder**
¼ tsp each **baking soda** and **salt**
½ cup **semisweet chocolate chips**
½ cup **milk chocolate chips** or **white chocolate chips**

method

TRIPLE-CHOCOLATE COOKIES: In large bowl, beat together butter, brown sugar and corn syrup until fluffy. Beat in egg and vanilla. Whisk together flour, cocoa powder, baking soda and salt; stir into butter mixture in 2 additions. Stir in semisweet chocolate chips and milk chocolate chips.

Drop by heaping 1 tbsp, about 2 inches (5 cm) apart, onto parchment paper–lined or greased baking sheets to make 20 cookies. Bake in 375°F (190°C) oven until no longer shiny and edges are firm to the touch, about 10 minutes.

Let cool on pans on racks for 2 minutes. Transfer to racks; let cool completely.

Spread about ¼ cup ice cream on bottom of each of half of the cookies. Sandwich with remaining cookies, pressing gently to spread ice cream to edge.

Roll edge of each sandwich in chocolate shot (if using). Wrap individually in plastic wrap and freeze in airtight container until firm, about 4 hours. *(Make-ahead: Freeze for up to 5 days.)*

MAKES 10 SERVINGS.
PER SERVING: about 374 cal, 5 g pro, 20 g total fat (12 g sat. fat), 47 g carb, 3 g fibre, 55 mg chol, 196 mg sodium. % RDI: 7% calcium, 13% iron, 12% vit A, 5% vit C, 17% folate.

273

CANADIAN LIVING • THE COMPLETE CHOCOLATE BOOK

A stunning yet easy to make dessert, this recipe is just a starting point. Customize it to your heart's content with any of your favourite ice cream flavour combinations.

Three-Ice Cream Terrine

ingredients

2 cups cubed (½ inch/1 cm) **brownies**
2 cups **chocolate ice cream,** softened
2 cups **coffee ice cream,** softened
2 cups **vanilla ice cream,** softened

MOCHA SAUCE:
1 tbsp **instant coffee granules**
⅓ cup **granulated sugar**
⅓ cup **corn syrup**
½ cup **whipping cream (35%)**
6 oz (170 g) **bittersweet chocolate,**
  chopped

method

Line 8- x 4-inch (1.5 L) loaf pan with plastic wrap, leaving 3-inch (8 cm) overhang. Sprinkle half of the brownies evenly in pan; press gently to pack. Spread with chocolate ice cream, smoothing top; freeze until firm, about 2 hours.

Spread coffee ice cream over chocolate ice cream, smoothing top; freeze until firm, about 2 hours.

Spread vanilla ice cream over coffee ice cream, smoothing top. Sprinkle with remaining brownies; press gently. Fold plastic overhang over top; freeze until firm, about 2 hours. *(Make-ahead: Overwrap with heavy-duty foil and freeze for up to 1 week.)*

MOCHA SAUCE: In small saucepan, dissolve coffee granules in ⅓ cup water; stir in sugar and corn syrup. Bring to boil; cook, stirring, for 1 minute. Add cream and chocolate; cook, stirring, over medium heat until melted and smooth, about 2 minutes. Let cool. *(Make-ahead: Refrigerate in airtight container for up to 1 week. To reheat, microwave on medium-high for 1 minute.)*

Turn terrine out onto chilled serving plate; peel off plastic wrap. Let stand in refrigerator until soft enough to slice, about 15 minutes. Serve slices with mocha sauce.

MAKES 12 SERVINGS.

PER SERVING: about 297 cal, 4 g pro, 19 g total fat (11 g sat. fat), 35 g carb, 3 g fibre, 37 mg chol, 76 mg sodium. % RDI: 9% calcium, 10% iron, 14% vit A, 5% vit C, 6% folate.

CHANGE IT UP
Chocolate Fudge Sauce
Omit instant coffee granules from mocha fudge sauce.

These sandwiches are so easy it's almost criminal. The chocolate cookies are delicious with all sorts of ice cream flavours – try raspberry ripple or black cherry for a fruity version. Make sure to use the boxed type of ice cream so you can slice it perfectly.

Mint Chocolate Sandwich Cookies

ingredients

1 box (2 L) **mint chocolate chip ice cream**

CHOCOLATE SANDWICH COOKIES:
¾ cup **butter,** softened
¾ cup **granulated sugar**
1 **egg**
1 tsp **vanilla**

1¼ cups **all-purpose flour**
¾ cup **cocoa powder**
¼ tsp **salt**

method

CHOCOLATE SANDWICH COOKIES: In bowl, beat butter with sugar until fluffy; beat in egg and vanilla. Whisk together flour, cocoa powder and salt; stir into butter mixture. Divide in half; shape into discs. Wrap and refrigerate until firm, about 1 hour.

Between parchment paper or waxed paper, roll out 1 disc at a time to scant ¼-inch (5 mm) thickness. Using floured 3-inch (8 cm) fluted round cutter or other shape, cut out shapes. Arrange, 1 inch (2.5 cm) apart, on 2 parchment paper–lined or greased rimless baking sheets. Bake on top and bottom racks in 350°F (180°C) oven, rotating and switching pans halfway through, until slightly puffed, about 10 minutes.

Let cool on pans on racks for 3 minutes. Transfer to racks; let cool completely. *(Make-ahead: Layer between waxed paper in airtight container and store for up to 5 days or freeze for up to 2 weeks.)*

Cut ice cream lengthwise into 6 scant 1-inch (2.5 cm) wide slices. Using same fluted cutter, cut out 12 shapes. Place ice cream shapes on bottoms of half of the cookies. Top with remaining cookies, pressing gently to spread ice cream to edge.

Wrap individually in plastic wrap; freeze in airtight container until firm, about 4 hours. *(Make-ahead: Freeze for up to 2 days.)*

MAKES 12 SERVINGS.
PER SERVING: about 416 cal, 6 g pro, 23 g total fat (14 g sat. fat), 52 g carb, 3 g fibre, 83 mg chol, 242 mg sodium. % RDI: 10% calcium, 17% iron, 23% vit A, 2% vit C, 16% folate.

We've translated Canada's favourite bar into a frozen True North dessert.
If you like, stir 2 oz (55 g) semisweet chocolate, chopped, into the softened ice cream
before spreading it over the crust.

Nanaimo Bar Ice Cream Cake

ingredients

¼ cup **butter**
2 tbsp **granulated sugar**
1 **egg yolk**
¾ cup **chocolate wafer crumbs**
½ cup **sweetened shredded coconut**
⅓ cup finely chopped **hazelnuts**

4 cups **vanilla ice cream,** softened
½ cup **whipping cream (35%)**
3 oz (85 g) **semisweet chocolate,** chopped

method

Line 9- x 5-inch (2 L) loaf pan with foil, leaving 1-inch (2.5 cm) overhang for handles; grease foil. Set aside.

In saucepan, melt butter with sugar over medium heat; remove from heat. Stir in egg yolk, chocolate wafer crumbs, shredded coconut and ¼ cup of the hazelnuts until moistened; press evenly into prepared pan. Bake in 350°F (180°C) oven until firm, about 25 minutes. Let cool completely in pan on rack.

Pack ice cream firmly over crust. Freeze until solid, about 4 hours.

In small saucepan, bring cream to boil; remove from heat. Add chocolate; whisk until smooth and melted. Let stand until cool and slightly thickened, about 30 minutes.

Pour chocolate sauce over ice cream layer, spreading evenly. Sprinkle with remaining hazelnuts. Freeze until firm, about 1 hour. *(Make-ahead: Cover with plastic wrap, overwrap in heavy-duty foil and freeze for up to 1 week.)*

To serve, let frozen cake stand in refrigerator for 30 minutes. Dip pan into warm water. Using foil as handles, transfer cake to cutting board. Dipping sharp knife into hot water and wiping dry between slices, cut into slices.

MAKES 12 SERVINGS.
PER SERVING: about 274 cal, 3 g pro, 20 g total fat (11 g sat. fat), 24 g carb, 1 g fibre, 63 mg chol, 99 mg sodium. % RDI: 7% calcium, 5% iron, 13% vit A, 4% folate.

277

Baked Alaska is one of those vintage desserts that just never gets old.
These mini versions are wonderful for a dinner party. Bake them up at the last minute and get
them to the table quickly so guests can dig in before the ice cream starts to melt.

Mini Baked Alaskas

ingredients

6 round (about 2 inch/5 cm) **chocolate wafer cookies**
6 scoops (each ⅓ cup) premium-quality **chocolate ice cream**

3 **egg whites**
½ cup **granulated sugar**

method

On parchment paper–lined rimmed baking sheet, top each cookie with 1 scoop of the ice cream. Freeze for 1 hour.

In bowl, beat egg whites until soft peaks form. Beat in sugar, 1 tbsp at a time, until stiff peaks form.

Using piping bag fitted with star tip, pipe meringue over ice cream to cover completely, ensuring that meringue seals to cookie ❶. Freeze until firm, about 4 hours.

Bake in 500°F (260°C) oven until browned, about 2 minutes. Serve immediately.

MAKES 6 SERVINGS.
PER SERVING: about 298 cal, 5 g pro, 14 g total fat (8 g sat. fat), 38 g carb, 2 g fibre, 70 mg chol, 97 mg sodium. % RDI: 6% calcium, 9% iron, 10% vit A, 1% folate.

279

Beating Egg Whites

Beating air into egg whites gives them height and structure in all kinds of recipes: cakes, mousses, meringues and more. Here's how to whip them into perfect shape.

1. **Start with a spotless bowl.** Metal or glass is best. Even a smear of grease or egg yolk mixed in with the whites can prevent them from reaching their full height, so make sure the bowl is washed, dried and gleaming.

2. **Use a big wire whisk.** A stand mixer with a whisk attachment makes this process fast and easy, and saves your arm muscles.

3. **Beat just until you see the results you want, then stop.** For soft peaks, you're looking for peaks that droop when you lift out the whisk. Stiff peaks are glossy and stand tall when you lift out the whisk.

4. **Add sugar slowly.** If you're incorporating sugar into the egg whites to achieve firm peaks, add it about 2 tbsp at a time, beating the mixture continuously.

This show-stopping dessert goes from freezer to oven to table for a fancy, no-fuss finale. Premium ice creams and sorbets, such as Häagen-Dazs, have less air whipped into them than lower quality brands, so they have a higher yield when beaten and will melt less quickly.

Chocolate Raspberry Pistachio Baked Alaska

ingredients

4 cups premium-quality **vanilla ice cream**, softened

½ cup shelled **pistachios**, coarsely chopped

Green food colouring (optional)

2 cups premium-quality **raspberry sorbet**, softened

CHOCOLATE CAKE:

4 oz (115 g) **bittersweet chocolate**, chopped

½ cup **butter**

2 each **eggs** and **egg yolks**

3 tbsp **granulated sugar**

⅓ cup **all-purpose flour**

2 tbsp **raspberry liqueur** or brandy (optional)

MERINGUE:

½ cup **liquid pasteurized egg whites** (or 4 egg whites)

¼ tsp **cream of tartar**

½ cup **instant dissolving (fruit/berry) sugar**

method

CHOCOLATE CAKE: Grease 9-inch (1.5 L) round cake pan; line bottom with parchment paper. Set aside.

In heatproof bowl over saucepan of hot (not boiling) water, melt chocolate with butter, stirring occasionally until smooth; set aside.

In large bowl, beat together eggs, egg yolks and sugar until doubled in volume and fluffy, about 8 minutes. Fold in flour. Remove ½ cup; beat into chocolate mixture; fold back into remaining egg mixture. Scrape into prepared pan, spreading evenly.

Bake in 350°F (180°C) oven until firm to the touch, 16 to 18 minutes. (Cake will be thin.) Let cool in pan on rack for 10 minutes. Transfer to rack; peel off paper. Let cool. *(Make-ahead: Wrap in plastic wrap and store for up to 24 hours.)*

Dampen then line 8-inch (20 cm) diameter 6-cup (1.5 L) bowl with plastic wrap. In separate bowl, beat together vanilla ice cream, pistachios, and desired amount of food colouring (if using). Pack into prepared bowl, shaping well in centre for sorbet. Line rounded outside of small (2½-cup) bowl with plastic wrap; press bowl into well to smooth ice cream mixture. Cover top with plastic wrap; freeze until firm, about 2 hours.

Beat sorbet until smooth. Remove small bowl and plastic wrap liner from ice cream well. Fill with sorbet, smoothing top. Cover and freeze until firm, about 2 hours. *(Make-ahead: Freeze for up to 24 hours.)*

Place cake on 10- or 12-inch (25 or 30 cm) ovenproof flat platter or round pizza pan; poke holes all over top with toothpick. Brush with liqueur (if using). Dip bowl of ice cream into warm water to loosen, about 20 seconds. Uncover and invert onto cake; remove plastic wrap. Wipe off any melted ice cream on plate. Freeze until hardened, about 30 minutes. *(Make-ahead: Wrap in plastic wrap then heavy-duty foil; freeze for up to 2 weeks.)*

MERINGUE: In bowl, beat egg whites with cream of tartar until soft peaks form; beat in sugar, 2 tbsp at a time, until stiff glossy peaks form (see Beating Egg Whites, page 279). Spread over ice cream, sealing to plate and making peaks and swirls with back of spoon. *(Make-ahead: Freeze for up to 8 hours.)* Bake in 475°F (240°C) oven until lightly browned, 3 to 5 minutes. Cut into wedges; serve immediately.

MAKES 12 SERVINGS.

PER SERVING: about 388 cal, 7 g pro, 25 g total fat (14 g sat. fat), 39 g carb, 2 g fibre, 115 mg chol, 111 mg sodium. % RDI: 8% calcium, 9% iron, 21% vit A, 3% vit C, 10% folate.

Angel food cake hiding a circle of ice cream – then smothered in whipped cream and served with fresh strawberries – is a true celebration of early summer. Best of all, this dessert can wait patiently in the freezer for any happy occasion.

Tunnel of Ice Cream Cake

ingredients

4 cups **chocolate ice cream,** softened
1½ cups **whipping cream (35%)**
2 tbsp **granulated sugar**

CAKE:
1¼ cups sifted **cake-and-pastry flour**
1½ cups **granulated sugar**
1½ cups **egg whites** (about 11)
1 tbsp **lemon juice**

1 tsp **cream of tartar**
½ tsp **salt**
2 tsp **vanilla**

GARNISH:
2 cups halved hulled **strawberries**
2 cups quartered hulled **strawberries**

method

CAKE: In bowl, sift flour with ¾ cup of the sugar; sift again into separate bowl. Set aside.

In large bowl, beat egg whites until foamy. Beat in lemon juice, cream of tartar and salt until soft peaks form. Beat in remaining sugar, 2 tbsp at a time, until stiff glossy peaks form. Sift flour mixture over top, one-quarter at a time, gently folding in each addition until blended. Fold in vanilla.

Pour into ungreased 10-inch (4 L) tube pan. Run spatula through batter to eliminate any large air pockets; smooth top. Bake in 350°F (180°C) oven until cake springs back when lightly touched, 40 to 45 minutes.

Turn pan upside down and let hang on legs attached to pan, or on inverted funnel or bottle, until completely cool. Remove from pan. (*Make-ahead: Store in airtight container for up to 2 days or freeze for up to 1 month.*)

Slice cake in half horizontally; turn both halves cut side up. Cut out tunnel from cut side of each, leaving ½-inch (1 cm) thick walls at sides and bottom. Reserve removed cake pieces for another use (see Tip, right).

Fill tunnels with softened ice cream; replace top half of cake over bottom half. Wrap in plastic wrap and freeze until firm, 2 hours.

Whip cream with sugar; spread over and inside centre tube of cake. (*Make-ahead: Freeze until solid; transfer to airtight container and freeze for up to 2 days. Let stand in refrigerator for 30 minutes before serving.*)

GARNISH: Surround bottom outside edge with strawberry halves; sprinkle strawberry quarters over top.

MAKES 12 SERVINGS.
PER SERVING: about 318 cal, 5 g pro, 16 g total fat (10 g sat. fat), 42 g carb, 2 g fibre, 53 mg chol, 139 mg sodium, 277 mg potassium. % RDI: 7% calcium, 9% iron, 17% vit A, 52% vit C, 13% folate.

How to Use Up Tasty Cake Scraps

Tear removed cake pieces into bite-size pieces and use them to make individual trifle cups. In parfait or wineglasses, layer cake pieces (splashed with your favourite liqueur), softly whipped cream and fresh berries.

Like the retro-cool ice cream of the same name, this dessert
has three flavours – two in the ice cream and one in the cake. Avoid low-fat ice creams
because they do not refreeze well.

Neapolitan Pistachio Frozen Bombe

ingredients

3 cups **chocolate ice cream**
2 cups **strawberry ice cream**
6 oz (170 g) **semisweet chocolate,** chopped
¾ cup **whipping cream (35%)**
½ cup chopped **pistachios**

CAKE:
1 **egg**
1 **egg yolk**
¼ cup **granulated sugar**
1 tsp **vanilla**
¼ cup **all-purpose flour**
¼ tsp **baking powder**
Pinch **salt**
1 tbsp **butter,** melted
2 tbsp finely chopped **pistachios**

method

CAKE: In bowl, beat egg with egg yolk until foamy. Beat in sugar, 2 tbsp at a time, until batter falls in ribbons when beaters are lifted, about 3 minutes. Beat in vanilla. Whisk together flour, baking powder and salt; sift half over egg mixture and fold in. Repeat with remaining flour mixture.

Transfer one-quarter of the batter to small bowl; fold in butter. Pour back over batter; sprinkle with pistachios and fold in. Scrape into greased 8-inch (2 L) springform pan.

Bake in 325°F (160°C) oven until cake springs back when lightly touched, about 30 minutes. Let cool in pan on rack for 10 minutes. Turn cake out onto rack; let cool completely.

Let chocolate and strawberry ice creams stand at room temperature until soft enough to scoop, about 20 minutes.

Dampen 7½-inch (1.5 L) bowl; line with plastic wrap, leaving 3-inch (8 cm) overhang. Line bowl with strawberry ice cream, spreading in even layer. Fill with chocolate ice cream, smoothing top. Trim cake to fit bowl; place over ice cream, pressing gently.

Cover with plastic wrap; freeze until firm, about 3 hours. *(Make-ahead: Freeze for up to 24 hours.)*

Place chocolate in heatproof bowl. In small saucepan, bring cream just to boil; pour over chocolate, whisking until smooth. Let cool for 10 minutes.

Remove plastic wrap from top of bombe. Invert bowl onto rack over rimmed baking sheet; remove bowl and peel off plastic wrap. Starting at top of dome, pour chocolate mixture over cake in spiral motion, spreading with palette knife to cover completely and letting excess drip off. Sprinkle bottom edge with pistachios. Freeze until set, about 15 minutes. *(Make-ahead: Wrap in plastic wrap and overwrap with heavy-duty foil; freeze for up to 2 weeks.)*

Transfer bombe to chilled flat serving plate. Let stand in refrigerator for 10 minutes before cutting into wedges.

MAKES 8 TO 12 SERVINGS.
PER EACH OF 12 SERVINGS: about 316 cal, 5 g pro, 21 g total fat (11 g sat. fat), 32 g carb, 2 g fibre, 79 mg chol, 71 mg sodium. % RDI: 9% calcium, 10% iron, 14% vit A, 2% vit C, 8% folate.

Praline is a wonderful southern candy that's not hard to make at home. You don't need a candy thermometer for it, but do keep an eye on the caramel so that it doesn't burn.

Frozen Chocolate Praline Meringue Torte

ingredients

8 cups **chocolate ice cream**

MERINGUES:
3 **egg whites**
Pinch **cream of tartar**
¾ cup **granulated sugar**
½ cup ground **pecans**
½ tsp **vanilla**

PRALINE:
½ cup chopped **pecans** or natural almonds
½ cup **granulated sugar**

method

MERINGUES: Line rimmed baking sheet with parchment paper. Using 8-inch (1.2 L) round cake pan as guide, trace 2 circles onto parchment paper. Turn paper over.

In bowl, beat egg whites with cream of tartar until soft peaks form. Beat in sugar, 2 tbsp at a time, until stiff glossy peaks form; fold in pecans and vanilla. Spoon onto circles, smoothing tops.

Bake on bottom rack in 225°F (110°C) oven until dry and crisp, 1½ to 2 hours. Turn off oven; let cool in oven, about 2 hours. *(Make-ahead: Store in airtight container in cool, dry place for up to 5 days.)*

PRALINE: Spread pecans on parchment paper–lined rimmed baking sheet. In heavy saucepan, stir sugar with 3 tbsp water over medium heat until dissolved, brushing down side of pan with pastry brush dipped in cold water. Bring to boil; boil vigorously, without stirring but brushing down side of pan often, until dark amber, about 8 minutes.

Pour over pecans; let cool. Break into pieces; chop coarsely and set aside. *(Make-ahead: Store in airtight container for up to 5 days.)*

Soften ice cream in refrigerator until spreadable, 30 minutes. Place 1 meringue on 10-inch (25 cm) plate; spread with half of the ice cream. Sprinkle half of the praline over top; press gently into ice cream. Top with remaining meringue; spread remaining ice cream over top and side, smoothing side. Cover with plastic wrap; freeze until very firm, about 8 hours. *(Make-ahead: Freeze for up to 2 days.)*

Dip 2 metal spatulas in warm water; wipe dry. Slide under bottom of cake to loosen; transfer to serving platter. Sprinkle with remaining praline pieces.

MAKES 12 SERVINGS.

PER SERVING: about 333 cal, 5 g pro, 16 g total fat (6 g sat. fat), 47 g carb, 2 g fibre, 30 mg chol, 80 mg sodium. % RDI: 9% calcium, 7% iron, 11% vit A, 2% vit C, 8% folate.

Dulce de leche is a gooey South American caramel made by boiling down sweetened condensed milk. It comes ready-made in jars at the supermarket, but here it's the main flavouring in one of the premium ice creams that make up the base of this pie.

Chocolate Caramel Ice Cream Pie

ingredients

2 cups **dulce de leche ice cream,** softened

3 bars (each 39 g) **chocolate-covered toffee** (such as Skor), chopped

6 cups **chocolate ice cream**

1 cup **chocolate sauce**

CRUST:
1½ cups **chocolate wafer crumbs**
¼ cup **butter,** melted

method

CRUST: Stir chocolate wafer crumbs with butter until moistened; press onto bottom and up side of 9-inch (23 cm) pie plate. Refrigerate until firm, about 30 minutes.

Spoon dulce de leche ice cream into crust, pressing and smoothing top. Sprinkle with half of the chopped chocolate-covered toffee bars. Freeze until firm, about 1½ hours.

Using ice cream scoop, scoop chocolate ice cream into balls and arrange in layers on top of dulce de leche ice cream. Sprinkle with remaining chopped chocolate bars. Freeze until firm, about 3 hours. *(Make-ahead: Wrap in plastic wrap; overwrap in heavy-duty foil or place in airtight container and freeze for up 1 week.)*

Serve topped with chocolate sauce.

MAKES 8 SERVINGS.
PER SERVING: about 706 cal, 10 g pro, 45 g total fat (26 g sat. fat), 73 g carb, 4 g fibre, 134 mg chol, 362 mg sodium. % RDI: 21% calcium, 18% iron, 29% vit A, 2% vit C, 13% folate.

285

Make It Your Own

Try a variety of flavours in this easy dessert. For example, replace dulce de leche with butterscotch ripple, caramel or pralines-and-cream ice cream. Replace the chocolate with heavenly hash or chocolate brownie ice cream.

Refreshing on the hottest summer day, this ice cream pie is, well, a piece of cake.
Use this recipe as a starting point and change up the flavours of the ice cream and sauce.

Mint Chocolate Chip Ice Cream Pie

ingredients

2 cups **chocolate wafer crumbs**
⅓ cup **butter,** melted
⅓ cup **chocolate sauce**
4 cups **mint chocolate chip ice cream,** softened

¾ cup **whipping cream (35%)**
1 tbsp **granulated sugar**
2 tsp **chocolate shot** (see Tip, page 265)

method

Stir chocolate wafer crumbs with butter until moistened; press over bottom and up side of 9-inch (23 cm) pie plate. Bake in 325°F (160°C) oven until firm, about 12 minutes. Let cool.

Spread chocolate sauce over crust. Using wooden spoon, beat ice cream until smooth; spread over chocolate sauce. Cover with plastic wrap; freeze until firm, about 1 hour.

Whip cream with sugar; spread over ice cream. Freeze until set, about 1 hour.

Garnish with chocolate shot. *(Make-ahead: Cover with plastic wrap and overwrap with heavy-duty foil; freeze for up to 1 day.)*

MAKES 12 SERVINGS.

PER SERVING: about 302 cal, 4 g pro, 19 g total fat (11 g sat. fat), 32 g carb, 1 g fibre, 50 mg chol, 213 mg sodium. % RDI: 7% calcium, 8% iron, 15% vit A, 7% folate.

Making Chocolate Wafer Crumbs

These crumbs are easy to find in the baking aisle of the grocery store, often under the brand name Oreo. But it's not hard to make them at home: Choose thin chocolate wafer cookies without any cream filling, then break them up and pulse them in the food processor until fine but not powdery. For coarser crumbs, seal the cookies in a plastic bag and crush with a rolling pin to the desired texture.

Test Kitchen TIP

Double your pleasure by swirling milk chocolate with white chocolate in this semifrozen dessert.
Garnish with fresh raspberries and Rich Double-Chocolate Sauce (page 36) if you like.

Double-Chocolate Semifreddo

ingredients

6 oz (170 g) **white chocolate,**
chopped
6 oz (170 g) **milk chocolate,**
chopped
4 **eggs**

¼ cup **granulated sugar**
1¾ cups **whipping cream (35%)**

method

Line 8- x 4-inch (1.5 L) loaf pan with plastic wrap, smoothing out any wrinkles. Set aside.

In separate heatproof bowls set over saucepan of hot (not boiling) water, melt white chocolate and milk chocolate, stirring until smooth. Let cool to room temperature.

In large heatproof bowl over saucepan of simmering water, beat eggs with sugar until consistency of softly whipped cream, about 5 minutes. Divide between 2 large bowls. Whisk white chocolate into 1 bowl; whisk milk chocolate into second bowl. Refrigerate until cold.

Whip cream. Divide half between white and milk chocolate mixtures; fold in. Fold one-third of the remaining whipped cream into milk chocolate mixture. Fold remaining whipped cream into white chocolate mixture.

Drop alternating spoonfuls of milk chocolate and white chocolate mixtures into prepared pan. Using knife, gently swirl. Place plastic wrap directly on surface; freeze until firm, about 6 hours. *(Make-ahead: Overwrap with heavy-duty foil and freeze for up to 1 week.)*

To serve, let soften in refrigerator for 30 minutes. Unwrap and invert onto serving platter. Peel off plastic wrap; slice.

MAKES 8 SERVINGS.
PER SERVING: about 455 cal, 7 g pro, 34 g total fat (20 g sat. fat), 33 g carb, 1 g fibre, 169 mg chol, 86 mg sodium. % RDI: 12% calcium, 4% iron, 25% vit A, 9% folate.

The Right Texture

When you beat the eggs with the sugar for this semifreddo, you want them to become fairly thick from the heat and the air that's being incorporated. The mixture should look like softly whipped cream – it should stand up slightly but any peaks should droop quickly.

Because you can tuck this dessert in the freezer, it's a busy host's best friend.
The taste and texture are heavenly: creamy, chocolaty, chilly and custardy.

Mocha Semifreddo

ingredients

10 oz (280 g) **semisweet chocolate,** chopped
¼ cup **instant coffee granules**
¼ cup boiling **water**
2 tbsp **cocoa powder**
4 **eggs**
⅓ cup **granulated sugar**
1½ cups **whipping cream (35%)**

CRUST:
1 cup **chocolate wafer crumbs**
2 tbsp **butter,** melted

GARNISH:
1 oz (30 g) **white chocolate,** melted
1 oz (30 g) **semisweet chocolate,** melted

method

CRUST: Grease 7-inch (1.5 L) springform pan; line side with parchment paper. Stir chocolate wafer crumbs with butter until moistened; press evenly into prepared pan. Bake in 350°F (180°C) oven until firm, about 7 minutes. Let cool in pan on rack.

In heatproof bowl over saucepan of hot (not boiling) water, melt semisweet chocolate, stirring occasionally until smooth; let cool to room temperature. Whisk together coffee granules, boiling water and cocoa; set aside.

In large heatproof bowl over saucepan of simmering water, beat eggs with sugar until thickened, about 5 minutes. Reduce speed to low; beat in coffee mixture and melted chocolate. Let cool to room temperature, about 20 minutes.

Whip cream; fold one-quarter into chocolate mixture. Gently fold in remaining whipped cream. Pour over crust, smoothing top.

GARNISH: Pipe or drizzle white chocolate and semisweet chocolate decoratively over top. Freeze until firm, at least 6 hours. *(Make-ahead: Wrap in plastic wrap and freeze in airtight container for up to 1 week.)*

Let soften in refrigerator for 1 hour. Remove side of pan; cut into wedges.

MAKES 8 SERVINGS.

PER SERVING: about 532 cal, 8 g pro, 39 g total fat (22 g sat. fat), 46 g carb, 3 g fibre, 176 mg chol, 117 mg sodium. % RDI: 7% calcium, 17% iron, 25% vit A, 6% folate.

These bites are great to have on hand as a healthier choice than ice cream, and kids will love to help make – and eat – them. Feel free to roll them in whatever topping you prefer.

Frozen Banana Bites

ingredients

¾ cup **semisweet chocolate chips**
2 tsp **vegetable oil**
¼ cup **sweetened flaked coconut,** toasted

¼ cup **salted roasted peanuts**
2 large **bananas,** cut in ½-inch (1 cm) thick slices

method

In heatproof bowl over saucepan of hot (not boiling) water, melt chocolate chips, stirring until smooth. Stir in oil.

Place coconut and peanuts in separate shallow bowls.

Using fork, dip banana slices into chocolate, turning to coat and letting excess drip back into bowl.

Using clean fork, roll banana slices in coconut and/or peanuts; place on parchment paper–lined baking sheet. Spear each banana slice with toothpick.

Freeze until chocolate is set and banana is frozen, about 1 hour. *(Make-ahead: Cover and freeze for up to 3 days.)*

MAKES ABOUT 16 PIECES.
PER PIECE: about 81 cal, 1 g pro, 5 g total fat (2 g sat. fat), 10 g carb, 1 g fibre, 0 mg chol, 16 mg sodium, 111 mg potassium. % RDI: 1% calcium, 3% iron, 2% vit C, 3% folate.

Use Firm Bananas

This recipe requires bananas that are ripe but on the firm side so that the frozen slices stand up to dipping and handling. Don't choose bananas with a lot of green on the peel, because their texture can be unpleasantly chalky. Look for peels that are yellow but not speckled with brown.

Test Kitchen TIP

Delightfully frosty, a Mocha Frappé is better than any frozen delight you'll find on a coffee shop menu. A Raspberry Chocolate Smoothie is, admittedly, an indulgent treat to start the day, but it is a delicious way to get a hit of calcium in the morning.

Mocha Frappé

Raspberry Chocolate Smoothie

ingredients

1 cup strong brewed **coffee,** cooled, and sweetened to taste (optional)
½ cup **ice cubes**
¼ cup **chocolate ice cream** or chocolate milk
Pinch **cinnamon**

2½ cups **chocolate milk**
1½ cups **frozen raspberries**
1 cup **vanilla yogurt**
1 tbsp **liquid honey**
2 tsp **cocoa powder**
1 tbsp **chocolate syrup**

method

In blender, blend together coffee, ice, ice cream and cinnamon until slushy.

Pour into tall glass.

MAKES 1 SERVING.
PER SERVING: about 71 cal, 2 g pro, 4 g total fat (2 g sat. fat), 9 g carb, trace fibre, 11 mg chol, 32 mg sodium, 199 mg potassium. % RDI: 4% calcium, 2% iron, 4% vit A, 5% folate.

In blender, blend together chocolate milk, raspberries, yogurt, honey and cocoa until smooth and frosty.

Pour into 2 tall glasses. Drizzle chocolate syrup over top.

MAKES 2 SERVINGS.
PER SERVING: about 449 cal, 17 g pro, 10 g total fat (6 g sat. fat), 77 g carb, 7 g fibre, 28 mg chol, 291 mg sodium. % RDI: 50% calcium, 13% iron, 22% vit A, 45% vit C, 24% folate.

Ice in Blended Drinks

Most blenders have an ice-crushing setting that can reduce your cubes to more manageable chips before you blend. If you prefer a really smooth frappé, crush the ice slightly before adding the rest of the ingredients to ensure no frozen chunks are suspended in your drink.

Feeling nostalgic? Old-Fashioned Milkshakes take you back to the era of soda fountains and carhops. If you prefer a nondairy beverage, a Chocolate Soy Banana Smoothie — or one of the tasty variations — is a delicious alternative.

Old-Fashioned Milkshakes

Chocolate Soy Banana Smoothie

ingredients

Old-Fashioned Milkshakes

2 cups halved hulled **strawberries**
½ cup **milk**
1 tbsp **liquid honey**
1 tsp **vanilla**
3 cups **chocolate ice cream** or vanilla ice cream

Chocolate Soy Banana Smoothie

1½ cups **chocolate soy beverage**
2 **bananas**
1 tsp **liquid honey**
¼ tsp **vanilla**
Pinch **cinnamon**

method

Old-Fashioned Milkshakes

In blender, combine strawberries, milk, honey and vanilla. Pulse 6 times.

Spoon in ice cream; blend until mixture is smooth and frosty.

MAKES 4 TO 6 SERVINGS.
PER EACH OF 6 SERVINGS: about 181 cal, 4 g pro, 8 g total fat (5 g sat. fat), 27 g carb, 2 g fibre, 24 mg chol, 60 mg sodium, 272 mg potassium. % RDI: 10% calcium, 6% iron, 9% vit A, 50% vit C, 11% folate.

Chocolate Soy Banana Smoothie

In blender, blend together chocolate soy beverage, bananas, honey, vanilla and cinnamon until smooth and frothy.

MAKES 2 SERVINGS.
PER SERVING: about 230 cal, 6 g pro, 2 g total fat (1 g sat. fat), 49 g carb, 2 g fibre, 0 mg chol, 94 mg sodium. % RDI: 20% calcium, 8% iron, 8% vit A, 20% vit C, 15% folate.

CHANGE IT UP
Chocolate Soy Strawberry Banana Smoothie
Substitute 1 cup frozen strawberries for 1 of the bananas.

Chocolate Soy Peanut Butter Banana Smoothie
Add 2 tbsp natural peanut butter.

Chocolate Soy Coffee Banana Smoothie
Add 1 tsp instant coffee granules.

A layered milkshake is deliciously beautiful. The higher-quality ice cream you use, the better the milkshake, so indulge in your favourite luxury brand. While you're in the kitchen, whip up a batch of Moustache Straw Cookies to slip over your straw for some hilarious sipping.

Neapolitan Milkshake

Moustache Straw Cookies

ingredients

½ cup **vanilla ice cream**
⅓ cup **2% milk**
½ cup **chocolate ice cream**
3 tbsp **1% chocolate milk**
½ cup **strawberry ice cream**

¾ cup **butter,** softened
1 cup **granulated sugar**
1 **egg**
1 tsp **vanilla**
2½ cups **all-purpose flour**
½ tsp **baking powder**
Pinch **salt**
Easy Royal Icing (below, left)
Brown paste food colouring

method

In blender, purée vanilla ice cream with half of the 2% milk until smooth. Pour into tall glass; freeze until almost firm, about 20 minutes.

In blender, purée chocolate ice cream with chocolate milk until smooth. Spoon over vanilla layer; freeze until almost firm, about 20 minutes.

In blender, purée strawberry ice cream with remaining 2% milk until smooth. Spoon over chocolate layer. Serve immediately.

MAKES 1 SERVING.
PER SERVING: about 652 cal, 14 g pro, 38 g total fat (23 g sat. fat), 66 g carb, 1 g fibre, 170 mg chol, 214 mg sodium, 661 mg potassium. % RDI: 42% calcium, 10% iron, 48% vit A, 10% vit C, 12% folate.

MAKE YOUR OWN
Easy Royal Icing
In bowl, beat ⅓ cup pasteurized egg whites until foamy, 30 to 60 seconds. Beat in 3½ cups icing sugar, 1 cup at a time, until thick and glossy, 6 to 8 minutes. Cover with damp cloth to prevent drying out.

In bowl, beat butter with sugar until fluffy; beat in egg and vanilla. Whisk together flour, baking powder and salt; stir into butter mixture in 3 additions. Divide in half; shape into discs. Wrap and refrigerate for 1 hour. *(Make-ahead: Refrigerate for up to 24 hours.)*

Let stand at room temperature for 15 minutes. Between parchment paper, roll out, 1 disc at a time, to ¼-inch (5 mm) thickness; peel off paper. Using floured moustache-shaped cookie cutter, cut out shapes, rerolling and cutting scraps. Arrange, 1 inch (2.5 cm) apart, on parchment paper–lined rimless baking sheet. Using end of straw, cut hole in centre of each. Bake in 375°F (190°C) oven until bottoms and edges are light golden, 10 minutes. Using end of straw, recut holes. Let cool on pan on rack for 1 minute. Transfer to rack; let cool completely.

Tint royal icing with food colouring; spoon into piping bag fitted with star tip. Pipe strips from centre out to edges. Let dry for 20 minutes. Insert straw through each cookie.

MAKES ABOUT 40 COOKIES.
PER COOKIE: about 161 cal, 2 g pro, 4 g total fat (2 g sat. fat), 31 g carb, trace fibre, 14 mg chol, 37 mg sodium, 16 mg potassium. % RDI: 3% iron, 3% vit A, 5% folate.

Serve a nutty Chocolate Brownie Martini as a cocktail version of dessert.
Use white crème de cacao if you prefer a clear drink. For a special Christmas gathering,
our Chocolate Mint Martini will have peppermint lovers lined up at the bar.

Chocolate Brownie Martini

ingredients

Ice cubes
1 oz (2 tbsp) **vanilla vodka** or vodka
1 oz (2 tbsp) **brown crème de cacao**
½ oz (1 tbsp) **Frangelico**
1 tbsp **whipping cream (35%)**
Shaved **dark chocolate** or Pencil-Thin
　　Chocolate Curls (see Making Perfect
　　Chocolate Curls, opposite)

method

Fill cocktail shaker with ice. Add vodka,
crème de cacao, Frangelico and cream; shake
vigorously to blend and chill.

Strain mixture into martini glass; garnish with
shaved chocolate.

MAKES 1 SERVING.
PER SERVING: about 279 cal, trace pro, 5 g total fat
(3 g sat. fat), 24 g carb, 0 g fibre, 19 mg chol, 10 mg
sodium, 25 mg potassium. % RDI: 1% calcium, 6% vit A.

Chocolate Mint Martini

Ice cubes
1 oz (2 tbsp) **vodka**
1 oz (2 tbsp) **white crème de cacao**
½ oz (1 tbsp) **white crème de menthe**

GARNISH:
White crème de menthe
Crushed **candy canes** or coarse red sugar

GARNISH: Moisten rim of martini glass with
crème de menthe; coat with candy cane.

Fill cocktail shaker with ice. Add vodka,
crème de cacao and crème de menthe; shake
vigorously to blend and chill.

Strain mixture into prepared martini glass.

MAKES 1 SERVING.
PER SERVING: about 234 cal, trace pro, trace total fat
(trace sat. fat), 22 g carb, 0 g fibre, 0 mg chol, 4 mg
sodium, 10 mg potassium.

MAKING PERFECT
Chocolate Curls

Chocolate curls give desserts a beautiful finish – and they couldn't be simpler to make. Here are two methods for creating different shapes and sizes.

Using chef's knife, chop 6 oz (170 g) bittersweet, semisweet or white chocolate into almond-size pieces. In heatproof bowl over saucepan of hot (not boiling) water, melt chocolate until about three-quarters is melted. Remove from heat; stir until smooth.

Sheet Method
Pour chocolate onto back of 15- x 10-inch (38 x 25 cm) rimmed baking sheet (do not use nonstick pan). With offset spatula or rubber spatula, spread evenly over pan ❶. Refrigerate until set, about 15 minutes. Place baking sheet on large damp towel that extends beyond edges of sheet; let stand for 3 minutes.

- **Short, Round Chocolate Curls:** Brace pan against body. Holding bowl of teaspoon at 45-degree angle to pan and working toward yourself, scrape about 4-inch (10 cm) lengths of chocolate into short, round curls ❷. Refrigerate pan if chocolate begins to soften. Use toothpick or offset spatula to transfer curls, in single layer, to waxed paper–lined rimmed baking sheet. Refrigerate.

- **Pencil-Thin Chocolate Curls:** Refrigerate pan before spreading with melted chocolate. Brace pan against body. At opposite end, place large chef's knife at 90-degree angle to pan; holding top of blade and handle steady, pull knife toward yourself, scraping chocolate into pencil-thin curls ❸. If chocolate is too brittle, let stand for a few minutes until softened.

- **Long Chocolate Curls:** Let pan stand for 5 minutes. Brace opposite side with hand. Holding stainless-steel spatula or bench scraper at 45-degree angle to pan, push spatula away from yourself, scraping chocolate into long curls.

Block Method
Pour melted chocolate into foil-lined 5¾- x 3¼-inch (625 mL) loaf pan. Refrigerate until set, about 4 hours. Unmould. Let stand until slightly softened, about 20 minutes.

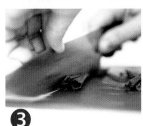

- **Long, Thin Chocolate Curls:** Holding chocolate with waxed paper to prevent melting, coarsely grate 1 long side into long, thin curls.

- **Short, Thick Chocolate Curls:** Holding chocolate with waxed paper to prevent melting and bracing block at comfortable angle, slowly draw blade of sharp vegetable peeler down 1 wide side to make short, thick curls ❹.

cakey

Chocolate Cherry Pancakes With Cherry Syrup **301**

Chocolate Cupid Cakes With Satin Glaze **302**

Cakey Chocolate Brownies **303**

Whoopie Pies With Cream Cheese Filling **304**

Mocha Snacking Cake **306**

Chocolate Cherry Fruit Cake **307**

Mini Steamed Chocolate Puddings **309**

Sour Cream Chocolate Crumb Cake **310**

Dark Chocolate Bûche de Noël **311**

Chocolate Strawberry Shortcake **312**

Chocolate Pistachio Loaf **314**

White Chocolate Almond Pound Cake **315**

Hot Fudge Banana Bundt Cake **317**

Chocolate Chocolate Loaf **318**

Chocolate Blackout Cake **319**

Chocolate Chip Angel Food Cake **320**

Chocolate Orange Bundt Cake **322**

Raspberry Chocolate Chip Bundt Cake **323**

Glazed Double-Chocolate Marble Cake **325**

Chocolate & Olive Oil Bundt Cake With Chocolate Sauce **326**

Chocolate-Glazed Chocolate Chip Muffins **327**

Chocolate Cupcakes With Double-Chocolate Icing **328**

Milk Chocolate Cupcakes **330**

Banana Chocolate Chip Muffins **331**

Banana & Chocolate Malt Cake Cones **333**

Chocolate Raspberry Curl Cake **334**

Chocolate Caramel Turtle Torte **335**

Our Favourite Chocolate Layer Cake **336**

Chocolate Torte With Pecans **338**

Chocolate EspressoTorte **339**

Hazelnut Torte With Caramel Milk Chocolate Buttercream **341**

Mascarpone cheese and cherry syrup add a touch of elegance to this otherwise humble family favourite. Top with shaved chocolate for a pretty finish.

Chocolate Cherry Pancakes
WITH CHERRY SYRUP

ingredients

1½ cups **all-purpose flour**

3 tbsp **granulated sugar**

1 tsp each **baking powder** and **baking soda**

¼ tsp **salt**

1¾ cups **buttermilk**

1 **egg**

2 tbsp **butter**, melted

2 tsp **vanilla**

¾ cup **sweet cherries**, pitted and halved

⅓ cup **dark chocolate chunks**

1 tbsp **canola oil**

½ cup **mascarpone cheese**

2 tbsp **maple syrup**

CHERRY SYRUP:

2 cups **sweet cherries,** pitted and halved

½ cup **maple syrup**

1 tsp **lemon juice**

method

CHERRY SYRUP: In saucepan, bring cherries and maple syrup to boil over medium-high heat; reduce heat and simmer, stirring often, until thickened, about 15 minutes. Stir in lemon juice. Set aside.

In large bowl, whisk together flour, sugar, baking powder, baking soda and salt. Whisk together buttermilk, egg, butter and 1 tsp of the vanilla; pour over dry ingredients and whisk until combined but still slightly lumpy. Fold in cherries and chocolate.

Lightly brush large nonstick skillet or griddle with some of the oil; heat over medium heat. Using scant ⅓ cup per pancake, pour in batter; spread slightly to form circles. Cook until bubbles appear on top, about 4 minutes.

Flip and cook until bottoms are golden, about 1 minute. Transfer to baking sheet; cover and keep warm in 250°F (120°C) oven.

In bowl, stir together mascarpone cheese, maple syrup and remaining vanilla. Serve with pancakes and cherry syrup.

MAKES 12 PANCAKES, OR 6 SERVINGS.
PER SERVING: about 244 cal, 5 g pro, 10 g total fat (5 g sat. fat), 34 g carb, 1 g fibre, 31 mg chol, 228 mg sodium, 199 mg potassium. % RDI: 8% calcium, 12% iron, 5% vit A, 3% vit C, 12% folate.

Easy Buttermilk Substitute

No worries if you forgot to put buttermilk on your grocery list; there's a simple substitution you can make. Pour 1 tbsp vinegar or lemon juice into a liquid measure, then pour in enough milk to make 1 cup. Let the mixture stand for 5 minutes to thicken. Use in place of 1 cup buttermilk in any baking recipe.

Test Kitchen TIP

Each of these diminutive angel food cakes serves two quite cosily.
For an even more sumptuous experience, serve with Raspberry Chantilly (below).

Chocolate Cupid Cakes
WITH SATIN GLAZE

ingredients

⅔ cup sifted **cake-and-pastry flour**
3 tbsp **cocoa powder**
1 cup **granulated sugar**
1 cup **egg whites** (about 7)
½ tsp **cream of tartar**
¼ tsp **salt**
1 tsp **vanilla**

CHOCOLATE SATIN:
4 oz (115 g) **bittersweet chocolate,** chopped
2 tbsp **corn syrup**
½ cup **whipping cream (35%)**

method

Into bowl, sift together flour, cocoa powder and ⅓ cup of the sugar; sift again. Set aside.

In large bowl, beat egg whites until foamy; beat in cream of tartar and salt until soft peaks form. Beat in remaining sugar, 2 tbsp at a time, until stiff glossy peaks form (see Beating Egg Whites, page 279). Fold in vanilla. Sift one-third of the flour mixture at a time over top, gently folding in each addition until blended.

Spoon mixture into large piping bag fitted with ¾-inch (2 cm) plain tip; pipe batter into 6 mini (1¼-cup/300 mL) angel food cake pans, filling halfway to tops. Bake in 350°F (180°C) oven until cakes spring back when lightly touched, about 20 minutes.

Invert pans; let cakes hang in pans until completely cool. Remove from pans. *(Make-ahead: Wrap individually in plastic wrap; store in single layer in airtight container for up to 2 days or freeze for up to 2 weeks.)*

CHOCOLATE SATIN: Place chocolate and corn syrup in heatproof bowl. In small saucepan, bring cream just to boil; pour over chocolate mixture, whisking until smooth. *(Make-ahead: Let cool. Refrigerate in airtight container for up to 3 days; gently rewarm to continue.)*

Place cakes on rack set over waxed paper. Spoon chocolate satin over cakes, using knife to spread and letting it drizzle down sides.

MAKES 6 CAKES, OR 12 SERVINGS.
PER SERVING: about 195 cal, 4 g pro, 7 g total fat (4 g sat. fat), 30 g carb, 1 g fibre, 13 mg chol, 88 mg sodium. % RDI: 2% calcium, 8% iron, 3% vit A, 3% folate.

MAKE YOUR OWN
Raspberry Chantilly
Press ½ cup thawed frozen raspberries through fine sieve to remove seeds. In bowl, beat ½ cup whipping cream (35%) with 2 tsp icing sugar until soft peaks form. Fold in raspberry purée. *(Make-ahead: Refrigerate in airtight container for up to 2 hours; whisk gently for a few seconds before serving.)*

MAKES 1 CUP.

Make Them Even Smaller

If you want to bake individual Cupid Cupcakes, spoon batter into 12 muffin cups. Reduce baking time to about 15 minutes.

This cross between chocolate cake and brownies is light and airy – nothing like your typical dense, fudgy brownie. Finish with either Coconut Pecan Icing or Chocolate Icing (below).

Cakey Chocolate Brownies

ingredients

⅓ cup **butter,** softened
1 cup **granulated sugar**
3 **eggs**
1 tsp **vanilla**

2 oz (55 g) **unsweetened chocolate,** melted and cooled
2 oz (55 g) **bittersweet chocolate,** melted and cooled
1 cup **all-purpose flour**
½ tsp **baking powder**
¼ tsp **salt**

method

In large bowl, beat butter with sugar until combined; beat in eggs, 1 at a time. Beat in vanilla; beat in unsweetened and bittersweet chocolates. Stir in flour, baking powder and salt. Spread in parchment paper–lined 8-inch (2 L) square cake pan.

Bake in 350°F (180°C) oven until cake tester inserted in centre comes out with a few moist crumbs clinging, about 20 minutes. Let cool in pan on rack. *(Make-ahead: Wrap and store for up to 2 days.)*

Cut into squares.

MAKES 20 SQUARES.
PER SQUARE: about 130 cal, 2 g pro, 6 g total fat (4 g sat. fat), 17 g carb, 1 g fibre, 36 mg chol, 67 mg sodium. % RDI: 1% calcium, 6% iron, 4% vit A, 7% folate.

MAKE YOUR OWN
Coconut Pecan Icing
In small saucepan over low heat, stir together ⅓ cup granulated sugar, ⅓ cup evaporated milk, 1 egg yolk and 2 tbsp butter. Cook, stirring constantly and without boiling, until thickened, about 8 minutes. Remove from heat. Stir in ¾ cup sweetened flaked coconut, ⅓ cup chopped toasted pecans and ½ tsp vanilla. Let cool.

MAKES ABOUT 1 CUP.

Chocolate Icing
In bowl, beat 1 cup icing sugar with ¼ cup butter. Beat in 1 oz (30 g) unsweetened chocolate, melted and cooled; 4 tsp hot water; and ½ tsp vanilla until fluffy.

MAKES ABOUT 1 CUP.

Made of two soft, cakelike cookies sandwiching a finger-licking-delicious cream cheese icing, whoopie pies are thought to have originated with the Amish in the United States.

Whoopie Pies
WITH CREAM CHEESE FILLING

ingredients

½ cup **unsalted butter**, softened
1 cup **granulated sugar**
1 **egg**
1 tsp **vanilla**
1¾ cups **all-purpose flour**
⅔ cup **cocoa powder**
1½ tsp **baking soda**
½ tsp **salt**
1 cup **buttermilk**

CREAM CHEESE FILLING:

1 pkg (250 g) **cream cheese,** softened
⅓ cup **unsalted butter,** softened
Pinch **salt**
2 cups **icing sugar**

method

In large bowl, beat butter with sugar until light and fluffy, about 2 minutes. Beat in egg; beat in vanilla. Whisk together flour, cocoa powder, baking soda and salt; stir into butter mixture alternately with buttermilk, making 3 additions of flour mixture and 2 of buttermilk.

Drop by heaping 2 tbsp, about 3 inches (8 cm) apart, onto parchment paper–lined rimless baking sheets to make 24 mounds. Bake in 350°F (180°C) oven until tops are slightly cracked and spring back when lightly touched, 12 to 14 minutes. Let cool on pans on racks.

CREAM CHEESE FILLING: In bowl, beat together cream cheese, butter and salt until smooth. Beat in icing sugar, 1 cup at a time, until smooth. Drop about 3 tbsp icing each onto flat side of half of the cookies; sandwich with tops.

MAKES 12 PIES.

PER PIE: about 422 cal, 6 g pro, 22 g total fat (13 g sat. fat), 55 g carb, 2 g fibre, 74 mg chol, 340 mg sodium, 211 mg potassium. % RDI: 5% calcium, 14% iron, 20% vit A, 20% folate.

Softening Cream Cheese

Like butter, cream cheese beats up light and fluffy in icings if it's softened first. Let the cream cheese stand on the counter for 30 minutes to 1 hour before you start. If you're in a rush, cube the cream cheese and scatter the cubes over a large plate; that should reduce the softening time a bit.

Test Kitchen TIP

With rich, dark coffee and chocolate, this moist cake is terrific on its own. But if you like, it's also nice dusted with icing sugar or dressed up with whipped cream and berries.

Mocha Snacking Cake

ingredients

⅔ cup **butter,** softened
1½ cups **granulated sugar**
2 **eggs**
1 tsp **vanilla**
1⅔ cups **all-purpose flour**
¾ cup **cocoa powder**

1 tsp **baking soda**
1 tsp **baking powder**
¼ tsp **salt**
1⅓ cups strong brewed **coffee,** cooled

method

Grease 8-inch (2 L) square cake pan; line bottom with parchment paper or waxed paper. Set aside.

In large bowl, beat butter with sugar until fluffy; beat in eggs, 1 at a time, just until incorporated. Stir in vanilla. Sift together flour, cocoa powder, baking soda, baking powder and salt; beat into butter mixture alternately with coffee, making 2 additions of flour mixture and 1 of coffee, until almost smooth. Pour into prepared pan; spread evenly and smooth top.

Bake in 350°F (180°C) oven until cake tester inserted in centre comes out clean, 45 to 50 minutes.

Let cool in pan on rack. (*Make-ahead: Wrap in plastic wrap and store for up to 3 days. Or overwrap with heavy-duty foil and freeze for up to 2 weeks.*)

MAKES 12 SERVINGS.
PER SERVING: about 275 cal, 4 g pro, 12 g total fat (7 g sat. fat), 41 g carb, 2 g fibre, 63 mg chol, 283 mg sodium. % RDI: 2% calcium, 13% iron, 11% vit A, 19% folate.

Make It Instant

Test Kitchen TIP

If you don't have strong brewed coffee on hand, make 1⅓ cups using boiling water and 2 tbsp instant coffee granules.

Depart from the tried and true with this dark fruit cake studded with dried cherries. Keep it for a special occasion and serve it in thin wedges along with ice cream drizzled with kirsch or chocolate liqueur.

Chocolate Cherry Fruit Cake

ingredients

½ cup **butter**
1½ cups **granulated sugar**
2 **eggs**
2 tsp **vanilla**
2 cups **all-purpose flour**
⅔ cup **cocoa powder**
1 tsp **baking soda**
½ tsp **salt**

1 cup **sour cream**
¼ cup **brandy**
3 cups chopped **pecans**
2 cups **dried sour cherries**

method

Grease 10-inch (4 L) tube pan; line bottom with parchment paper. Set aside.

In large bowl, beat butter with sugar until fluffy. Beat in eggs, 1 at a time; beat in vanilla. Sift together flour, cocoa powder, baking soda and salt; stir into butter mixture in 3 additions, alternating with 1 addition of sour cream, then 1 addition of brandy. Sprinkle with pecans and cherries; stir just until combined. Scrape into prepared pan; smooth top.

Tap pan lightly on counter to remove any air bubbles. Bake in 300°F (150°C) oven until cake tester inserted in centre comes out clean, about 1½ hours.

Let cool in pan on rack for 30 minutes. Transfer, right side up, to rack; let cool completely. Wrap in plastic wrap and overwrap with foil; store in cool place for up to 2 weeks. *(Make ahead: Freeze for up to 1 month.)*

MAKES 24 SERVINGS.
PER SERVING: about 278 cal, 4 g pro, 16 g total fat (5 g sat. fat), 32 g carb, 3 g fibre, 32 mg chol, 166 mg sodium. % RDI: 3% calcium, 9% iron, 10% vit A, 5% vit C, 10% folate.

Lining Tube Pans

For this and some other cakes, you need to line just the bottom of a tube pan with parchment paper, which can seem a bit finicky. But it's not. Simply place a sheet of parchment paper on your work surface; using a pencil, trace around the bottom of the pan and cut out the circle. Turn the pan over and match up the edge of the circle with the edge of the pan; trace the inner circle on the paper and cut out. Voilà – a perfect fit.

Test Kitchen TIP

Steamed puddings are an old-fashioned holiday treat, but you don't have to wait till December to make them. The batter for these mini cakes can also be made into a single big pudding.

Mini Steamed Chocolate Puddings

ingredients

White Chocolate Pouring Custard
(page 63)

PUDDING:
⅓ cup **butter,** softened
1 cup packed **brown sugar**
2 **eggs**
6 oz (170 g) **bittersweet chocolate,** melted
1 tbsp **orange liqueur** (or orange
juice concentrate)
2 tsp grated **orange zest**

1¼ cups **all-purpose flour**
⅓ cup **cocoa powder**
1½ tsp **baking powder**
¾ cup **milk**

CHOCOLATE SYRUP:
⅓ cup **granulated sugar**
2 oz (55 g) **bittersweet chocolate** or
semisweet chocolate, chopped
1 tbsp **orange liqueur** (or orange
juice concentrate)

method

PUDDING: In large bowl, beat butter with sugar until fluffy. Beat in eggs, 1 at a time; beat in chocolate, liqueur and orange zest. Whisk together flour, cocoa powder and baking powder. With wooden spoon, stir into butter mixture alternately with milk, making 3 additions of flour mixture and 2 of milk.

Spoon ½ cup pudding mixture into each of 6 greased 1-cup (250 mL) mini Bundt pans. Cover tightly with foil, leaving 1-inch (2.5 cm) overhang; press down side. Tie kitchen string around foil.

Place on rack in roasting pan; add enough boiling water to come halfway up sides of Bundt pans. Cover roasting pan with foil; steam over medium-low heat until edges of puddings pull away from sides of pans, about 1 hour. Transfer Bundt pans to rack; let cool slightly. Remove foil; invert onto rack.

CHOCOLATE SYRUP: Meanwhile, in saucepan, bring sugar and ⅓ cup water to boil; stir in chocolate. Boil hard until consistency of maple syrup, 2 minutes. Stir in liqueur. Brush over puddings until absorbed. *(Make-ahead: Let cool. Wrap in plastic wrap; refrigerate for up to 1 week. Or overwrap in heavy-duty foil and freeze for up to 1 month; thaw. To reheat, turn out onto serving plate; cover with microwaveable bowl. Microwave on high until hot, 5 minutes.)*

To serve, spoon pouring custard into pools on dessert plates; top with puddings.

MAKES 6 SERVINGS.

PER SERVING: about 931 cal, 16 g pro, 51 g total fat (28 g sat. fat), 119 g carb, 8 g fibre, 97 mg chol, 273 mg sodium. % RDI: 24% calcium, 43% iron, 28% vit A, 32% folate.

CHANGE IT UP
Steamed Chocolate Pudding
Spoon pudding mixture into greased 6-cup (1.5 L) pudding ring mould or Bundt pan. Cover with lid. (For Bundt pan, make 1-inch/2.5 cm pleat across middle of large piece of foil and fit over top. Trim edge, leaving 3-inch/8 cm overhang; press down side. Tie string securely around pan about 1 inch/2.5 cm below rim; fold foil overhang up over string.) Place on rack in deep pot; pour in enough boiling water to come halfway up side of mould. Cover and bring to boil; reduce heat and simmer, adding boiling water as necessary to maintain level, until skewer inserted in centre comes out clean, 1½ to 2 hours. Remove from pot; let cool slightly. Remove lid; invert onto rack. Brush with chocolate syrup.

MAKES 6 TO 8 SERVINGS.

This simple cake is perfect for laid-back munching. The sweet crumb topping makes it look, feel and taste like the best coffee cake you've ever tried.

Sour Cream Chocolate Crumb Cake

ingredients

½ cup **unsalted butter**, softened
½ cup **granulated sugar**
1 **egg**
1 **egg yolk**
1⅓ cups **all-purpose flour**
½ tsp **baking soda**
¼ tsp **salt**
½ cup **sour cream**
3 oz (85 g) **bittersweet chocolate**, melted

TOPPING:
½ cup packed **brown sugar**
¼ cup **granulated sugar**
¼ tsp **cinnamon**
Pinch **salt**
½ cup **unsalted butter**, melted and warm
1⅓ cups **all-purpose flour**
⅓ cup **ground almonds**

method

TOPPING: In bowl, stir together brown sugar, granulated sugar, cinnamon and salt; stir in butter. Stir in flour and almonds; using hands, press mixture together. Let cool.

In large bowl, beat butter with sugar until combined. Beat in egg and egg yolk. Whisk together flour, baking soda and salt. Stir into butter mixture alternately with sour cream, making 3 additions of flour mixture and 2 of sour cream. Stir in chocolate.

Spread in parchment paper–lined 8-inch (2 L) square cake pan. Crumble topping evenly over batter.

Bake in 350°F (180°C) oven until cake tester inserted in centre comes out clean, 35 to 40 minutes. Let cool in pan on rack.

MAKES 12 SERVINGS.
PER SERVING: about 387 cal, 5 g pro, 21 g total fat (12 g sat. fat), 46 g carb, 2 g fibre, 77 mg chol, 116 mg sodium, 105 mg potassium. % RDI: 4% calcium, 14% iron, 16% vit A, 29% folate.

CHANGE IT UP
Sour Cream Chocolate Chunk Crumb Cake
Substitute ⅓ cup chopped bittersweet chocolate for the melted chocolate.

Cake Testers

A cake tester is a simple tool – just a piece of metal wire with a handle – made for checking the doneness of cakes. (Of course, a plain old skewer or toothpick works just as well.) And while some old-timey cookbooks say you can even use a broom straw, we recommend sticking with a tester designed just for food.

Test Kitchen TIP

A traditional holiday recipe, this popular Yule log is a cinch to make in stages.
It can be ready to assemble a day ahead, leaving you free to attend to other celebratory cooking.

Dark Chocolate Bûche de Noël

ingredients

¼ cup **milk**
2 tbsp **butter**
¾ cup sifted **cake-and-pastry flour**
1 tsp **baking powder**
¼ tsp **salt**
5 **eggs**
¾ cup **granulated sugar**
1 tbsp **icing sugar**

ICING:
1 cup **butter,** softened
⅓ cup **whipping cream (35%)**
2 tsp **vanilla**
2 cups **icing sugar**
4 oz (115 g) **unsweetened chocolate,**
  melted and cooled

CHOCOLATE BARK:
8 oz (225 g) **bittersweet chocolate,**
  chopped

method

In heatproof bowl over saucepan of simmering water, heat milk with butter, stirring until melted. Remove pan from heat, leaving bowl on top to keep warm enough that finger can remain in bowl for no longer than 10 seconds.

Whisk together flour, baking powder and salt; set aside. Separate 3 of the eggs, dropping yolks and whites into separate large bowls. Beat egg whites until foamy; beat in ¼ cup of the granulated sugar, 1 tbsp at a time, until soft peaks form.

Beat egg yolks, remaining eggs and remaining granulated sugar until pale and thick enough that batter leaves ribbons on surface when beaters are lifted, 5 minutes. Fold in one-third of the whites; fold in remaining whites.

Sift flour mixture over top; fold in until combined. Pour in milk mixture; fold in until blended. Spread evenly on parchment paper–lined 15- x 10-inch (38 x 25 cm) rimmed baking sheet. Bake in 350°F (180°C) oven until golden and cake springs back when lightly touched, about 12 minutes.

Loosen edges with knife; invert onto flour-dusted tea towel. Starting at corner, carefully peel off paper. Starting at short side, roll up cake in towel; let cool on rack. *(Make-ahead: Wrap in plastic wrap and store at room temperature for up to 24 hours.)*

ICING: In bowl, beat butter until fluffy; gradually beat in cream. Beat in vanilla. Beat in icing sugar, 1 cup at a time; beat in chocolate until fluffy.

CHOCOLATE BARK: In heatproof bowl over saucepan of hot (not boiling) water, melt chocolate, stirring occasionally. Pour onto parchment paper–lined 15- x 10-inch (38 x 25 cm) rimmed baking sheet, spreading to scant ⅛-inch (3 mm) thickness. Refrigerate until set, about 10 minutes. Break or tear chocolate into about 3- x 1-inch (8 x 2.5 cm) pieces. Arrange in single layer on baking sheet; cover loosely with plastic wrap and refrigerate until firm. *(Make-ahead: Refrigerate for up to 2 days.)*

Unroll cake; spread with 1½ cups of the icing. Reroll without towel; place, seam side down, on platter. Spread remaining icing all over log. Cover log with chocolate bark. Refrigerate until cold. *(Make-ahead: Cover with plastic wrap; refrigerate for up to 1 day.)*

Dust bark with icing sugar just before serving.

MAKES 12 SERVINGS.
PER SERVING: about 499 cal, 7 g pro, 37 g total fat (22 g sat. fat), 45 g carb, 4 g fibre, 141 mg chol, 280 mg sodium. % RDI: 5% calcium, 19% iron, 23% vit A, 9% folate.

Strawberries and ice cream are delicious partners for these rich, fluffy biscuits.
They're a nice, chocolaty change of pace from plain shortcakes.

Chocolate Strawberry Shortcake

ingredients

3 cups sliced **strawberries**
3 tbsp **granulated sugar**
4 cups **vanilla ice cream**
½ cup **chocolate sauce** (such as Rich
  Double-Chocolate Sauce, page 36)

CHOCOLATE BISCUITS:
2¼ cups **all-purpose flour**
½ cup **cocoa powder**
½ cup **granulated sugar**
2½ tsp **baking powder**

½ tsp each **baking soda** and **salt**
½ cup cold **unsalted butter,**
  cubed
1 cup **buttermilk**
1 **egg**
1 tsp **vanilla**

TOPPING:
1 tbsp **whipping cream (35%)**
2 tsp **granulated sugar**

method

CHOCOLATE BISCUITS: In large bowl, whisk together flour, cocoa powder, sugar, baking powder, baking soda and salt. Using pastry blender or 2 knives, cut in butter until crumbly. Whisk together buttermilk, egg and vanilla; add to flour mixture, stirring with fork to form soft dough.

With lightly floured hands, press dough into ball. On lightly floured surface, knead gently 10 times. Pat into 1-inch (2.5 cm) thick round. Using 3-inch (8 cm) round cookie cutter, cut out rounds, patting out and cutting scraps. Place on parchment paper–lined rimless baking sheet.

TOPPING: Brush biscuits with cream; sprinkle with sugar. Bake in 400°F (200°C) oven until puffed and cake tester inserted into several comes out clean, 15 to 20 minutes. Let cool on pan on rack. (*Make-ahead: Set aside for up to 6 hours.*)

Meanwhile, mix strawberries with sugar; cover and let stand until juicy, about 20 minutes. (*Make-ahead: Let stand for up to 2 hours.*)

Split biscuits horizontally in half; place bottom halves on plates. Layer with strawberries, ice cream and biscuit tops; drizzle chocolate sauce over tops.

MAKES 8 SERVINGS.
PER SERVING: about 566 cal, 10 g pro, 24 g total fat (14 g sat. fat), 83 g carb, 5 g fibre, 88 mg chol, 474 mg sodium. % RDI: 20% calcium, 23% iron, 20% vit A, 62% vit C, 44% folate.

Pistachios dot this dark, chocolaty loaf with pretty green flecks. Cut generous slices and serve them with cups of tea or espresso for an afternoon indulgence.

Chocolate Pistachio Loaf

ingredients

1 cup shelled **pistachios**
¾ cup **butter,** softened
1 cup **granulated sugar**
2 **eggs**
1 tbsp **vanilla**
1¾ cups **all-purpose flour**
½ cup **cocoa powder**

1 tsp **baking soda**
½ tsp **salt**
¾ cup **sour cream**
1 cup **semisweet chocolate chips**

method

Toast pistachios on rimmed baking sheet in 350°F (180°C) oven, stirring once, until fragrant, about 8 minutes. Place on clean tea towel; rub briskly to remove as much of the skin as possible. Let cool.

Meanwhile, in bowl, beat butter with sugar until light and fluffy; beat in eggs, 1 at a time, beating well after each. Beat in vanilla. Sift together flour, cocoa powder, baking soda and salt. Stir into butter mixture alternately with sour cream, making 3 additions of flour mixture and 2 of sour cream. Sprinkle chocolate chips and pistachios over batter; fold in.

Scrape into parchment paper–lined or greased 9- x 5-inch (2 L) loaf pan, smoothing top. Bake in 350°F (180°C) oven until cake tester inserted in centre comes out clean, about 70 minutes.

Let cool in pan on rack for 10 minutes. Transfer to rack; let cool completely. *(Make-ahead: Wrap in plastic wrap and store for up to 2 days or overwrap with heavy-duty foil and freeze for up to 1 month.)*

MAKES 1 LOAF, ABOUT 12 SLICES.
PER SLICE: about 403 cal, 7 g pro, 24 g total fat (12 g sat. fat), 44 g carb, 4 g fibre, 68 mg chol, 330 mg sodium. % RDI: 4% calcium, 19% iron, 14% vit A, 2% vit C, 15% folate.

Test Kitchen TIP

Shelled Pistachios

Look for shelled pistachios in the baking aisle of the supermarket or in a specialty store. If you can't find them, buy 2 cups unsalted pistachios and shell them yourself.

With all the buttery denseness of a plain pound cake, this one has a bit of added glamour in the form of white chocolate. It's a rich little cake, so a small slice is satisfying.

White Chocolate Almond Pound Cake

ingredients

1 cup **butter,** softened
1½ cups **granulated sugar**
3 **eggs**
½ tsp **almond extract**
2½ cups **all-purpose flour**
½ cup **ground almonds**
2 tsp **baking powder**
¼ tsp **salt**

½ cup **milk**
½ cup **slivered almonds**
½ cup **white chocolate chips**

TOPPING:
⅓ cup **white chocolate chips,** melted
¼ cup **slivered almonds,** toasted

method

In bowl, beat butter with sugar until fluffy. Beat in eggs, 1 at a time, beating well after each. Beat in almond extract.

Whisk together flour, ground almonds, baking powder and salt; stir into butter mixture alternately with milk, making 3 additions of flour mixture and 2 of milk. Stir in slivered almonds and white chocolate chips.

Scrape into parchment paper–lined 9- x 5-inch (2 L) loaf pan. Bake in 325ºF (160ºC) oven until golden and cake tester inserted in centre comes out clean, about 1½ hours.

Let cool in pan on rack; turn out onto plate and let cool completely.

TOPPING: Drizzle white chocolate down centre of loaf; sprinkle with almonds. *(Make-ahead: Wrap in plastic wrap and store for up to 3 days or overwrap in heavy-duty foil and freeze for up to 2 weeks.)*

Cut into 12 slices; cut each in half.

MAKES 24 SERVINGS.
PER SERVING: about 239 cal, 4 g pro, 13 g total fat (6 g sat. fat), 27 g carb, 1 g fibre, 48 mg chol, 140 mg sodium. % RDI: 4% calcium, 6% iron, 9% vit A, 9% folate.

Banana cake is invariably moist and buttery, and this one is no exception.
Add swirls of chocolate inside and a fudgy chocolate sauce crowning the top,
and you have a spectacular dessert that's spectacularly easy to make.

Hot Fudge Banana Bundt Cake

ingredients

1 cup **unsalted butter**, softened
1¾ cups **granulated sugar**
6 **eggs**
3 cups **all-purpose flour**
1½ tsp **baking powder**
¾ tsp **baking soda**
¾ tsp **salt**
1½ cups mashed **bananas** (about
   5 small)
1½ tsp **vinegar**

HOT FUDGE SAUCE:
1½ cups **whipping cream (35%)**
1¼ cups **granulated sugar**
4 oz (115 g) **unsweetened chocolate,**
   coarsely chopped
2 oz (55 g) **bittersweet chocolate,**
   coarsely chopped
2 tbsp **butter**
2 tbsp **corn syrup**
½ tsp **vanilla**

method

HOT FUDGE SAUCE: In heavy saucepan, combine cream, sugar, unsweetened chocolate, bittersweet chocolate, butter and corn syrup; heat over low heat, whisking constantly, until sugar is dissolved and chocolate is melted. Boil over medium-high heat, whisking constantly, until reduced to 2½ cups, about 8 minutes. Let cool until room temperature but still pourable. *(Make-ahead: Refrigerate in airtight container for up to 1 week; gently rewarm to liquefy.)* Stir in vanilla.

In bowl, beat butter with sugar until light and fluffy. Beat in eggs, 1 at a time, beating well after each. Whisk together flour, baking powder, baking soda and salt. Stir bananas with vinegar. Stir flour mixture into egg mixture alternately with banana mixture, making 3 additions of flour mixture and 2 of banana mixture.

Pour one-quarter of the batter into greased and floured 10-inch (3 L) Bundt pan; leaving ½-inch (1 cm) border around edge of pan, drizzle ¼ cup of the fudge sauce over batter. Repeat layers twice. Top with remaining batter. Run thin knife or skewer through batter to create swirls. Bake in 350°F (180°C) oven until cake tester inserted in centre comes out clean, about 1 hour.

Let cool in pan on rack for 30 minutes. Invert pan onto rack; remove pan. Let cool completely. *(Make-ahead: Wrap in plastic wrap and store for up to 2 days or overwrap in heavy-duty foil and freeze for up to 2 weeks.)*

Serve thick slices with remaining slightly warm fudge sauce.

MAKES 12 SERVINGS.
PER SERVING: about 704 cal, 9 g pro, 38 g total fat (23 g sat. fat), 88 g carb, 4 g fibre, 192 mg chol, 320 mg sodium. % RDI: 6% calcium, 19% iron, 31% vit A, 3% vit C, 21% folate.

There's no way to pack more chocolate into this moist loaf. Serve it for tea or as a simple, polished dessert with creamy mascarpone cheese and fresh raspberries.

Chocolate Chocolate Loaf

ingredients

½ cup **butter,** softened
1¼ cups packed **brown sugar**
2 **eggs**
2 tsp **vanilla**
1¾ cups **all-purpose flour**
¾ cup **cocoa powder**
1 tsp **baking powder**

½ tsp each **baking soda** and **salt**
1 cup **sour cream**
¾ cup **semisweet chocolate chips**
¼ cup chopped **pecan halves**

method

In large bowl, beat butter with brown sugar until fluffy. Beat in eggs, 1 at a time; beat in vanilla. Sift together flour, cocoa powder, baking powder, baking soda and salt until no streaks remain; stir into butter mixture alternately with sour cream, making 2 additions of flour mixture and 1 of sour cream. Fold in chocolate chips and pecans. Scrape into parchment paper–lined or greased 9- x 5-inch (2 L) loaf pan.

Bake in 350°F (180°C) oven until cake tester inserted in centre comes out clean, about 70 minutes.

Transfer to rack; let cool completely. *(Make-ahead: Wrap in plastic wrap and store in airtight container for up to 3 days or overwrap with foil and freeze for up to 1 month.)*

MAKES 1 LOAF, OR 12 SLICES.
PER SLICE: about 345 cal, 5 g pro, 16 g total fat (9 g sat. fat), 47 g carb, 3 g fibre, 63 mg chol, 273 mg sodium. % RDI: 6% calcium, 19% iron, 11% vit A, 22% folate.

Chocolate cake crumbs covering three layers of dark, tender cake and a smooth, rich filling earn this superb dessert the name "blackout." It doesn't get any more chocolaty than this!

Chocolate Blackout Cake

ingredients

4 oz (115 g) **unsweetened chocolate,** chopped
⅓ cup **butter**
2 cups **granulated sugar**
1 tsp **vanilla**
2 **eggs,** lightly beaten
2 cups **all-purpose flour**
2 tsp **baking powder**
2 tsp **baking soda**
½ tsp **salt**

ICING:
1½ cups **granulated sugar**
1⅓ cups **whipping cream (35%)**
6 oz (170 g) **unsweetened chocolate,** chopped
⅔ cup **butter,** softened
1 tsp **vanilla**

method

Place chocolate and butter in heatproof bowl. In saucepan, bring sugar and 2 cups water to boil, stirring until sugar is dissolved; pour over chocolate mixture, whisking until melted and smooth. Stir in vanilla. Let cool slightly. Beat in eggs.

Whisk together flour, baking powder, baking soda and salt; beat into chocolate mixture until smooth. Divide between 2 greased 8-inch (1.2 L) round cake pans. Bake in 350°F (180°C) oven until tops spring back when lightly touched, about 35 minutes.

Let cool in pans on racks for 30 minutes. Transfer to racks; let cool completely. *(Make-ahead: Wrap with plastic wrap and store for up to 1 day or overwrap with heavy-duty foil and freeze for up to 2 weeks.)*

ICING: In saucepan, bring sugar and cream just to boil. Remove from heat; whisk in chocolate, butter and vanilla until melted and smooth. Transfer to bowl; refrigerate until cold, about 2 hours. Beat until thick and glossy, about 5 minutes.

Slice each cake in half horizontally; set 1 layer aside. Place 1 layer on cake plate; slide strips of waxed paper between cake and plate. Spread top with heaping 1 cup of the icing; level icing. Repeat layers once. Top with third cake layer; spread top and sides with remaining icing. Refrigerate for 10 minutes.

Crumble reserved cake layer into crumbs; sprinkle over top and press small handfuls onto side of cake, pressing lightly to adhere. Remove paper strips. *(Make-ahead: Cover loosely and refrigerate for up to 2 days.)*

Serve at room temperature.

MAKES 12 SERVINGS.
PER SERVING: about 659 cal, 6 g pro, 39 g total fat (23 g sat. fat), 82 g carb, 4 g fibre, 111 mg chol, 515 mg sodium. % RDI: 6% calcium, 18% iron, 25% vit A, 13% folate.

Beating the egg whites in a stand mixer gives great height to this updated classic cake. An electric hand mixer still creates a pillowy texture, but the cake will not be quite as high.

Chocolate Chip Angel Food Cake

ingredients

1¼ cups sifted **cake-and-pastry flour**
1½ cups **granulated sugar**
1½ cups **egg whites** (about 11)
1 tbsp **lemon juice**
1 tsp **cream of tartar**
½ tsp **salt**
½ cup **mini semisweet chocolate chips** or regular semisweet chocolate chips
2 tsp **vanilla**

GLAZE:
2 oz (55 g) **bittersweet chocolate,** coarsely chopped
⅓ cup **whipping cream (35%)**
1 tsp **corn syrup**

method

Into bowl, sift flour with ¾ cup of the sugar; sift again into separate bowl. Set aside.

In large bowl, beat egg whites until foamy. Add lemon juice, cream of tartar and salt; beat until soft peaks form. Beat in remaining sugar, 2 tbsp at a time, until stiff glossy peaks form (see Beating Egg Whites, page 279). Sift flour mixture over top, one-quarter at a time, gently folding in each addition until blended. Fold in chocolate chips and vanilla.

Pour into ungreased 10-inch (4 L) tube pan. Run spatula through batter to eliminate any large air bubbles ❶; smooth top. Bake in 350°F (180°C) oven until cake springs back when lightly touched, 45 to 50 minutes.

Turn pan upside down and let hang on legs attached to pan or on bottle until cooled ❷. Remove from pan; invert onto cake plate. *(Make-ahead: Wrap with plastic wrap and store in airtight container for up to 2 days or overwrap with foil and freeze for up to 1 month.)*

GLAZE: In heatproof bowl over saucepan of hot (not boiling) water, melt chocolate. Stir in cream and corn syrup until smooth. Spread over top of cake, letting drip down side. *(Make-ahead: Cover loosely in plastic wrap and store for up to 24 hours.)*

MAKES 12 SERVINGS.
PER SERVING: about 239 cal, 5 g pro, 7 g total fat (4 g sat. fat), 41 g carb, 1 g fibre, 9 mg chol, 148 mg sodium. % RDI: 1% calcium, 10% iron, 2% vit A, 7% folate.

HOW-TO

Chocolate and orange is a reliably tasty flavour pairing. The bright candied zest on top of this simple cake perfectly complements the chocolate chunks hidden within.

Chocolate Orange Bundt Cake

ingredients

1 cup **butter**, softened
1¼ cups packed **brown sugar**
3 **eggs**
1 tbsp **orange liqueur**
1½ cups **all-purpose flour**
¾ cup **cocoa powder**
1½ tsp **baking powder**
¾ tsp **baking soda**
½ tsp **salt**
1¼ cups **sour cream**

1 cup **dark chocolate chunks**
1 tbsp grated **orange zest**

CANDIED ORANGE ZEST:
½ cup **orange zest strips** (about 2 oranges)
1 cup **granulated sugar**

CHOCOLATE ORANGE GLAZE:
6 oz (170 g) **bittersweet chocolate**, chopped
2 tbsp **corn syrup**
⅓ cup **whipping cream (35%)**
3 tbsp **orange liqueur**

method

In large bowl, beat butter with brown sugar until fluffy; beat in eggs, 1 at a time. Beat in liqueur. Whisk together flour, cocoa powder, baking powder, baking soda and salt; stir into butter mixture alternately with sour cream, making 3 additions of flour mixture and 2 of sour cream. Stir in chocolate chunks and orange zest. Scrape into greased and floured 10-inch (3 L) Bundt pan. Bake in 325°F (160°C) oven until cake tester inserted in centre comes out clean, about 1 hour.

Let cool in pan on rack for 10 minutes. Invert pan onto rack; remove pan. Let cool completely. *(Make-ahead: Wrap in plastic wrap and store for up to 2 days or freeze in airtight container for up to 2 weeks.)*

CANDIED ORANGE ZEST: Meanwhile, in small saucepan, cover orange zest with cold water; bring to boil and drain. Repeat twice. Remove 1 tbsp of the sugar; set aside. In saucepan, bring 1 cup water and remaining sugar to boil. Add orange zest; reduce heat and simmer until zest is translucent and deepens in colour, about 10 minutes. Strain; spread zest on parchment paper. Let cool. Toss zest with reserved sugar.

CHOCOLATE ORANGE GLAZE: In heatproof bowl over saucepan of hot (not boiling) water, melt chocolate with corn syrup. In saucepan, bring cream just to boil; pour over chocolate mixture, stirring until smooth. Remove from heat. Stir in liqueur. Let cool until lukewarm and glaze runs slowly off back of spoon, about 15 minutes.

Place cake on rack over waxed paper. Pour glaze over top, letting excess drip down side; top with candied orange zest. Refrigerate until glaze is set, about 20 minutes.

MAKES 10 TO 12 SERVINGS.
PER EACH OF 12 SERVINGS: about 561 cal, 7 g pro, 33 g total fat (20 g sat. fat), 64 g carb, 5 g fibre, 106 mg chol, 367 mg sodium, 430 mg potassium. % RDI: 10% calcium, 26% iron, 20% vit A, 10% vit C, 20% folate.

Frozen raspberries make this handsome cake a reality year-round.
Of course, you can use fresh raspberries or, for a change of flavour, fresh wild blueberries
when they're in season.

Raspberry Chocolate Chip Bundt Cake

ingredients

2 pkg (each 300 g) **frozen unsweetened raspberries**
3 tbsp **icing sugar**
¾ cup **butter**, softened
1 cup **granulated sugar**
3 **eggs**
2 tsp **vanilla**
2¼ cups **all-purpose flour**
2 tsp **baking powder**

1½ tsp **baking soda**
½ tsp **salt**
1½ cups **sour cream**
1½ cups **semisweet chocolate chips**
¼ cup **light cream (10%)**

method

Measure 1 cup of the raspberries; thaw in sieve set over bowl, reserving juice. Thaw remaining berries; purée in food processor, adding reserved juice. Press through separate fine-mesh sieve into bowl to remove seeds; stir in icing sugar. Set aside sauce and reserved raspberries separately.

In bowl, beat butter with sugar until light and fluffy; beat in eggs, 1 at a time. Beat in vanilla. Whisk together flour, baking powder, baking soda and salt; stir into butter mixture alternately with sour cream, making 2 additions of flour mixture and 1 of sour cream. Stir in 1 cup of the chocolate chips.

Spread half of the batter in greased 10-inch (3 L) Bundt pan; sprinkle with reserved drained berries. Spread remaining batter over top. Bake in 350°F (180°C) oven until top springs back when lightly touched, about 40 minutes.

Let cool in pan on rack for 10 minutes. Invert pan onto rack; remove pan. Let cool completely. *(Make-ahead: Wrap in plastic wrap and store for up to 1 day or freeze in airtight container for up to 2 weeks. Thaw before continuing.)*

Place cake on cake plate; slide strips of waxed paper between cake and plate. In saucepan over low heat, melt remaining chocolate chips with cream, stirring until smooth; pour over cake and drizzle down side. Serve with reserved raspberry sauce.

MAKES 12 SERVINGS.
PER SERVING: about 447 cal, 6 g pro, 24 g total fat (14 g sat. fat), 55 g carb, 2 g fibre, 99 mg chol, 435 mg sodium. % RDI: 8% calcium, 15% iron, 18% vit A, 17% vit C, 20% folate.

Smooth Move

Raspberries have so many tiny seeds, which can make sauces and purées unpleasantly gritty. To strain them out, pour the puréed raspberries into a fine-mesh sieve, then press the pulp with the back of a spoon or a firm rubber spatula. Occasionally scrape the seedless purée off the bottom of the sieve with a clean spoon or spatula and into the bowl below.

323

White and dark chocolate batters swirl together in this ganache-glazed cake, which is delish with chocolate whipped cream or ice cream. To make the optional white chocolate shards, use a vegetable peeler to peel the edge of a square of chocolate.

Glazed Double-Chocolate Marble Cake

ingredients

2 oz (55 g) **unsweetened chocolate,** chopped

3 oz (85 g) **white chocolate,** chopped

⅔ cup **butter,** softened

1½ cups **granulated sugar**

3 **eggs**

2 tsp **vanilla**

2¼ cups **all-purpose flour**

1 tsp each **baking powder** and **baking soda**

½ tsp **salt**

1 cup **buttermilk**

White chocolate shards (optional)

GANACHE:

2 oz (55 g) **bittersweet chocolate,** chopped

¼ cup **whipping cream (35%)**

method

In separate bowls over saucepan of hot (not boiling) water, melt unsweetened chocolate and white chocolate, stirring occasionally until smooth; let cool to room temperature.

In large bowl, beat butter with sugar until fluffy. Beat in eggs, 1 at a time, beating well after each. Beat in vanilla.

Spoon half of the butter mixture into separate bowl; stir in unsweetened chocolate. Stir white chocolate into remaining butter mixture.

Whisk together flour, baking powder, baking soda and salt. Stir half into dark chocolate mixture alternately with half of the buttermilk, making 2 additions of flour mixture and 1 of buttermilk. Repeat with white chocolate mixture, remaining flour mixture and buttermilk.

Drop spoonfuls of dark and white batters into greased and floured 10-cup (2.5 L) fancy or classic Bundt or tube pan. With tip of knife, swirl batters to marble. Bake in 325°F (160°C) oven until cake tester inserted in centre comes out clean, about 55 minutes.

Let cool in pan on rack for 10 minutes. Invert pan onto rack; remove pan. Let cool completely. *(Make-ahead: Wrap in plastic wrap and store for up to 1 day or overwrap with heavy-duty foil and freeze for up to 1 month.)*

GANACHE: Place bittersweet chocolate in heatproof bowl. In saucepan, bring cream just to boil; pour over chocolate, stirring until melted and smooth. Let stand for 10 minutes; brush over cake.

Sprinkle white chocolate shards (if using) over cake. Let stand until ganache is set, about 40 minutes. *(Make-ahead: Cover cake with bowl or place in airtight container and store for up to 1 day.)*

MAKES 16 SERVINGS.

PER SERVING: about 304 cal, 5 g pro, 15 g total fat (9 g sat. fat), 39 g carb, 1 g fibre, 64 mg chol, 275 mg sodium. % RDI: 5% calcium, 9% iron, 10% vit A, 12% folate.

This dairy-free cake, with its dense crumb and deep, dark chocolate flavour, is the perfect ending to a celebratory dinner.

Chocolate & Olive Oil Bundt Cake
WITH CHOCOLATE SAUCE

ingredients

1¼ cups **all-purpose flour**
¾ cup **cocoa powder**, sifted
¼ cup **ground almonds**
1½ tsp **baking powder**
¾ tsp **baking soda**
½ tsp **salt**
1¼ cups packed **brown sugar**
1 cup **olive oil**
3 **eggs**
1 tbsp **lemon juice**

½ cup **sliced almonds**
2 tsp **icing sugar**

CHOCOLATE SAUCE:

½ cup **soy milk**
3 tbsp **corn syrup**
5 oz (140 g) **70% dark chocolate**, finely chopped
1 tbsp **dairy-free butter-flavoured spread** (such as Earth Balance)
¼ tsp **vanilla**

method

In bowl, whisk together flour, cocoa powder, ground almonds, baking powder, baking soda and salt. Remove 2 tbsp and use to flour greased 10-cup (2.5 L) fancy Bundt pan.

In large bowl, beat together brown sugar, oil, eggs, ⅓ cup water and lemon juice; stir in remaining flour mixture until combined. Stir in sliced almonds. Scrape into prepared pan.

Bake in 325°F (160°C) oven until cake tester inserted in centre comes out clean, about 55 minutes. Invert onto rack; remove pan. Let cool completely. *(Make-ahead: Wrap in plastic wrap and store for up to 2 days or freeze in airtight container for up to 2 weeks.)* Dust with icing sugar.

CHOCOLATE SAUCE: In small saucepan, bring soy milk and corn syrup to boil. Remove from heat; whisk in chocolate, butter-flavoured spread and vanilla until melted and smooth. Let cool slightly. Serve with cake.

MAKES 8 TO 10 SERVINGS.
PER EACH OF 10 SERVINGS: about 544 cal, 8 g pro, 35 g total fat (8 g sat. fat), 56 g carb, 5 g fibre, 55 mg chol, 313 mg sodium, 401 mg potassium. % RDI: 9% calcium, 31% iron, 5% vit A, 17% folate.

Change the Pan, Change the Cake

Fancy Bundt pans come in all sorts of shapes, including stars, flowers and cathedral windows. But if you don't have one, a regular Bundt pan or any 10-cup (3 L) tube-shaped pan will work just fine for this cake.

OK, so these muffins are really cupcakes in disguise. Let's just call them muffins with attitude. Get the kids to help you make them – they're a terrific introduction to baking basics.

Chocolate-Glazed Chocolate Chip Muffins

ingredients

½ cup **butter,** softened
1 cup **granulated sugar**
2 **eggs**
1 cup **milk**
1¾ cups **all-purpose flour**
2 tsp **baking powder**
¼ tsp **salt**

1 cup **semisweet chocolate chips**
3 oz (85 g) **semisweet chocolate,** chopped
3 tbsp **whipping cream (35%)**

method

In bowl, beat butter with sugar until light and fluffy, about 3 minutes. Beat in eggs, 1 at a time. Gradually stir in milk (mixture may appear curdled).

In large bowl, whisk together flour, baking powder and salt; make well in centre. Pour milk mixture into well and stir just until moistened (mixture will appear separated). Fold in chocolate chips.

Divide among 12 large paper-lined muffin cups. Bake in 350°F (180°C) oven until tops are firm to the touch, 22 to 25 minutes. Transfer to rack; let cool completely.

In small saucepan, melt semisweet chocolate with cream over medium-low heat, stirring until smooth; let cool for 10 minutes. Spread over muffins.

MAKES 12 MUFFINS.
PER MUFFIN: about 335 cal, 5 g pro, 17 g total fat (10 g sat. fat), 45 g carb, 2 g fibre, 58 mg chol, 175 mg sodium, 145 mg potassium. % RDI: 6% calcium, 11% iron, 10% vit A, 20% folate.

Muffin Liner Sizes

Paper muffin liners come in a range of sizes, from small to extra-large. This recipe makes a substantial muffin, so you'll need large liners to surround the contents and prevent spillovers.

Test Kitchen TIP

Milk chocolate and unsweetened chocolate pair up to make one of the most luscious chocolate icings you'll ever lick off your fingers. Dress up your cupcakes for a party with chocolate shot and delicate silver dragées.

Chocolate Cupcakes
WITH DOUBLE-CHOCOLATE ICING

ingredients

2 oz (55 g) **bittersweet chocolate,** chopped
¼ cup strong brewed **coffee** or water
½ cup **milk**
⅓ cup **cocoa powder**
⅓ cup **unsalted butter,** softened
¾ cup **granulated sugar**
2 **eggs**
1 tsp **vanilla**
1 cup **all-purpose flour**
½ tsp each **baking soda** and **baking powder**
⅛ tsp **salt**

DOUBLE-CHOCOLATE ICING:
½ cup **unsalted butter,** softened
1¾ cups **icing sugar**
Pinch **salt**
2 oz (55 g) **milk chocolate,** melted and cooled
1 oz (30 g) **unsweetened chocolate,** melted and cooled
1 tsp **milk** (approx)

method

In heatproof bowl over saucepan of hot (not boiling) water, melt chocolate with coffee, whisking until smooth. Whisk milk with cocoa until smooth; stir into chocolate mixture.

In large bowl, beat butter with sugar until light, about 2 minutes. Beat in eggs, 1 at a time; beat in vanilla. Whisk together flour, baking soda, baking powder and salt; stir into butter mixture alternately with chocolate mixture, making 3 additions of flour mixture and 2 of chocolate mixture, stirring until no streaks remain.

Divide among 12 paper-lined muffin cups. Bake in 350°F (180°C) oven until cake tester inserted in centre of several comes out clean, about 18 minutes.

Let cool in pan on rack for 5 minutes. Transfer to rack; let cool completely.

DOUBLE-CHOCOLATE ICING: In bowl, beat together butter, icing sugar and salt until fluffy, about 4 minutes. Beat in milk chocolate and unsweetened chocolate; beat in milk until smooth, adding up to 1 tsp more if necessary. Spread over cupcakes.

MAKES 12 CUPCAKES.
PER CUPCAKE: about 353 cal, 4 g pro, 19 g total fat (11 g sat. fat), 46 g carb, 2 g fibre, 67 mg chol, 111 mg sodium, 142 mg potassium. % RDI: 4% calcium, 11% iron, 13% vit A, 13% folate.

This is a traditional chocolate cupcake that works as a base for
any kind of icing you like. Here, we've paired it with a simple smooth chocolate glaze.

Milk Chocolate Cupcakes

ingredients

2 oz (55 g) **semisweet chocolate,** chopped
1 oz (30 g) **milk chocolate,** chopped
½ cup **butter,** softened
½ cup **granulated sugar**
2 **eggs**
1 tsp **vanilla**
¾ cup **all-purpose flour**

½ tsp **baking powder**
½ tsp **baking soda**
¼ tsp **salt**
½ cup **sour cream**

SMOOTH CHOCOLATE GLAZE:
3 oz (85 g) **bittersweet chocolate,** chopped
1 tbsp **butter**
⅓ cup **whipping cream (35%)**

method

In bowl over saucepan of hot (not boiling) water, melt semisweet chocolate with milk chocolate, stirring until smooth. Let cool to room temperature.

In large bowl, beat butter with sugar until fluffy; beat in eggs, 1 at a time. Beat in vanilla; beat in chocolate mixture. Whisk together flour, baking powder, baking soda and salt; stir into butter mixture alternately with sour cream, making 3 additions of flour mixture and 2 of sour cream.

Divide among 12 paper-lined or greased muffin cups. Bake in 350°F (180°C) oven until cake tester inserted in centre of several comes out clean, 20 to 25 minutes. Transfer to rack; let cool.

SMOOTH CHOCOLATE GLAZE: Place chocolate and butter in heatproof bowl. In saucepan, bring cream just to boil; pour over chocolate mixture, whisking until melted and smooth. Let cool slightly, about 10 minutes.

Dip cupcake tops into warm glaze; let stand until set.

MAKES 12 CUPCAKES.
PER CUPCAKE: about 262 cal, 4 g pro, 18 g total fat (11 g sat. fat), 23 g carb, 2 g fibre, 67 mg chol, 193 mg sodium, 65 mg potassium. % RDI: 4% calcium, 6% iron, 12% vit A, 10% folate.

CHANGE IT UP
Chilled Chocolate Spread
Refrigerate glaze until thickened but not firm, 15 to 20 minutes. Spread over cupcakes.

Sweet, tender banana muffins are the perfect backdrop for some delicious chocolate chips, don't you think? Make sure your bananas are really ripe for the best flavour.

Banana Chocolate Chip Muffins

ingredients

2½ cups **all-purpose flour**
1 cup packed **brown sugar**
1½ tsp **baking powder**
1 tsp **baking soda**
½ tsp **salt**
2 **eggs**
1 cup **buttermilk**

1 cup mashed **bananas**
⅓ cup **vegetable oil**
1 tsp **vanilla**
¾ cup **semisweet chocolate chips**

method

In large bowl, whisk together flour, brown sugar, baking powder, baking soda and salt. In separate bowl, beat eggs; blend in buttermilk, bananas, oil and vanilla. Pour over flour mixture; sprinkle with chocolate chips. Stir just until flour mixture is moistened.

Divide among 12 greased or paper-lined muffin cups, filling three-quarters full. Bake in 375°F (190°C) oven until tops are firm to the touch, 20 to 25 minutes.

Let cool in pan on rack for 5 minutes. Transfer to rack; let cool completely.

MAKES 12 MUFFINS.
PER MUFFIN: about 305 cal, 5 g pro, 11 g total fat (3 g sat. fat), 50 g carb, 2 g fibre, 32 mg chol, 264 mg sodium. % RDI: 6% calcium, 14% iron, 2% vit A, 2% vit C, 16% folate.

Mashing Bananas

A fork does a good job of mashing ripe bananas, but a small potato masher is even faster and more efficient.

This combo of two favourite treats – cupcakes and ice cream cones – is the best of both worlds. To pack them for travel, snuggle them in the bottom of a cookie tin, then insert a few toothpicks around the edge and one in the centre to support the plastic wrap on top and keep the icing perfect.

Banana & Chocolate Malt Cake Cones

ingredients

⅔ cup **butter,** softened
1 cup packed **brown sugar**
2 **eggs**
1 cup mashed **bananas**
1 tsp **vanilla**
1⅔ cups **all-purpose flour**
¾ tsp **baking powder**
½ tsp **baking soda**
¼ tsp each **salt** and **cinnamon**
⅓ cup **buttermilk**
18 **flat-bottom ice cream cups**

CHOCOLATE MALT ICING:
¾ cup **chocolate malt drink mix**
  (such as Ovaltine)
2 tbsp **cocoa powder,** sifted
¼ cup **icing sugar**
½ cup **unsalted butter,** softened
⅓ lb (150 g) **milk chocolate,** melted
  and cooled
2 tsp **coloured sprinkles**

method

In large bowl, beat butter with brown sugar until fluffy; beat in eggs, 1 at a time. Beat in bananas and vanilla. Whisk together flour, baking powder, baking soda, salt and cinnamon; stir into butter mixture alternately with buttermilk, making 2 additions of flour mixture and 1 of buttermilk. Scoop into ice cream cups. Set in mini muffin cups.

Bake in 350°F (180°C) oven until cake tester inserted in centre of several cakes comes out clean, about 24 minutes. Let cool on rack.

CHOCOLATE MALT ICING: Meanwhile, in bowl, whisk malt drink mix with cocoa powder; stir in ¼ cup boiling water until smooth. Let cool. Whisk in icing sugar.

In separate bowl, beat butter until creamy; beat in icing sugar mixture. Beat in chocolate until smooth and soft peaks form when beaters are lifted, about 2 minutes.

Spoon icing into piping bag fitted with plain tip; pipe icing onto cones. Garnish with coloured sprinkles. *(Make-ahead: Store in airtight container for up to 24 hours.)*

MAKES 18 CONES.
PER CONE: about 337 cal, 4 g pro, 16 g total fat (10 g sat. fat), 46 g carb, 2 g fibre, 55 mg chol, 197 mg sodium, 224 mg potassium. % RDI: 5% calcium, 12% iron, 12% vit A, 2% vit C, 21% folate.

Even novice bakers will find this impressive curl-covered cake surprisingly straightforward to make. Garnish it with fresh raspberries when they're in season.

Chocolate Raspberry Curl Cake

ingredients

1½ cups **butter,** softened
2¼ cups **granulated sugar**
3 **eggs**
¼ cup thawed **raspberry cocktail concentrate**
2 tsp **vanilla**
3 cups **all-purpose flour**
¾ cup **cocoa powder**
1½ tsp each **baking powder** and **baking soda**
½ tsp **salt**

2 cups **sour cream**
2½ batches **Short, Round Chocolate Curls** (see Making Perfect Chocolate Curls, page 297)

FILLING & ICING:
1 lb (450 g) **bittersweet chocolate** or semisweet chocolate, chopped
2⅓ cups **sour cream**
¼ cup **granulated sugar**
1 tsp **vanilla**
⅓ cup **seedless raspberry jam**

method

Grease sides of three 9-inch (1.5 L) round cake pans; line bottoms with parchment paper. Set aside.

In large bowl, beat butter with sugar until fluffy. Beat in eggs, 1 at a time; beat in raspberry concentrate and vanilla. In separate bowl, sift together flour, cocoa powder, baking powder, baking soda and salt; sift again. Stir into butter mixture alternately with sour cream, making 3 additions of flour mixture and 2 of sour cream. Scrape into prepared pans; smooth tops.

Bake in 350°F (180°C) oven until cake tester inserted in centre comes out clean, 30 to 35 minutes. Let cool in pans on racks for 20 minutes. Turn out onto racks; let cool completely. Peel off paper. *(Make-ahead: Wrap individually in plastic wrap and refrigerate for up to 1 day or overwrap with heavy-duty foil and freeze for up to 2 weeks.)*

FILLING & ICING: In large heatproof bowl over saucepan of hot (not boiling) water, melt chocolate, stirring occasionally until smooth. Remove from heat. Whisk in half of the sour cream; whisk in remaining sour cream until smooth. Whisk in sugar and vanilla.

Brush any crumbs from cake layers. Place 1 layer on flat cake plate. Slide strips of waxed paper between cake and plate. Spread top of layer with ⅓ cup of the icing; spread jam over bottoms of remaining 2 layers. Place 1 layer, jam-side down, over icing.

Spread ⅓ cup of the icing on top of second layer; top with third layer, jam-side down. Spread remaining icing over side and top of cake.

Using toothpick, lift chocolate curls and gently press against side of cake. Remove paper strips. Refrigerate for 30 minutes. *(Make-ahead: Cover loosely with plastic wrap and refrigerate for up to 24 hours. Let come to room temperature before serving.)*

MAKES 16 SERVINGS.
PER SERVING: about 798 cal, 12 g pro, 59 g total fat (35 g sat. fat), 76 g carb, 11 g fibre, 114 mg chol, 431 mg sodium. % RDI: 13% calcium, 40% iron, 25% vit A, 2% vit C, 21% folate.

Warning: This cake is for serious chocolate and caramel lovers. This special creation has a velvety texture, crunchy pecans, smooth whipped cream and a sophisticated caramel drizzle.

Chocolate Caramel Turtle Torte

ingredients

4 oz (115 g) **unsweetened chocolate,** coarsely chopped
2¼ cups **all-purpose flour**
2¼ cups packed **brown sugar**
1 tsp **baking soda**
½ tsp **baking powder**
¼ tsp **salt**
1 cup **sour cream**
½ cup **butter,** softened
3 **eggs**

1 tsp **vanilla**
2 cups **pecan pieces**

CARAMEL:
1½ cups **granulated sugar**
⅔ cup **whipping cream (35%)**
¼ cup **butter**

TOPPINGS:
2½ cups **whipping cream (35%)**
¾ cup **Chocolate Shards** (below)
⅓ cup **pecan halves,** toasted

method

Grease sides of three 9-inch (1.5 L) round cake pans; line bottoms with parchment paper. Set aside.

In heatproof bowl over saucepan of hot (not boiling) water, melt chocolate; let cool slightly. In bowl, whisk flour, sugar, baking soda, baking powder and salt. Beat in sour cream and butter to make thick batter. Beat in eggs, 1 at a time, beating well after each; beat in chocolate and vanilla. Beat for 2 minutes, scraping down side of bowl occasionally. Gradually stir in 1 cup water.

Divide evenly among prepared pans; sprinkle pecans over tops. Bake in 350°F (180°C) oven until cake tester inserted in centre comes out clean, 30 to 35 minutes. Let cool in pans on racks for 15 minutes. Turn out onto racks; peel off paper. Let cool completely. *(Make-ahead: Wrap in plastic wrap and store for up to 1 day.)*

CARAMEL: In heavy saucepan, stir sugar with ⅓ cup water over medium heat until dissolved, brushing down side of pan with pastry brush dipped in cold water. Bring to boil; boil hard, without stirring but brushing down side of pan, until dark amber, 10 minutes. Standing back and averting face, add cream; whisk until smooth. Whisk in butter until smooth. Let cool. *(Make-ahead: Refrigerate in airtight container for up to 3 days. Reheat slightly.)*

TOPPINGS: Whip cream. Place 1 cake layer, pecan side up, on cake plate. Drizzle with 2 tbsp of the caramel. Spread 1 cup of the whipped cream over top. Drizzle with 2 tbsp of the caramel, being careful not to let any drip down side. Repeat layers once.

Top with remaining cake layer. Spread remaining cream over top and side, smoothing surface. Drizzle 2 tbsp of the caramel over top. Garnish with chocolate shards and pecans. Serve with remaining caramel.

MAKES 12 TO 16 SERVINGS.
PER EACH OF 16 SERVINGS: about 685 cal, 7 g pro, 45 g total fat (21 g sat. fat), 71 g carb, 3 g fibre, 124 mg chol, 251 mg sodium. % RDI: 9% calcium, 18% iron, 27% vit A, 2% vit C, 15% folate.

MAKE YOUR OWN
Chocolate Shards
In heatproof bowl over saucepan of hot (not boiling) water, melt 4 oz (115 g) semisweet chocolate, chopped. Spread on baking sheet; refrigerate until firm, about 15 minutes. Place sheet on damp towel; let stand for 3 minutes. Bracing pan against body, slowly scrape metal spatula through chocolate toward body to make shards. Refrigerate for 3 to 4 minutes if too soft to scrape.

MAKES 1½ CUPS.

One of The Test Kitchen's best-loved creations, this cake is a masterpiece that never goes out of style. We're sure it will be one of your favourites too.

Our Favourite Chocolate Layer Cake

ingredients

1 cup **butter**, softened
1½ cups **granulated sugar**
2 **eggs**
1 tsp **vanilla**
2 cups **all-purpose flour**
½ cup **cocoa powder**
1 tsp each **baking powder** and
   baking soda
¼ tsp **salt**
1½ cups **buttermilk**

CHOCOLATE ICING:
1½ cups **butter**, softened
½ cup **whipping cream (35%)**
1 tbsp **vanilla**
3 cups **icing sugar**
6 oz (170 g) **unsweetened chocolate**,
   melted and cooled

method

Grease two 9-inch (1.5 L) round cake pans; line with parchment paper. Set aside.

In large bowl, beat butter with sugar until fluffy. Beat in eggs, 1 at a time; beat in vanilla. Sift together flour, cocoa powder, baking powder, baking soda and salt. Stir into butter mixture alternately with buttermilk, making 3 additions of flour mixture and 2 of buttermilk. Scrape into prepared pans. Bake in 350°F (180°C) oven until cake tester inserted in centre comes out clean, 30 to 35 minutes.

Let cool in pans on racks for 20 minutes. Turn out onto racks; peel off paper. Let cool completely. *(Make-ahead: Wrap individually in plastic wrap and refrigerate for up to 1 day or overwrap in heavy-duty foil and freeze for up to 2 weeks.)* Cut each cake horizontally into 2 layers ❶.

CHOCOLATE ICING: In bowl, beat butter until fluffy; gradually beat in cream. Beat in vanilla. Beat in icing sugar, 1 cup at a time. Beat in chocolate until fluffy.

Place 1 cake layer, cut side up, on cake plate; slide strips of waxed paper between cake and plate. Spread cut side with about ¾ cup of the icing; cover with remaining cake half, cut side down. Spread top with another ¾ cup of the icing. Repeat with remaining layers.

Spread remaining icing over side and top. Remove paper strips. *(Make-ahead: Cover loosely in plastic wrap and refrigerate for up to 2 days. Let come to room temperature before serving.)*

MAKES 16 TO 20 SERVINGS.

PER EACH OF 20 SERVINGS: about 464 cal, 4 g pro, 31 g total fat (19 g sat. fat), 47 g carb, 2 g fibre, 89 mg chol, 296 mg sodium. % RDI: 5% calcium, 11% iron, 23% vit A, 14% folate.

CHANGE IT UP
Chocolate Cupcakes
Spoon batter into 24 greased or paper-lined muffin cups. Bake for about 20 minutes. Transfer to racks; let cool completely. Spread icing over tops.

MAKES 24 CUPCAKES.

HOW-TO

This rich, dense cake is the perfect dessert to pair with a light and fruity local or Belgian raspberry beer (such as Mort Subite Framboise). Top each slice with a dollop of whipped cream.

Chocolate Torte With Pecans

ingredients

6 oz (170 g) **bittersweet chocolate,** chopped

2 oz (55 g) **milk chocolate,** chopped

⅔ cup **whipping cream (35%)**

¼ cup **unsalted butter**

3 **eggs**

⅓ cup packed **brown sugar**

3 tbsp **all-purpose flour**

1 tbsp **bourbon** or coffee liqueur

1 cup coarsely chopped **pecans**

method

In heatproof bowl over saucepan of hot (not boiling) water, melt together bittersweet chocolate, milk chocolate, cream and butter, stirring occasionally until smooth.

In large bowl, whisk together eggs, brown sugar, flour and bourbon; stir in chocolate mixture just until combined. Fold in pecans.

Scrape into greased 8-inch (2 L) springform pan. Bake in 275°F (140°C) oven until centre is firm to the touch, about 1 hour.

Let cool in pan on rack for 15 minutes. Turn out onto serving plate; let cool. *(Make-ahead: Cover and refrigerate for up to 2 days.)*

MAKES 12 TO 14 SERVINGS.

PER EACH OF 14 SERVINGS: about 252 cal, 4 g pro, 29 g total fat (9 g sat. fat), 17 g carb, 2 g fibre, 64 mg chol, 23 mg sodium. % RDI: 4% calcium, 7% iron, 8% vit A, 5% folate.

Decorating With Icing Sugar

Creating a pretty pattern of icing sugar on top of our Chocolate Espresso Torte (opposite) makes it a knockout. On paper, trace a 9-inch (23 cm) circle. Draw desired pattern, leaving a 1-inch (2.5 cm) border. With an X-acto knife, cut out pattern. (Large doilies will give a similar, more detailed effect.) Centre the template on top of the cake. Spoon about 1 tbsp icing sugar into a small fine-mesh sieve and gently shake over the template until the cake is lightly dusted. Carefully lift the template straight up and discard any excess sugar.

Test Kitchen TIP

Cocoa powder gives this soft, fudgy cake a deep colour and intense flavour.
The cake may sink slightly in the centre; if it does, turn it over and garnish with strawberries
and chocolate syrup. The variation makes a lovely Passover dessert.

Chocolate Espresso Torte

ingredients

1 cup **walnuts**
1¼ cups **granulated sugar**
2 tbsp **cornstarch**
½ tsp **cinnamon**
¼ tsp **salt**
1 cup **butter**
¼ cup brewed **espresso** or very strong
   brewed coffee

1 cup **cocoa powder**
4 **eggs,** separated

CHOCOLATE SYRUP:
⅓ cup **cocoa powder**
⅓ cup **liquid honey**

method

In food processor, whirl walnuts with 1 tbsp
of the sugar until powdery; whirl in cornstarch,
cinnamon and salt. Transfer to large bowl;
set aside.

In small saucepan, melt butter with espresso.
Add cocoa powder; whisk until smooth.
Let cool.

Meanwhile, in large bowl, beat egg yolks with
¾ cup of the remaining sugar until thick and
pale; beat in chocolate mixture. Stir into
walnut mixture.

In bowl, beat egg whites until soft peaks
form. Beat in remaining sugar, 1 tbsp at a
time, until stiff glossy peaks form. Fold
one-third into chocolate mixture; fold in
remaining whites. Scrape into parchment
paper–lined or greased 9-inch (2.5 L)
springform pan; smooth top. Bake in 350°F
(180°C) oven until cake tester inserted in
centre comes out clean, about 1¼ hours.

Let cool in pan on rack for 10 minutes.
Remove side of pan; let cool completely.
*(Make-ahead: Cover with plastic wrap and
store for up to 1 day.)*

CHOCOLATE SYRUP: In saucepan, bring
½ cup water, cocoa powder and honey to boil;
boil until syrupy, about 3 minutes. *(Make-
ahead: Let cool. Refrigerate in airtight
container for up to 2 days.)* Serve with torte.

MAKES 8 TO 10 SERVINGS.
PER EACH OF 10 SERVINGS: about 431 cal, 7 g pro,
30 g total fat (14 g sat. fat), 44 g carb, 4 g fibre, 122 mg
chol, 217 mg sodium, 381 mg potassium. % RDI:
4% calcium, 18% iron, 20% vit A, 12% folate.

CHANGE IT UP
Passover Chocolate Espresso Torte
Substitute potato starch for the cornstarch,
soft pareve margarine for the butter, and
kosher pareve cocoa powder (such as
Ghirardelli) for the regular cocoa powder.

Buttercream is the most delicious icing for a cake, and this caramel milk chocolate version
is no exception. It gives the nutty cake a wonderful creaminess.

Hazelnut Torte
WITH CARAMEL MILK CHOCOLATE BUTTERCREAM

ingredients

½ cup **all-purpose flour**
⅓ cup toasted skinned **hazelnuts**
4 tsp **cornstarch**
6 **egg yolks**
⅔ cup **granulated sugar**
5 **egg whites**
¼ cup **unsalted butter**, melted and warm

SYRUP:
2 tbsp **granulated sugar**
1 tbsp **hazelnut liqueur**

CARAMEL MILK CHOCOLATE BUTTERCREAM:
8 oz (225 g) **milk chocolate**, chopped
2 oz (55 g) **bittersweet chocolate**, chopped
½ cup **granulated sugar**
1 cup **whipping cream (35%)**
Pinch **salt**
2 tbsp **hazelnut liqueur**
¾ cup finely chopped toasted skinned
    hazelnuts (see Tip, page 72)
36 toasted **hazelnuts**

341

method

In food processor, pulse together flour,
hazelnuts and cornstarch until finely ground,
about 30 seconds. Set aside.

Beat egg yolks until thick and light coloured,
about 2 minutes. Beat in all but 3 tbsp of
the sugar until thickened and batter falls in
ribbons when beaters are lifted, about
4 minutes. Transfer to bowl.

In clean bowl, beat egg whites until foamy;
beat in 2 tbsp of the remaining sugar until
stiff peaks form. Beat in yolk mixture. Sift
one-quarter of the flour mixture over top and
fold in; repeat twice. Pour in warm butter,
leaving white sediment behind. Fold in
remaining flour mixture until blended.

Pour onto parchment paper–lined 15- x
10-inch (38 x 25 cm) rimmed baking sheet;
spread evenly. Bake in 350°F (180°C) oven
until springy to the touch and cake pulls away
from sides of pan, about 15 minutes. Let cool
on pan on rack. Sprinkle with remaining
sugar. *(Make-ahead: Wrap in plastic wrap and
store for up to 24 hours.)* Remove from pan.
Trim edges; cut crosswise into thirds. Loosen
from paper with spatula.

SYRUP: In small saucepan, heat sugar with
½ cup water until dissolved. Stir in hazelnut
liqueur; set aside.

CARAMEL MILK CHOCOLATE BUTTERCREAM:
Place milk chocolate and bittersweet
chocolate in heatproof bowl. In saucepan over
medium heat, cook sugar with ¼ cup water,
without stirring but brushing down side of pan
with pastry brush dipped in cold water, until
deep amber, about 7 minutes. Remove from
heat. Averting face, stir in cream and salt.
Simmer over medium-low heat, stirring
constantly, until caramel dissolves. Pour over
chocolate mixture, whisking until smooth;
whisk in liqueur. Cover and refrigerate just
until cool but still loose, about 1 hour (do not
refrigerate longer because buttercream will
harden). Beat until soft peaks form.

Place one-third of the cake on platter. Slide
strips of waxed paper between cake and
platter. Brush cake with one-third of the
syrup. Spread ⅔ cup buttercream over top.
Repeat layers once. Brush remaining cake
layer with syrup; invert onto top. Spread
remaining buttercream over top and sides of
cake. Press chopped hazelnuts onto sides;
garnish top with toasted hazelnuts. *(Make-
ahead: Cover; refrigerate for up to 24 hours.)*

MAKES 12 SERVINGS.
PER SERVING: about 458 cal, 7 g pro, 29 g total fat
(13 g sat. fat), 45 g carb, 3 g fibre, 141 mg chol, 49 mg
sodium, 208 mg potassium. % RDI: 8% calcium,
11% iron, 15% vit A, 17% folate.

Thank You

Chocolate makes almost everyone drool. So bringing together a group of people to work on a chocolate cookbook was an easy task.

As always, the first people I need to thank for their hard work and dedication are our Food director, Annabelle Waugh, and her team in The Canadian Living Test Kitchen. Chocolate is a passionate indulgence for every one of our food specialists – Rheanna Kish, Amanda Barnier, Irene Fong and Jennifer Bartoli – and our consulting food specialist, Melanie Stuparyk. Their imagination and their tireless quest for perfection when creating Tested-Till-Perfect recipes make it a pleasure to cook these delicious confections at home.

Next, a huge helping of thanks to our brilliant art director, Colin Elliott, who was the brains behind the fun, funky and beautiful design of this book. From hand-crafting pretty graphics to making the final layout tweaks, Colin did it all. Working with him is a treat that's even nicer than a piece of chocolate.

Thanks go out to the talented photographers and stylists who captured the essential beauty of the chocolate recipes in this book. I'm grateful to photographers Ryan Szulc and Edward Pond, food stylist Claire Stubbs and prop stylist Catherine Doherty for shooting a gorgeous set of new images especially for this collection. Their work and the work of many other photographers and stylists (see page 351 for a complete list) are what make each page almost lick-worthy.

A round of applause goes to our ever-diligent copy editors for keeping our grammar and spelling in check. Lisa Fielding went through every chapter, and Jill Buchner pitched in at the last second with the final straggler pages, making sure everything was just-so.

My gratitude also goes to champion indexer Beth Zabloski, who whipped up a fabulously detailed index so you can figure out where each and every recipe resides, and to Sharyn Joliat of Info Access, who analyzed each recipe for its nutrient content. Thank you also to the team at Random House Canada, who helped our pretty book find a home in bookstores and homes across the country.

My thanks and a box of homemade chocolates go to the management team: Transcontinental Books vice-president Marc Laberge, publishing director Mathieu de Lajartre and assistant editor Céline Comtois. Their devotion and hard work give our team the tools we need to turn the germ of an idea into a beautiful finished book.

Finally, sincerest thanks to *Canadian Living* group publisher Caroline Andrews, associate publisher Susan Antonacci and editor-in-chief Jennifer Reynolds for their passion for this and many other projects. Their support means the world to all of us.

– Tina Anson Mine,
project editor

Index

A

almond liqueur
    Chocolate Almond Tartlets, 221
almond paste versus marzipan, 202
almonds
    Apricot Almond Scones, 245
    Cherry Almond White Chocolate Biscotti, 111
    Chocolate Almond Tartlets, 221
    Chocolate & Olive Oil Bundt Cake
        With Chocolate Sauce, 326
    Chocolate Chestnut Fingers, 130
    Chocolate Fruit & Nut Tart, 228
    English Toffee, 98
    Ice Cream Truffles, 265
    Marbled Almond Bark, 99
    Matzo Chocolate Almond Buttercrunch, 104
    Reverse Nanaimo Bars, 215
    Sour Cherry Almond Clusters, 95
    Sour Cherry & Almond Chocolate Bar, 94
    White Chocolate Almond Pound Cake, 315
    White Chocolate Cherry Torte, 45
    White Chocolate Praline Truffles, 193
almonds, chocolate-covered
    Double-Chocolate Almond Shortbread
almonds, ground
    Basler Brunsli, 258
    Chocolate & Olive Oil Bundt Cake
        With Chocolate Sauce, 326
    Chocolate Ganache Macarons, 126
    Chocolate Macarons, 126
    Flourless Chocolate Truffle Cake, 25
    Gluten-Free Chocolate Glitter Cookies, 150
    Passover Flourless Chocolate Truffle Cake, 25
    Really Good Rum Balls, 184
    Sour Cream Chocolate Chunk Crumb Cake, 310
    Sour Cream Chocolate Crumb Cake, 310
    White Chocolate Almond Pound Cake, 315
    White Chocolate Cherry Torte, 45
amaretti cookies
    Amaretti White Chocolate Coffee Parfaits, 87
    Bittersweet Amaretti Bark, 99
    Caramel Chocolate Custard, 30
    Ice Cream Truffles, 265
amaretti cookies, how to cut, 99
amaretto
    Chocolate Fondue, 62
angel food cake
    Chocolate Chip Angel Food Cake, 320
    Chocolate Cupid Cakes With Satin Glaze, 302
    Tunnel of Ice Cream Cake, 281
apricots, dried
    Apricot Almond Scones, 245
    Candied Ginger & White Chocolate
        Hermits, 160
    Pistachio Apricot Clusters, 95

B

Bailey's Original liqueur. *See* Irish cream liqueur.
baked Alaskas
    Chocolate Raspberry Pistachio
        Baked Alaska, 280
    Mini Baked Alaskas, 279
baklava
    Chocolate Hazelnut Baklava, 96
banana chips
    Banana Brownies, 138
    Monkey Bars, 162
bananas
    Banana & Chocolate Malt Cake Cones, 333
    Banana Brownies, 138
    Banana Chocolate Chip Muffins, 331
    Banana Chocolate Chunk Bread Pudding, 23
    Chocolate Banana Cream Pie, 64

Chocolate Soy Banana Smoothie, 293
Chocolate Soy Coffee Banana Smoothie, 293
Chocolate Soy Peanut Butter Banana
    Smoothie, 293
Chocolate Soy Strawberry Banana Smoothie, 293
Double–Chocolate Chip Waffles With Bananas
    and Strawberry Coulis, 93
Frozen Banana Bites, 290
Hot Fudge Banana Bundt Cake, 317
S'mores Chocolate Fondue, 41
bananas, baking with, 138
barks
    Bittersweet Amaretti Bark, 99
    Black Forest Bark, 101
    Candied Orange & Ginger Bark, 182
    Chocolate Bark, 311
    Marbled Almond Bark, 99
    Tropical Fruit Bark, 101
    Two-Tone Peppermint Bark, 181
Bartlett pears
    Chocolate Cream Pear Tart, 225
Basler Brunsli, 258
beating egg whites, 279
Best Chocolate Brownies, The, 145
beverages
    Chocolate Brownie Martini, 296
    Chocolate Mint Martini, 296
    Chocolate Soy Banana Smoothie, 293
    Chocolate Soy Coffee Banana Smoothie, 293
    Chocolate Soy Peanut Butter Banana
        Smoothie, 293
    Chocolate Soy Strawberry Banana Smoothie, 293
    Hot Chocolate, 82
    Malted Hot Chocolate, 81
    Marshmallow Hot Chocolate Mix, 81
    Mocha Frappé, 292
    Neapolitan Milkshake, 295
    Old-Fashioned Milkshakes, 293
    Raspberry Chocolate Smoothie, 292
    White Chocolate Mocha Mugs, 80
Big Chocolate Chip Orange Cookies, 125
biscotti. *See also* cookies.
    Cherry Almond White Chocolate Biscotti, 111
    Chocolate, Star Anise & Orange Biscotti, 112
    Cranberry White Chocolate Biscotti, 109
    Itty-Bitty Hazelnut Cioccolata Biscotti, 110
biscuits
    Chocolate Biscuits, 312
Bittersweet Amaretti Bark, 99
bittersweet chocolate, 39
    Banana Brownies, 138
    Banana Chocolate Chunk Bread Pudding, 23
    Basler Brunsli, 258
    Best Chocolate Brownies, 145
    Bittersweet Amaretti Bark, 99
    Black Forest Bark, 101
    Black Forest Mousse Parfaits, 78
    Boca Negra With Rum-Soaked Cherries, 180
    Boozy Chocolate Sauce, 34
    Cakey Chocolate Brownies, 303
    Candied Orange & Ginger Bark, 182
    Candy-Covered Fudge, 205
    Caramel Chocolate Custard, 30
    Cardamom Chocolate Pots de Crème, 66
    Chai Tea Chocolate Truffles, 198
    Chocolate Almond Tartlets, 221
    Chocolate Bar Brownies, 140
    Chocolate Breakfast Braid, 135
    Chocolate Cappuccino Cheesecake, 53
    Chocolate Caramel & Cashew Torte, 14
    Chocolate Caramel Bites, 143
    Chocolate Caramel Cookies, 26
    Chocolate Caramel Pecan Clusters, 28
    Chocolate Cherry Rounds, 255

Chocolate Chestnut Fingers, 130
Chocolate Chestnut Mousse, 69
Chocolate Chip Angel Food Cake, 320
Chocolate Cigar Cookies, 115
Chocolate Cinnamon Buns, 33
Chocolate Coconut Mounds, 146
Chocolate-Covered Homemade
    Marshmallows, 27
Chocolate Cream Pear Tart, 225
Chocolate Cupcakes With Double-Chocolate
    Icing, 328
Chocolate Cupid Cakes With Satin Glaze, 302
Chocolate Fondue, 62
Chocolate Fruit & Nut Tart, 228
Chocolate Fudge Sauce, 274
Chocolate Ganache Macarons, 126
Chocolate Orange Bundt Cake, 322
Chocolate Overload Cookies, 122
Chocolate Peanut Butter Pie, 61
Chocolate Pecan Mounds, 252
Chocolate Raspberry Curl Cake, 334
Chocolate Raspberry Pistachio Baked
    Alaska, 280
Chocolate Shortbread Fingers, 233
Chocolate Soufflé Cakes With Sherry Cream, 83
Chocolate Stripe Shortbread, 240
Chocolate Toffee Pecan Tart, 12
Chocolate Toffee Squares, 22
Chocolate Torte With Pecans, 338
Cinnamon Chocolate Pots de Crème, 66
Classic Chocolate Soufflé, 85
Coconut Rum Truffles, 201
Cranberry Jewel Fudge, 205
Dark & Stormy Truffle Cups, 196
Dark Chocolate Bûche de Noël, 311
Double-Chocolate Coffee Ice Cream Stacks, 268
Double-Chocolate Éclairs, 89
Double-Chocolate Ice Box Cookies, 256
Double-Chocolate Walnut Chunks, 175
Dry Gin Martini Truffle Cups, 196
Earl Grey Chocolate Truffles, 198
Easy Chocolate Walnut Fudge, 212
English Toffee, 98
Flourless Chocolate Lava Cakes, 17
Flourless Chocolate Truffle Cake, 25
German Chocolate Brownies, 154
Glazed Double-Chocolate Marble Cake, 325
Gluten-Free Chocolate Glitter Cookies, 150
Hazelnut Mochaccino Fudge, 213
Hazelnut Torte With Caramel Milk Chocolate
    Buttercream, 341
Hot Fudge Banana Bundt Cake, 317
Irish Cream Brownie Bites, 148
Irish Cream Chocolate Truffles, 192
Malted Hot Chocolate, 81
Maple Chocolate Butter Tarts, 13
Milk Chocolate Cheesecake, 50
Milk Chocolate Cupcakes, 330
Milk Chocolate Tart Brûlée, 58
Mini Steamed Chocolate Puddings, 309
Mocha Chocolate Crackles, 131
Mocha Mousse, 70
Mocha Mousse Cake, 48
Mocha Sauce, 274
Molten Chocolate Cakes, 19
No-Bake Chocolate Marble Cheesecake Pie, 56
Nut Fudge, 205
Orange Blossom Truffle Cups, 196
Passover Dairy-Free Gluten-Free Flourless
    Chocolate Lava Cakes, 17
Passover Flourless Chocolate Truffle Cake, 25
Peanut Butter Brownies, 153
Really Good Rum Balls, 184
Rich Double-Chocolate Sauce, 36

Rocky Road Cheesecake, 47
Scoop & Freeze Double-Chocolate
    Cookies, 119
Scotch on the Rocks Truffle Cups, 196
Silky Dark Chocolate Sauce, 38
Smooth Chocolate Glaze, 330
S'mores Chocolate Fondue, 41
Snowball Chocolate Fudge, 205
Sour Cream Chocolate Chunk Crumb Cake, 310
Sour Cream Chocolate Crumb Cake, 310
Spicy Chocolate Cinnamon Shortbread, 241
Steamed Chocolate Pudding, 309
Sublime Brownies & Bourbon Sauce
    Sundaes, 271
Terrine au Chocolat, 179
The Best Chocolate Brownies, 145
Thick & Fudgy Bittersweet Chocolate
    Sauce, 38
Three-Ice Cream Terrine, 274
Triple-Chocolate Cookies, 128
Triple-Decker Ice Cream Stacks, 268
Two-Tone Mocha Cheesecake, 46
Two-Tone Peppermint Bark, 181
Warm Cinnamon Chocolate Sauce, 35
White Chocolate Mocha Mugs, 80
black currant jam
    Chocolate Macarons, 126
Black Forest Bark, 101
Black Forest Mousse Parfaits, 78
Black Forest Trifle, 76
blackberries
    Triple-Berry Chocolate Tart, 234
blondies. See also brownies; squares.
    Ginger Macadamia Blondies, 157
    Rocky Road Blondies, 159
    White Chocolate Cranberry Blondies, 142
bloom, 95, 200
blueberries
    Triple-Berry Chocolate Tart, 234
blueberry jam
    White Chocolate Ice Cream With Blueberry
        Swirl, 266
Boca Negra With Rum-Soaked Cherries, 180
Boozy Chocolate Sauce, 34
bourbon
    Chocolate Banana Cream Pie, 64
    Chocolate Silk Tartlet Trio, 223
    Chocolate Torte With Pecans, 338
    Sublime Brownies & Bourbon Sauce
        Sundaes, 271
brandy
    Black Forest Trifle, 76
    Brandied Cherry Compote, 45
    Caramel Chocolate Custard, 30
    Chocolate Cherry Fruit Cake, 307
    Chocolate Fruit & Nut Tart, 228
    White Chocolate Cherry Torte, 45
Brazilian Brigadeiros, 187
bread pudding
    Banana Chocolate Chunk Bread Pudding, 23
breads. See also loafs; muffins; pastries; scones.
    Bread Machine Chocolate Breakfast Braid
        Dough, 135
    Bread Machine Chocolate Monkey Bread
        Dough, 137
    Chocolate Breakfast Braid, 135
    Chocolate Monkey Bread, 137
    Nutty Caramel Monkey Bread, 137
brownies. See also blondies; squares.
    Banana Brownies, 138
    Best Chocolate Brownies, The, 145
    Cakey Chocolate Brownies, 303
    Chocolate Bar Brownies, 140
    German Chocolate Brownies, 154
    Gluten-Free Super Fudgy Chocolate
        Brownies, 139
    Irish Cream Brownie Bites, 148
    Peanut Butter Brownies, 153
    Sublime Brownies & Bourbon Sauce
        Sundaes, 271
    Three-Ice Cream Terrine, 274

Bundt cakes
    Chocolate & Olive Oil Bundt Cake
        With Chocolate Sauce, 326
    Chocolate Orange Bundt Cake, 322
    Glazed Double-Chocolate Marble Cake, 325
    Hot Fudge Banana Bundt Cake, 317
    Mini Steamed Chocolate Puddings, 309
    Raspberry Chocolate Chip Bundt Cake, 323
    Steamed Chocolate Pudding, 309
Bundt pans, 326
butter, 236
butter, how to cube cold, 248
butter tarts
    Maple Chocolate Butter Tarts, 13
buttercream. See also icings.
    Hazelnut Torte With Caramel Milk Chocolate
        Buttercream, 341
buttermilk substitute, 301
butterscotch
    Chocolate Caramel Layered Pudding, 86
    Ginger Butterscotch Squares, 167
    White Chocolate Butterscotch Oatmeal
        Chippers, 168

C

cake decorating, 82, 338
cake testers, 310
cakes. See also cheesecakes; cupcakes; terrines;
    tortes.
    Boca Negra With Rum-Soaked Cherries, 180
    Chocolate & Olive Oil Bundt Cake
        With Chocolate Sauce, 326
    Chocolate Babka, 134
    Chocolate Blackout Cake, 319
    Chocolate Cherry Fruit Cake, 307
    Chocolate Chip Angel Food Cake, 320
    Chocolate Chocolate Loaf, 318
    Chocolate Cupid Cakes With Satin Glaze, 302
    Chocolate Orange Bundt Cake, 322
    Chocolate Peanut Butter Pudding Cake, 18
    Chocolate Pistachio Loaf, 314
    Chocolate Pound Cake, 76, 77
    Chocolate Raspberry Curl Cake, 334
    Chocolate Raspberry Pistachio Baked
        Alaska, 280
    Chocolate Soufflé Cakes With Sherry Cream, 83
    Chocolate Strawberry Shortcake, 312
    Dark Chocolate Bûche de Noël, 311
    Flourless Chocolate Lava Cakes, 17
    Flourless Chocolate Truffle Cake, 25
    Glazed Double-Chocolate Marble Cake, 325
    Hot Fudge Banana Bundt Cake, 317
    Mini Steamed Chocolate Puddings, 309
    Mocha Mousse Cake, 48
    Mocha Snacking Cake, 306
    Molten Chocolate Cakes, 19
    Nanaimo Bar Ice Cream Cake, 277
    Neapolitan Pistachio Frozen Bombe, 282
    Our Favourite Chocolate Layer Cake, 336
    Passover Dairy-Free Gluten-Free Flourless
        Chocolate Lava Cakes, 17
    Passover Flourless Chocolate Truffle Cake, 25
    Raspberry Chocolate Chip Bundt Cake, 323
    Slow Cooker Chocolate Peanut Butter
        Pudding Cake, 18
    Slow Cooker Hot Cocoa Cake, 20
    Sour Cream Chocolate Chunk Crumb Cake, 310
    Sour Cream Chocolate Crumb Cake, 310
    Steamed Chocolate Pudding, 309
    Tunnel of Ice Cream Cake, 281
    White Chocolate Almond Pound Cake, 315
    Whoopie Pies With Cream Cheese Filling, 304
Cakey Chocolate Brownies, 303
cakey recipes, 298–341
Candied Ginger & White Chocolate Hermits, 160
Candied Orange & Ginger Bark, 182
Candied Orange Zest, 322
candied pineapple
    Tropical Fruit Bark, 101

candies. See also barks; clusters; fudge; truffles.
    Brazilian Brigadeiros, 187
    Chocolate Caramel Bites, 143
    Chocolate Cherry Cups, 202
    Chocolate-Covered Homemade
        Marshmallows, 27
    Crispy Coffee Truffle Slice, 206
    English Toffee, 98
    Ganache-Filled Chocolates, 195
    Gluten-Free Chocolate-Dipped Peanut Butter
        Balls, 188
    Peanut Butter Cups, 217
    Praline, 284
    Really Good Rum Balls, 184
    Sour Cherry & Almond Chocolate Bar, 94
Candy-Covered Fudge, 205
candy, how to crush, 181
cappuccino
    Chocolate Cappuccino Cheesecake, 53
caramel
    Caramel Chocolate Custard, 30
    Chewy Caramel Pecan Squares, 156
    Chocolate & Salted Caramel Swirl
        Ice Cream, 263
    Chocolate, Caramel & Cashew Torte, 14
    Chocolate Caramel Bites, 143
    Chocolate Caramel Cookies, 26
    Chocolate Caramel Ice Cream Pie, 285
    Chocolate Caramel Layered Pudding, 86
    Chocolate Caramel Pecan Clusters, 28
    Chocolate Caramel Turtle Torte, 335
    Chocolate Cheesecake With Caramel
        Pecan Sauce, 11
    Frozen Chocolate Praline Meringue Torte, 284
    Hazelnut Torte With Caramel Milk Chocolate
        Buttercream, 341
    Milk Chocolate Tart Brûlée, 58
    Nutty Caramel Monkey Bread, 137
    Peanut Butter Caramel Sauce, 35
    Rocky Road Cheesecake, 47
    Salted Caramel Sauce, 263
caramel, working with, 14
Cardamom Chocolate Pots de Crème, 66
cashews
    Chocolate, Caramel & Cashew Torte, 14
    Triple-Nut Chocolate Fudge, 209
    White Chocolate Chai Fudge, 208
chai
    Chai Tea Chocolate Truffles, 198
    White Chocolate Chai Fudge, 208
Checkerboard Cookies, 253
cheesecake, how to cut, 47
cheesecakes
    Chocolate Cappuccino Cheesecake, 53
    Chocolate Cheesecake With Caramel
        Pecan Sauce, 11
    Chocolate Hazelnut Swirl Cheesecake, 54
    Milk Chocolate Cheesecake, 50
    Mini White Chocolate Cheesecake, 51
    No-Bake Chocolate Marble Cheesecake Pie, 56
    Rocky Road Cheesecake, 47
    Two-Tone Mocha Cheesecake, 46
cherries
    Black Forest Bark, 101
    Black Forest Mousse Parfaits, 78
    Black Forest Trifle, 76
    Boca Negra With Rum-Soaked Cherries, 180
    Cherry Almond White Chocolate Biscotti, 111
    Cherry White Chocolate Scones, 245
    Chocolate Cherry Cups, 202
    Chocolate Cherry Fruit Cake, 307
    Chocolate Cherry Pancakes With Cherry
        Syrup, 301
    Chocolate Cherry Rounds, 255
    Chocolate Walnut Tart, 242
    Dark Chocolate & Dried Cherry Scones, 248
    Pecan Cherry Chocolate Hermits, 160
    Sour Cherry Almond Clusters, 95
    Sour Cherry & Almond Chocolate Bar, 94
    White Chocolate Cherry Torte, 45

cherry brandy
    Black Forest Trifle, 76
    White Chocolate Cherry Torte, 45
chestnut purée
    Chocolate Chestnut Fingers, 130
    Chocolate Chestnut Mousse, 69
Chewy Caramel Pecan Squares, 156
Chilled Chocolate Spread, 330
chilly recipes, 260–297
Chocolate Almond Tartlets, 221
Chocolate & Olive Oil Bundt Cake With
    Chocolate Sauce, 326
Chocolate & Salted Caramel Swirl Ice Cream, 263
Chocolate Babka, 134
Chocolate Banana Cream Pie, 64
chocolate bar. See also barks.
    Sour Cherry & Almond Chocolate Bar, 94
Chocolate Bar Brownies, 140
Chocolate Bark, 311
Chocolate Biscuits, 312
Chocolate Blackout Cake, 319
Chocolate Breakfast Braid, 135
Chocolate Brownie Martini, 296
Chocolate Cake, 280
Chocolate Cappuccino Cheesecake, 53
Chocolate, Caramel & Cashew Torte, 14
Chocolate Caramel Bites, 143
Chocolate Caramel Cookies, 26
Chocolate Caramel Ice Cream Pie, 285
Chocolate Caramel Layered Pudding, 86
Chocolate Caramel Pecan Clusters, 28
Chocolate Caramel Turtle Torte, 335
Chocolate Cheesecake With Caramel Pecan Sauce, 11
Chocolate Cherry Cups, 202
Chocolate Cherry Fruit Cake, 307
Chocolate Cherry Pancakes With Cherry Syrup, 301
Chocolate Cherry Rounds, 255
Chocolate Chestnut Fingers, 130
Chocolate Chestnut Mousse, 69
Chocolate Chip Angel Food Cake, 320
Chocolate Chip Cookies, 272
Chocolate Chip Ice Cream Sandwiches, 272
Chocolate Chocolate Loaf, 318
Chocolate Cigar Cookies, 115
Chocolate Cinnamon Buns, 33
Chocolate Coconut Cream Pie, 59
Chocolate Coconut Mounds, 146
chocolate-covered almonds
    Double-Chocolate Almond Shortbread, 236
chocolate-covered espresso beans
    Lightened-Up Mocha Mousse, 70
    Mocha Mousse, 70
Chocolate-Covered Homemade Marshmallows, 27
Chocolate Cream Pear Tart, 225
Chocolate Crust, 234
Chocolate Cupcakes, 336
Chocolate Cupcakes With Double-Chocolate
    Icing, 328
Chocolate Cupid Cakes With Satin Glaze, 302
chocolate curls, how to make perfect, 297
Chocolate Espresso Glaze, 25
Chocolate Espresso Torte, 339
Chocolate Fondue, 41, 62
Chocolate Fruit & Nut Tart, 228
Chocolate Fudge Sauce, 274
Chocolate Ganache Macarons, 126
Chocolate Gingerbread Pretzels, 103
Chocolate Gingersnap Hearts, 118
Chocolate Glaze, 89
Chocolate-Glazed Chocolate Chip Muffins, 327
Chocolate Goat's Milk Fudge, 204
Chocolate Hazelnut Baklava, 96
Chocolate Hazelnut Palmiers, 117
chocolate hazelnut spread
    Chocolate Banana Cream Pie, 64
    Chocolate Hazelnut French Toast, 31
    Chocolate Hazelnut Rugalach, 161
    Chocolate Hazelnut Swirl Cheesecake, 54
    Chocolate Hazelnut Trifle, 77
    Hazelnut Chocolate Mousse, 72
    White Chocolate Hazelnut Pie, 232

Chocolate Hazelnut Tassies, 249
Chocolate Hearts, 82
chocolate, how to chop, 252
chocolate, how to grate and shave, 80
chocolate, how to melt, 94
chocolate, how to temper, 95
Chocolate Icing, 303, 336
Chocolate Key Lime Tarts, 231
Chocolate Macarons, 126
chocolate malt
    Banana & Chocolate Malt Cake Cones, 333
    Malted Hot Chocolate, 81
Chocolate Mint Martini, 296
Chocolate Mint Nanaimo Bars, 216
Chocolate Monkey Bread, 137
Chocolate Mousse Pie, 229
Chocolate Orange Bundt Cake, 322
Chocolate Orange Glaze, 322
Chocolate Overload Cookies, 122
Chocolate Pastry, 59, 221, 229, 231, 242
Chocolate Pastry Cream, 225
Chocolate Peanut Butter Pie, 61
Chocolate Peanut Butter Pudding Cake, 18
Chocolate Pecan Mounds, 252
Chocolate Pistachio Loaf, 314
Chocolate Pound Cake, 76, 77
Chocolate Raspberry Curl Cake, 334
Chocolate Raspberry Pistachio Baked Alaska, 280
Chocolate Ricotta Tart, 239
Chocolate Sandwich Cookies, 276
Chocolate Satin, 302
chocolate sauces. See dessert sauces.
Chocolate Shards, 335
Chocolate Shortbread Fingers, 233
chocolate shot, 265
    Brazilian Brigadeiros, 187
    Ice Cream Truffles, 265
    Mint Chocolate Chip Ice Cream Pie, 287
    Really Good Rum Balls, 184
    Triple-Chocolate Cookie Ice Cream
        Sandwiches, 273
Chocolate Silk Tartlet Trio, 223
Chocolate Sorbet, 264
Chocolate Soufflé Cakes With Sherry Cream, 83
Chocolate Soy Banana Smoothie, 293
Chocolate Soy Coffee Banana Smoothie, 293
Chocolate Soy Peanut Butter Banana Smoothie, 293
Chocolate Soy Strawberry Banana Smoothie, 293
Chocolate Spice Pastry Cream, 89
Chocolate, Star Anise & Orange Biscotti, 112
Chocolate Strawberry Shortcake, 312
Chocolate Stripe Shortbread, 240
Chocolate Syrup, 309, 339
Chocolate Toffee Pecan Tart, 12
Chocolate Toffee Squares, 22
Chocolate Torte With Pecans, 338
chocolate, types of, 39
chocolate wafer cookies
    Mini Baked Alaskas, 279
    Triple-Decker Ice Cream Stacks, 268
chocolate wafer crumbs, 287
    Chocolate Cappuccino Cheesecake, 53
    Chocolate Caramel Ice Cream Pie, 285
    Chocolate Mint Nanaimo Bars, 216
    Chocolate Peanut Butter Pie, 61
    Grasshopper Truffle Tart, 55
    Milk Chocolate Cheesecake, 50
    Mint Chocolate Chip Ice Cream Pie, 287
    Mocha Ice Cream Squares, 269
    Mocha Semifreddo, 289
    Monkey Bars, 162
    Nanaimo Bar Ice Cream Cake, 277
    No-Bake Chocolate Marble Cheesecake Pie, 56
    Rocky Road Cheesecake, 47
    Two-Tone Mocha Cheesecake, 46
Chocolate Walnut Fudge Scones, 250
Chocolate Walnut Tart, 242

cinnamon
    Chocolate Cinnamon Buns, 33
    Cinnamon Chocolate Pots de Crème, 66
    Cinnamon Pistachio Truffles, 190
    Spicy Chocolate Cinnamon Shortbread, 241
    Warm Cinnamon Chocolate Sauce, 35
    White Chocolate Cinnamon Butter Truffles, 200
citrus zest strips, how to cut, 266
Classic Chocolate Chip Cookies, 169
Classic Chocolate Soufflé, 85
Classic Nanaimo Bars, 210
clusters. See also candies; cookies.
    Chocolate Caramel Pecan Clusters, 28
    Fruit & Nut Clusters, 95
    Pistachio Apricot Clusters, 95
    Sour Cherry Almond Clusters, 95
coarse sugar, where to find, 196
Cocoa Orange Truffles, 189
Cocoa Pecan Macaroons, 147
cocoa powder, 39, 187
Cocoa Sugar Cookies, 122
coconut, 146
    Chocolate Coconut Cream Pie, 59
    Chocolate Coconut Mounds, 146
    Chocolate Mint Nanaimo Bars, 216
    Classic Nanaimo Bars, 210
    Coconut Rum Truffles, 201
    Coconut Rum Truffles, 201
    Double-Chocolate Walnut Chunks, 175
    Frozen Banana Bites, 290
    German Chocolate Brownies, 154
    Ice Cream Truffles, 265
    Nanaimo Bar Ice Cream Cake, 277
    Reverse Nanaimo Bars, 215
    White Chocolate Butterscotch Oatmeal
        Chippers, 168
    White Chocolate Coconut Sauce, 34
coconut, desiccated, 216
coffee, brewed
    Black Forest Mousse Parfaits, 78
    Chocolate Cupcakes With Double-Chocolate
        Icing, 328
    Classic Chocolate Soufflé, 85
    Mocha Chocolate Crackles, 131
    Mocha Frappé, 292
    Mocha Mousse Cake, 48
    Mocha Snacking cake, 306
    Mostaccioli, 114
    Slow Cooker Hot Cocoa Cake, 20
    Terrine au Chocolat, 179
    White Chocolate Mocha Mugs, 80
coffee cakes
    Chocolate Babka, 134
    Sour Cream Chocolate Chunk Crumb Cake, 310
    Sour Cream Chocolate Crumb Cake, 310
coffee granules, instant
    Amaretti White Chocolate Coffee Parfaits, 87
    Chocolate Silk Tartlet Trio, 223
    Chocolate Soy Coffee Banana Smoothie, 293
    Crispy Coffee Truffle Slice, 206
    Hazelnut Mochaccino Fudge, 213
    Milk Chocolate Coffee Ganache, 206
    Milk Chocolate Mocha Silk, 223
    Mocha Rosettes, 185
    Mocha Sauce, 274
    Mocha Semifreddo, 289
    Silky Mocha Mousse, 67
    Three–Ice Cream Terrine, 274
    Two-Tone Chocolate Espresso Panna Cotta, 71
    Two-Tone Mocha Cheesecake, 46
coffee liqueur
    Boozy Chocolate Sauce, 34
    Lightened-Up Mocha Mousse, 70
    Mocha Mousse, 70
    Mocha Mousse Cake, 48
    Two-Tone Mocha Cheesecake, 46
compote
    Brandied Cherry Compote, 45
cookie crumbs, how to make, 51
cookie decorating, 123
cookie scoops, 120

cookies. *See also* biscotti; clusters; macarons;
macaroons; shortbread.
Basler Brunsli, 258
Big Chocolate Chip Orange Cookies, 125
Candied Ginger & White Chocolate
Hermits, 160
Checkerboard Cookies, 253
Chocolate Caramel Cookies, 26
Chocolate Cherry Rounds, 255
Chocolate Chestnut Fingers, 130
Chocolate Chip Ice Cream Sandwiches, 272
Chocolate Cigar Cookies, 115
Chocolate Coconut Mounds, 146
Chocolate Gingerbread Pretzels, 103
Chocolate Gingersnap Hearts, 118
Chocolate Hazelnut Rugalach, 161
Chocolate Overload Cookies, 122
Chocolate Pecan Mounds, 252
Classic Chocolate Chip Cookies, 169
Cocoa Sugar Cookies, 122
Dairy-Free Chocolate Meringues, 107
Dark & Dangerous Triple-Chocolate
Cookies, 172
Double-Chocolate Ice Box Cookies, 256
Double-Chocolate Minties, 170
Double-Chocolate Walnut Chunks, 175
Gluten-Free Chocolate Glitter Cookies, 150
Gluten-Free White Chocolate Pistachio
Cookies, 151
Hazelnut Chocolate Pizzelle, 106
Matzo Chocolate Almond Buttercrunch, 104
Mint Chocolate Sandwich Cookies, 276
Mocha Chocolate Crackles, 131
Mocha Rosettes, 185
Mostaccioli, 114
Moustache Straw Cookies, 295
No-Bake Fudge Crispies, 102
Oatmeal Chocolate Chip Cookies, 164
Pecan Cherry Chocolate Hermits, 160
Scoop & Freeze Double-Chocolate Cookies, 119
S'mores Chocolate Fondue, 41
Sparkly Chocolate Blossoms, 257
Surprise Peanut Butter Cookies, 165
Toffee Chocolate Chip Toonies, 120
Toffee, Macadamia & White Chocolate
Chunk Cookies, 173
Triple-Chocolate Cookie Ice Cream
Sandwiches, 273
Triple-Chocolate Cookies, 128
Vanilla Candy Ice Cream Sandwiches, 272
White Chocolate Butterscotch Oatmeal
Chippers, 168
White Chocolate, Cranberry & Pistachio
Cookies, 127
Whoopie Pies With Cream Cheese Filling, 304
cookies, how to store, 150
corn syrup, types of, 26
coulis
Strawberry Coulis, 93
cranberries
Black Forest Bark, 101
Candied Orange & Ginger Bark, 182
Cranberry Jewel Fudge, 205
Cranberry White Chocolate Biscotti, 109
Cranberry White Chocolate Tarts, 226
White Chocolate, Cranberry & Pistachio
Cookies, 127
White Chocolate Cranberry Blondies, 142
cranberries, buying dried, 226
cream cheese
Chocolate Cappuccino Cheesecake, 53
Chocolate Cheesecake With Caramel Pecan
Sauce, 11
Chocolate Hazelnut Rugalach, 161
Chocolate Hazelnut Swirl Cheesecake, 54
Chocolate Hazelnut Tassies, 249
Chocolate Peanut Butter Pie, 61
Milk Chocolate Cheesecake, 50
Mini White Chocolate Cheesecake, 51
No-Bake Chocolate Marble Cheesecake Pie, 56

Rocky Road Cheesecake, 47
Two-Tone Mocha Cheesecake, 46
Whoopie Pies With Cream Cheese Filling, 304
cream cheese, how to soften, 304
creamy recipes, 42–89
Crème Anglaise, 19
crème de cacao
Chocolate Brownie Martini, 296
Chocolate Mint Martini, 296
crème de menthe
Chocolate Mint Martini, 296
Grasshopper Truffle Tart, 55
Crispy Coffee Truffle Slice, 206
Crispy Dark Chocolate Ganache, 206
crumbly recipes, 218–259
crunchy recipes, 90–131
cupcakes. *See also* muffins.
Banana & Chocolate Malt Cake Cones, 333
Chocolate Cupcakes, 336
Chocolate Cupcakes With Double-Chocolate
Icing, 328
Milk Chocolate Cupcakes, 330
currants, dried
Chocolate Fruit & Nut Tart, 228
custard
Black Forest Trifle, 76
Caramel Chocolate Custard, 30
Chocolate Banana Cream Pie, 64
Chocolate Hazelnut Trifle, 77
Classic Nanaimo Bars, 210
Mini Steamed Chocolate Puddings, 309
Reverse Nanaimo Bars, 215
Steamed Chocolate Pudding, 309
White Chocolate Cherry Torte, 45
White Chocolate Pomegranate Trifle, 75
White Chocolate Pouring Custard, 63

D

dairy-free recipes
Chocolate & Olive Oil Bundt Cake
With Chocolate Sauce, 326
Chocolate Sorbet, 264
Chocolate Soy Banana Smoothie, 293
Chocolate Soy Coffee Banana Smoothie, 293
Chocolate Soy Peanut Butter Banana
Smoothie, 293
Chocolate Soy Strawberry Banana
Smoothie, 293
Dairy-Free Chocolate Meringues, 107
Passover Dairy-Free Gluten-Free Flourless
Chocolate Lava Cakes, 17
Dark & Dangerous Triple-Chocolate Cookies, 172
Dark & Stormy Truffle Cups, 196
dark chocolate, 39
Black Forest Trifle, 76
Chocolate & Olive Oil Bundt Cake With
Chocolate Sauce, 326
Chocolate & Salted Caramel Swirl Ice Cream, 263
Chocolate Brownie Martini, 296
Chocolate Cheesecake With Caramel Pecan
Sauce, 11
Chocolate Cherry Cups, 202
Chocolate Cherry Pancakes With Cherry
Syrup, 301
Chocolate Goat's Milk Fudge, 204
Chocolate Hazelnut Trifle, 77
Chocolate Orange Bundt Cake, 322
Chocolate Silk Tartlet Trio, 223
Chocolate Sorbet, 264
Chocolate, Star Anise & Orange Biscotti, 112
Cinnamon Pistachio Truffles, 190
Crispy Coffee Truffle Slice, 206
Dairy-Free Chocolate Meringues, 107
Dark Chocolate & Dried Cherry Scones, 248
Dark Chocolate Bûche de Noël, 311
Dark Chocolate Silk, 223
Dark Chocolate Truffles, 190
Double-Chocolate Almond Shortbread, 236
Double-Chocolate Minties, 170
Ganache-Filled Chocolates, 195

Gingerbread Truffles, 197
Glazed Double-Chocolate Marble Cake, 325
Gluten-Free Super Fudgy Chocolate
Brownies, 139
Grasshopper Truffle Tart, 55
Hazelnut Truffles, 190
Peanut Butter Cups, 217
Reverse Nanaimo Bars, 215
Silky Chocolate Mousse, 67
Sour Cherry Almond Clusters, 95
Sour Cherry & Almond Chocolate Bar, 94
Triple-Berry Chocolate Tart, 234
White Chocolate Cinnamon Butter Truffles, 200
decorating cakes and tarts, 82
decorating cookies, 123
decorating with icing sugar, 338
desiccated coconut, 216
dessert sauces. *See also* compote; coulis; fondue;
ganache; glazes; icings.
Boozy Chocolate Sauce, 34
Bourbon Sauce, 271
Caramel Pecan Sauce, 11
Chocolate Fudge Sauce, 274
Chocolate Sauce, 326
Chocolate Syrup, 309, 339
Hot Fudge Sauce, 317
Mocha Fudge Sauce, 38
Mocha Sauce, 274
Peanut Butter Caramel Sauce, 35
Rich Double-Chocolate Sauce, 36
Salted Caramel Sauce, 263
Silky Dark Chocolate Sauce, 38
Strawberry Sauce, 268
Thick & Fudgy Bittersweet Chocolate
Sauce, 38
Warm Cinnamon Chocolate Sauce, 35
White Chocolate Coconut Sauce, 34
dessert sauces, gifting, 36
dessert sauces, reheating, 271
docking dough, 228
Double-Chocolate Almond Shortbread, 236
Double–Chocolate Chip Waffles With Bananas and
Strawberry Coulis, 93
Double-Chocolate Coffee Ice Cream Stacks, 268
Double-Chocolate Éclairs, 89
Double-Chocolate Ice Box Cookies, 256
Double-Chocolate Icing, 328
Double-Chocolate Minties, 170
Double-Chocolate Semifreddo, 288
Double-Chocolate Walnut Chunks, 175
dough, how to dock, 233
doughs
Bread Machine Chocolate Breakfast Braid
Dough, 135
Bread Machine Chocolate Monkey Bread
Dough, 137
Sweet Yeast Dough, 135
Dry Gin Martini Truffle Cups, 196

E

Earl Grey Chocolate Truffles, 198
Easy Chocolate Walnut Fudge, 212
Easy Royal Icing, 295
éclairs
Double-Chocolate Éclairs, 89
egg whites, how to beat, 279
English Toffee, 98
espresso beans, chocolate-covered
Lightened-Up Mocha Mousse, 70
Mocha Mousse, 70
espresso, brewed
Chocolate Espresso Torte, 339
Passover Chocolate Espresso Torte, 339
espresso powder, instant
Chocolate Cappuccino Cheesecake, 53
Flourless Chocolate Truffle Cake, 25
Irish Cream Brownie Bites, 148
Mocha Fudge Sauce, 38
Passover Flourless Chocolate Truffle Cake, 25

F

Flourless Chocolate Lava Cakes, 17
Flourless Chocolate Truffle Cake, 25
fondue
 Chocolate Fondue, 62
 S'mores Chocolate Fondue, 41
fondue for a party, 62
Frangelico. *See* hazelnut liqueur.
frappé
 Mocha Frappé, 292
French toast
 Chocolate Hazelnut French Toast, 31
Frozen Banana Bites, 290
Frozen Chocolate Praline Meringue Torte, 284
Fruit & Nut Clusters, 95
fruit cake
 Chocolate Cherry Fruit Cake, 307
fudge
 Candy-Covered Fudge, 205
 Chocolate Fudge Sauce, 274
 Chocolate Goat's Milk Fudge, 204
 Chocolate Walnut Fudge Scones, 250
 Cranberry Jewel Fudge, 205
 Easy Chocolate Walnut Fudge, 212
 Hazelnut Mochaccino Fudge, 213
 Hot Fudge Banana Bundt Cake, 317
 Mocha Fudge Sauce, 38
 No-Bake Fudge Crispies, 102
 Nut Fudge, 205
 S'mores Fudge, 209
 Snowball Chocolate Fudge, 205
 Triple-Nut Chocolate Fudge, 209
 White Chocolate Chai Fudge, 208
fudge, how to cut, 205
fudge secret weapon, 208

G

ganache. *See also* icings; glazes.
 Chocolate Caramel & Cashew Torte, 14
 Chocolate Ganache Macarons, 126
 Chocolate Hazelnut Tassies, 249
 Chocolate Peanut Butter Pie, 61
 Chocolate Silk Tartlet Trio, 223
 Chocolate Toffee Pecan Tart, 12
 Chocolate Toffee Squares, 22
 Cocoa Orange Truffles, 189
 Crispy Coffee Truffle Slice, 206
 Double-Chocolate Minties, 170
 Ganache-Filled Chocolates, 195
 Ganache Topping, 142
 German Chocolate Brownies, 154
 Glazed Double-Chocolate Marble Cake, 325
 Grasshopper Truffle Tart, 55
 Irish Cream Brownie Bites, 148
 Irish Cream Chocolate Truffles, 192
 Milk Chocolate Cheesecake, 50
 Mocha Mousse Cake, 48
 Triple Berry Chocolate Tart, 234
 White Chocolate Tartlets With Strawberries, 220
German Chocolate Brownies, 154
German Chocolate Icing, 154
Giant Swiss Chocolate Chunk Shortbread, 244
gifting dessert sauces, 36
gin
 Dry Gin Martini Truffle Cups, 196
ginger
 Candied Ginger & White Chocolate
  Hermits, 160
 Candied Orange & Ginger Bark, 182
 Chai Tea Chocolate Truffles, 198
 Chocolate Gingerbread Pretzels, 103
 Chocolate Gingersnap Hearts, 118
 Chocolate Sorbet, 264
 Dark & Stormy Truffle Cups, 196
 Ginger Butterscotch Squares, 167
 Ginger Macadamia Blondies, 157
 Ginger Vanilla Ice Cream Stacks, 268
Gingerbread Truffles, 197
ginger liqueur
 Dark & Stormy Truffle Cups, 196

glacé cherries, where to find, 255
Glazed Double-Chocolate Marble Cake, 325
glazes. *See also* ganache; icings.
 Chocolate Espresso Glaze, 25
 Chocolate Glaze, 89
 Chocolate Orange Glaze, 322
 Chocolate Satin, 302
 Ganache Glaze, 12
 Smooth Chocolate Glaze, 330
gluten-free
 Basler Brunsli, 258
 Gluten-Free Chocolate-Dipped Peanut Butter
  Balls, 188
 Gluten-Free Chocolate Glitter Cookies, 150
 Gluten-Free Super Fudgy Chocolate
  Brownies, 139
 Gluten-Free White Chocolate Pistachio
  Cookies, 151
 Passover Dairy-Free Gluten-Free Flourless
  Chocolate Lava Cakes, 17
goat's milk
 Chocolate Goat's Milk Fudge, 204
gooey recipes, 8–41
graham cracker crumbs
 Chocolate Cheesecake With Caramel Pecan
  Sauce, 11
 Chocolate Hazelnut Swirl Cheesecake, 54
 Classic Nanaimo Bars, 210
 Reverse Nanaimo Bars, 215
graham crackers
 S'mores Fudge, 209
Grand Marnier. *See* orange liqueur.
Grasshopper Truffle Tart, 55
grinding spices, 157
ground almonds. *See* almonds, ground.

H

hand mixer versus stand mixer, 55
hazelnut liqueur
 Chocolate Brownie Martini, 296
 Chocolate Hazelnut Swirl Cheesecake, 54
 Chocolate Hazelnut Tassies, 249
 Chocolate Hazelnut Trifle, 77
 Chocolate Mousse Pie, 229
 Ganache-Filled Chocolates, 195
 Hazelnut Chocolate Pizzelle, 106
 Hazelnut Torte With Caramel Milk Chocolate
  Buttercream, 341
 Hazelnut Truffles, 189, 190
 White Chocolate Hazelnut Pie, 232
 White Chocolate Praline Truffles, 193
hazelnuts. *See also* chocolate hazelnut spread.
 Chocolate Cigar Cookies, 115
 Chocolate Hazelnut Baklava, 96
 Chocolate Hazelnut French Toast, 31
 Chocolate Hazelnut Palmiers, 117
 Chocolate Hazelnut Rugalach, 161
 Chocolate Hazelnut Tassies, 249
 Chocolate Hazelnut Trifle, 77
 Chocolate Mousse Pie, 229
 Chocolate Ricotta Tart, 239
 Hazelnut Chocolate Mousse, 72
 Hazelnut Chocolate Pizzelle, 106
 Hazelnut Mochaccino Fudge, 213
 Hazelnut Torte With Caramel Milk Chocolate
  Buttercream, 341
 Hazelnut Truffles, 189, 190
 Itty-Bitty Hazelnut Cioccolata Biscotti, 110
 Milk Chocolate Tart Brûlée, 58
 Nanaimo Bar Ice Cream Cake, 277
 White Chocolate Hazelnut Pie, 232
 White Chocolate Praline Truffles, 193
hazelnuts, how to skin, 72
hot chocolate
 Hot Chocolate, 82
 Malted Hot Chocolate, 81
 Marshmallow Hot Chocolate Mix, 81
 White Chocolate Mocha Mugs, 80
Hot Fudge Banana Bundt Cake, 317
Hot Fudge Sauce, 317

how to

 beat egg whites, 279
 buy and store nuts, 212
 buy white chocolate, 101
 check yeast strength, 134
 chop chocolate, 252
 cube cold butter or lard, 248
 cut amaretti cookies, 99
 cut cheesecake, 47
 cut citrus zest strips, 266
 cut fudge, 205
 decorate cakes and tarts, 82
 decorate cookies, 123
 decorate with icing sugar, 338
 dock dough, 228
 grate chocolate, 80
 keep walnuts fresh, 175
 line pans with parchment paper, 145, 307
 make cookie crumbs, 51
 make perfect chocolate curls, 297
 melt chocolate, 94
 prevent chocolate from seizing, 220
 recrisp pizzelle, 106
 reheat dessert sauce, 271
 seed a pomegranate, 75
 shave chocolate, 80
 skin hazelnuts, 72
 soften cream cheese, 304
 soften ice cream, 269
 store cookies, 150
 temper chocolate, 95

I

ice cream
 Chocolate & Salted Caramel Swirl Ice
  Cream, 263
 Chocolate Caramel Ice Cream Pie, 285
 Chocolate Chip Ice Cream Sandwiches, 272
 Chocolate Raspberry Pistachio Baked
  Alaska, 280
 Chocolate Sorbet, 264
 Chocolate Strawberry Shortcake, 312
 Double-Chocolate Coffee Ice Cream Stacks, 268
 Frozen Chocolate Praline Meringue Torte, 284
 Ginger Vanilla Ice Cream Stacks, 268
 Ice Cream Truffles, 265
 Mini Baked Alaskas, 279
 Mint Chocolate Chip Ice Cream Pie, 287
 Mint Chocolate Sandwich Cookies, 276
 Mocha Frappé, 292
 Mocha Ice Cream Squares, 269
 Nanaimo Bar Ice Cream Cake, 277
 Neapolitan Milkshake, 295
 Neapolitan Pistachio Frozen Bombe, 282
 Old-Fashioned Milkshakes, 293
 Sublime Brownies & Bourbon Sauce
  Sundaes, 271
 Three–Ice Cream Terrine, 274
 Triple-Chocolate Cookie Ice Cream
  Sandwiches, 273
 Triple-Decker Ice Cream Stacks, 268
 Tunnel of Ice Cream Cake, 281
 Vanilla Candy Ice Cream Sandwiches, 272
 White Chocolate Ice Cream With Blueberry
  Swirl, 266
ice cream, how to soften, 269
icing sugar, decorating with, 338
icings. *See also* ganache; glazes.
 Caramel Milk Chocolate Buttercream, 341
 Chocolate Icing, 303, 336
 Chocolate Malt Icing, 333
 Coconut Pecan Icing, 303
 Double-Chocolate Icing, 328
 Easy Royal Icing, 295
 Fudge Icing, 250
 German Chocolate Icing, 154
instant coffee granules. *See* coffee granules, instant.

347

CANADIAN LIVING • THE COMPLETE CHOCOLATE BOOK

instant dissolving (fruit/berry) sugar, 240
    Chocolate Raspberry Pistachio Baked Alaska, 280
    Chocolate Stripe Shortbread, 240
    Marshmallow Hot Chocolate Mix, 81
instant espresso powder. See espresso powder, instant.
Irish cream liqueur
    Irish Cream Brownie Bites, 148
    Irish Cream Chocolate Truffles, 192
    Molten Chocolate Cakes, 19
Itty-Bitty Hazelnut Cioccolata Biscotti, 110

K

key lime
    Chocolate Key Lime Tarts, 231
kirsch
    Basler Brunsli, 258
    Black Forest Mousse Parfaits, 78
    Cherry Almond White Chocolate Biscotti, 111

L

lard, how to cube cold, 248
large-flake rolled oats, 164
    Oatmeal Chocolate Chip Cookies, 164
    White Chocolate Butterscotch Oatmeal
        Chippers, 168
lemon
    Lemon Poppy Seed Scones, 245
    White Chocolate Lemon Tart, 224
Lightened-Up Mocha Mousse, 70
lime
    Chocolate Key Lime Tarts, 231
loafs
    Chocolate Chocolate Loaf, 318
    Chocolate Pistachio Loaf, 314

M

macadamia nuts
    Ginger Macadamia Blondies, 157
    Toffee, Macadamia & White Chocolate
        Chunk Cookies, 173
    Tropical Fruit Bark, 101
macarons
    Chocolate Ganache Macarons, 126
    Chocolate Macarons, 126
macaroons
    Cocoa Pecan Macaroons, 147
malt chocolate
    Banana & Chocolate Malt Cake Cones, 333
    Malted Hot Chocolate, 81
mango, dried
    Tropical Fruit Bark, 101
maple syrup
    Chocolate Cherry Pancakes With Cherry
        Syrup, 301
    Maple Chocolate Butter Tarts, 13
Marbled Almond Bark, 99
marshmallows
    Chocolate-Covered Homemade
        Marshmallows, 27
    Marshmallow Hot Chocolate Mix, 81
    Rocky Road Blondies, 159
    Rocky Road Cheesecake, 47
    S'mores Chocolate Fondue, 41
    S'mores Fudge, 209
    Snowball Chocolate Fudge, 205
martinis
    Chocolate Brownie Martini, 296
    Chocolate Mint Martini, 296
    Dry Gin Martini Truffle Cups, 196
marzipan
    Chocolate Cherry Cups, 202
mascarpone cheese
    Chocolate Cherry Pancakes With Cherry
        Syrup, 301
Matzo Chocolate Almond Buttercrunch, 104
melting chocolate, 94
melty recipes, 176–217

meringue
    Chocolate Raspberry Pistachio Baked Alaska, 280
    Dairy-Free Chocolate Meringues, 107
    Frozen Chocolate Praline Meringue Torte, 284
    Mini Baked Alaskas, 279
    Mocha Rosettes, 185
milk chocolate, 39
    Banana & Chocolate Malt Cake Cones, 333
    Chai Tea Chocolate Truffles, 198
    Chocolate Caramel Layered Pudding, 86
    Chocolate Cherry Cups, 202
    Chocolate Chestnut Mousse, 69
    Chocolate Cupcakes With Double-Chocolate
        Icing, 328
    Chocolate Fondue, 62
    Chocolate Gingersnap Hearts, 118
    Chocolate Hazelnut Baklava, 96
    Chocolate Hazelnut Swirl Cheesecake, 54
    Chocolate Overload Cookies, 122
    Chocolate Silk Tartlet Trio, 223
    Chocolate Sorbet, 264
    Chocolate Stripe Shortbread, 240
    Chocolate Torte With Pecans, 338
    Classic Chocolate Soufflé, 85
    Coconut Rum Truffles, 201
    Crispy Coffee Truffle Slice, 206
    Double-Chocolate Semifreddo, 288
    Double-Chocolate Walnut Chunks, 175
    Earl Grey Chocolate Truffles, 198
    Fruit & Nut Clusters, 95
    Ganache-Filled Chocolates, 195
    Giant Swiss Chocolate Chunk Shortbread, 244
    Ginger Butterscotch Squares, 167
    Gingerbread Truffles, 197
    Hazelnut Torte With Caramel Milk Chocolate
        Buttercream, 341
    Irish Cream Chocolate Truffles, 192
    Milk Chocolate Cheesecake, 50
    Milk Chocolate Cupcakes, 330
    Milk Chocolate Pudding, 86
    Milk Chocolate Scones, 247
    Milk Chocolate Tart Brûlée, 58
    Mocha Mousse Cake, 48
    Peanut Butter Cups, 217
    Rich Double-Chocolate Sauce, 36
    Silky Chocolate Mousse, 67
    Silky Mocha Mousse, 67
    Swiss Chocolate Chunk Shortbread, 244
    Triple-Chocolate Cookie Ice Cream
        Sandwiches, 273
    Triple-Chocolate Cookies, 128
    Two-Tone Chocolate Espresso Panna Cotta, 71
    Two-Tone Mocha Cheesecake, 46
    Warm Cinnamon Chocolate Sauce, 35
    White Chocolate Cinnamon Butter Truffles, 200
milkshakes
    Neapolitan Milkshake, 295
    Old-Fashioned Milkshakes, 293
Mini Baked Alaskas, 279
Mini Steamed Chocolate Puddings, 309
Mini White Chocolate Cheesecake, 51
mint
    Chocolate Mint Martini, 296
    Chocolate Mint Nanaimo Bars, 216
    Double-Chocolate Minties, 170
    Mint Chocolate Chip Ice Cream Pie, 287
    Mint Chocolate Sandwich Cookies, 276
    Two-Tone Peppermint Bark, 181
    White Chocolate Tartlets With Strawberries, 220
mocha
    Chocolate Silk Tartlet Trio, 223
    Hazelnut Mochaccino Fudge, 213
    Lightened-Up Mocha Mousse, 70
    Mocha Chocolate Crackles, 131
    Mocha Frappé, 292
    Mocha Fudge Sauce, 38
    Mocha Ice Cream Squares, 269
    Mocha Mousse, 70
    Mocha Mousse Cake, 48
    Mocha Rosettes, 185
    Mocha Semifreddo, 289

    Mocha Snacking Cake, 306
    Silky Mocha Mousse, 67
    Three–Ice Cream Terrine, 274
    Two-Tone Mocha Cheesecake, 46
    White Chocolate Mocha Mugs, 80
Molten Chocolate Cakes, 19
Monkey Bars, 162
Mostaccioli, 114
mousse
    Black Forest Mousse Parfaits, 78
    Chocolate Almond Tartlets, 221
    Chocolate Chestnut Mousse, 69
    Chocolate Mousse Pie, 229
    Hazelnut Chocolate Mousse, 72
    Lightened-Up Mocha Mousse, 70
    Mocha Mousse, 70
    Mocha Mousse Cake, 48
    Orange Chocolate Mousse, 70
    Raspberry Chocolate Mousse, 70
    Silky Chocolate Mousse, 67
    Silky Mocha Mousse, 67
    White Chocolate Mousse, 78
Moustache Straw Cookies, 295
muffins
    Banana Chocolate Chip Muffins, 331
    Chocolate-Glazed Chocolate Chip Muffins, 327

N

Nanaimo bars
    Chocolate Mint Nanaimo Bars, 216
    Classic Nanaimo Bars, 210
    Nanaimo Bar Ice Cream Cake, 277
    Reverse Nanaimo Bars, 215
Neapolitan Milkshake, 295
Neapolitan Pistachio Frozen Bombe, 282
No-Bake Chocolate Marble Cheesecake Pie, 56
No-Bake Fudge Crispies, 102
Nut Fudge, 205
nuts, buying and storing, 212
Nutella. See chocolate hazelnut spread.
Nutty Caramel Monkey Bread, 137

O

Oatmeal Chocolate Chip Cookies, 164
Oatmeal Chocolate Chip Shortbread, 237
oats, 164
Old-Fashioned Milkshakes, 293
orange
    Big Chocolate Chip Orange Cookies, 125
    Candied Orange & Ginger Bark, 182
    Chai Tea Chocolate Truffles, 198
    Chocolate Orange Bundt Cake, 322
    Chocolate, Star Anise & Orange Biscotti, 112
    Cocoa Orange Truffles, 189
    Earl Grey Chocolate Truffles, 198
    Orange Blossom Truffle Cups, 196
    Orange Chocolate Mousse, 70
    White Chocolate Pouring Custard, 63
orange liqueur
    Chocolate Orange Bundt Cake, 322
    Cocoa Orange Truffles, 189
    Cranberry White Chocolate Tarts, 226
    Mini Steamed Chocolate Puddings, 309
    Orange Blossom Truffle Cups, 196
    Orange Chocolate Mousse, 70
    Steamed Chocolate Pudding, 309
    White Chocolate Ice Cream With Blueberry
        Swirl, 266
    White Chocolate Pouring Custard, 63
Our Favourite Chocolate Layer Cake, 336

P

palmiers
    Chocolate Hazelnut Palmiers, 117
pancakes
    Chocolate Cherry Pancakes With Cherry
        Syrup, 301

panna cotta
    Two-Tone Chocolate Espresso Panna Cotta, 71
papaya, dried
    Tropical Fruit Bark, 101
parchment paper, lining pans with, 145, 307
parchment paper, tracing on, 115
parfaits
    Amaretti White Chocolate Coffee Parfaits, 87
    Black Forest Mousse Parfaits, 78
Passover Chocolate Espresso Torte, 339
Passover Dairy-Free Gluten-Free Flourless
    Chocolate Lava Cakes, 17
Passover Flourless Chocolate Truffle Cake, 25
pastries. *See also* breads; pies; scones; tarts.
    Chocolate Cinnamon Buns, 33
    Chocolate Hazelnut Baklava, 96
    Chocolate Hazelnut Palmiers, 117
    Chocolate Hazelnut Tassies, 249
    Double-Chocolate Éclairs, 89
pastry
    Chocolate Pastry, 59, 221, 229, 231, 242
    Quick Puff Pastry, 117
    Single-Crust All-Purpose Pastry, 226
    Sour Cream Pastry, 13
    Sweet Pastry, 228
pastry cream
    Chocolate Hazelnut Trifle, 77
    Chocolate Pastry Cream, 225
    Chocolate Spice Pastry Cream, 89
peanut butter
    Chocolate Peanut Butter Pie, 61
    Chocolate Peanut Butter Pudding Cake, 18
    Chocolate Soy Peanut Butter Banana
        Smoothie, 293
    Gluten-Free Chocolate-Dipped Peanut Butter
        Balls, 188
    Peanut Butter Brownies, 153
    Peanut Butter Caramel Sauce, 35
    Peanut Butter Cups, 217
    Slow Cooker Chocolate Peanut Butter
        Pudding Cake, 18
    Surprise Peanut Butter Cookies, 165
peanut butter, baking with, 61
peanut butter chips
    Gluten-Free Chocolate-Dipped Peanut Butter
        Balls, 188
    Monkey Bars, 162
peanuts
    Chocolate Peanut Butter Pie, 61
    Frozen Banana Bites, 290
    Fruit & Nut Clusters, 95
    Monkey Bars, 162
    Peanut Butter Brownies, 153
    Peanut Butter Cups, 217
    Surprise Peanut Butter Cookies, 165
pears, Bartlett
    Chocolate Cream Pear Tart, 225
pecans
    Chewy Caramel Pecan Squares, 156
    Chocolate Caramel Bites, 143
    Chocolate Caramel Pecan Clusters, 28
    Chocolate Caramel Turtle Torte, 335
    Chocolate Cheesecake With Caramel Pecan
        Sauce, 11
    Chocolate Cherry Fruit Cake, 307
    Chocolate Chip Ice Cream Sandwiches, 272
    Chocolate Chocolate Loaf, 318
    Chocolate Pecan Mounds, 252
    Chocolate Silk Tartlet Trio, 223
    Chocolate Toffee Pecan Tart, 12
    Chocolate Torte With Pecans, 338
    Cocoa Pecan Macaroons, 147
    Coconut Pecan Icing, 303
    Frozen Chocolate Praline Meringue Torte, 284
    German Chocolate Brownies, 154
    Nut Fudge, 205
    Nutty Caramel Monkey Bread, 137
    Pecan Cherry Chocolate Hermits, 160
    Triple-Nut Chocolate Fudge, 209
    Vanilla Candy Ice Cream Sandwiches, 272

White Chocolate Butterscotch Oatmeal
    Chippers, 168
    White Chocolate Silk, 223
peppermint extract
    Chocolate Mint Nanaimo Bars, 216
    Double-Chocolate Minties, 170
    Two-Tone Peppermint Bark, 181
Peppermint Ganache, 170
phyllo pastry
    Chocolate Hazelnut Baklava, 96
pies. *See also* tarts.
    Chocolate Banana Cream Pie, 64
    Chocolate Caramel Ice Cream Pie, 285
    Chocolate Coconut Cream Pie, 59
    Chocolate Mousse Pie, 229
    Chocolate Peanut Butter Pie, 61
    Mint Chocolate Chip Ice Cream Pie, 287
    No-Bake Chocolate Marble Cheesecake Pie, 56
    White Chocolate Hazelnut Pie, 232
pineapple, candied
    Tropical Fruit Bark, 101
Piped Chocolate Trees, 82
pistachios
    Candied Orange & Ginger Bark, 182
    Chocolate Pistachio Loaf, 314
    Chocolate Raspberry Pistachio Baked Alaska, 280
    Cinnamon Pistachio Truffles, 190
    Cranberry White Chocolate Biscotti, 109
    Dry Gin Martini Truffle Cups, 196
    Gluten-Free White Chocolate Pistachio
        Cookies, 151
    Neapolitan Pistachio Frozen Bombe, 282
    Pistachio Apricot Clusters, 95
    Terrine au Chocolat, 179
    White Chocolate, Cranberry & Pistachio
        Cookies, 127
pizzelle
    Hazelnut Chocolate Pizzelle, 106
pomegranate, how to seed a, 75
pomegranate seeds
    White Chocolate Pomegranate Trifle, 75
poppy seeds
    Lemon Poppy Seed Scones, 245
pots de crème
    Cardamom Chocolate Pots de Crème, 66
    Cinnamon Chocolate Pots de Crème, 66
pound cakes
    Chocolate Pound Cake, 76, 77
    White Chocolate Almond Pound Cake, 315
pouring custard
    White Chocolate Pouring Custard, 63
praline
    Frozen Chocolate Praline Meringue Torte, 284
    White Chocolate Praline Truffles, 193
pretzels
    Chocolate Gingerbread Pretzels, 103
prunes
    Chocolate Fruit & Nut Tart, 228
pudding cake layers, the secret to, 18
puddings
    Banana Chocolate Chunk Bread Pudding, 23
    Caramel Pudding, 86
    Cardamom Chocolate Pots de Crème, 66
    Chocolate Caramel Layered Pudding, 86
    Chocolate Peanut Butter Pudding Cake, 18
    Cinnamon Chocolate Pots de Crème, 66
    Milk Chocolate Pudding, 86
    Mini Steamed Chocolate Puddings, 309
    Slow Cooker Chocolate Peanut Butter
        Pudding Cake, 18
    Steamed Chocolate Pudding, 309

Q

quick-cooking rolled oats, 164
    Oatmeal Chocolate Chip Shortbread, 237

R

raisins
    Fruit & Nut Clusters, 95
raspberries
    Chocolate Silk Tartlet Trio, 223
    Raspberry Chantilly, 302
    Raspberry Chocolate Chip Bundt Cake, 323
    Raspberry Chocolate Mousse, 70
    Raspberry Chocolate Smoothie, 292
    Triple-Berry Chocolate Tart, 234
raspberry jam
    Chocolate Raspberry Curl Cake, 334
    Triple-Berry Chocolate Tart, 234
raspberry liqueur
    Chocolate Raspberry Pistachio Baked Alaska, 280
    Raspberry Chocolate Mousse, 70
Really Good Rum Balls, 184
Reverse Nanaimo Bars, 215
rice crisp cereal
    Crispy Coffee Truffle Slice, 206
    No-Bake Fudge Crispies, 102
Rich Double-Chocolate Sauce, 36
ricotta cheese
    Chocolate Ricotta Tart, 239
Rocky Road Blondies, 159
Rocky Road Cheesecake, 47
rugalach
    Chocolate Hazelnut Rugalach, 161
rum, 184
    Boca Negra With Rum-Soaked Cherries, 180
    Boozy Chocolate Sauce, 34
    Chocolate Chestnut Mousse, 69
    Coconut Rum Truffles, 201
    Really Good Rum Balls, 184

S

Salted Caramel Sauce, 263
sauces. *See* dessert sauces.
scones. *See also* breads.
    Apricot Almond Scones, 245
    Cherry White Chocolate Scones, 245
    Chocolate Walnut Fudge Scones, 250
    Dark Chocolate & Dried Cherry Scones, 248
    Lemon Poppy Seed Scones, 245
    Milk Chocolate Scones, 247
Scoop & Freeze Double-Chocolate Cookies, 119
Scotch on the Rocks Truffle Cups, 196
seizing chocolate, how to prevent, 220
semifreddo
    Double-Chocolate Semifreddo, 288
    Mocha Semifreddo, 289
semisweet chocolate, 39
    Black Forest Bark, 101
    Chocolate Banana Cream Pie, 64
    Chocolate Coconut Cream Pie, 59
    Chocolate-Glazed Chocolate Chip Muffins, 327
    Chocolate Hazelnut Palmiers, 117
    Chocolate Hazelnut Tassies, 249
    Chocolate Mint Nanaimo Bars, 216
    Chocolate Mousse Pie, 229
    Chocolate Ricotta Tart, 239
    Chocolate Shards, 335
    Chocolate Silk Tartlet Trio, 223
    Cinnamon Pistachio Truffles, 190
    Classic Nanaimo Bars, 210
    Cocoa Orange Truffles, 189
    Dark Chocolate Truffles, 190
    Double-Chocolate Minties, 170
    Gluten-Free Chocolate-Dipped Peanut Butter
        Balls, 188
    Hazelnut Truffles, 189, 190
    Hot Chocolate, 82
    Itty-Bitty Hazelnut Cioccolata Biscotti, 110
    Marbled Almond Bark, 99
    Milk Chocolate Cupcakes, 330
    Mocha Fudge Sauce, 38
    Mocha Semifreddo, 289
    Nanaimo Bar Ice Cream Cake, 277
    Neapolitan Pistachio Frozen Bombe, 282
    S'mores Fudge, 209

Triple-Nut Chocolate Fudge, 209
White Chocolate Lemon Tart, 224
semisweet chocolate chips
Banana Brownies, 138
Banana Chocolate Chip Muffins, 331
Big Chocolate Chip Orange Cookies, 125
Bread Machine Chocolate Monkey Bread
Dough, 137
Chewy Caramel Pecan Squares, 156
Chocolate Chip Angel Food Cake, 320
Chocolate Chip Ice Cream Sandwiches, 272
Chocolate Chocolate Loaf, 318
Chocolate-Glazed Chocolate Chip Muffins, 327
Chocolate Monkey Bread, 137
Chocolate Pistachio Loaf, 314
Classic Chocolate Chip Cookies, 169
Cocoa Pecan Macaroons, 147
Dark & Dangerous Triple-Chocolate Cookies, 172
Double–Chocolate Chip Waffles With
Bananas & Strawberry Coulis, 93
Frozen Banana Bites, 290
Matzo Chocolate Almond Buttercrunch, 104
Monkey Bars, 162
Mostaccioli, 114
No-Bake Fudge Crispies, 102
Oatmeal Chocolate Chip Cookies, 164
Oatmeal Chocolate Chip Shortbread, 237
Raspberry Chocolate Chip Bundt Cake, 323
Rocky Road Blondies, 159
Slow Cooker Hot Cocoa Cake, 20
Toffee Chocolate Chip Toonies, 120
Triple-Chocolate Cookie Ice Cream
Sandwiches, 273
Sherry Cream, 83
shortbread
Chocolate Shortbread Fingers, 233
Chocolate Stripe Shortbread, 240
Double-Chocolate Almond Shortbread, 236
Giant Swiss Chocolate Chunk Shortbread, 244
Oatmeal Chocolate Chip Shortbread, 237
Spicy Chocolate Cinnamon Shortbread, 241
Swiss Chocolate Chunk Shortbread, 244
shortbread cookie crumbs
Mini White Chocolate Cheesecake, 51
shortcake
Chocolate Strawberry Shortcake, 312
sifting cocoa powder, 187
silk
Chocolate Silk Tartlet Trio, 223
Silky Chocolate Mousse, 67
Silky Dark Chocolate Sauce, 38
Silky Mocha Mousse, 67
Single-Crust All-Purpose Pastry, 226
slow cooker, baking with a, 20
Slow Cooker Chocolate Peanut Butter Pudding
Cake, 18
Slow Cooker Hot Cocoa Cake, 20
Smooth Chocolate Glaze, 330
smoothies
Chocolate Soy Banana Smoothie, 293
Chocolate Soy Coffee Banana Smoothie, 293
Chocolate Soy Peanut Butter Banana
Smoothie, 293
Chocolate Soy Strawberry Banana Smoothie, 293
Raspberry Chocolate Smoothie, 292
S'mores Chocolate Fondue, 41
S'mores Fudge, 209
Snowball Chocolate Fudge, 205
sorbet. See also ice cream.
Chocolate Raspberry Pistachio Baked Alaska, 280
Chocolate Sorbet, 264
soufflés
Chocolate Soufflé Cakes With Sherry Cream, 83
Classic Chocolate Soufflé, 85
Sour Cherry Almond Clusters, 95
Sour Cherry & Almond Chocolate Bar, 94
Sour Cream Chocolate Chunk Crumb Cake, 310
Sour Cream Chocolate Crumb Cake, 310
Sour Cream Pastry, 13
Sparkly Chocolate Blossoms, 257
spices, grinding, 157

Spicy Chocolate Cinnamon Shortbread, 241
squares. See also brownies; fudge.
Chewy Caramel Pecan Squares, 156
Chocolate Mint Nanaimo Bars, 216
Chocolate Toffee Squares, 22
Classic Nanaimo Bars, 210
Crispy Coffee Truffle Slice, 206
Ginger Butterscotch Squares, 167
Ginger Macadamia Blondies, 157
Mocha Ice Cream Squares, 269
Monkey Bars, 162
Reverse Nanaimo Bars, 215
Rocky Road Blondies, 159
stand mixer versus hand mixer, 55
star anise
Cardamom Chocolate Pots de Crème, 66
Chocolate, Star Anise & Orange Biscotti, 112
Steamed Chocolate Pudding, 309
steel-cut oats, 164
storing cookies, 150
strawberries
Chocolate Soy Strawberry Banana Smoothie, 293
Chocolate Strawberry Shortcake, 312
Double–Chocolate Chip Waffles With Bananas
and Strawberry Coulis, 93
Flourless Chocolate Lava Cakes, 17
Old-Fashioned Milkshakes, 293
Strawberry Sauce, 268
Triple-Decker Ice Cream Stacks, 268
Tunnel of Ice Cream Cake, 281
White Chocolate Tartlets With Strawberries, 220
sundaes
Sublime Brownies & Bourbon Sauce
Sundaes, 271
Surprise Peanut Butter Cookies, 165
sweet chocolate, 39
Sweet Pastry, 228
Sweet Yeast Dough, 135
Swiss Chocolate Chunk Shortbread, 244
syrups
Cherry Syrup, 301
Chocolate Syrup, 309, 339

T

tarts. See also pies.
Chocolate Almond Tartlets, 221
Chocolate Cream Pear Tart, 225
Chocolate Fruit & Nut Tart, 228
Chocolate Hazelnut Tassies, 249
Chocolate Key Lime Tarts, 231
Chocolate Ricotta Tart, 239
Chocolate Silk Tartlet Trio, 223
Chocolate Toffee Pecan Tart, 12
Chocolate Walnut Tart, 242
Cranberry White Chocolate Tarts, 226
Grasshopper Truffle Tart, 55
Maple Chocolate Butter Tarts, 13
Milk Chocolate Tart Brûlée, 58
Triple-Berry Chocolate Tart, 234
White Chocolate Lemon Tart, 224
White Chocolate Tartlets With Strawberries, 220
tarts, how to decorate, 82
tempering chocolate, 95
terrines
Terrine au Chocolat, 179
Three–Ice Cream Terrine, 274
The Best Chocolate Brownies, 145
Thick & Fudgy Bittersweet Chocolate Sauce, 38
Three–Ice Cream Terrine, 274
toffee
Chocolate Caramel Ice Cream Pie, 285
Chocolate Toffee Pecan Tart, 12
Chocolate Toffee Squares, 22
English Toffee, 98
Mocha Ice Cream Squares, 269
Toffee Chocolate Chip Toonies, 120
Toffee, Macadamia & White Chocolate Chunk
Cookies, 173

tortes
Chocolate, Caramel & Cashew Torte, 14
Chocolate Caramel Turtle Torte, 335
Chocolate Espresso Torte, 339
Chocolate Torte With Pecans, 338
Frozen Chocolate Praline Meringue Torte, 284
Hazelnut Torte With Caramel Milk Chocolate
Buttercream, 341
Passover Chocolate Espresso Torte, 339
White Chocolate Cherry Torte, 45
trifles
Black Forest Trifle, 76
Chocolate Hazelnut Trifle, 77
White Chocolate Pomegranate Trifle, 75
Triple-Berry Chocolate Tart, 234
Triple-Chocolate Cookie Ice Cream Sandwiches, 273
Triple-Chocolate Cookies, 128
Triple-Decker Ice Cream Stacks, 268
Triple-Nut Chocolate Fudge, 209
Tropical Fruit Bark, 101
truffles
Chai Tea Chocolate Truffles, 198
Cinnamon Pistachio Truffles, 190
Cocoa Orange Truffles, 189
Coconut Rum Truffles, 201
Crispy Coffee Truffle Slice, 206
Dark & Stormy Truffle Cups, 196
Dark Chocolate Truffles, 190
Dry Gin Martini Truffle Cups, 196
Earl Grey Chocolate Truffles, 198
Flourless Chocolate Truffle Cake, 25
Gingerbread Truffles, 197
Grasshopper Truffle Tart, 55
Hazelnut Truffles, 189, 190
Ice Cream Truffles, 265
Irish Cream Chocolate Truffles, 192
Molten Chocolate Cakes, 19
Orange Blossom Truffle Cups, 196
Passover Flourless Chocolate Truffle Cake, 25
Scotch on the Rocks Truffle Cups, 196
White Chocolate Cinnamon Butter Truffles, 200
White Chocolate Praline Truffles, 193
tube pan, how to line a, 307
Tunnel of Ice Cream Cake, 281
Two-Tone Chocolate Espresso Panna Cotta, 71
Two-Tone Mocha Cheesecake, 46
Two-Tone Peppermint Bark, 181

U

unsweetened chocolate, 39
Banana Brownies, 138
Best Chocolate Brownies, The, 145
Cakey Chocolate Brownies, 303
Caramel Chocolate Custard, 30
Checkerboard Cookies, 253
Chocolate Bar Brownies, 140
Chocolate Blackout Cake, 319
Chocolate Caramel Turtle Torte, 335
Chocolate Cupcakes, 336
Chocolate Cupcakes With Double-Chocolate
Icing, 328
Chocolate Icing, 303
Dark Chocolate Bûche de Noël, 311
German Chocolate Brownies, 154
Glazed Double-Chocolate Marble Cake, 325
Hot Fudge Banana Bundt Cake, 317
Irish Cream Brownie Bites, 148
Mocha Rosettes, 185
Our Favourite Chocolate Layer Cake, 336
Peanut Butter Brownies, 153
Sublime Brownies & Bourbon Sauce
Sundaes, 271
The Best Chocolate Brownies, 145

V

Vanilla Candy Ice Cream Sandwiches, 272
vanilla extract, 140
Vanilla-Poached Pears, 225

vanilla wafers
  Chewy Caramel Pecan Squares, 156
vodka
  Chocolate Brownie Martini, 296
  Chocolate Mint Martini, 296

W

waffles
  Double–Chocolate Chip Waffles With Bananas and Strawberry Coulis, 93
walnuts
  Big Chocolate Chip Orange Cookies, 125
  Chocolate Cinnamon Buns, 33
  Chocolate Espresso Torte, 339
  Chocolate Fruit & Nut Tart, 228
  Chocolate Walnut Fudge Scones, 250
  Chocolate Walnut Tart, 242
  Classic Nanaimo Bars, 210
  Double-Chocolate Walnut Chunks, 175
  Easy Chocolate Walnut Fudge, 212
  Gluten-Free Super Fudgy Chocolate Brownies, 139
  Maple Chocolate Butter Tarts, 13
  Mostaccioli, 114
  Nut Fudge, 205
  Passover Chocolate Espresso Torte, 339
  Triple-Chocolate Cookies, 128
  Triple-Nut Chocolate Fudge, 209
walnuts, how to keep fresh, 175
Warm Cinnamon Chocolate Sauce, 35
white chocolate, 39
  Amaretti White Chocolate Coffee Parfaits, 87
  Black Forest Mousse Parfaits, 78
  Candied Ginger & White Chocolate Hermits, 160
  Cherry Almond White Chocolate Biscotti, 111
  Cherry White Chocolate Scones, 245
  Chocolate Cappuccino Cheesecake, 53
  Chocolate Overload Cookies, 122
  Chocolate Silk Tartlet Trio, 223
  Cranberry Jewel Fudge, 205
  Cranberry White Chocolate Biscotti, 109
  Cranberry White Chocolate Tarts, 226
  Crispy Coffee Truffle Slice, 206
  Dark & Dangerous Triple-Chocolate Cookies, 172
  Double-Chocolate Semifreddo, 288
  German Chocolate Brownies, 154
  Ginger Macadamia Blondies, 157
  Glazed Double-Chocolate Marble Cake, 325
  Gluten-Free White Chocolate Pistachio Cookies, 151
  Grasshopper Truffle Tart, 55
  Marbled Almond Bark, 99
  Mini White Chocolate Cheesecake, 51
  No-Bake Fudge Crispies, 102
  Pistachio Apricot Clusters, 95
  Reverse Nanaimo Bars, 215
  Toffee, Macadamia & White Chocolate Chunk Cookies, 173
  Tropical Fruit Bark, 101
  Two-Tone Peppermint Bark, 181
  White Chocolate Almond Pound Cake, 315
  White Chocolate Butterscotch Oatmeal Chippers, 168
  White Chocolate Chai Fudge, 208
  White Chocolate Cherry Torte, 45
  White Chocolate Cinnamon Butter Truffles, 200
  White Chocolate Coconut Sauce, 34
  White Chocolate, Cranberry & Pistachio Cookies, 127
  White Chocolate Cranberry Blondies, 142
  White Chocolate Hazelnut Pie, 232
  White Chocolate Ice Cream With Blueberry Swirl, 266
  White Chocolate Lemon Tart, 224
  White Chocolate Mocha Mugs, 80
  White Chocolate Mousse, 78
  White Chocolate Pomegranate Trifle, 75
  White Chocolate Pouring Custard, 63
  White Chocolate Praline Truffles, 193
  White Chocolate Tartlets With Strawberries, 220
white chocolate, buying, 101
Whoopie Pies With Cream Cheese Filling, 304

Y

yeast strength, how to check, 134
Yule log
  Dark Chocolate Bûche de Noël, 311

Z

zest strips, how to cut citrus, 266

Credits

Recipes

All recipes developed by The Canadian Living Test Kitchen

Photography

Michael Alberstat: page 238 (main).

Ryan Brook: pages 324 and 337 (how-to).

Jeff Coulson: back cover (portrait); pages 5, 15 (main), 16, 21, 44, 65, 149, 166, 207, 291, 294 and 300.

Mike DeLuca/Transcontinental Interactive: page 84 (how-tos).

Yvonne Duivenvoorden: pages 24, 29, 32 (main), 37, 57, 60, 68, 92, 105, 121, 124, 129, 152 (main), 186, 199 (main), 222 (main), 227, 243, 251, 254, 259, 267 (main), 270, 275, 278 (main), 283, 286, 308, 313 and 329.

Joe Kim: pages 158, 194, 235, 246 and 332.

Jim Norton: page 49.

Edward Pond: front cover; back cover (food: top left, top centre and bottom left); pages 10, 40, 52, 73, 79, 88, 141, 199 (how-tos), 262, 297, 305, 316, 321 (main) and 340.

Jodi Pudge: pages 84 (main), 174 and 337 (main).

David Scott: page 230.

Ryan Szulc: back cover (top right); pages 4, 6, 7, 8, 15 (how-tos), 32 (how-tos), 42, 74, 90, 97, 100, 108, 113, 116, 117, 132, 136, 144, 152 (how-tos), 155, 163, 171, 176, 178, 183, 191, 203, 211, 214, 218, 222 (how-tos), 238 (how-to), 260, 267 (how-to), 278 (how-to), 298 and 321 (how-tos).

Thinkstock: pages 2 and 39.

Food Styling

Julie Aldis: pages 32 (main), 238 (main) and 283.

Donna Bartolini: pages 57, 297 and 308.

Ashley Denton: pages 158, 194, 262, 332 and 337 (main).

Carol Dudar: pages 270 and 275.

David Grenier: page 324.

Adele Hagan: pages 49, 84 (main) and 291.

Heather Howe: page 199 (how-tos).

Lucie Richard: pages 29, 52, 60, 92, 121, 124, 129, 174, 251, 254, 259, 267 (main), 286 and 329.

Claire Stancer: pages 222 (main) and 243.

Claire Stubbs: front cover; back cover (top left, top centre and bottom left); pages 6, 7, 8, 10, 15 (how-tos), 16, 24, 32 (how-tos), 37, 40, 42, 68, 73, 79, 88, 90, 97, 100, 105, 108, 116, 117, 132, 136 (how-tos), 141, 149, 152, 166, 176, 178, 186, 199 (main), 203, 218, 222 (main), 227, 235, 238 (how-to), 260, 267 (how-to), 278, 298, 305, 313, 316, 321 and 340.

Melanie Stuparyk: pages 15 (main), 21, 44, 65, 207, 300 and 337 (how-to).

Rosemarie Superville: page 230.

Nicole Young: back cover (top right); pages 4, 74, 113, 136 (main), 144, 155, 163, 171, 183, 191, 203, 211, 214 and 246.

Prop Styling

Laura Branson: pages 21, 44, 49, 65, 84 (main), 92, 246, 291 and 300.

Catherine Doherty: front cover; back cover (food); pages 6, 7, 8, 10, 15, 16, 24, 32 (how-tos), 40, 42, 73, 74, 88, 90, 97, 100, 105, 108, 113, 116, 117, 124, 132, 136 (how-tos), 141, 152 (how-tos), 155, 158, 163, 171, 174, 176, 178, 183, 191, 194, 203, 207, 214, 218, 222 (how-tos), 238 (how-to), 254, 260, 262, 267 (how-to), 278 (how-to), 298, 305, 316, 321 (how-tos), 324, 332 and 337 (main).

Marc-Philippe Gagné: pages 37, 129 and 238 (main).

Mandy Gyulay: page 121.

Madeleine Johari: pages 4, 136 (main), 144, 211 and 235.

Maggi Jones: pages 297 and 321 (main).

Oksana Slavutych: pages 32 (main), 52, 57, 60, 68, 152 (main), 199 (main), 222 (main), 227, 230, 243, 251, 259, 267 (main), 270, 275, 278 (main), 283, 286, 308 and 313.

Genevieve Wiseman: pages 29, 79, 149, 166, 186, 329 and 340.

Our **Tested-Till-Perfect** guarantee means we've tested every recipe, using the same grocery store ingredients and household appliances as you do, until we're sure you'll get perfect results at home.

ABOUT OUR NUTRITION INFORMATION

To meet nutrient needs each day, moderately active women 25 to 49 need about 1,900 calories, 51 g protein, 261 g carbohydrate, 25 to 35 g fibre and not more than 63 g total fat (21 g saturated fat). Men and teenagers usually need more. Canadian sodium intake of approximately 3,500 mg daily should be reduced, whereas the intake of potassium from food sources should be increased to 4,700 mg per day.

CANADIAN LIVING ✓ TESTED TILL PERFECT EST. 1975 TEST KITCHEN

Percentage of recommended daily intake (% RDI) is based on the values used for Canadian food labels for calcium, iron, vitamins A and C, and folate.

Figures are rounded off. They are based on the first ingredient listed when there is a choice and do not include optional ingredients or those with no specified amounts.

ABBREVIATIONS:

cal = calories
pro = protein
carb = carbohydrate
sat. fat = saturated fat
chol = cholesterol

Canadian Living

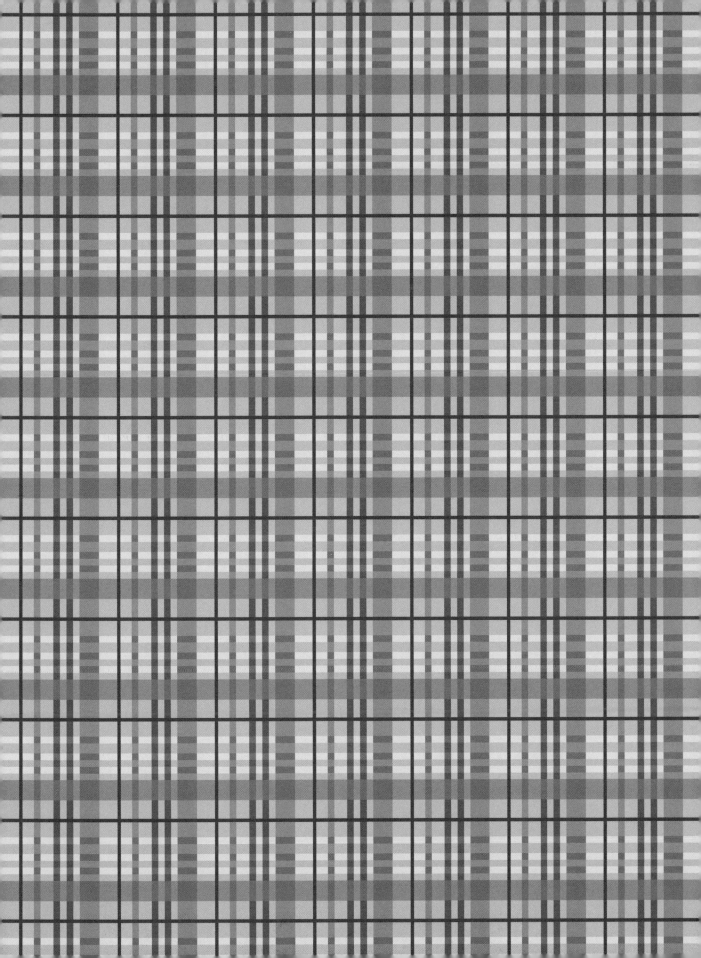

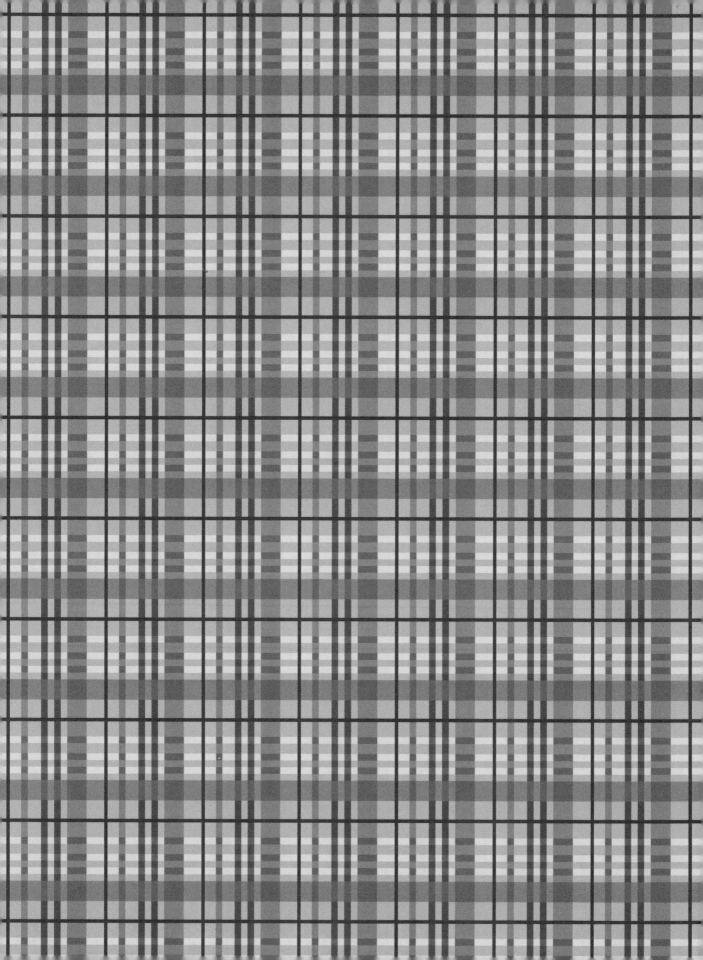